The Politics of Verification

The Politics of Verification

Nancy W. Gallagher

The Johns Hopkins University Press

Baltimore and London

© 1999 The Johns Hopkins University Press
All rights reserved. Published 1999
Printed in the United States of America on acid-free paper
9 8 7 6 5 4 3 2 1

The Johns Hopkins University Press
2715 North Charles Street
Baltimore, Maryland 21218-4363
www.press.jhu.edu

Library of Congress Cataloging-in-Publication Data
will be found at the end of this book.
A catalog record for this book is available from the British Library.

ISBN 0-8018-6017-2

For Tony

Contents

Preface and Acknowledgments ix

Acronyms and Abbreviations xv

1
Verification: The Key to Cooperation? 1

2
Substance, Structure, and Strategy in Verification Politics 27

3
How the Politics of Verification Shape Prenegotiation 57

4
"Scientific" Approaches to Verification Decisions 91

5
The Corrosive Effects of Coercive Diplomacy 119

6
The Politics of Verification during Détente 149

7
Cooperative Verification at the Cold War's Conclusion 184

8
Working with the Politics of Verification 214

Notes 247

Bibliography 285

Index 303

Preface and Acknowledgments

BARGAINING IS THE CURRENCY OF HUMAN INTERACTION—in friendships, families, markets, and politics. When neither side is able and willing to get its way by force, cooperation requires compromise and confidence that agreements will be honored. How does that confidence develop? This book sheds light on this basic question by exploring the politics of verification in international relations, that is, the processes through which suspicious states and contentious groups decide how to judge compliance with their cooperative accords.

Everyone makes choices about the amount and type of verification they need for cooperation. Some relationships are so harmonious that neither side doubts the other's reliability. Trust, though, is rarely the sole source of confidence among bargainers with a mix of common and conflicting interests. Participants can easily assess compliance for themselves when agreements involve transparent behaviors. A farmer who agrees to sell twenty healthy lambs for a thousand dollars, for example, leaves little room for argument. Yet few bargains are this simple, direct, and measurable. The terms can be ambiguous, as when labor unions exchange wage restraint for job security. Compliance may be hard to monitor fairly and thoroughly, as with tax laws and traffic rules. Participants may tolerate some uncertainty if cooperation is beneficial, minor violations are unimportant, and information is hard to get. They may offer each other evidence to validate their claims of compliance. They may delegate authority to a neutral entity, such as an oversight committee or a jury. They may devise a set of mutually acceptable procedures for making joint assessments. Or they may refuse to cooperate because they fear exploitation.

Decisions about arms control verification are especially important and difficult because an inability to agree or a false confidence in compliance could both be catastrophic. Accords that restrict, reduce, or ban military activities can lower the likelihood of war, lessen the destruction should war occur, decrease the cost of security, and maybe even turn foes into friends over time. The tighter the constraints on competition are, though, the stronger temptations to cheat and fears of exploitation will be. Because "nobody wants to be a sucker," policy makers and constituents will support arms control only if they are confident that the verification arrangements offer a strong inducement for mutual cooperation and a satisfactory way to resolve compliance concerns.

Groups in domestic debates and international negotiations often have very different verification requirements. Peace activists, for example, believe that nuclear weapons are so dangerous that the superpowers should radically reduce their arsenals even if this requires some trust, uncertainty, or delegation of authority. More moderate members of the American arms control community want greater transparency so that U.S. leaders can deter cheating, detect violations, and reassure citizens when all is well. But many states and some U.S. groups fear that transparency will increase vulnerability to military attack, economic espionage, and other hostile acts. Some argue that each state should substantiate its own compliance. Others question whether adversaries can ever agree on the "truth" about compliance, or if misperceptions and self-serving analyses will always bias their conclusions.

Conflicting verification preferences create a daunting challenge: arms control supporters must satisfy every state at the bargaining table and any domestic group whose approval is needed to implement an accord. Arms control opponents can block cooperation by preventing agreement on verification either at home or abroad. In the past, domestic and international agreement on verification has occurred only when the risks of cheating were low, such as when treaty-limited activities offered little military advantage, or after the urge to compete was gone. But arguments about verification are still complicating negotiations and slowing ratification, even though the major powers all officially want to ban chemical weapons, end nuclear tests, halt proliferation, and work together on other security problems. This book explains why the politics of verification has had a net negative effect on cooperation and suggests how it should be changed to promote more significant arms control in the future.

I argue that the ideas about verification that have dominated U.S. policy debates contain a core contradiction that makes domestic support for arms control depend on verification arrangements which negotiating partners are likely to oppose. Americans often depict verification as a technical problem of increasing transparency to reveal the "truth" about compliance. Yet they also insist that the United States must make its own compliance judgments because the process is highly subjective and prone to distortion by self-interested states. The more significant arms restrictions would be, the more Americans want to maximize their access to compliance information and their freedom to use that information as they see fit. Other states react by trying to protect sensitive information and increase their control over decision making, especially when their ideas about verification emphasize the risks of transparency or the value of joint compliance evaluations. These reactions set off warning bells in the United States, where resistance to American verification demands is taken as a sign of dubious intentions. Arms control seems riskier, so Americans insist on even more information and more adversarial decision-making procedures, and a deadlock results.

Does this counter-cooperative dynamic occur because states want arms control only on terms that give them a competitive advantage—the reason Realists give for the failures of Cold War arms control? Or does it arise when states want mutually beneficial accords but misperceive one another's motives and misunderstand one another's verification concerns—the Liberal's explanation? This book synthesizes these perspectives by showing how each describes the behavior of a different kind of player. The key features of American arms control debates can be captured by using three ideal types to define the middle and ends of a security spectrum. "Cautious Cooperators" believe that a bargain could be beneficial but are uncertain about others' intentions and afraid of exploitation. Their support for a treaty depends on the details of verification. "Arms Control Advocates" think that the benefits of a particular accord greatly outweigh the potential costs and risks. Their concerns about verification are easily satisfied, so they use arguments about verifiability to reassure Cautious Cooperators. "Unilateralists" are so skeptical about arms control that it is difficult, if not impossible, to meet their verification concerns. Since they expect rival states to resist intrusive verification, they also have strategic incentives to exacerbate Cautious Cooperators' anxieties and increase their verification demands. This makes arms control less attractive to Cautious Cooperators in other states and gives foreign Unilateralists more evidence that the United States wants to exploit arms control for competitive purposes.

The best way to trace the connections between domestic debates and international negotiations is to follow a single issue over an extended time. The test ban case is the only arms control problem that has been on the agenda in one form or another since nuclear negotiations started and that has been pursued in bilateral, trilateral, and multilateral forums. The wealth of primary resources includes negotiating records, declassified documents, congressional hearings, memoirs, newspaper accounts, opinion polls, and interviews. With strong arguments for and against a test ban, the case has the key features of any "mixed motive" problem. Many verification options are available; in fact, the United States had national technical means to monitor Soviet tests more than a decade before satellites could be used to verify arms control. Yet even in this "easy" case, winning coalitions have been hard to form and blocking coalitions have been difficult to sustain. Thus, the case holds important lessons for more difficult verification problems in the post–Cold War world.

No explanation that trivializes the politics of verification can account for the range of test ban outcomes. Ambitious proposals for international control of all dangerous nuclear activities produced no serious negotiations until separate test ban talks began in 1958. There were two failed trilateral attempts at a Comprehensive Test Ban, in 1958–63 and 1978–80. The 1963 Limited Test Ban Treaty was signed and ratified without formal verification provisions. Two minor bilateral accords, the Threshold Test Ban Treaty and the Peaceful Nuclear Explosions Treaty, were signed in the 1970s but not ratified until 1990. Verification breakthroughs in the mid-1980s revived negotiations but secured no new limits. Multilateral CTB negotiations started in 1994 and recently culminated in a CTBT with broad international support but restrictive entry-into-force conditions that may keep key verification provisions from ever taking effect.

The mixed results of recent arms control efforts show that agreement on verification is possible but not automatic in the post–Cold War world. I hope that this book helps scholars and policy makers understand why arguments about verification persist and how they can be provisionally resolved. It offers no easy answers: trade-offs are inevitable because adversarial verification cannot support major cooperation, yet joint monitoring and assessment necessarily involve some uncertainty and a chance that one group's judgment will differ from another's. Attempts to downplay these dilemmas or "depoliticize" verification play into Unilateralists' blocking strategies. Education can keep Cautious Cooperators from assuming that anyone who shares their verification concerns is serious about arms control and that anyone who disagrees with their verification demands wants to take advantage of them, but it will not make conflicting ideas and interests disappear. The best long-term solution is to approach the politics of verification like any other form of bargaining: (1) build winning coalitions around compromise positions that are acceptable to different groups for divergent reasons, and (2) move gradually toward more cooperative verification and more significant arms control.

This book has been many years in the making. My work on it started in the late 1980s, a time when arms control policy and international relations theory were much different than they are today. My close involvement with the University of Illinois' interdisciplinary program in Arms Control, Disarmament, and International security provided financial support through the MacArthur Foundation, as well as diverse intellectual resources related to the politics of nuclear test ban verification. Jeremiah Sullivan taught me about verification technology and gave me numerous contacts in the scientific world; Roger Kanet and John Lepingwell provided insights into the Soviet side of arms control; and Stephen Cohen encouraged me to include the perspectives of nonsuperpowers. Mary Anderson, Judy Jones, and Merrily Shaw served as a delightful antidote to the loneliness often associated with dissertation work.

Over the years, this book has changed almost as much as the world has. Its evolution benefitted from the chance to give papers at American Political Science Association and International Studies Association meetings. I received useful feedback from scientists who attended presentations at Lawrence Livermore and Sandia National Laboratories. Vicki Golich, Richard Harknett, Linda Brady, and David Welch provided helpful suggestions and invaluable encouragement early in the revision process. Wesleyan University contributed to the book's development with funds for research assistance and interview expenses. Erhardt Konerding, Wesleyan's documents librarian, was remarkably resourceful and helpful. Students in my arms control classes and cooperation theory seminars fed my enthusiasm and pressed me to explain my arguments more clearly. A colleague in the Government Department, James McGuire, went over the penultimate draft with a careful eye and helped make the manuscript more accessible to interested nonspecialists. Andrew Szegedy-Maszak of the Classics Department restored my confidence in my darkest hour, and he has helped me move forward ever since.

A postdoctoral research fellowship from Women in International Security for the 1995–96 academic year greatly facilitated my study of post–Cold War verification politics. WIIS provided research funds, contacts in the arms control policy community, and a supportive work environment. It encouraged me to bring theorists and policy makers together for a workshop, "Bridging the Gaps on Arms Control," at which many of the ideas in this book were presented. Since WIIS is housed in the Center for International and Security Studies at the University of Maryland, I also benefitted greatly from the expertise of Steve Fetter, Mac Destler, and George Quester.

My understanding of arms control policy making and negotiation has been greatly enhanced through access to declassified documents and extensive interviews. I am grateful for the generosity of the Cold War historians who shared documents uncovered through the Freedom of Information Act by placing them in the National Security Archives. The policy makers and analysts who consented to be interviewed are too numerous to mention here, and some prefer to remain nameless. I would like to give special thanks to Thomas Cochran, Pierce Corden,

Allan Krass, Michael Krepon, Milo Nordyke, Christopher Paine, Amy Sands, James Schear, Jacob Scherr, Roland Timerbayev, Gregory van der Vink, and Herbert York. Warren Heckrotte not only granted several interviews but also gave detailed comments on the penultimate manuscript and responded to numerous queries. Rebecca Johnson graciously shared her insider's knowledge of test ban negotiations in the 1990s, even after realizing that my book would necessitate a change in her proposed dissertation topic.

Numerous people have assisted in the production of this book. Karen Hultgren and Marisa Uchin served as research assistants, and Noreen O'Connor helped make the manuscript a manageable size. For the Johns Hopkins University Press, Wendy Jacobs clarified prose and ensured consistency throughout the book; thanks also go to Henry Tom, executive editor, and Julie McCarthy, senior production editor.

Edward Kolodziej, my dissertation director, mentor, and friend, has been a constant source of inspiration, encouragement, and practical assistance. From him I learned to think theoretically about the policy-making process and to prefer synthetic perspectives on politics over single-factor explanations. In research and in real life, I have always appreciated his mix of clear-eyed realism and humane idealism. He is truly the intellectual grandfather of this book.

My deepest appreciation goes to family and friends. Ellen Riggle, Cecelia Miller, Brian Stewart, Jane Brawerman, Wendy Rayack, and Amy Schmidt-Stowe have stood by me through thick and thin. My parents, brother, and sister may never wade through the acronyms and theoretical terms associated with the politics of arms control verification, but they have always shown the unflagging confidence in my work that every author needs. Tony Daley has done everything from improving my writing and typing my bibliography to cooking countless dinners and driving me to obscure FedEx boxes on New Year's Eve. More important, he has also reminded me that the truest measure of a political scientist's work is its ability to illuminate and alleviate suffering, injustice, and insecurity. My son, Ted, has kept me grounded during a very cerebral exercise, and my daughter, Arianne, arrived just in time to help check the copyediting.

Acronyms and Abbreviations

AAAS	American Association for the Advancement of Science
ABM	antiballistic missile
ACA	Arms Control Association
ACDA	Arms Control and Disarmament Agency
ADA	Atomic Development Authority
AEC	Atomic Energy Commission
AFTAC	Air Force Technical Applications Center
ALC	Acheson-Lilienthal Committee
ARPA	Advanced Research Projects Agency
BWC	Biological and Toxic Weapons Convention
CCD	Conference of the Committee on Disarmament
CD	Conference on Disarmament
CFE	Conventional Forces in Europe
CIA	Central Intelligence Agency
COG	chief of government
CORRTEX	Continuous Reflectrometry for Radius v. Time Experiments
CTB	Comprehensive Test Ban
CTBT	Comprehensive Test Ban Treaty
CWC	Chemical Weapons Convention
DARPA	Defense Advanced Research Projects Agency
DOD	Department of Defense
DOE	Department of Energy
EIF	Entry into Force
EMP	electromagnetic pulse
ENDC	Eighteen-Nation Disarmament Committee
ERDA	Energy Research and Development Administration
EURATOM	European Atomic Energy Community

FAS	Federation of American Scientists
G-21	Group of 21 Nonaligned States
GAC	General Advisory Committee
GCD	General and Complete Disarmament
GSE	Ad Hoc Group of Scientific Experts
GSETT-3	Third Technical Test of GSE Prototype Network
HNE	hydronuclear experiment
IAEA	International Atomic Energy Agency
ICBM	Intercontinental Ballistic Missile
IDC	International Data Center
IMS	International Monitoring System
INF	Intermediate-Range Nuclear Forces Treaty
JCAE	Joint Committee on Atomic Energy
JCS	Joint Chiefs of Staff
JVE	Joint Verification Experiment
kt	kiloton
LANL	Los Alamos National Laboratory
LLNL	Lawrence Livermore National Laboratory
LTBT	Limited Test Ban Treaty
MAD	Mutual Assured Destruction
M_b	magnitude of compressional body wave (P-wave)
MIRV	multiple independently targetable re-entry vehicles
M_s	magnitude of Rayleigh surface wave
mt	megaton
NATO	North Atlantic Treaty Organization
NNWS	non-nuclear weapons state
NPT	Nonproliferation Treaty
NRDC	Natural Resources Defense Council
NSA	National Security Archives
NSC	National Security Council
NSS	National Seismic Station
NTBC	Nuclear Test Ban Committee
NTM	national technical means of verification
NTS	Nevada Test Site
NTT	Nuclear Testing Talks
NWS	nuclear weapons state
NUTS	Nuclear Utilization Targeting Selection

OSI	on-site inspection
OTA	Office of Technology Assessment
PNE	peaceful nuclear explosion
PNET	Peaceful Nuclear Explosions Treaty
PSAC	President's Science Advisory Committee
SALT	Strategic Arms Limitation Treaty
SCC	Standing Consultative Commission
SCFR	Senate Committee on Foreign Relations
SDI	Strategic Defense Initiative
SLBM	submarine-launched ballistic missile
SIPRI	Stockholm International Peace Research Institute
SRPAG	Seismic Research Program Advisory Group
START	Strategic Arms Reduction Treaty
SVA	special verification agreement
TTBT	Threshold Test Ban Treaty
TWG	Technical Working Group
UNAEC	United Nations Atomic Energy Commission
UNIDIR	United Nations Institute for Disarmament Research
UNGA	United Nations General Assembly
UNSCOM	United Nations Special Commission
USGS	United States Geological Survey
WTO	Warsaw Treaty Organization
WWSSN	Worldwide Standardized Seismograph Network

The Politics of Verification

1

Verification

The Key to Cooperation?

IN A WORLD IN WHICH STATES FACE CONFLICTING PRESSURES to maximize military capabilities and negotiate mutual restraints, the prospects for arms control often hinge on verification. Accords are easier to negotiate and ratify when participants have confidence in their ability to monitor behavior and judge compliance. In the standard American formulation, verification is the "critical element of arms control": effective cooperation will enhance national security only if U.S. leaders have the means to deter cheating, detect violations, and reassure constituents about mutual compliance.[1]

Although verification is often considered primarily a technical problem, politics become important whenever suspicious states and contentious domestic groups have conflicting preferences about the amount and type of verification that would make the benefits of arms control outweigh the costs and risks. With no overarching authority to impose a solution or a set of shared principles from which one best answer can be definitively derived, verification arrangements must be developed through bargaining, coercion, persuasion, coalition-building, and other political processes. This book examines the causes of verification arguments, the processes through which they are perpetuated or provisionally resolved, and the effects on cooperation.

The checkered history of nuclear arms control can be read as the story of verification politics. Conflicts between American demands for "foolproof" verification and Soviet denunciation of "legalized espionage" provided the most visible reason for failure in the first decade of nuclear disarmament talks.[2] During the 1960s and 1970s, the superpowers accepted partial arms control measures only when satellites, seismic monitors, and other remote sensing technologies could satisfy their contradictory verification concerns. When bilateral relations soured in the early 1980s, U.S. conservatives used doubts about verification to attack détente-era treaties and condition future cooperation on unprecedented inspection rights. The intensity of the superpower rivalry decreased in the mid-1980s, as agreement on increasingly elaborate bilateral verification created the confidence needed for stricter constraints on more threatening activities. Then, in the immediate post–Cold War years, the relative ease with which 130 countries granted international agents unprecedented inspection rights and decision-making authority for the 1993 Chemical Weapons Convention (CWC) spurred hopes that traditional obstacles to cooperative security were finally eroding.

Arms control opponents ridicule the notion that verification can be a driving force for cooperation. In their view, Cold War verification controversies were predictable attempts to sabotage negotiations or gain an advantage at the bargaining table. Skeptics claim that verification breakthroughs came only after Mikhail Gorbachev rejected excess secrecy and exorbitant military expenditures and Ronald Reagan dropped his "evil empire" approach to the USSR. Arms control opponents saw support for these verification regimes as a fleeting relic of post–Cold War euphoria: if relations remained good, nobody would want to pay for inspections and expensive monitoring equipment; if relations soured, no one would trust verification arrangements designed during a friendlier time. Indeed, many old Cold Warriors have borne out their own contradictory predictions. One contingent argues that Russia's shift from communism to capitalism obviates the need for formal arms control and verification, while another contends that Russian leaders' failure to ratify and implement post–Cold War accords shows that they still cannot be trusted, regardless of their verification promises. In short, critics contend that agreement on verification is a consequence rather than a cause of cooperation. If so, the politics of verification is just a sideshow that distracts from the real reasons for weapons development and arms control.

Despite the intensity and importance of these debates, nobody has studied the politics of verification as a basic problem for international relations theory. The few scientists and policy analysts who wrote about this subject in the mid-1980s argued that verification preferences are derived from prior beliefs about arms control, deterrence, and Soviet intentions. They urged U.S. leaders to depoliticize verification decisions by building a domestic consensus on these larger policy issues and finding "win-win" technologies to monitor compliance without revealing other sensitive information. Ironically, even those analysts who were the strongest arms control supporters concluded that agreement on verification is essential for cooperation but most likely when it is least necessary—when distrust and incentives to compete are already low.

On the surface, the disappointing record of Cold War arms control supports the pessimistic conclusion that agreement on verification is possible only for narrow, noncontroversial accords tailored to available monitoring technologies. If one digs deeper, however, a more complex and promising picture emerges. I argue that the persistent problems in reaching domestic and international agreement on verification for truly significant arms control accords have arisen from the particular ideas and strategies that have dominated the politics of verification, rather than from the more immutable features of international relations.

This book starts from the premise that the politics of verification pose a fundamental problem for any cooperative enterprise. Decisions about principles and procedures for evaluating compliance are intensely contested for their own sake and their connection to other controversial questions. Similar arguments have recurred repeatedly, despite major changes in the identity of participants and the political context, because conflicting positions reflect enduring disagreements about the nature of international relations and about verification itself. Domestic debates and international negotiations are interconnected; therefore, moves made in one political arena affect the chances of agreement in the other. Attempts to depoliticize verification have always failed, often with counter-cooperative consequences. Instead, provisional agreements have come through a political process of coalition-building among players with conflicting ideas about verification and international relations. Despite difficult conditions during the Cold War, arms control supporters made noteworthy progress toward agreement on verification for measures that would have fundamentally altered nuclear competition. Each iteration forced arms control opponents to devise new blocking strategies, a task that benefitted greatly from the rigidly opposing ideas about verification that dominated debates in the United States and the USSR.

The political-military context for arms control has improved since the end of the Cold War, yet many of the old verification arguments nearly torpedoed U.S. ratification of the CWC, delayed negotiation of the 1996 Comprehensive Test Ban Treaty (CTBT), and threaten the CTBT's ratification. Familiar arguments about the amount and type of verification are also emerging as cooperative accords are considered for other issue areas, such as the environment, trade, and human rights. All this suggests an urgent need to challenge the view of verification as a technical solution to political dilemmas of arms control, illuminate the deep structure of verification arguments, educate decision makers about inevitable trade-offs, and develop coalition-building strategies that do not require shared beliefs about international relations.

Three Views of the Politics of Verification

Americans have always been deeply divided over the value of arms control but have been united in the belief that any possible benefits from mutual cooperation depend not only on shared interests but also on reliable means to judge and enforce compliance.[3] Arms control can lower the likelihood of conflict, the lethality of war, and the costs of security.[4] It may even help transform enemies into friends over time. Yet leaders often fear cheating, unfavorable relative gains, or domestic opposition to an accord. Decision makers with conflicting incentives to coordinate behavior and to act unilaterally face an arms control dilemma. The intensity of that dilemma, and hence the significance of a treaty, depends on the mix of motives held or perceived by participants. In other words, the more an accord would actually change behavior from choices that would have been made in the absence of an agreement, the greater both the potential gains and the potential costs and risks. To reap the benefits of arms control, participants must fulfill their bargains and avoid false accusations. But incentives to cheat and fears of exploitation rise as the significance of cooperation increases. The difficulty of designing equitable, effective, and efficient verification arrangements grows as the demand for verification intensifies. The challenge for negotiators involved in the politics of verification is to reach domestic and international agreement on principles and procedures that promote significant accords, encourage compliance, and increase confidence despite strong suspicions and temptations to defect.[5]

Can this challenge can be met? The politics of verification have played a central role in efforts to build coalitions for and against nuclear arms control because Americans typically agree that reliable verification is a prerequisite for cooperation. They disagree, however, about whether satisfactory arrangements can be obtained for a particular agreement. The popularity of President Reagan's "trust but verify" slogan stemmed from its appeal to groups seeking major reductions in superpower arsenals, as well as those who were ambivalent about arms control or opposed to any significant cooperation with a potential adversary. All three groups valued verification but differed in their requirements and their expectations about the USSR's response to their preferred arrangements. The "trust but verify" slogan refocused debate from arms control, which a majority of Americans supported, to verification requirements, which a majority could be persuaded to expand beyond anything that the Soviets would likely accept.

Arguments among policy makers about the prospects for agreement on verification correspond to debates among theorists about the possibilities for international cooperation in an anarchic world. The assumption that stable cooperation is easier inside sovereign states than among them reflects the extent to which domestic leaders have the legitimacy and power needed for authoritative judgments and effective sanctions. National governments have formal institutions to clarify rules, catch criminals, adjudicate disputes, punish violators, and compensate victims. These systems are far from perfect, and compliance with domestic rules depends as much on shared benefits, habits, and morality as it does on threats and sanctions.[6] Moreover, adherence to international agreements reflects common interests, organizational incentives, and inertia, as well as fear of detection and punishment.[7] Still, a crucial question about world politics is whether sovereign states can devise their own verification arrangements to secure and sustain cooperation without a supranational network of global legislators, police, lawyers, judges, and jailers.

Conflicting answers to this question reflect divergent beliefs about world politics that correspond to three traditions in Western international relations theory: Hobbesian, Grotian, and Kantian.[8] These academic approaches make different assumptions about international relations that lead to divergent conclusions about the politics of verification. I use this threefold categorization, rather than the more common dichotomies between realists and idealists, or neorealists and liberal institutionalists, to highlight crucial distinctions between Kantian and Grotian attitudes toward arms control and verification. This classic categorization is also appropriate for developing generalizations about the politics of verification because it relates disagreements to philosophical controversies that have endured for centuries rather than to policy disputes that are more context specific.

When practitioners think about arms control and verification, they use assumptions about world politics to make sense of complex, ambiguous, or indeterminate information.[9] Few interesting questions can be answered solely on the basis of uncontroversial "facts"; rather, research in social psychology has shown that "interpretation of reality tends to be more theory driven than data driven."[10] Policy makers' worldviews may rest on systematic theorizing or reflect a jumble of ideas absorbed from others with divergent belief structures. Participants in the politics of verification are usually less self-consciously theoretical than the classical terms imply. Therefore, I will refer to decision makers, policy analysts, and concerned citizens as "Unilateralists" (Hobbesians), "Cautious Cooperators" (Grotians), and "Arms Control Advocates" (Kantians).

These ideal types are actually shorthand for different positions along a security spectrum. Most participants describe themselves as Cautious Cooperators, but a close look at the assumptions they make often reveals a strong tendency toward one end of the spectrum. Oftentimes, too, Cautious Cooperators reason like Arms Control Advocates when they consider minor arms control measures and use the Unilateralists' worst-case assumptions when they think about major disarmament proposals. Although individual theorists and practitioners do not always fit neatly into one of these categories, using ideal types as an analytical device helps highlight key points of disagreement and explain why similar arguments about verification occur in very different policy contexts. It also directs attention to logical flaws in each of the traditional approaches. A recent issue of *International Security* published representative essays on post–Cold War verification by prominent analysts. The remainder of this section uses these essays to illustrate how conflicting conceptions of verification reflect alternative worldviews.

Hobbesians and Unilateralists

Hobbesian theorists see international relations as a zero-sum game among states with conflicting interests and little interdependence. Anarchy creates a self-help system wherein security and prosperity depend on relative power. These theorists' attitude toward arms control and verification reflects two dictums from Hobbes's *Leviathan*: "Where there is no common power, there is no law" beyond national survival and "covenants without swords [to enforce them] are but words." Hobbesians assume that states will rarely sign arms control accords unless they can get terms that give them an advantage over other participants, catch all cheating, and punish every violation in a way that restores their relative advantage.[11] The politics of verification is simply one more arena in which states compete. When public opinion forces leaders to negotiate, Hobbesians predict that they will try to score public relations points by offering to sign popular arms control measures if the other side accepts extremely disadvantageous verification arrangements. Should national leaders decide that a treaty would codify a power advantage or provide political benefits with no effect on military capabilities, they will seek a verification regime that maximizes their own monitoring capabilities, denies the other side access to sensitive information, and preserves their autonomy to act and judge others in ways that suit their competitive goals. Hobbesians may also try to use verification as a cover for aggressive behavior, such as collecting "collateral" information (e.g., military and economic intelligence not related to treaty compliance) or disrupting military preparations that are not banned by the accord.[12]

The *International Security* essay by Kenneth Adelman, director of the Arms Control and Disarmament Agency (ACDA) from 1983 to 1987, presented a Unilateralist's view of verification that clearly rests on Hobbesian assumptions.[13] He asserted that the end of the Cold War made verification more difficult and less important than it had been during the Reagan years. Although the Soviets were willing to permit intrusive inspections, Adelman insisted that the United States still could not reliably verify the kinds of cooperative accords that would enhance its security. This situation was due partly to changes in military technology, such as the trend toward strategic systems that were smaller, more mobile, and harder for satellite monitoring to detect. He also alleged, however, that the Soviets routinely continued to violate their agreements and that they only seemed more cooperative under Gorbachev because their concealment and deception practices had improved. From Adelman's perspective, the Soviets had little reason to honor their agreements because the popularity of arms control in the United States prevented democratic leaders from taking effective enforcement measures, despite clear evidence of noncompliance. Therefore, he recommended that American leaders place less emphasis on formal treaties and more on informal reciprocal reductions that posed little risk to national security and would be easily reversible should new threats arise.

As Adelman's recommendations indicate, Hobbesian theorists and Unilateralist practitioners do not see verification as the basis for lasting cooperation because self-help monitoring, judgment, and enforcement systems are inherently imperfect. They also assume that adversaries will manipulate any joint verification processes by feeding in false information or biasing judgments in their favor.[14] Thus, they argue that the competitive nature of international politics creates a paradoxical situation in which states are most likely to agree on verification measures when they least need them—when relations are friendly or when accords only constrain inconsequential activities.[15]

This pessimistic view of the politics of verification exaggerates the difference between domestic and international systems. Fear of detection and punishment is not the sole reason why most citizens obey rules; nor do national legislators refrain from passing laws against murder and other major crimes simply because some criminals will not be caught, convicted, and punished enough to prevent future transgressions. Arms control opponents also rarely compare the benefits, costs, and risks of imperfectly verified cooperation with those of unconstrained competition. If these considerations are included, possibilities for agreement on verification increase.

Grotians and Cautious Cooperators

Grotian theorists believe that states have a combination of common and conflicting interests that create the need and opportunity for global "governance without government"—a society among sovereign states based on reciprocal self-restraint.[16] Grotians maintain that cooperation is possible when participants can do better (in absolute terms, especially over the long run) by coordinating their behavior than through unilateral actions. Since states could gain even more (at least in the short run) by defecting while others cooperate, Grotians want behavior to be transparent so that players can use reciprocal strategies to establish and enforce cooperation.[17] States will be less afraid of exploitation if they can detect violations before lasting harm is done. Leaders with mixed motives will also be more likely to honor accords if they expect cheating to be punished and compliance to be rewarded. Finally, because no state wants to be taken advantage of, verification can build domestic support for arms control by providing evidence that can be publicized to reassure citizens that other states are upholding their obligations. Verification cannot completely replace centralized judgment and enforcement: justice will be crude and uneven when states judge their own disputes and lack the solidarity, capability, and will to punish violations consistently.[18] Still, Grotians believe that sovereign states can perform most compliance functions themselves with as much success and fewer negative side effects than would occur under world government.[19]

The essays by Ivan Oelrich and Lewis Dunn provided two Cautious Cooperators' perspectives on verification. Whereas Grotian theorists often see transparency measures in a purely positive light, practitioners are more apt to recognize that sharing information about military activities involves costs and risks as well as benefits. But Oelrich was confident that verification dilemmas could easily be solved in the post–Cold War security context.[20] He maintained that verification was the limiting factor in Cold War arms control. Advances in monitoring technology and Soviet acceptance of intrusive verification forced Americans to decide how much verification they really needed for a particular treaty and whether they actually wanted to negotiate every arms control measure that could be verified. Agreement on verification should be easier to reach because low-level violations would have little military significance and verification had lost its political function as an indicator of Soviet commitment to arms control. Oelrich claimed that verification decisions were becoming more "matter of fact" and "technical" as negotiations grew less confrontational and ratification debates became less ideological. Arms control need no longer be confined to measures that could be monitored by national technical means (NTM), because countries had recognized the value of "cooperative monitoring."[21] By this, Oelrich meant that each party to an agreement actively increases the other's access to information that substantiates their compliance by exchanging data, for example, or permitting aerial surveillance and on-site inspections (OSIs). He still considered verification fundamentally to be a self-help activity, however, on the grounds that each state should decide for itself whether cooperation is occurring and what to do if it is not.

Dunn was more ambivalent about the prospects for verification.[22] He contended that current arms control proposals were at the outer limits of verifiability, due partly to the technical characteristics of the weapons under consideration and partly to increased American concerns about intrusive monitoring measures. Dunn believed that minor violations could have major political significance even when they had little military importance, so his verification requirements were higher than Oerlich's. But because Dunn wanted national leaders to weigh the political and military benefits of arms control against the risks of imperfect compliance, he did not agree with Adelman that treaties necessarily need foolproof verification. Instead, he urged the United States to compensate for the uncertainties of verification by investing in unilateral "safeguards," such as chemical weapons defenses or facilities to resume nuclear tests on short notice.

As these examples illustrate, some Grotians and Cautious Cooperators see verification as a technical fix to the dilemmas of cooperation under anarchy, whereas others recognize that mixed motives complicate verification, just as they confuse other arms control decisions. In either view, however, the possibility of solving verification problems depends on the contextual factors that determine costs and benefits attributed to a particular arms control measure, the perceived probabilities and consequences of noncompliance, and the potential methods for achieving the desired degree of transparency.

Grotians make a convincing case for the importance of verification but rarely explain how self-interested states and contentious domestic groups can agree on verification when they have conflicting interests and contradictory ideas about international politics. For example, advances in satellite technology facilitated strategic arms control (SALT I in 1972 and SALT II in 1979), but only after the superpowers had achieved understanding on the legitimacy of NTM and "passive cooperation" to enhance transparency.[23] SALT I was ratified by the U.S. Senate whereas SALT II was not, partly because U.S. leaders could secure domestic support for verification based solely on NTM for the former but not the latter. Grotian analyses that treat verification as a substitute for trust forget that no feasible monitoring system offers perfect certainty about compliance behavior.[24] Thus, Grotians face a chicken-and-egg problem wherein verification is needed to enhance trust and cooperation, but cooperation and trust are needed to secure agreement on verification.

When Grotians address the politics of verification, they usually depict it as a second-order free-rider problem: because monitoring and enforcement are costly, everyone will be tempted to let others bear the burdens of verification.[25] Elinor Ostrom predicts that individuals will verify compliance if the added costs of monitoring are low or if they receive additional benefits, such as extra information that improves their strategic calculations or rewards them for catching malefactors.[26] Applying this solution to arms control would be only partly effective and potentially destabilizing. Making monitoring a natural by-product of ongoing activities limits arms control to what is already being watched by military and intelligence personnel. Moreover, providing private benefits to those who pay for monitoring raises incentives to use verification for competitive purposes. As one U.S. Department of Defense (DOD) staffer saw it, the only difference between verification and espionage was whether he could speak openly about the source of his information on Soviet military activities.[27]

The Grotian emphasis on transparency also blurs the difference between monitoring (collecting information) and verification (judging compliance).[28] Even when participants have extensive information about treaty-relevant behavior, they may disagree about how that information should be interpreted and how compliance disputes should be resolved. Negotiators frequently use ambiguous or incomplete treaty language to bridge minor disputes, preserve flexibility, or protect core elements of an accord against future developments. Furthermore, monitoring systems are often good enough to detect signs of suspicious activity but not to provide definitive evidence that a violation has (or has not) occurred. The most common Grotian solution is to establish a consultative committee of national representatives to seek clarification of controversial activities. The assumption that each state must ultimately make its own verification decisions, though, means that conflicts of interest can easily lead to self-serving interpretations and acrimonious arguments about whether the evidence of noncompliance is strong enough to support inspections, sanctions, or treaty abrogation.

Kantians and Arms Control Advocates

Kantian theorists believe that states and individuals in world politics have more shared interests and fewer genuine conflicts than Hobbesians and Grotians perceive. Some Kantians think that this harmony of interests reflects human sociability and potential altruism. Others hold that extensive interdependence makes cooperation the preferred mode of interaction even for purely self-interested (egoistic) actors. Kantians argue that arms races and wars result only rarely from hostile motives and occur usually when security elites misperceive defensive actions or pursue selfish policies that hurt their populations (e.g., self-enrichment by a industrial-military complex). Whereas Grotians support modest arms control to manage the costs and risks of unilateral security, Kantians see major arms control and disarmament accords as a key component of cooperative security regimes. Such regimes presume fundamentally compatible security objectives and increase security through threat prevention. Members avoid misperceptions and internal pressures for "inappropriate" military systems (e.g., the amounts and types of weapons not needed for homeland defense) by negotiating complex agreements about the size, concentration, technical configuration, and operational practices of their militaries.[29] If a state is bent on aggression, Kantians argue, such shared understandings should help other countries identify and unite against the threat to their mutual security.

Since Kantians assume that states rarely make bargains that are not in their interest to keep, the main function of verification is reassurance that cooperation is occurring, rather than detection or deterrence of violations.[30] Should compliance concerns arise because states interpret ambiguous rules differently or lack the capability to follow complex regulations, Kantians advocate satisfactory adjustments to make cooperative security operate more smoothly. The minimum amount of verification needed is low, because the expected benefits greatly outweigh the anticipated risks. But some Kantians advise using extra verification to promote international openness, strengthen international organizations, and democratize security policy in countries whose civilian oversight of military decisions is weak. Optimism about the prospects for agreement on verification comes from enthusiasm about new monitoring technologies and a belief that transparency is fast becoming a global norm.[31] It also reflects the belief that changing conceptions of sovereignty increase pressures for compliance, decrease resistance to cooperative monitoring, and encourage national leaders to delegate authority for verification to international agents.[32]

The essay by Abram Chayes and Antonia Handler Chayes represents the reasoning of Arms Control Advocates. Their Kantian assumptions led them to support a shift from an adversarial, law-enforcement model of verification to a managerial approach patterned after dispute resolution in complex regulatory regimes.[33] In the Chayes's view, on-site inspections (OSIs) were not needed to catch militarily significant violations because low-level noncompliance could not disrupt the stability of deterrence, and the Soviet record of compliance had been good even without OSIs. Still, they saw Gorbachev's acceptance of intrusive verification as an "extremely hopeful development" that would increase opportunities to work with the Soviets in clarifying ambiguous activities, in improving capabilities for compliance, and in fine-tuning rules to minimize future friction. If formal dispute resolution procedures failed to resolve compliance concerns, the authors argued, crude unilateral responses, such as treaty withdrawal or economic sanctions, would be counterproductive. Therefore, they advised injured states to "resort to a higher authority" by working with "whatever political and diplomatic pressures can be brought to bear."[34] The implication was that the ultimate guarantor of international cooperation is enlightened public opinion, solidarity among like-minded states, and international organizations with growing enforcement capabilities.

Cooperative security and managerial verification are attractive concepts, but their acceptance and success require a harmony of interest on key security issues, accurate perceptions, and high levels of trust. Therefore, academics and practitioners who dispute Kantian assumptions about international politics maintain that such proposals rest on hopeful visions rather than hard-headed analysis. One common charge is that cooperative security and managerial verification cannot cope effectively with hard cases, for example, "rogue" states that do not have purely defensive intentions or desire to be good international citizens. Another criticism is that states still lack the clarity of common principles and the level of solidarity needed to agree on inappropriate behavior and unite behind effective countermeasures. Kantians counter allegations of idealism with real-world examples of cooperative security and managerial verification, but these are only partial applications to low-risk agreements among friendly states. We still lack persuasive evidence that states will trust collective security and delegate verification authority for major military agreements when national survival is at stake. But when states try to hedge their bets by keeping residual offensive capabilities or by reserving the right to respond unilaterally if dispute resolution procedures and diplomatic pressure fail, Kantian proposals become Grotian practices.

Ongoing Arguments among the Three Traditions

Hobbesian, Grotian, and Kantian assumptions create the conflicting views of verification summarized in Table 1.1. My goal is not to determine which theory most accurately captures the inherent nature of verification politics and international relations. Instead, this book attempts to show that the politics of arms control is shaped by ongoing arguments among the three traditions.

Distinguishing among three radically different ways of thinking about verification, each of which is logical if the starting assumptions are accepted, has important implications. It does not mean that the politics of verification occurs primarily in participants' minds; their preferences reflect both objective factors, such as the capabilities of a particular monitoring technology, and subjective factors, such as their evaluation of the risks of cooperation, given that uncertainty about compliance. It does, however, undermine the notion that objective factors determine an optimal solution to verification problems—a "strategic baseline" against which any other outcome can be measured as a deviation

Table 1.1 Three Views of Verification

	Hobbesians and Unilateralists	Grotians and Arms Control Advocates	Kantians and Cautious Cooperators
Assumptions about international relations	Pure conflict Relative gains matter Low interdependence Preserve autonomy	Mixed motives Seek absolute gains Some interdependence Reciprocal self-restraint possible	Mostly harmonious Egoism and altruism High interdependence Complex agreements Changing sovereignty
Potential for cooperation	Highly unlikely Strong states impose and enforce favorable terms Ends when states can gain advantage by cheating or abrogating accord	When unilateral choices yield suboptimal results Decrease temptation to defect/fear of exploitation	Cooperation is widespread already More possible if states minimize misperceptions and increase cooperative capabilities Compliance is high
Main functions of verification	Detect violations Provide evidence of cheating needed for effective response Lower public support for bad treaties Collect collateral information	Enable reciprocity Deter violations Timely detection to avoid exploitation Domestic reassurance Focus on militarily significant issues	Reassure participants that everyone is cooperating Manage compliance disputes Promote openness, democracy, and international authority
Preferred type of verification	Purely adversarial Entire process must be self-help Any violation must be confronted and punished	Mainly adversarial Cooperative measures aid transparency Consultation and clarification Judgment and response are national responsibilities	Managerial Monitoring, assessment, and response best done jointly Few violations show aggressive motives or have military significance
Prospects for agreement on verification	Extremely low unless leaders give in to popular pressure for bad accords Politics of verification mainly for public relations	Moderate and context-dependent Easier for low-risk accords that can be monitored with NTM	High Cooperation very beneficial Need not detect minor violations Advances in win-win monitoring Less resistance to intrusive measures

from rationality and attributed to misperceptions or domestic politics. It also explains why there is neither a scholarly consensus about what verification is nor a single cumulative body of knowledge about what works best under different circumstances. The current controversy between proponents of "enforcement" and "managerial" approaches to verification shows that scholars still speak past each other because they make divergent assumptions about motivations and decision making.[35]

Verification debates cannot be permanently settled because preferences reflect "essentially contested concepts" with "an ideological element which renders empirical evidence irrelevant as a means of resolving the dispute."[36] Furthermore, world politics contains elements of conflict, harmony, and mutual self-restraint, so observers can find evidence to support each worldview. Finally, all three traditional understandings of verification are flawed, so policy makers often shift positions or support hybrid policies. Therefore, the success or failure of verification accords reflects the temporary alignment of actors with different ideas about international relations rather than permanent features of world politics. Those who wish to enhance arms control must determine why, in the past, blocking coalitions formed more frequently than winning ones and whether that pattern can be broken.

Previous Research: The Politicization of Verification

Despite decades of detailed research on verification technology and policy options, we know little about the politics of verification.[37] Most international relations theorists who have written about verification either ignore politics or treat it as a constraint on leaders' ability to maximize gains despite imperfect verification.[38] The few analysts who wrote about the politics of verification in the 1980s focused on a pressing policy problem: the Reagan administration's approach to verification was so at odds with previous U.S. policy and Soviet preferences that existing treaties were threatened and future arms control efforts doomed unless practitioners could find new grounds for agreement or take verification out of the political arena.[39] What I call the "first wave" authors had insights that should inform any theory of verification: (1) arms control verification is not a purely objective and technical process; (2) arguments over verification have a deep structure; and (3) disagreements about verification can be sincere, cynical, or both. But their main conclusion—verification is a peripheral problem that can and should be depoliticized—rested on unreliable assumptions and risked turning the verification paradox into a self-fulfilling prophecy.

In contrast to the common assumption that arms control verification is like scientific verification—a technical process of collecting facts to confirm or disprove claims about treaty compliance—first-wave analysts showed that compliance assessments are inherently subjective and susceptible to manipulation. Identical monitoring information could support conflicting compliance judgments, because U.S. decision makers were influenced by several factors: knowledge of other Soviet military and political actions, assumptions about Soviet intentions, lessons drawn from past interactions, the current political context, and idiosyncratic interpretations of treaty provisions. As Stephen Meyer noted, "hard" intelligence is often ambiguous, whereas "soft" inputs are highly volatile, and the relative weight given to each component changes over time.[40]

First-wave authors recognized that verification disputes stem from conflicting assumptions. As Lynn Eden pointed out, "Beneath the fragmentary arguments, beneath the flotsam and jetsam of competing claims advanced in debates over specific issues, is a deeper structure of argument which, when directly examined, makes orderly and comprehensible what is otherwise chaotic and unclear."[41] Each author depicted this deep structure differently, but the basic approach was to reduce the arguments between the superpowers and among U.S. policy makers to one question—"How much is enough?"—and explain answers in terms of contextual differences or disagreements on other policy issues.

At the international level, some first-wave authors explained U.S. attempts to maximize verification and Soviet efforts to minimize it as a legitimate reflection of different security concerns, whereas others saw contradictory U.S. and Soviet preferences as a cynical strategy to deadlock negotiations. For example, Mikhail Kokeyev and Andrei Androsov attributed the Soviet fear of espionage to the USSR's weaker strategic position during the 1950s and 1960s. Walter Slocombe asserted that the United States needed more formal verification than did the Soviets because the USSR was closed and secretive, whereas the United States was open and democratic.[42] Alva Myrdal, a Swedish diplomat, took a dimmer view of both sides' motives for making incompatible verification demands: "Behind their outwardly often fierce disagreements . . . there has always been a secret and undeclared collusion between the superpowers. Neither has wanted to be constrained by effective disarmament measures."[43]

First-wave authors also explained U.S. domestic disputes over "adequate" or "effective" verification standards as surrogate debates or sabotage techniques. In the 1960s and 1970s, U.S. verification capabilities were considered adequate if they could detect militarily significant violations in a timely fashion. Supporters argued that this put the Soviets in a double bind, because "to go undetected, any Soviet cheating would have to be on so small a scale that it would not be militarily significant. Cheating on such a level would hardly be worth the political risks involved. On the other hand, any cheating serious enough to affect the military balance would be detectable in sufficient time to take whatever action the situation required."[44] The first Reagan administration, however, insisted that any violation would be militarily or politically significant. Thus, truly effective verification must provide unambiguous evidence of even small violations, so that U.S. leaders could rally public support for treaty withdrawal, increased defense spending, sanctions, or other vigorous responses.[45]

The "adequate" versus "effective" debate was often depicted as a surrogate for deeper disagreements about U.S. nuclear strategy. Policy makers and attentive citizens who advocated adequate verification usually believed that deterrence was the only rational use for nuclear weapons and that both superpowers would be deterred as long as neither could destroy the other's retaliatory capability. In this Mutual Assured Destruction (MAD) strategy, which dominated official policy from the early 1960s through the mid-1970s, small quantitative advantages are unimportant, stockpiles that exceed the assured destruction threshold are useless, and types of weapons suited more for a first strike than a retaliatory blow are destabilizing.[46] Because the benefits of arms control are high and the military significance of minor violations is low, little verification is needed for high limits on warheads, restrictions on strategic defenses, or bans on very accurate delivery systems.

Verification standards rise as requirements for deterrence increase. Critics of MAD-based policies argued that threats to destroy Soviet cities in response to attacks on U.S. weapons or American allies were not credible, because they would invite destruction of U.S. population centers in return. To enhance deterrence and minimize damage should war occur, proponents of flexible response, or "NUTS"-type strategies, sought U.S. superiority—in all aspects of conventional, tactical, and strategic warfare; in advanced counterforce targeting capabilities; and in passive and active defense (e.g., hardened bunkers, fallout shelters, and antiballistic missile systems).[47] Policy makers and citizens who supported some form of NUTS might welcome arms control that preserved American superiority or secured asymmetrical reductions from the Soviets. Their verification requirements would be much higher than those of MAD supporters, however, both because their threshold for militarily significant cheating was lower and because failure to punish every violation could raise destabilizing doubts about American will.

First-wave analysts also linked verification arguments to differences of opinion about Soviet intentions.[48] Beliefs about Soviet motivations influenced verification preferences by shaping deterrence requirements: the more aggressive the Soviets, the more capability and will were needed to deter them. Assumptions about Soviet risk-taking propensities also had a direct effect on verification standards because they influenced expectations about cheating. Policy makers and citizens who believed that the Soviets were concerned solely about their own security or were risk-adverse saw less need for elaborate verification systems than did Americans who expected the Soviets to run high risks for small military or political advantages over the West.

Less generous analyses questioned whether one or both sides really cared about verification. Arms control supporters often complained that demands for "effective" verification were designed to deadlock negotiations by insisting on measures that the Soviets would refuse. For example, Michael Gordon called verification a common "fuzzword" in arms control debates: because everyone favored reliable verification, "stressing the need for stringent verification requirements that are unlikely to be met can be a politically convenient way to oppose agreements—without being perceived as opposing them."[49] Likewise, critics accused those who were satisfied with adequate verification of being so eager for arms control that they would accept accords that constrained the United States while the Soviets secretly developed new weapons.

Regardless of whether first-wave analysts saw verification arguments primarily as surrogates or stall tactics, they agreed that the politics of verification was a derivative problem whose solution depended on policy questions that were logically prior and substantively more important. Of the pro–arms control analysts, Allan Krass was most explicit: "Verification is not the 'critical element of arms control.' The critical element is an acknowledgment of the uselessness of marginal military advantages between nuclear armed states. Once this fact of life is recognized and accepted, verification will begin to look like a solvable problem."[50] At the opposite end of the political spectrum, Colin Gray was even more blunt.[51] He dismissed verification as a nonissue, incapable of deterring violations, because American leaders do not respond effectively to evidence of noncompliance. He denounced the politics of verification as a "scam," claiming that liberals pay lip service to it but condone violations while conservatives use it to undermine interest in arms control. He concurred that verification debates cover up deeper disagreements about the logic of arms control but urged Americans to oppose treaties unless they would provide a military advantage, even if the Soviets did not comply.

First-wave analysts concluded that verification decisions could and should be depoliticized by shifting attention to policy questions that determine verification preferences. They urged national leaders to build a new domestic consensus about "what we can expect from arms control, how much risk we are willing to accept, and how much uncertainty we can tolerate."[52] Answers would let policy makers calculate what detection probability would make the expected benefits of cooperation outweigh the costs and risks. Negotiators could then determine whether the Soviets would accept measures that provided the desired level of certainty.

Treating the politics of verification as a derivative problem has unnecessarily bleak implications. If verification preferences rest solely on prior beliefs about security policy, agreement is only possible when everyone already thinks that compliance offers mutual benefits, temptations to cheat are minimal, and risks of exploitation are low. For policy makers, this implies a trade-off between significance and confidence: an accord can constrain security options that states are motivated to pursue *or* contain verification measures that satisfy everybody.[53] For theorists, it suggests a problematic paradox. If verification is a prerequisite for cooperation but suspicious states and contentious domestic groups can only agree on verification after incentives to compete are gone, arms control and other regimes cannot have an independent effect on state behavior.

Three weaknesses in first-wave analyses caution against hasty acceptance of unreliable conclusions. First, their view of verification politics was too narrow. Reducing arguments about verification to surrogates and sabotage tactics ignores substantive dilemmas that make decisions about verification inherently controversial. Designing an arms control verification regime involves many trade-offs found in domestic law enforcement or regulatory management systems, such as the tension between individual privacy (sovereignty) and effective monitoring. Deriving verification preferences from positions on other policy issues also overlooks the extent to which these other policy disputes also reflect fundamentally different views of international relations. Calls for "adequate" or "effective" verification may correlate with support for MAD or NUTS policies, but deterrence preferences reflect Kantian, Grotian, or Hobbesian assumptions about security environments and strategies. Assumptions about international politics also lead to policy choices that change the political, technological, and military context for the politics of verification. For example, decisions about which monitoring technologies to develop and how to assess their capabilities depend on assumptions about the relationship between verification and cooperation. In short, little about arms control verification is purely technical.

Second, first-wave authors oversimplified the structure of verification arguments in numerous ways. The tendency to dichotomize positions and pit minimalists against maximalists overlooked important nuances and underestimated the importance of middle-ground participants in domestic debates and international negotiations. Explanations of verification arguments as either surrogate debates or stall tactics minimized both the difficulty of differentiating between sincere and cynical motives and the extent to which cynical verification arguments work only if target audiences actually believe what they are hearing. Focusing on domestic and international arguments about the amount of verification ignored equally consequential disagreements about the best type of compliance evaluation. Finally, analyzing domestic and international arguments separately obscured how developments in one political arena affected the prospects for agreement in the other.

Third, because first-wave authors said little about the strategies used to turn verification arguments into arms control outcomes, they risked turning the verification paradox into a self-fulfilling prophecy. Even when support for arms control is high, leaders will not start serious negotiations unless they believe (rightly or wrongly) that they can negotiate and ratify appropriate verification measures without too much difficulty. Thus, reinforcing the notion of an unavoidable trade-off between the significance of an arms control measure and the prospects for agreement on verification, without examining whether that relationship has actually held true over time, encourages a lowest-common-denominator approach to cooperation. Treating the politics of verification as a derivative problem also discouraged many scholars from giving the issue the attention it deserved. Before concluding that significant cooperation must await an end to the politics of verification brought by breakthroughs in monitoring technology, dramatic improvements in adversarial relations, or domestic consensus on security policy, we need a deeper understanding of verification arguments and opportunities for agreement.

Research Design and Case Selection

This book uses a two-pronged approach to develop a more accurate and complete picture of verification politics. Chapter Two synthesizes history and theory into a general framework for analyzing the substantive questions addressed by the politics of verification, the basic structure of verification arguments, and the strategies used to promote or avoid provisional agreement. The primary theoretical task is to illuminate interrelationships among ideas, interests, internal policy-making processes, and international negotiations. A theoretical framework that stresses interactive effects does not lend itself to hypothesis testing or parsimonious predictions about how changes in one variable would affect arms control outcomes. Nevertheless, the shortcomings of first-wave explanations and the strength of newer scholarship showing that interests and ideas are mutually constitutive suggest that a synthetic approach is the most productive way to understand the politics of verification.[54]

Chapters Three through Eight analyze the politics of nuclear test ban verification to explain why stable and significant agreements were difficult to reach during the Cold War and remain surprisingly elusive. Each theoretical tradition offers a simple answer to this question; all of them treat the politics of verification as an epiphenomenon. Hobbesians see the test ban case as a classic example of the verification paradox and argue that the struggle for competitive advantage prevented agreement on verification, except for restrictions on types of tests that the superpowers were ready to forego for other reasons. Grotians focus on context and argue that agreement on verification was possible only when the arms race reached a point at which both sides could benefit from a particular type of test restriction and available technology could monitor compliance without intolerable expense or espionage concerns. Kantians emphasize cognitive factors: superpower leaders had a strong common interest in ending the arms race, but ignorance, misperceptions, and mistrust prevented agreement on test ban verification, except when crisis-induced learning, advice from scientific experts, or pressure from grassroots activists helped them overcome these obstacles. A detailed analysis of the nuclear test ban case shows that such simple stories are consistently incomplete and misleading. Each explanation reflects how one group in the politics of verification thought about the problem, but to understand the twists and turns of policy making, negotiation, and ratification, one must examine how ideas about verification itself shaped the shifting pattern of winning and blocking coalitions.

The theoretical framework developed in Chapter Two analyzes the politics of verification as a two-level game among groups defined by their answers to basic questions about international cooperation. Recurrent arguments over the nature, scope, functions, and forms of verification involve dilemmas about decision-making authority (what type?) as well as level of uncertainty (how much?). States and domestic groups have substantive or "sincere" reasons for engaging in verification debates, because different ways of evaluating compliance reflect diverse principles and distribute the benefits, costs, and risks of cooperation in divergent ways. They may also have strategic (cynical) incentives to facilitate or complicate agreement on verification, as a prerequisite for arms control. Thus, Arms Control Advocates try to increase Cautious Cooperators' confidence in verification arrangements that also satisfy negotiating partners, whereas Unilateralists try to exacerbate Cautious Cooperators' anxieties and generate verification requirements that are technologically impossible, economically impractical, or politically unobtainable.

The structure of verification arguments is complicated still further because the ideas about verification that prevail in one country may be quite different from those that dominate elsewhere. For example, Americans stressed the positive functions of verification during the Cold War, whereas the Soviets were more concerned about verification abuse. Therefore, U.S. attempts to negotiate verification details before committing to arms control were at odds with Soviet desires to negotiate arms restrictions before accepting intrusive inspections. Similarities in conceptions of verification can also create conflicts. For example, both superpowers viewed verification as an adversarial process and often engaged in zero-sum struggles for control over international verification processes. The superpowers' eventual convergence on reciprocal verification (United States verifies Soviet compliance and vice versa) satisfied them but posed new problems for multilateral negotiations.

To determine how verification arguments affect arms control outcomes, I contrast depoliticization strategies suggested by first-wave research with coalition-building strategies that change the likelihood of agreement, despite mixed motives and conflicting worldviews. I show that ideas about verification have important effects, not only on the definition of interests and the determination of initial bargaining positions but also on the types of coalition-building strategies that are selected and their effects on arms control outcomes. In addition to interest-based strategies such as linkage and side payments, more idea-based moves that I term *identification, alliance, alignment,* and *avoidance strategies* play a major role in the politics of verification. Every strategy is theoretically available to each group, so process-oriented variables like leadership, savvy strategy selection, and skillful execution are important. Certain conditions, however— especially dominant conceptions of verification, knowledge of monitoring options, and the political context for coalition formation—give particular groups a systematic advantage. The sheer complexity of verification politics also means that many strategies have unintended effects.

My analysis of the domestic verification debates focuses mainly on the United States because of the pluralistic nature of American policy making and the relative availability of information. Whenever possible, I show that the same analytical approach can shed light on verification debates in other countries, although the divisions and the decision-making process differ somewhat. Even during the Cold War, some Western analysts found evidence of disagreement among Soviet security elites. After the mid-1980s, the policy of *glasnost* (openness) and the collapse of the USSR slowly increased foreign access to information and former Soviet policy makers' ability to discuss arms-control decision making in the USSR. A growing literature argues that domestic-international interactions played a crucial role in Gorbachev's revision of Soviet security policy and continue to influence Russian arms control decisions in positive and negative ways.

Similar divisions exist elsewhere. For example, domestic debates over India's nuclear weapons program pit those who favor abstinence (Arms Control Advocates) against those who prefer nuclear ambiguity (Cautious Cooperators) or overt weaponization (Unilateralists).

Since the analytical framework encompasses many factors, this book uses a detailed case study of one issue area to assess the framework's utility and validity. A single case study, even one that can be divided into numerous sub-cases with different outcomes, cannot "test" the causal relationships and relative importance of so many inter-related variables. It can, however, serve as a plausibility probe and a heuristic device for stimulating creative thinking about a subject on which little prior theoretical work has been done.[55] Following a single issue over time allows one to examine the effects of continuity and change in the variables that Hobbesians, Grotians, and Kantians emphasize, and to analyze how ideas and choices made about verification at one moment changed future arguments, options, and outcomes. It also allows one to analyze verification arguments in enough detail to see that progress occurred on important problems, even though domestic and international agreement was rarely reached on every aspect of verification for major arms control accords.

Why the Test Ban Case?

The nuclear test ban case is well suited for building theory about verification and cooperation. As in other mixed-motive arms control issues, strong incentives push both for and against an end to nuclear tests.[56] Supporters argue that a CTB would hinder the development of more dangerous and destabilizing weapons, discourage proliferation, decrease tensions, and end environmental damage from nuclear tests. Opponents counter that a ban would rule out modernization programs needed for deterrence stability, decrease confidence in the safety and reliability of stockpiled weapons, encourage proliferation, and prevent research on more discriminating weapons that could reduce destruction should deterrence fail. The strategic impact of a CTB is lower now than in the 1950s, when fewer countries had nuclear weapons programs, nuclear arsenals were much smaller, weapons technology was less sophisticated, and little was known about nonexplosive methods of testing weapons design. But decreased strategic significance has not ended arguments about the costs, benefits, and risks of nuclear testing.

Given these mixed motives, questions about verification have played a large role in test ban politics. For decades, Soviet and American Arms Control Advocates insisted that seismology, atmospheric sampling, and satellites could verify a CTB without excessive expense or intrusion. American Cautious Cooperators worried that NTM might not be enough to detect small seismic signals and determine whether they were caused by an earthquake or an explosion. U.S. Unilateralists devised elaborate cheating scenarios to contend that the Soviets might conduct very large clandestine explosions even if a CTB verification regime included NTM, in-country monitoring stations, and on-site inspections. From the late 1950s through 1980, both superpowers claimed to want a CTB as soon as verification questions could be resolved. After the Reagan administration repudiated a CTB as incompatible with deterrence, Arms Control Advocates used the politics of verification to send the superpowers back to the negotiating table, and to secure agreement on a treaty.

The test ban case is the only arms control issue that spans the entire nuclear age and includes bilateral, trilateral, and multilateral negotiations. Two generations of CTB negotiations among the United States, the USSR, and Great Britain (1958–63 and 1977–80) both collapsed. The 1963 Limited Test Ban Treaty (LTBT) was negotiated, signed, and ratified in three months. The superpowers reached agreement on unprecedented verification measures for the 1974 Threshold Test Ban Treaty (TTBT) and the 1976 Peaceful Nuclear Explosions Treaty (PNET), but these minor treaties were not ratified until 1990. During the 1980s, Americans and Soviets agreed to two "try before you buy" collaborative verification projects, but the results failed to translate directly into new test limitations. In January 1994, multilateral CTB negotiations started in the Conference on Disarmament (CD) and finished in September 1996 with the signing of a CTB that cannot enter into force unless improbable conditions are met. Thus, the test ban issue includes numerous subcases with differing outcomes that cannot be fully explained by changes in military balances, monitoring technology, or U.S.-Soviet relations. Instead, I argue that ideas and coalition-building strategies used with varying degrees of effectiveness in the politics of verification explain the timing, scope, significance, and stability of attempts at test ban cooperation.

Historical Overview and Argument

Chapter Three focuses on the first prenegotiation phase of test ban politics (1945–58) to show that arguments about verification played a crucial role in determining when serious arms control negotiations would start and what they would cover. For the first decade, Unilateralists got their preferred outcome (negotiations for public relations purposes only) by convincing Cautious Cooperators to support disarmament and verification policies that left no room for common ground with the USSR. Arms Control Advocates slowly defeated this blocking strategy by depicting a test ban as an independent "first step" arms control measure that could bring mutual benefits and be verified through mutually acceptable means. A commitment to CTB negotiations did not come, however, until key players agreed (for different reasons) to an international conference at which scientists reached consensus on a CTB verification system.

Chapters Four and Five contrast the politics of verification during two administrations with different types of mixed motives in the first generation of CTB negotiations. President Eisenhower was ambivalent and his advisers were divided about the benefits of arms control. Knowledge about test ban verification was limited, so arms control opponents could manipulate scientific uncertainty to increase the anxiety of Cautious Cooperators. Progress toward agreement on verification was slow and easily disrupted. Still, negotiators came close to agreement on a phased test ban treaty that would have placed more significant constraints on weapons development than did any other accord reached during the Cold War. President Kennedy was less ambivalent about a CTB, and his advisers were less divided than those of the Eisenhower administration. Nevertheless, negotiators never neared agreement on comprehensive test ban verification, even after the Cuban Missile Crisis. Kennedy's mix of arms control advocacy and unilateralism sent the Soviets conflicting signals, increased their fears of espionage, and created a legacy of mistrust in Congress that no obtainable verification could overcome. The LTBT was signed and ratified, but at the cost of unilateral safeguards that hurt the prospects for more significant test restrictions.

Chapter Six explores the politics of test ban verification from 1963 to 1980 in light of struggles among groups with conflicting ideas about security in a world of nuclear parity. For years after the LTBT was signed, superpower leaders called for an "adequately verified CTB" but perpetuated verification disputes in order to finesse conflicting pressures for competition and cooperation. When superpower leaders got serious about test ban negotiations, they found creative solutions to difficult verification problems, and the Soviets accepted important elements of arms control verification that became part of their *glasnost* approach in the 1980s. But these achievements were vulnerable, because neither Arms Control Advocates nor Unilateralists wanted to set precedents that would contradict their long-term policy goal (full cooperation based on flexible verification requirements or a perpetuation of verification arguments to block any arms control). Domestic debates were still dominated by technical, adversarial conceptions of verification; therefore U.S. Unilateralists could erode popular support for arms control by discrediting TTBT compromises, complicating CTB verification questions, and exacerbating doubts about compliance.

Chapter Seven examines the politics of test ban verification as a cause and a consequence of the Cold War's conclusion. It shows how the Reagan administration tried to institutionalize a highly adversarial approach to arms control and security, with unexpected effects in the United States and abroad. It then explores two collaborative verification projects that CTB supporters and opponents used for contradictory purposes. The in-country seismic monitoring project by the Natural Resources Defense Council (NRDC) and the Soviet Academy of Sciences reveals the limited extent to which transnational collaboration between nongovernmental organizations can push a recalcitrant administration toward cooperation. The Reagan administration's Joint Verification Experiment (JVE) of an on-site alternative to seismic monitoring started as a way to block progress toward a new round of CTB negotiations. When Gorbachev called the administration's bluff, however, the technical findings and the political symbolism of the project raised the pressure for new test restrictions.

Chapter Eight uses the multilateral CTB talks to show that Cold War ideas and strategies still complicate negotiations, decrease the significance of agreements, raise the probability of ratification fights, and threaten the stability of cooperation. When negotiations started in 1994, observers thought that substantive verification questions could be easily solved, thanks to advances in seismology and precedents for managed-access inspections. They also predicted that the superpowers' decreased interest in testing and increased concern about proliferation would raise strategic pressures for agreement on verification and lower the likelihood of sabotage tactics. But talks proceeded more slowly than expected, and many serious arguments about verification occurred. Some disputes, such as the conflict between Western attempts to maximize inspection rights and other states' efforts to restrict them, replayed U.S.-Soviet debates in a new security context. Others, such as whether requests for OSIs must be legitimated with evidence from the international monitoring system or could be based on classified information from national intelligence sources, were exacerbated by the inequalities that characterize multilateral negotiations. The chair for the negotiations finally drafted a treaty text that won support from most states, but only after the United States modified its most rigid self-help positions on verification. Unless an effort is made to educate more Americans about the inevitability of verification trade-offs and the need for more cooperative approaches to monitoring and assessment, however, Unilateralists may once again use these verification compromises as the basis for a ratification battle.

Conclusion

The politics of verification provide a unique perspective on the complex determinants of security decisions, because preferences reflect both the technical, political, and military context in which arms control debates occur and the enduring worldviews that shape policy preferences. But the politics of verification is not just an epiphenomenon. The ideas and strategies that have dominated the politics of verification have had an independent effect on arms control decisions. Progress toward mutual restraint was slower, accords were less significant, and cooperation was less stable than it might have been because Unilateralists (often with the unwitting assistance of Arms Control Advocates) made domestic support for verification depend on measures that decreased the probability of international agreement (and vice versa). This study shows how this frustrating situation developed, reveals that partial progress toward domestic and international agreement occurred despite vigorous attempts to block it, and suggests steps to facilitate the formation of winning verification coalitions for more significant arms control accords.

This study also has important implications for international relations theory and arms control policy. It challenges both the hope that verification can be an easy solution to the dilemmas of cooperation in an anarchic world and the fear that agreement on verification will be impossible in mixed-motive situations. Because verification is central to the prospects for and the consequences of cooperation, it is intensely and unavoidably controversial. The following chapters show that verification arguments have their roots in conflicting conceptions of international politics. They explain how the ideas about verification that dominated domestic debates and international negotiations during the Cold War favored the Unilateralists' blocking strategies in the short term but repeatedly nurtured new pressures for arms control. They also demonstrate that when key players were seriously interested in cooperation, negotiators devised new concepts, principles, and practices to bridge competing concerns about test ban verification. This study explains why such innovations were necessary, relates ad hoc solutions to a more general theory of verification politics, and suggests strategies to increase support for compromise and collaboration on verification.

2

Substance, Structure, and Strategy in Verification Politics

DECIDING HOW TO EVALUATE COMPLIANCE is a basic problem for any cooperative enterprise. Similar dilemmas arise inside states, where all citizens must obey a highly developed set of laws, and in international society, where choices are constrained by a patchwork of rules binding only states that have accepted them. Designing a verification regime raises fundamental questions about the social construction of knowledge. What kinds of information can participants use to assess compliance? Who will collect the evidence? What principles and procedures will be used to analyze the raw data? What are the rights of the accused? Who will judge compliance according to what standards? What appeals procedures are available when judgments conflict? These issues are debated constantly by philosophers and legal scholars. They are less well understood yet are equally important for arms control verification.

When Hobbesians draw too sharply the dichotomy between domestic and international politics, they forget that decisions about compliance evaluation are always controversial. Domestic legal systems based on English, Roman, Islamic, or Confucian traditions generate divergent laws, levels of compliance, police practices, and judgments. Where several legal systems claim authority in the same case, such as when certain crimes are committed on American Indian reservations or when family law issues are contested by Muslim citizens of some African countries, participants often appeal to whichever system is most familiar or favorable. Recurrent debates in the United States over constitutional interpretation and sentencing biases show that even when power and authority are centralized, the methods used to judge compliance are contested for the underlying principles they represent and the impact they will have on outcomes. In short, conflicting ideas and interests always cause substantive arguments over compliance evaluation.

When Grotians and Kantians overlook a key difference between domestic and international politics, however, they underestimate the potential for verification arguments. The international system has no comprehensive verification system that automatically takes effect when a treaty is signed, so national leaders must develop customized verification arrangements for each new accord. Some policy makers' support for arms control depends on whether their substantive concerns about verification can be satisfied. Others care less about how compliance is evaluated than about whether cooperation occurs at all, so they have strategic incentives to adopt whatever stance toward verification facilitates or obstructs agreement.

Developing a general theory of the politics of verification involves identifying common questions that must be answered through political processes, showing that verification arguments are structured around predictable disagreements, and determining what types of strategies are used with what effects on the prospects for cooperation. Rather than trying to test incomplete explanations against each other, the analytical framework developed here seeks to integrate conflicting positions in policy debates and contending theories of international cooperation. It suggests that verification preferences have both objective and subjective components that cannot be easily disentangled. It shows that decisions about verification are inherently political and unavoidably politicized because of their implications for other contested issues. It also indicates that the politics of verification occur simultaneously at the domestic and the international levels, and that strategies used to promote or obstruct agreement at one level have consequences, often ill understood, for coalition-building at the other level.

Substantive Questions for the Politics of Verification

The most basic question—What is verification?—evokes conflicting answers.[1] Physicist Allan Krass has described it as the "action of demonstrating compliance with treaty obligations."[2] An American Association for the Advancement of Science (AAAS) primer defined it as "the technological and intelligence process that establishes the fact of compliance."[3] Congressional analysts Mark Lowenthal and Joel Witt reduced it to a "shorthand expression both for alleged instances of Soviet noncompliance and for US reactions or inactions."[4] Roland Timerbayev, a senior Soviet diplomat, portrayed it as "measures to assure the fulfillment of disarmament agreements."[5]

Definitional disagreements can reflect competing interests or contradictory ideas. Some authors try to establish their preferences as the starting point for discussion. Lowenthal and Witt reinforced Reagan-era efforts to shift attention from compliance information to noncompliance accusations; Timerbayev explicitly excluded proposals to monitor activities outside existing arms control accords; and Krass implied that validating cooperation matters more than catching cheaters. Definitions may also inadvertently reflect ideas that are false or overly restrictive. The AAAS authors equated compliance assessments with laboratory verification of research hypotheses, whereas the congressional analysts assumed that "facts" about Soviet behavior are less important than American leaders' response.

When arguments over verification occur, participants commonly accuse one another of ulterior motives. But there are good reasons to take seriously both sides' claims that their position is motivated, at least in part, by substantive considerations. First, comparable debates about evaluating compliance with domestic laws occur even though citizens need not endorse customized judgment principles and procedures for new laws to take effect.[6] Second, decisions about verification pose logical dilemmas whenever conflicting values or contradictory objectives are involved. Third, Soviet verification preferences reflected similar principles from the mid-1940s to the mid-1980s, regardless of how leaders felt about specific arms control measures:

1. Verification should not infringe on national sovereignty or promote interference in internal affairs.

2. Verification cannot occur apart from arms control.

3. The scope and forms of verification should match the significance of the arms control agreement.

4. The detailed elaboration of verification provisions is possible only after agreement in principle on the scope of cooperation.

5. States make agreements with the intention of upholding them; therefore, verification should not be based on total mistrust.

6. International forms of verification should be limited.

7. Given modern monitoring technology, no serious violation can remain undetected for long.[7]

In Chapter One I argued that no single "verification theology" has shaped U.S. policy, contrary to the claims of some arms control critics.[8] Still, one can identify dominant trends in American verification proposals and contrast them with Soviet preferences. (These issues are covered more closely in Chapters Three through Eight.) My purpose here is to show that the politics of verification must find provisional solutions to a complex set of interconnected questions for which there are no easy answers.

The Nature of Verification

American commentators often remarked that the biggest difference in superpower attitudes toward verification was that the United States cared and the Soviets did not.[9] The West placed more emphasis on formal verification, but the

Soviets also wanted to know whether the United States was honoring its treaty commitments. Soviet and American approaches were so different, each side rarely appreciated the other's concerns.

The most basic dispute was about whether verification is a technical or political process. U.S. policy makers depicted verification as an objective way to ascertain the "truth" about compliance or at least obtain a desired "confidence level" in their compliance judgments.[10] They argued that verification requirements could be derived from objective criteria, such as the frequency of small earthquakes or the size of a country's civilian nuclear program. Portraying verification demands as scientifically correct and thus nonnegotiable makes for a stronger bargaining position. For example, the Reagan administration asserted that verification was "neutral," so Soviet acquiescence to U.S. verification demands should not require reciprocal concessions.[11] But there are also substantive reasons why this conception of verification appeals to Americans. It suits the scientific rationalism that has shaped American strategic culture, including the technical approach to arms control developed in the late 1950s.[12] It fits well with Western empiricism and liberal faith in the unproblematic nature of knowledge.[13] It also offers the attractive (but false) hope that verification dilemmas can be resolved by scientific methods that transcend political differences.

The USSR maintained that verification is inherently subjective and political. Russian-language treaty texts and articles about arms control used the word *kontrol* (oversight) rather than *proverka* (verification) because the Soviets rejected the positivistic implications drawn by the West.[14] The Soviets recognized the strategic side of verification arguments and maintained that a state's attitude toward disarmament is what ultimately determines its position on verification."[15] But Soviet policy also held that political factors have a decisive impact on verification decisions, even when both sides want an accord. In contrast to the Western assumption that openness and transparency always increase cooperation, the USSR maintained that verification is a double-edged sword that can be used for good or ill, depending on political relations.[16] In an environment of distrust and competition, the Soviets argued, it would be foolish to allow foreign inspectors into sensitive military and industrial sites. Soviet leaders expected that representatives of capitalist and communist countries would interpret ambiguous behavior differently, because they saw the world from conflicting perspectives.[17] They also predicted that verification could be used to erode popular support for arms control by increasing suspicion, institutionalizing mistrust, and fueling poisonous propaganda campaigns based on false accusations—predictions borne out by the Reagan administration.

The Scope of Verification

In domestic political systems, arguments about the line between lawful surveillance of suspected criminals and illegal invasion of privacy involve philosophical debates about community needs and individual freedoms. In arms control, the tension is between expanding verification while protecting states' prerogatives to keep secrets, exclude outsiders, and reject foreign interference in domestic affairs. Among enemies, either extreme is dangerous: limiting the scope of verification enables cheating; expanding the scope facilitates spying and other verification abuse. Even in less adversarial arms control, a trade-off remains between maximizing the resources for dispute resolution and minimizing the burdens of regulatory management.

Verification includes fixed costs, such as trained personnel and sophisticated equipment. Attempts to prevent inspectors from collecting collateral information can raise costs and complicate daily operations at military bases, chemical companies, and nuclear reactors. Although these expenses are small compared with U.S. defense budgets, they reduce the "peace dividend" that arms control provides.[18] Some states also perceive less measurable but equally worrisome costs when verification infringes on sovereignty or discriminatory principles produce more intrusive monitoring requirements for "rogue states" than for "good citizens."

The known costs of verification often cause less concern than the risk that verification will be abused for competitive gain. Where secrecy is a security asset, transparency poses military risks. For example, an American at the 1958 Surprise Attack Conference later testified that the Soviets saw secrecy as "a form of 'hardening' of their bases which we do not have. Thus they regard any encroachment upon this secrecy as a unilateral disarmament step . . . which must be compensated for by other measures."[19] Even sharing information about compliance can be risky. For example, the exchange of location data needed to monitor limits on mobile missiles makes these systems more vulnerable to preemptive attack.

Verification also poses political risks. The Reagan administration's practice of issuing annual reports about alleged Soviet treaty violations created negative publicity, even when the accusations could not be substantiated. Increased contact during intrusive monitoring may cause friction, harassment, and mistrust. Moreover, data exchanges, site visits, and scientific exchanges can sow seeds of political subversion in states whose leaders restrict information and contact with foreigners as a means of social control.

Finally, monitoring involves economic risks, especially when treaty-limited technology has both military and civilian uses. During negotiations for the 1968 Treaty on the Nonproliferation of Nuclear Weapons (NPT), countries with advanced nuclear energy programs objected that verification would increase industrial espionage, accounting expenses, and sales restrictions; less-developed states feared that measures to facilitate verification would hinder modernization. Similarly, current efforts to negotiate a binding verification protocol for the 1972 Biological and Toxic Weapons Convention (BWC) have run into trouble because pharmaceutical companies worry about trade secrets, whereas developing countries fear that they will be denied access to equipment, pathogens, and toxins with legitimate medical uses.

In short, determining the appropriate scope of verification poses trade-offs between making verification workable (i.e., maximizing the positive effects on compliance) and keeping it tolerable (i.e., minimizing expense, inconvenience, espionage, and interference). Official preferences have alternated between the extremes in the United States and the USSR. In the pre-nuclear era, the Soviets claimed to favor extensive verification, and the Americans opposed any infringement of national sovereignty. During the Cold War, the Soviets charged that verification would be "legalized espionage" unless the scope matched the significance of arms control and the details were determined *after* a commitment to cooperation was made.[20] The United States, by contrast, preferred to design and sometimes even test elaborate verification arrangements *before* making a commitment to modest arms control measures—what came to be called the "try before you buy" approach to verification.[21] In the mid-1980s, Washington and Moscow seemed to switch roles again. When the USSR offered "triple verification," the United States backed away from its inspection demands.[22] The Bush administration even chose to pursue many important arms control goals through reciprocal unilateral initiatives that included no joint steps to enhance verification.[23] These reversals suggest that superpower leaders managed ambivalence about the scope of verification by emphasizing one side of the dilemma and expecting the other to counterbalance them.

The Functions of Verification

How one delineates the scope of verification depends on how one thinks that verification works. Such debates are common in domestic politics. Is the primary function of the penal system to prevent crimes by getting criminals off the streets or to deter them by convincing potential felons that crime will not pay? Is it the main job of regulatory agencies to hand out huge fines for environmental misdeeds or to educate polluters about the errors of their ways? In international negotiations, the fundamental question has been whether verification regimes must control capabilities by making noncompliance impossible (a standard that is often technically, economically, or politically unobtainable) or have the more realistic but less reliable objective of making defection less attractive than cooperation.

Early nuclear disarmament discussions used the term *control* rather than *verification* because most states would only agree to disarm if international arrangements could guarantee good behavior.[24] National leaders have often imposed verification as control on defeated rivals, but they have yet to accept such sweeping measures to judge and enforce their own cooperation. For example, the resolution ending the Persian Gulf War gave the United Nations Special Commission (UNSCOM) nearly unlimited powers to uncover, destroy, and permanently disable Iraqi programs for weapons of mass destruction.[25] But nothing at the 1995 NPT extension conference showed that current signatories, let alone nonparticipants like India and Israel, are ready to renounce the transfer of all fissile materials, grant unlimited inspection rights, or give up the right to withdraw legally if national security is at stake.

During early nuclear negotiations, U.S. insistence on "foolproof" detection systems was tantamount to demanding that the Soviets submit to verification as control. Stipulating that arms control could not proceed without perfect verification created a "gamesman's paradise" in which opponents could block any accord by imagining some way that an aggressive and ingenious adversary could spoof or evade the monitoring system.[26]

The growing Soviet nuclear capability prompted some Americans to rethink the function of verification. By the mid-1950s, U.S. officials openly admitted that no verification system could physically prevent the USSR from violating a ban on nuclear weapons, because international agents could never be sure that they had monopolized all fissile materials, destroyed all stockpiles, and found all scientists with bomb-building abilities. As scholars and policy makers began to think more seriously about using partial arms control measures to enhance deterrence stability, they suggested that imperfect verification might be acceptable if the risk of detection was high enough to deter major violations and nuclear arsenals remained large enough to make minor violations militarily insignificant. The Soviets quickly endorsed verification as deterrence and argued that even a low detection probability would counteract incentives for noncompliance. But even after the views of both superpowers converged in the idea that verification should provide detection, deterrence, and reassurance, they assigned different priorities to these functions.

The idea of verification as deterrence has frequently failed to moderate U.S. verification demands. Many Americans relied on worst-case assumptions when deciding what detection probability would deter militarily significant violations.

Furthermore, policy makers who did not hold these worst-case assumptions often asked for extra verification to reassure nervous constituents or to avoid being called soft on communism.

The "detection, deterrence, reassurance" formula is also extremely elastic. The most common expansion sought reassurance about other countries' future intentions, not just their current compliance behavior. Proponents argued that if verification promotes cooperation through detection, deterrence, and reassurance, then anyone who is serious about arms control should agree to any verification requests. Thus, the Reagan administration tried to make Soviet support for intrusive monitoring into a "litmus test" of their intentions, even when NTM could have detected most violations.[27]

More ambitious Americans at both ends of the security spectrum have viewed verification as a tool for political transformation. If democratic states have more peaceful relations with each other, they maintained, then the best way to promote cooperation is to push authoritarian regimes in a democratic direction. A 1961 article argued that Soviet officials could not mobilize grassroots pressure for arms control in the West without popularizing the practice at home. If Western leaders challenged Khrushchev to say that all peace-loving citizens should cooperate with arms control inspectors, his propaganda objectives might compel him to allow some interaction with foreign inspectors. This would open Soviet society, complicate surprise attack, increase positive contacts between Soviet and U.S. citizens, and weaken internal factions who exaggerated enemy images to promote aggressive policies.[28] This proposal sounded fanciful at the time, yet Ronald Lehman, director of ACDA under President Bush, later claimed that "verification *glasnost* led to and reinforced political *glasnost*, and vice versa," through very similar mechanisms.[29]

Where the United States emphasized benign functions, the USSR feared competitive abuses and favored using verification more for reassurance than for detection and deterrence. When Soviet leaders who favored cooperation faced internal criticism, however, they sometimes bragged that their monitoring capabilities could prevent Western deceptions.[30] A few East bloc authors suggested one ambitious function: watching for new military technology that could alter the strategic impact of an agreement.[31] But this would require intrusive inspections in research laboratories, arms factories, and weapons testing facilities, so Soviet leaders never pushed for it.

The Forms of Verification

Differing beliefs about the nature, scope, and functions of verification lead to conflicting calculations concerning the level of certainty about compliance needed to make the benefits of arms control outweigh the costs and risks. Decisions about the type of verification that will be most workable and tolerable are equally important. The politics of verification often seems like a numbers game because the media finds it easier to contrast maximalist and minimalist proposals for OSI quotas, for example, than to explain arcane arguments about OSI procedures. But compliance information is useless if participants lack confidence in the people who collect, process, and evaluate it.

The Soviets' view of verification as a political and potentially dangerous process led them to prefer modest forms of verification with maximum host country involvement. The USSR frequently offered to exchange data that substantiated its claims of compliance but opposed mandatory data requests and independent validation. After initial resistance, Soviet policy makers endorsed satellite surveillance, atmospheric sampling, and other remote monitoring methods. Although Moscow never categorically opposed OSIs, it treated them as a last resort and tried to restrict them to routine observation of regulated activities away from military locations. The USSR sought to control when foreign inspectors entered Soviet territory, where they went, and what they saw. It also wanted host-country nationals to take pictures, collect samples, operate equipment, and transmit data under international supervision. The USSR traditionally supported forums in which treaty signatories could consult about compliance concerns, but it refused to let international verification agents make authoritative judgments or impose sanctions without Soviet consent.[32] By the 1980s, Soviet skepticism about organizations such as the International Atomic Energy Agency (IAEA) had softened, but the USSR still wanted decision-making procedures that would prevent the West from using such agencies for their own purposes.

Americans usually preferred measures that were more intrusive and less susceptible to subversion by the host government, especially when there was little chance that such measures would be applied to the United States. From 1945 until the late 1950s and again in the 1980s, OSIs were considered an essential component of any verification regime. The United States always sought to ensure that OSIs would be easy to trigger, hard to refuse, quick to start, comprehensive, and controlled by trustworthy states. It has also tried to maximize access to and control over other types of compliance information, both by favoring extensive international monitoring systems and by reserving the right to base accusations on national intelligence without revealing the source of that information.

Some Kantians have even proposed what might be called civilian-based verification, such as urging peace-minded citizens to inform on their own governments or encouraging scientists to exchange information about potential arms control violations on a global electronic "*vernet.*"[33] Inspectors monitoring German disarmament after World War I did receive some information from citizens who needed money or opposed militarism. When UNSCOM officials have received comparable tips, however, they have turned out to be ruses used by Iraqi counterintelligence to lead inspectors astray.[34]

The responsibilities that Americans would entrust to international verification agents have decreased as U.S. confidence in international organizations has declined. In the test ban case, for example, the United States went from proposing an international control commission many times the size of the U.N. secretariat, which would handle the entire verification process, to preferring a small organization to facilitate the exchange of data from national monitoring stations. But even when American preferences for reciprocal self-help verification have been strongest, some policy makers have argued that multilateralizing certain aspects of verification would increase international support should the United States determine that a violation had occurred.

This overview of verification arguments is far from exhaustive. Related issues, such as the allocation of verification expenses, were contentious during the Cold War and are becoming even more controversial in multilateral negotiations among states with asymmetrical intelligence assets and economic resources. Three points are most important for my purposes. First, substantive questions matter to anyone facing an arms control dilemma, because alternative arrangements embody divergent principles and distribute the benefits, costs, and risks of cooperation in different ways. Second, substantive disagreements involve fundamentally different assumptions about verification itself. Third, verification arguments include controversies over how information will be collected, judgments made, and compliance concerns resolved—questions about allocating decision-making authority, not just reducing uncertainty to tolerable levels. These points suggest that verification disputes are much deeper, more complicated, and less easily depoliticized than is often assumed.

An End to the Politics of Verification?

Many observers predicted that the politics of verification would wither away after the Cold War, because competitive pressures had declined and verification preferences converged. As early as 1981, Timerbayev rejoiced that Soviet principles such as proportionality, sovereign equality, and noninterference in internal affairs had gained broad international support.[35] Over the next few years, Soviet decisions to reduce secrecy, increase transparency, permit more inspections, and support multilateral monitoring organizations inspired the director of the U.N. Institute for Disarmament Research (UNIDIR) to declare that "an important facet of the dramatic progress in disarmament negotiations in the last few years is the remarkable consensus achieved on the hitherto contentious issue of verification."[36] Meanwhile, the popularity of Reagan's "trust but verify" policy prompted Adelman to declare that "verification is one of the few areas of arms control on which there is a consensus."[37] What one observer called "the verification revolution" led numerous others to expect that domestic debates and international negotiations over verification would become more "businesslike" and constructive.[38]

When groups whose verification preferences have traditionally been far apart all rejoice that their perspective has triumphed, one must be skeptical. The end of the Cold War has added new twists to the politics of verification without resolving basic dilemmas. For example, although the victorious Persian Gulf War coalition could impose the most effective verification arrangements it could imagine, disagreements occurred between UNSCOM representatives, who favored a law enforcement approach, and IAEA officials, who preferred a more managerial model.[39] The fall 1997 crisis over the composition of UNSCOM inspection teams and their access to "presidential palaces" suspected of hiding forbidden materials tapped into growing disputes in the victorious coalition: did Iraq retain any sovereign rights regarding verification, and what more must it do to demonstrate compliance with the relevant U.N. resolutions? U.S. domestic debates about verification are more muted in the mid-1990s than they were a decade earlier. But President Clinton's decision to postpone the CWC ratification vote until after the 1996 election is evidence that the politics of verification remain potent. The only way to know what has changed and why is to look more closely at the structure of verification arguments and the strategies used to perpetuate or resolve them.

The Structure of Verification Arguments

One of the most contentious questions in current international relations theory is whether outcomes are determined by structural givens, such as anarchy and power distributions, or developed through agent-centered processes, such as learning, bargaining, and institution-building.[40] Although both clearly affect the politics of verification, the main discussion of process-oriented variables is taken up later in this chapter. Here I examine the structure of verification arguments and build on research showing that social structures can include ideational—not just material—factors. Rather than defining structure in terms of shared understandings at the domestic or international level, however, my framework integrates the two levels of analysis and suggests that verification arguments are shaped by patterns of conflicting and common ideas inside and among states. It reintroduces the strategic side of verification politics by showing how ideas about verification can be advanced for both sincere and self-interested reasons. It also considers how material factors, such as the distribution of power among states and groups in the policy-making process, condition potential outcomes in the politics of verification.

Ideas, Interests, and Domestic-International Interconnections

Although few theorists still advocate a rigid separation among levels of analysis, they disagree about the relative weight and causal relationships among interests, ideas, domestic politics, and international interactions.[41] The structure of verification arguments is best understood by considering increasingly complex and consequential relationships among these variables. With a synthetic framework for analysis, one can think systematically about enduring dilemmas, common themes, and possible causes of change in the politics of verification. But the more complex the structure and causal pathways are, the harder it is to specify precisely how the variables will interact to produce particular arms control outcomes.

Traditional system-level theories assume that material factors, such as the superpower nuclear balance and the state of monitoring technology, are the main determinants of verification decisions.[42] Ideas and internal politics matter only as a means to account for residual variance. When decision makers fail to do what systemic theories predict, their behavior is often blamed on individual idiosyncrasies, cognitive constraints, or domestic resistance.[43] For example, Stephen Meyer proposed a monitoring system for mobile intercontinental missiles that optimized two conflicting values—verification and invulnerability—only to conclude that negotiating such an optimal accord with the Soviets would be easier than selling it to Congress.[44]

Ideas and internal politics are taken more seriously by theorists who see systemic factors as indeterminate.[45] The absence of a world government does not force members to pursue their goals through competitive or cooperative means. Similarly, the sheer destructiveness of nuclear weapons does not compel states to start arms races, negotiate partial restraints, or disarm unilaterally. Because Hobbesian, Grotian, and Kantian theories would prescribe different but equally rational responses to security problems, one needs additional factors to explain verification preferences.

Constructivists focus on the meaning that political actors attach to "facts" about international relations. These theorists argue that state and nonstate actors' interests, identities, and ideas about appropriate behavior reflect social structures, such as norms, institutions, and cultural practices, that are collective rather than purely subjective.[46] For example, Alexander Wendt has argued that international politics often follow Hobbesian predictions not because anarchy necessitates such behavior but because policy makers use realist assumptions to interpret other states' behavior and determine their own response, thus creating a self-fulfilling prophecy.[47] Constructivists attribute cooperation to changes in social structure that decrease conflicts of interest and minimize problematic behavior. Thus, Ann Florini suggests that the prospects for arms control have improved dramatically because the "long-dominant norm of the sovereign right of states to maintain secrecy about all security matters has gradually ceded ground to a new norm of transparency."[48] To the extent that this normative shift has occurred, it has increased the number of states for whom enhancing transparency is a national interest and raised the likelihood that other states would see secretive behavior as more costly than beneficial.

When systemic factors are indeterminate, arms control outcomes can also be explained by structural factors at the domestic level. Some second-image accounts analyze conflicting preferences and distributions of power among bureaucratic actors or interest groups; others focus more on shared ideas, such as national strategic culture, organizational norms, and enemy images.[49] Interest and ideas can be combined by examining how "myths"—that is, incorrect or untestable assumptions about the way the world works—give particular groups a systematic advantage in the domestic policy-making process. Some analysts view strategic myths as false or fuzzy concepts that players purposefully embrace to achieve other policy goals.[50] Others argue that the abstraction, ambiguity, and uncertainty associated with nuclear deterrence force policy makers to rely more on unproven assumptions and unsubstantiated assertions than on empirical evidence about alternative nuclear postures. Disproportionate influence over national nuclear policy is then given to mythmakers—individual policy entrepreneurs whose expertise, position, and rhetorical skills help them create, spread, and perpetuate particular strategic beliefs.[51] The world has had even less experience with verification for major arms control accords than with nuclear deterrence. Thus, arguments over verification can be conceptualized as competitions among proponents of different untested and potentially untestable assumptions about what verification is and how different arrangements affect the benefits, costs, and risks of arms control.

In "second-image reversed" theories, external factors change the domestic determinants of arms control by strengthening particular factions or disabusing players of faulty assumptions.[52] International events might cause domestic politics to "drop out" by ending debates about the adversary's intentions, demonstrating that self-serving security strategies are inherently unworkable, or by mobilizing citizens to work together against a threat to shared values.[53] In less extreme cases, information gained during initial rounds of bargaining can reduce uncertainty about the other side's power and preferences, helping central decision makers select and build domestic support for an optimal bargaining strategy.[54]

Conceptualizing the structure of verification arguments as a two-level game suggests that the causal arrows flow in both directions. Instead of using domestic politics solely to account for national interests or using system-level factors just to explain the outcome of internal policy debates, this approach assumes that national leaders have their own preferences but are simultaneously constrained by what other states will negotiate and what constituents will ratify.[55] Here, the structure of the game is determined by the mix of common and conflicting interests and the allocation of power among national representatives at the negotiating table; it is also determined by the configuration of preferences and the decision-making rules of each participating state. When the chief of government (COG) is significantly more competitive or cooperation-minded than powerful domestic groups, the policy-making process may permit enough autonomy to negotiate effectively despite internal opposition. The result will be "involuntary defection," however, if an accord falls outside the domestic "win-set"—the range of possible agreements that have sufficient support to survive the ratification process.[56] In arms control negotiations, all too often dissatisfaction with verification has been a major justification for ratification failure or delay. Similarly, several U.S. presidents have cited verification problems as a reason for avoiding serious arms control efforts, only to learn that "no negotiation" is not an acceptable outcome for their domestic constituents.

The original two-level game framework assumes the players have fixed interests but that clever COGs can promote their preferred outcome at one level by changing the structure of the game at the other level. For example, a COG-as-Dove (one who wants more cooperation than his constituents do) might selectively release sensitive security information to emphasize a verification system's capabilities and downplay its weaknesses. When the COG's preferred negotiating outcome falls within a broad range of agreements that constituents would approve, he or she might try to gain negotiating leverage by "tying their own hands"—misrepresenting or deliberately shrinking the set of verification compromises that could be ratified. COGs can also change the structure of domestic preferences in the other state by altering expectations about the benefits of cooperation. For example, Gorbachev's unilateral arms control initiatives were a form of suasion meant to decrease U.S. verification demands by reassuring Americans about his peaceful intentions. In contrast, some of Khrushchev's belligerent behavior had negative reverberation, causing ambivalent Americans to doubt his motives for wanting arms accords.

The original two-level game framework must be modified in several ways to fit the politics of verification. Most work on two-level games has defined players in terms of interests rather than ideas and assumed that interests remain constant over time. Arguments over verification, however, clearly have both substantive and strategic components. Moreover, substantive disagreements over verification reflect both interests and ideas. Therefore, the best way to analyze the structure of verification arguments is to integrate a modified two-level approach with insights about the impact of worldviews and myths on domestic debates and international negotiations.

My framework builds on the Arms Control Advocate, Cautious Cooperator, and Unilateralist ideal types introduced in Chapter One. It categorizes players according to the basic assumptions used to justify their verification preferences without presuming to know what combination of ideas and interests led them to adopt these "first principles." This approach sidesteps the heated but probably unwinnable theoretical dispute between rationalists and reflectivists about whether ideas are simply "hooks" that actors use to promote preexisting interests or the fundamental source of all values and behavioral choices.[57] It acknowledges that participants in verification politics are often uncertain about each others' motives. It also respects evidence that players themselves may not know why they behave in a particular way.[58] One cannot—and need not—know for sure whether participants in verification politics reason from interests, ideas, or emotions to determine the structure of verification arguments and analyze the strategies used to promote or block agreement.

The traditional image of a unitary COG who seeks to maximize fixed interests also exaggerates the coherence of Executive Branch policy makers on verification issues. Instead, there is often an internal struggle to determine what the administration's preferences are and how vigorously they will be pursued. Although verification arguments among Arms Control Advocates, Cautious Cooperators, and Unilateralists inside the Executive Branch frequently pit one bureaucracy against another, at the senior levels where policy is actually made, preferences are influenced at least as much by worldview as by the role that an adviser currently holds.[59]

Traditional bureaucratic models also cannot account for other important features in the politics of verification. Representatives of the same organization have had fundamental disagreements, as evidenced by divisions inside Eisenhower's

State and Defense Departments between those who thought that nuclear sufficiency made it possible to relax verification for partial arms control and those
who favored an all-or-nothing approach to verification and disarmament. No
bureaucracy or interest group has ever been the sole voice expressing a particular point of view; each ideal type has always had proponents in the Executive
Branch, Congress, the scientific community, the media, and the public. Finally,
the same agency has sometimes reversed positions in a subsequent administration, even though its organizational interests and the majority of personnel have
not changed. For example, ACDA was one of the agencies most eager to negotiate verification compromises during the Carter administration and most recalcitrant in the early Reagan years.

Neither COGs nor members of the Executive Branch are the only ones who
can play cross-level games. Jeffrey Knopf has shown that social groups, such as
the Nuclear Freeze Movement, can be active players, especially when wooed by
the rival COG.[60] Other recent research has suggested that the impact of transnational actors and coalitions depends in part on domestic structures that determine who gets access, which ideas resonate inside a state, and what the requirements are for coalitions capable of changing policy.[61] Alliance politics also
increase the complexity of domestic-international interactions. In negotiations
leading to the 1987 Intermediate-Range Nuclear Forces Treaty (INF), for example, Richard Eichenberg found that domestic pressures created problems for alliance partners who then made statements (Reagan's antinuclear rhetoric) or
adopted policies (the dual-track decision and the zero option) with repercus-
sions at home and abroad.[62]

In short, the politics of verification can be conceptualized as a multilevel
game in which groups are defined through first principles and numerous participants are trying simultaneously to promote their preferred outcome by
changing the Executive Branch's preferences, the domestic configuration, or the
correlation of forces at the international level. The remainder of this chapter
elaborates a general framework for analyzing structures and strategies in the politics of verification. But the detailed examination of the test ban case shows that
even though the two-level games approach is a useful metaphor for organizing
information and thinking systematically about domestic-international interconnections, it falls short of being a full-blown theory that can capture the full
complexity of verification politics and provide detailed predictions or prescriptions about a specific policy issue. Thus, Chapter Eight suggests that the image
of a Rubik's cube, in which each component is connected to everything else and
outcomes are highly contingent, might be a more accurate metaphor for the politics of verification.

The First Level: Substantive and Strategic Players in Domestic Debates

Domestic actors who influence arms control policy—including Executive Branch officials, members of Congress, technical experts, and attentive citizens in the United States today, but limited to political and military elites when the policy-making process is more closed—can be categorized by their answers to three questions:

1. Is mutual cooperation desirable?
2. Are potential partners seriously interested in cooperation?
3. Would cheating or unequal relative gains pose serious risks?

These questions encompass the policy debates that first-wave analysts blamed for verification disputes. Relating verification preferences to more basic questions increases generalizability, however, and explains why similar arguments recur in different policy contexts. It also offers a way to differentiate between players whose predisposition toward verification derives from preexisting attitudes toward arms control and those whose support for cooperation depends on finding workable and tolerable verification.

Arms Control Advocates value cooperative measures to minimize the chance of nuclear war, reduce potential destruction, decrease defense budgets, and improve adversarial relationships. Some Arms Control Advocates hope ultimately to eliminate all nuclear weapons; others would rather keep small, secure retaliatory capabilities. They assume that the logic of nuclear vulnerability is so obvious that other countries also understand the need for cooperation. Given that the superpowers can destroy each other many times over, Arms Control Advocates see few incentives for noncompliance and little chance that minor cheating or relative gains would destabilize deterrence. In short, because Arms Control Advocates value cooperation, expect voluntary compliance, and discount low-level cheating, their support for arms control does not hinge on verification details. The nearer they are to the cooperative end of the spectrum, the more *flexible* about verification they will be, supporting whatever arrangements increase the chances for negotiation and ratification.

Cautious Cooperators, in contrast, care deeply about the substance of verification. They agree with Arms Control Advocates about the need for arms control but worry about other states' intentions and deterrence stability. For Cautious Cooperators, the destructive power of nuclear weapons creates incentives and opportunities for both cooperation and competition. They assume that foreign leaders have mixed motives and may be tempted to exploit an agreement. Cheating is a serious concern for Cautious Cooperators because noncompliance would either provide a military advantage or indicate willingness to violate treaties for little military gain. Because Cautious Cooperators experience the dilemmas of arms control so intensely, they are extremely *attentive* to verification issues. The more they doubt others' motives and deterrence stability, the more confidence in verification they will demand.

Unilateralists neither desire mutual restraint nor believe that other countries want mutual cooperation. Their antipathy to arms control can have many sources, including a Hobbesian conception of international politics or a parochial interest in funding for weapons development. Unilateralists assume that adversaries will exploit each other whenever possible and believe that small differences in nuclear capabilities can provide political leverage or military advantage. Thus, their opposition to arms control is frequently overdetermined, regardless of verification capabilities. If so, Unilateralists will use *rigid* verification demands to sabotage negotiations or maximize national advantage when some limits are inevitable. Table 2.1 summarizes the key divisions in domestic debates and the resulting verification predispositions.

At the domestic level, structure affects preference formation inside the Executive Branch and the prospects for ratification once an accord has been signed. Analyzing the structure of domestic verification debates on a particular arms control issue involves estimating how many players can be considered Arms Control Advocates, Cautious Cooperators, and Unilateralists; determining where the heavyweights (players with special influence) are; and ascertaining the distance between groups on different principles. These variables depend partly on

Table 2.1 Divisions in Domestic Verification Debates

	Arms Control Advocates	Cautious Cooperators	Unilateralists
Is mutual cooperation desirable?	Yes	Yes	No
Does the other side want arms control?	Yes	Maybe	No
Would cheating or unequal relative gains matter?	No	Yes	Yes
Resulting verification predisposition	Flexible	Attentive	Rigid

the significance of the proposed treaty. For example, an Arms Control Advocate for the CWC who doubts that the United States would ever use chemical weapons might be a Cautious Cooperator or a weak Unilateralist about deep conventional cuts or total nuclear disarmament. These variables will also reflect domestic factors, including presidential commitment and leadership on arms control, Executive Branch organization for security policy making, the partisan balance in the Senate, the rules for ratification, and the extent to which foreign policy elites are open to expert opinion and interest group pressure. But even when verification decisions occur inside a closed circle of elites, public opinion remains important because of elites' strategic incentives to adopt verification stands that increase popular support for other security policies.

When first-wave analysts urged national leaders to build a domestic consensus about arms control, they wanted to simplify the structure of verification arguments by getting agreement on first principles. This is highly unlikely, though, since consensus on these questions has eluded theorists and practitioners for hundreds of years. Scholars have noted a "persistent conflict in the security politics of democratic societies: between the liberal, 'idealist' visions of security achieved through trade, negotiation, or international law, and the 'realist' vision of security achieved through a balance of power."[63] Sometimes, the lines of conflict have been sharply drawn; at other times, a pseudoconsensus has formed around concepts and programs that combine deterrence with negotiation. Arms Control Advocates and Unilateralists make strategic use of verification arguments because it is easier to convince Cautious Cooperators about an accord's (un)verifiability than to end their ambivalence about cooperation. But coalition-building strategies based on promises or doubts about verification must be plausible to be potent. In other words, Arms Control Advocates or Unilateralists can only win the support of Cautious Cooperators if the arguments they make about verification resonate with Cautious Cooperators' assumptions.

The Second Level: National Myths and International Arguments

National negotiating positions are shaped not only by competition among domestic groups with different first principles but also by assumptions about verification shared by groups across the domestic security spectrum. As the overview of standard U.S.-Soviet arguments indicated, one can generalize about national approaches to verification, even though Arms Control Advocates, Cautious Cooperators, and Unilateralists have different reasons for endorsing particular assumptions and varying degrees of commitment to a specific approach. In other words, international arguments over verification also have substantive and strategic components because some national policy makers genuinely believe their verification myths, whereas others find them convenient, if not completely true.

In U.S. policy debates, the dominant myth has been that verification is a technical process of increasing transparency whose functions are purely benign and which should ultimately be each country's own responsibility. This conception fits well with Grotian assumptions about international politics and suits Cautious Cooperators' desire for a low-risk technical solution to arms control dilemmas. Arms Control Advocates strongly endorse the notion that verification increases transparency in order to enhance cooperation. They may personally favor a more managerial approach, but they often use self-help language, to appeal to Cautious Cooperators. Unilateralists do not believe that anything connected with security can be apolitical or purely benign, but they espouse this view of verification as a way to raise U.S. demands and maximize national control over verification if cooperation occurs.

The power of American verification myths has often prevented scholars, policy makers, and citizens from recognizing that other countries have different but equally plausible ways of thinking about verification. As we have seen, the traditional Soviet view assumed that verification was intensely political, potentially malign, and unavoidably adversarial. American allies have typically agreed with the United States about the broad objectives of verification; some, however, have questioned the U.S. view that "more is better," especially when their own territory would be subject to stringent monitoring whereas that of the United States would not.[64] The superpowers' preference for reciprocal monitoring and assessment has also frustrated countries that prefer a more multilateral approach. Some Western states, such as Sweden and Australia, have a benign, technical view of verification but want to give international organizations more responsibility. By contrast, countries such as China and India assume that verification is political and potentially malign but want tight international control, so that a hostile country cannot initiate an OSI or punish a violation without overwhelming support from other states.

The more Americans insist that verification is purely benign, technical, and self-help in nature, the harder it is to negotiate with countries whose ideas about verification differ. Conflicting verification myths often create a counter-cooperative spiral, as the types of proposals that appealed to Cautious Cooperators in one country exacerbate the anxieties of Cautious Cooperators elsewhere. The more significant a potential accord, the more Americans want to maximize access to compliance information and control over the verification process. For countries where verification is viewed as a political and potentially malign activity, such demands raise the fixed costs of cooperation and the risks that the verification process will be used for competitive purposes. Such states' resistance to verification demands that seem reasonable to American Cautious Cooperators raises new doubts, however, about these states' reliability as arms control partners and causes Americans to want even more intrusion and control over verification.

Table 2.2 illustrates how the domestic and international levels can be combined. For simplicity's sake, Table 2.2 only includes arguments about the amount of verification. Disagreements about whether verification is mainly technical or political, predominantly adversarial or managerial, and primarily unilateral or multilateral can cause further conflict and misunderstanding.

This two-level framework resolves the first-wave debate about whether verification arguments are surrogate issues or sabotage tactics. Cautious Cooperators in the United States and the USSR had legitimate reasons for substantive disagreements, and Unilateralists exploited these differences to deadlock negotiations. Since Unilateralists in the United States and the USSR shared a highly adversarial view of international politics, they knew how to ensure a hostile response by taking positions that sounded reasonable to their own Cautious Cooperators but repelled states with different assumptions about other aspects of verification.

This framework also shows how oversimplified conceptions of verification hinder cooperation. Unilateralists have enjoyed a structural advantage, because the myth that verification is benign and technical prevents U.S. Cautious Cooperators from recognizing that support for stringent verification does not always indicate sincere interest in arms control, any more than resistance to American

Table 2.2 Preferences in International Verification Politics

International Arguments about Verification	Divisions in Domestic Debates		
	Arms Control Advocates	Cautious Cooperators	Unilateralists
Purely benign	7	8	9
Involves trade-offs	6	5	4
Primarily malign	3	2	1

Note Expressed desire to maximize verification 1 = least, 9 = most verification demands necessarily signals uncooperative intentions. Arms Control Advocates have had a structural disadvantage: because Americans rarely talk about verification trade-offs, Unilateralists could routinely trump Arms Control Advocates by convincing Cautious Cooperators that the United States needed more compliance information or control over the verification process than negotiating partners would permit. U.S. leaders often boxed themselves into a corner by starting with extreme verification demands for strategic reasons, then confronting substantive dilemmas as negotiations got more serious. American political leaders have been forced to think more carefully about verification trade-offs whenever technical and diplomatic constraints on intrusive monitoring methods have decreased. But because Executive Branch officials have done little to educate Congress and attentive citizens about these trade-offs, the president's ability to negotiate and ratify verification compromises has been hurt by critics who attack him for weakening earlier verification demands.

Insufficient discussion of verification trade-offs has also obscured important divisions among Unilateralists that can be used to facilitate agreement. When an accord seems inevitable, former opponents often part company over the amount and type of verification that the United States should demand, depending on how their subgroup will be affected. Representatives of the U.S. chemical industry had little incentive to help solve verification problems for a treaty that would only complicate their operations, until the Persian Gulf War convinced American leaders that the United States should not use chemical weapons under any circumstances. Once the superpowers agreed that an imperfectly verified ban on chemical weapons was better than no agreement, the chemical industry wanted to design monitoring arrangements that seemed workable and tolerable to them. The small group of security specialists who remained staunch Unilateralists toward a CWC delayed ratification by arguing that the verification provisions were too weak to catch all cheating but too intrusive and expensive for U.S. chemical firms. Their lack of industrial allies on the latter issue decreased the plausibility of this claim and contributed to their defeat.[65]

In short, the structure of verification arguments is more complex than previously assumed. My multidimensional framework captures controversies about amounts and types of verification, combines substantive and strategic motives, and stresses multiple interconnections between domestic and international politics. It also shows how narrow, unidimensional conceptions of verification can oversimplify domestic debates in ways that hurt the prospects for arms control. Structure alone does not determine outcomes, but it stacks the deck in ways that favor some groups and facilitate strategies to promote or block cooperation.

Strategies and Outcomes

When participants reason from different first principles, two types of strategies can promote or obstruct agreement. First-wave analysts focused primarily on efforts to depoliticize verification decisions by reducing conflicts of interests and ideas. This obscured the role that political decisions play in determining when conflicts can be avoided, reduced, or resolved. It also perpetuated the verification paradox by restricting arms control to narrow, lowest-common-denominator measures that could be monitored with win-win technology. When incentives for both cooperation and unilateral action are strong, the prospects for arms control depend on political strategies to build winning coalitions among groups with divergent interests and ideas about international politics. But ideas about verification do more than just influence initial policy preferences and bargaining positions. They also have important effects on the types of coalition-building strategies that are selected and their impact on arms control outcomes.

Proposals to Depoliticize Verification Decisions

The first wave's primary prescription was to establish a consensus on first principles from which common verification requirements could be derived. When participants in verification politics call for consensus, they usually want everybody else to adopt their assumptions. Unilateralists thought that if Americans would just "face the facts" about the futility of arms control, most verification debates would become irrelevant. Arms Control Advocates hoped that domestic and international convergence on MAD would allay concerns about low-level cheating or spying. But the likelihood of a general consensus on verification is extremely low, since it would require resolving several essentially contested questions simultaneously. Moreover, domestic consensus can be counterproductive if it precludes flexibility in negotiations: any strategy to move countries closer to agreement on verification by strengthening the influence of domestic groups with more compatible preferences depends on internal divisions to succeed. Therefore, one must determine what conditions encourage new thinking about verification principles and whether convergence on a particular set of ideas helps or hinders cooperation.

If popular agreement on first principles is impossible, another common proposal is to remove verification decisions from the political arena and entrust them to like-minded experts. This approach may mean delegating decisions to some subset of policy elites; for example, weapons scientists and intelligence officers have often tried to claim a special responsibility for verification decisions. Alternatively, policy makers may enlist outside experts. Research on epistemic communities suggests that increasing the influence of technical specialists with shared values, causal beliefs, notions of validity, and objectives can facilitate agreement on verification.[66] For example, Emanuel Adler argues that a group of pro–arms control scientists and security analysts helped to convince superpower leaders that limits on nuclear tests and ABM systems would benefit both countries and could be monitored without undue intrusion or expense.[67] The hope that science can rise above politics explains why some arms control supporters emphasize technical aspects of compliance assessment and advocate a verification-first approach to arms control negotiations.

Politics, however, creeps into technical problems in numerous ways. Political decisions often determine what type of research gets funded, whether researchers have a pro– or anti–arms control bent, how widely the findings are disseminated, and how the results affect policy decisions. One of the interesting features of seismology is that a huge influx of federal funding in the late 1950s turned an underdeveloped branch of geophysics into a popular and dynamic field. Although policy makers tried to channel this research in ways that supported their preferred outcomes, independent centers of seismological expertise developed that could challenge official claims about verification capabilities and compliance judgments.

Politics also affects which lessons are learned by policy makers and whether policy change results.[68] Decision makers often resist ceding control to technical experts (especially non-nationals) or sacrificing autonomy to international regimes, even when doing so would increase policy effectiveness. Public opinion is a critical intervening variable: citizens can force leaders to consult experts when the "dread factor" is high, but they rarely control which experts are chosen.[69] On verification, as on many other scientific questions, epistemic dissension has been more common than consensus.[70] When technical experts disagree, competing states, policy makers, and social groups will favor scientists who are likely to promote their preferred verification arrangements. High uncertainty and complexity also multiply opportunities for players to release information selectively, use numbers incorrectly, or postpone decisions until further research is done. Moreover, technical complexity or consensus among a small group of scientists is no more likely to favor cooperation than will consensus among senators or attentive citizens. Thus, one needs to determine which questions about verification are truly technical and which are inherently political. One also must explain when and how technical arguments become politically potent.

The development of win-win monitoring methods is a third strategy to decrease conflicts over verification. Satellites provide the most dramatic example, but negotiators have devised many creative ways to bridge seemingly contradictory verification concerns. The availability of appropriate nonintrusive monitoring technologies makes this easier. But it does not avoid countless questions about how the equipment will be used, what steps each side will take to make treaty-relevant behavior more transparent while protecting collateral information, who will analyze the data, and what will happen if the monitoring system yields ambiguous results. From a negotiator's perspective, the crucial variable is often political will: when leaders really want an accord, their representatives manage to find mutually acceptable verification arrangements. Many agreements are never ratified, however, because critics reject the compromises that make the technical arrangements workable and tolerable. Thus, one must investigate the conditions that favor compromise and creativity in negotiations, as well as the factors that affect domestic support for the resulting verification arrangements.

Coalition-Building Strategies

There is no way to get domestic and international agreement on verification for significant arms control without politics entering into the picture. Efforts to alter first principles, shrink or shift the circle of decision makers, or limit cooperation to measures where win-win monitoring methods exist may be sincere but misguided attempts to avoid conflict. Such efforts may also be covertly political strategies to promote a particular outcome by reshaping the structure of verification arguments. In either case, they are a subset of strategies used to form winning or blocking coalitions among groups with conflicting verification preferences.

Assembling a winning verification coalition is not easy. The provisions must be acceptable to each national negotiating team, despite conflicting interests and contradictory ideas about the nature, scope, functions, and forms of verification. Furthermore, the arrangements must enjoy whatever level of domestic support is required for ratification and implementation.[71] At a minimum in the United States, this involves a two-thirds majority in the Senate. But presidents usually want overwhelming Senate support for arms control treaties and are rarely willing to negotiate, much less try to ratify, a treaty that is disliked by top security advisers. Therefore, negotiation and ratification will not occur unless Arms Control Advocates can satisfy most Cautious Cooperators, secure the endorsement of key individuals (such as the Joint Chiefs of Staff and the chairman of the Senate Foreign Relations Committee), and neutralize doubts about verification raised by treaty opponents.

Negative outcomes (decisions that obstruct arms control) are more common because opponents can block cooperation at either the international or the domestic level. Unilateralists can prevail in the short term by ensuring that the only verification provisions that could "win" at home would be rejected by the other side, and vice versa. But negative outcomes will not be stable unless Unilateralists can convince Cautious Cooperators that no matter how much they desire arms control, there is no point in reopening talks, because agreement on verification is impossible.

In interest-based analyses of coalition politics, the rational strategy is to make just enough promises, threats, and concessions to achieve a winning coalition without alienating existing supporters, spreading the benefits of cooperation too thin, or making contradictory commitments. Many traditional coalition-building strategies can be used on verification. Discussing verification before or after determining the scope of arms control represents a form of agenda-setting. Targeted side payments, such as presidential pledges to increase general funds for intelligence agencies in return for their confident assessment of a treaty's verifiability, are common. Linkage influences the politics of verification when proponents of particular monitoring arrangements argue that they will also lead to increased democratization, technological cooperation, or economic gain. Designing fair allocation rules, such as requiring the states or groups who are most interested in a particular verification measure to bear the greatest costs, has also been helpful.

Interest-based strategies work best when players are easy to identify, groups have fixed interests but variable policy preferences, and support for cooperation stems from hard-headed calculations about material benefits. Coalition formation operates somewhat differently in the politics of verification because participants are often unclear about each others' motives (strategic or substantive, interest- or idea-based). It is also harder to make fine-grained calculations and concessions when groups form around principles rather than economic interests. Uncertainty stems not just from uneven access to information but also from lack of experience with nuclear arms control and verification. These conditions make rational-actor models of coalition-building inappropriate for an analysis of verification politics. They encourage unusual types of coalition-building that can be termed identification, alliance, alignment, and avoidance strategies. They also increase the likelihood that these strategies will have unexpected effects on arms control outcomes.

Identification strategies are used because the number of people who claim to take verification seriously is far greater than the number who really do. The first step in forming a coalition is to determine which players actually have very flexible preferences, which are sincerely concerned about the substance of verification, and which will rigidly oppose any obtainable set of arrangements. The most common type of identification strategy involves inviting others to study or implement verification as a test of their intentions. For example, the NRDC hoped that Soviet participation in their in-country seismic monitoring project would convince American Cautious Cooperators that Gorbachev was serious about mutual cooperation. But assessing interest in arms control from attitudes toward verification can be misleading. The benign conception of verification that dominated U.S. debates let American Unilateralists use verification-first proposals to mislabel some Cautious Cooperators in the USSR as arms control opponents. The reverse occurs when American arms control opponents use verification proposals to misidentify themselves as Cautious Cooperators. For example, some members of the American pharmaceutical industry have offered to try out proposals for adding managed-access inspections to the BWC, but policy makers who want a new verification protocol suspect that industry members secretly hope to derail the project by identifying verification problems without finding solutions.

Alliance strategies are used to build domestic and international coalitions among groups that already have compatible verification preferences. Side payments can sometimes convince less committed Unilateralists to support minor accords. But the fear of verification precedents that could bring more significant restrictions makes this less common than interest-based analyses predict. Because Arms Control Advocates and Unilateralists each share one first principle with Cautious Cooperators, most alliance strategies seek to narrow the distance on other principles or convince groups that a particular proposal is consistent with different underlying assumptions. Cautious Cooperators are uncertain about other states' intentions, which explains why Arms Control Advocates use other countries' support for verification as evidence of their interest in arms control. It also explains why misidentification has been such a successful blocking strategy for the Unilateralists.

Transboundary alliances can form among like-minded players, such as members of an epistemic community or international peace activists. They can also be forged across group lines when a proposal appeals to different groups for diverse reasons. The challenges of forming transboundary and transgroup alliances help explain why Gorbachev directed numerous unilateral initiatives in different issue areas to an amorphous group of American Cautious Cooperators instead of targeting a few concessions to swing voters.[72]

Alignment strategies attempt to reshape the structure of domestic and international arguments over verification. One can mount public education campaigns to increase the number of policy makers and influential outsiders who share one's first principles—a weak version of the consensus-building efforts advocated by first-wave authors. Or one can try to ensure that the real heavyweights have congenial verification preferences by educating existing decision makers, switching which roles have the most responsibility for verification decisions, or changing which individuals are in key roles.

None of these alignment strategies is easy. Apparent swings in public opinion on arms control mask the fact that a majority of Americans have been consistently ambivalent and do not want leaders to go too far in either direction.[73] Many policy makers have been skeptical of new ideas and slow to seek outside advice; only Eisenhower repeatedly responded to arms control dilemmas by making major changes in his advising system. Peter Haas found that epistemic communities could only influence policy makers' attitudes when they lacked clear-cut preferences on a particular issue and expert advice helped them to achieve other goals. When governmental learning happened, it was relatively unsophisticated and occurred less through education than through the replacement of old policy makers with new thinkers from the epistemic community.[74] Steven Weber's study of superpower arms control reached similar conclusions: most governmental learning was tactical (involving new ideas about how to operate given a set of assumptions about nuclear weapons and power) rather than strategic (involving alterations in those basic assumptions). Moreover, the United States and the USSR each experienced only one "critical learning period" during which strategic learning was possible; these occurred at different times (the mid-1960s in the United States and the mid-1980s in the USSR) and produced new assumptions that were still out of sync with the other side.[75] In the politics of verification, elections can alter the balance of influence among the three groups temporarily, but the requirements for ratification of a positive or negative outcome mean that no group can be ignored for long.

Avoidance strategies are used when policy makers do not want to make a clear-cut choice between cooperation and competition. The most common approach is to profess support for arms control once unrealistic verification demands have been met. Presidents may care most about preserving harmony among advisers, agencies, or attentive groups with irreconcilable arms control preferences. Or they may feel personally conflicted about the contradictions inherent in arms control and deterrence, since the former involves cooperating with an adversary and the latter requires credible threats to undertake irrational actions. Unilateralists may also use avoidance strategies as a second-best option when they face unavoidable pressures for arms control but do not want decisions that permanently foreclose their preferred outcome.

In theory, each type of strategy is available to every group attempting to influence verification decisions. In practice, however, ambivalence encourages Cautious Cooperators to be passive, play avoidance games, or quietly work on verification details. Arms Control Advocates and Unilateralists are more confident in their policy preferences, so they are frequently the more active and vocal participants in domestic verification debates. The tendency for the most visible players to have the strongest strategic motives explains why the politicization of verification has received more attention than have the more subtle political dilemmas.

Contextual factors can give any group a temporary advantage. For example, whichever group dominates the Executive Branch has some control over what verification technologies are developed and how their capabilities are perceived by Cautious Cooperators. In a technologically advanced democracy, though, there is a limit to anyone's ability to manipulate uncertainty or misrepresent empirical data. The international context also clearly affects both the salience of arms control and the values that Cautious Cooperators assign to the benefits, costs, and risks of specific verification arrangements. But the politics of verification has shown more continuity than change, despite the major contextual changes brought by the end of the Cold War. Moreover, some of the most effective strategies have involved attempts to change how different groups perceive contextual factors and even to alter the actual political, military, and technological context in which the politics of verification occur.

Some authors have hypothesized that Unilateralists will always have the edge in security issues. For example, Jack Snyder argues that "hawks" in hostile countries can form de facto alliances by giving belligerent speeches, whereas "doves" will have trouble forming transnational alliances because they lack opportunities to interact, have limited economic ties and vast sociocultural differences, and risk charges of disloyalty by talking to the other side.[76] In the Cold War, fear of communism gave Unilateralists a systematic advantage by promoting worst-case scenario thinking and ensuring that no politician could afford to be soft on verification. But many of the Unilateralists' most important advantages stemmed from the ideas about verification that dominated domestic debates and international negotiations.

Conclusion

The politics of verification defy a simple explanation. Every attempt to reach agreement on verification raises questions about the nature, scope, function, and appropriate forms of compliance evaluation. But these substantive questions are often oversimplified in ways that distort verification decisions. Because Cautious Cooperators care about the substance of verification, Arms Control Advocates and Unilateralists can make strategic use of verification arguments to form winning or blocking coalitions. Identification, alliance, alignment, and avoidance strategies are all used, sometimes with unexpected and counterproductive effects.

For any particular verification decision, the specific form that these general features will take depends *in part* on contextual factors, such as the significance of treaty provisions, the availability of different monitoring technologies, the degree of tension or trust between negotiating partners, and the domestic decision-making system. Contrary to those who believe that verification is peripheral and derivative, however, one cannot account fully for test ban verification outcomes by looking at shifts in the nuclear balance, crises in superpower relations, breakthroughs in monitoring technology, or changes in domestic leadership.

To demonstrate that the politics of verification have unique dynamics with an independent effect on cooperation, Chapters Three through Seven consider substantive concerns about the type and amount of verification and assess the structure of verification arguments during prenegotiation, negotiation, and ratification periods. Each chapter also traces the processes through which verification arguments were perpetuated or provisionally resolved. The aim is to determine the degree to which verification decisions can be depoliticized and the extent to which they are inherently political. These historical chapters demonstrate that failure to reach agreement on verification for significant test limits stemmed from the particular ideas and strategies employed, not from an inescapable verification paradox, an unfortunate combination of contextual circumstances, or an unwarranted lack of trust. Chapter Eight uses these insights to analyze the mixed results of post–Cold War efforts to conclude a CTB, as well as to suggest changes that could promote more positive outcomes in verification politics.

3

How the Politics of Verification Shape Prenegotiation

THE INTERESTS, IDEAS, AND INTERNAL PROCESSES that determine whether states start serious negotiations matter as much as anything that happens at the bargaining table. The process of prenegotiation helps adversaries recognize a shared interest in cooperation and perceive each other as worthy of some trust.[1] It can be triggered by a crisis or series of policy failures which convince political leaders that unilateral actions are ineffective or dangerous, a hope that prenegotiation would lower the risks involved in formal negotiations, or a belief that prenegotiation will bring extranegotiatory benefits such as favorable public opinion. Prenegotiation helps to establish agendas; clarify interests; change perceptions about the costs, benefits, and risks of negotiation; influence expectations of reciprocity; alter domestic support for conciliation; and build bridges from conflict to cooperation using small, provisional concessions. In the test ban case, prenegotiation began soon after World War II, endured a decade during which the superpowers exchanged non-negotiable proposals for comprehensive disarmament, and concluded with a commitment in 1958 to negotiate a CTB as an independent, "first step" measure.

The politics of verification has received little attention in previous studies of prenegotiation. Offers to discuss or implement monitoring mechanisms are occasionally mentioned as a low-risk way to indicate trustworthiness and to start cooperating. For example, William Zartman and Maureen Berman suggest that Soviet objections to verification raised doubts about their intentions that could only be removed "if it were conclusively shown that the refusal were for other reasons."[2] More typically, though, questions about verification are viewed as a secondary concern that can be addressed after formal negotiations begin.

The test ban case suggests that the politics of verification are more important to prenegotiation than previously assumed and that early attention to verification can hinder as well as help progress toward cooperation. Arguments about verification played a crucial role in domestic decisions about the dangers and opportunities posed by nuclear weapons. Each new stage in the arms race strengthened a sense of nuclear crisis without ending debates about the mix of cooperation and competition that would best serve security. Arms Control Advocates, Cautious Cooperators, and Unilateralists wanted to participate in prenegotiations for different reasons; thus, all three triggers existed, but they often worked at cross-purposes. Given these domestic divisions and the level of distrust that characterized superpower relations, serious efforts to find mutually acceptable arms control measures could not start until Arms Control Advocates convinced Cautious Cooperators that there was a reasonable prospect of agreement on verification. As long as Unilateralists could argue persuasively that Soviet resistance to Western verification demands indicated hostile intentions and that agreement on verification was impossible, they could reap public relations benefits from talking about nuclear disarmament while avoiding negotiated limits. Prenegotiation ended successfully, not because preferences suddenly changed or trust slowly developed, but because a winning coalition of players concluded (over-optimistically) that agreement on workable and tolerable CTB verification was within reach.

Discouraging Precedents from Past Negotiations

The destruction of Hiroshima and Nagasaki graphically demonstrated the unprecedented power and the catastrophic potential of nuclear weapons. Intense debates occurred in high-level meetings and on the streets about whether the best prospect for security lay in vigorous national nuclear programs or sweeping international control over nuclear activities. Strong popular support for cooperation left Western leaders with little choice but to raise the issue in the fledgling U.N. The real decisions for political leaders were whether to take the talks seriously or to treat them as a public relations ploy, and whether to postpone work on their own nuclear programs while they explored the prospects for cooperation.

Arms Control Advocates were at a disadvantage in these policy debates because they had little historical evidence to suggest that the major powers could reach agreement on verification. Most previous attempts to reduce international conflict had emphasized legal prohibitions on the use of force, not limits on weapons possession.[3] The most successful arms control accord, the Rush-Bagot Agreement of 1817, banned warships on the Great Lakes—a narrow measure that could be monitored informally by smaller boats in the region. The 1922 Washington Naval Treaty also lacked formal verification and proved less stable because incentives to cheat were higher and likelihood of detection lower than for Rush-Bagot.[4] The Hague Conferences of 1899 and 1907 established the International Commission of Inquiry. The commission had modest fact-finding powers, but OSIs were voluntary and the host country had to cooperate only "as fully as they may think practicable" if the inquiry did not "impair its sovereign rights or safety."[5]

The only prenuclear treaties with rigorous verification were imposed on defeated states after World War I.[6] The Inter-Allied Commission of Control had almost unlimited powers. The German government was required to cooperate fully and pay the commission's operating expenses. What might be called "verification by military occupation" ensured that the Germans carried out finite tasks, such as destroying war matériel and converting arms works into farm tool factories.[7] But Germany evaded many prohibitions by building a shadow army, using plants and training grounds in the USSR, and raising private funds for military use.[8] Moreover, the unprecedented extent of the Control Commission's verification powers may have reduced German incentives to comply and the inspectors' will to persist.[9] As it became increasingly clear that the victors would not accept comparable disarmament and verification measures for themselves, those commissioners who favored a managerial approach saw their activities as less legitimate and those of German noncompliance as more understandable.[10] Reluctance to verify and enforce provisions that did more to punish Germany than to promote cooperative security meant that inspections ended in 1927, despite growing evidence of noncompliance.

The most interesting early parallels to the politics of test ban verification occurred during general disarmament negotiations after World War I. The public perception that excess arming had caused the conflict created domestic pressures for negotiations, but national leaders were less confident about the value of disarmament and had divergent verification preferences. The United States depicted sovereignty as inviolable and "international good faith and respect for treaties" as sufficient incentives for compliance.[11] The Soviets called for strict international supervision but provided few details. Most major European states wanted to balance secrecy, sovereignty, and security by establishing a weak agency that could make inquiries but not conduct mandatory inspections. Only the French insisted on a verification authority with broad, well-defined powers, because they were the most directly threatened by German rearmament. The French also originated arguments about the confidence-building role of verification and warned that doubts about compliance might lead to defensive cheating.[12]

When disarmament talks deadlocked over conflicting preferences, issues were referred to technical committees.[13] One diplomat lamented that technical experts were occupationally ill equipped with diplomatic skills. He wrote, "Regarded as a time-wasting device, [the technical committees'] success was staggering.... But as any contribution to disarmament, they were doomed to sterility from the very beginning."[14]

After World War II, the prospects for agreement on nuclear verification seemed even slimmer. The United States used the failures of interwar arms control as proof that all cooperation must involve extensive verification, while the USSR used it as evidence against exchanging military information prior to commitments about disarmament.[15] The success of the Manhattan Project had shown that atomic bombs could be developed in secrecy and used without warning, thereby raising the requirements for workable verification. But the closed nature of the Stalinist state reduced access to "soft" sources of compliance information, such as military attachés, diplomatic missions, and disgruntled citizens, thus making inspections more necessary but less likely. Many Cautious Cooperators decided that verifiable arms control was not a realistic option, no matter how desirable it might be. As one secret British study concluded, no workable verification would be accepted by the USSR, and any tolerable system would "develop into a highly dangerous sham, productive of endless suspicion and friction."[16]

Alternative Plans for International Control of Nuclear Activities

American Arms Control Advocates believed that the dangers of unconstrained nuclear weapons development were so severe that the great powers must find the creative ideas and political will needed for agreement on verification. This position was represented by the Acheson-Lilienthal Committee (ALC), a group of scientists and policy makers assembled in early 1946 to recommend international controls that the United States could trust and the Soviets would accept.[17] The ALC knew their task was daunting—David Lilienthal later likened it to asking someone who has previously only jumped ten feet to leap a twenty-foot chasm—but they were confident that it could be done because "the alternative was so bad."[18]

The ALC report started with the "facts" as the authors saw them.[19] International cooperation to control atomic weapons was imperative given their unprecedented destructiveness, the absence of effective defense, and the fleeting nature of the U.S. monopoly. The development of atomic energy for peaceful purposes, however, was largely "interchangeable and interdependent" with its exploitation for military uses. Because clandestine bomb building could not be detected from afar, an international agency would need full accountability for all fissile material.

In an analysis that paralleled the experience with German disarmament after World War I, the ALC argued that adversarial verification would "destroy the confidence and cooperation" required for stable arms control. "So long as intrinsically dangerous activities may be carried on by nations," the ALC predicted, "rivalries are inevitable and fears are engendered that place so great a pressure upon a system of international enforcement by police methods that no degree of ingenuity or technical competence would possibly hope to cope with them."[20] Ensuring that "peaceful" programs did not disguise military projects would require countless foreigners with special privileges to scrutinize industrial operations, monitor mining, and track all personnel with relevant expertise. This would be obnoxious to inspectors and inspectees alike. Frictions and incidents would arise, and morale would suffer. Yet even such draconian measures could not provide complete confidence because "the people charged with policing an agreement . . . couldn't possibly know as much as those they were trying to police."[21]

The ALC foresaw that sovereign states would voluntarily renounce nuclear weapons only if a managerial approach was used to lower the costs and risks of verification relative to the benefits of cooperation. Therefore, the committee wanted to entrust all dangerous nuclear activities to an international Atomic Development Authority (ADA). Its role would be to prevent national nuclear weapons development and promote peaceful uses of atomic energy, but not to open Soviet society or reduce other U.S.-Soviet tensions.[22] With an ADA monopoly of weapons-grade fissile materials, only a few routine inspections would be necessary. Seizure of dangerous materials or refusal to cooperate with the ADA would provide early warning of nuclear weapon ambitions. Empowering the ADA to conduct groundbreaking atomic research would increase the value of cooperation. It would also improve the quality of verification by attracting the brightest scientists who could discover new paths to nuclear weapons before potential proliferants did. In short, a collaborative approach to verification would make international control of atomic energy less costly, more attractive, and more secure.

The ALC report was based on Arms Control Advocates' assumptions that the risks of unfettered nuclear weapons development outweighed the risks of imperfect verification and that once others understood these "facts," they would reach the same conclusions.[23] This diverse group of experts glossed over several substantive dilemmas, however, in the hope that their recommendations would carry more weight if they spoke with one voice.[24] The report underestimated a dual-use problem with verification information: to establish a cooperative verification agency, the United States must disclose nuclear secrets that could shorten the time required for others to build a bomb.[25] It barely mentioned the dilemmas associated with a safe transition from a U.S. monopoly to international control of nuclear weapons. The authors recognized the need for enforcement yet said nothing about responses to noncompliance; they did not want to imply mistrust and doubted that the Soviets would grant an international agency the right to punish violations.[26]

Most Americans were more divided and ambivalent about nuclear weapons, cooperation, and verification than the ALC acknowledged. When asked whether the United States should stop making atomic bombs and destroy its stockpile, between 20 and 30 percent favored abolition, whereas 60 to 70 percent wanted production to continue.[27] When asked where the best prospects for security lay, however, a large majority (67 percent) favored international control versus national nuclear weapons development (28 percent). Support for inspection in principle was even stronger, but only about 50 percent would accept international control over U.S. atomic factories, and 40 percent would give nuclear information to the global agency. Fewer still were willing to let teams search U.S. facilities if they might learn how to make a bomb. These views are not surprising, because the 1946 Atomic Energy Act had restricted the sharing of nuclear information even with close allies.

President Truman chose Bernard Baruch, a conservative businessman, to translate the ALC plan into a negotiating proposal that U.S. lawmakers and taxpayers would support. Like Truman and many other policy elites, Baruch was more of a Unilateralist at heart.[28] He assumed that the United States could protect its atomic secrets and deny the Soviets access to fissile materials for ten years—long enough for the USSR to moderate its behavior or the West to find an "antidote" to nuclear bombs.[29] Cooperation should be on U.S. terms, and Soviet objections should be used to build domestic support for confrontational strategies, such as Baruch's preferred option—a nuclear Pax Atomica.

The Baruch delegation to the U.N. Atomic Energy Commission changed the ALC plan in ways that pleased U.S. Cautious Cooperators but ensured Soviet rejection. To avoid movement toward an "international socialized State," it returned responsibility for mining and refining fissionable materials to private industries. This change vastly increased the number and intrusiveness of inspections.[30] On the controversial issues that the ALC downplayed, the changes were even more dramatic. Baruch put enforcement "at the heart" of his proposal and insisted on veto-free procedures for "immediate, swift, and sure punishment" of any violations.[31] The USSR was required to suspend atomic research and permit a survey of their fissionable resources at the start, but the United States would not reveal any nuclear information or transfer any weapons until the full international system was operating to its satisfaction. Finally, the United States would not relinquish its "winning weapon" without "a guarantee of safety, not only against the offenders in the atomic area but against the illegal users of other weapons—bacteriological, biological, gas—perhaps?—why not?—against war itself."[32]

The Soviet response was predictably negative.[33] They agreed that international control of atomic energy was technologically feasible and would require some verification and enforcement. But because Stalin's advisers were less afraid of a nuclear arms race than of external control over Soviet economic development, they opposed most elements in Baruch's plan.[34] The Soviets refused to relinquish their veto if the Security Council deliberated about a possible violation. They wanted to continue national research related to nuclear weapons and rejected international controls over peaceful programs. They would tolerate data submissions, statistical checks, and periodic OSIs at declared facilities, but not continuous monitoring or OSIs at undeclared sites. Finally, they wanted to outlaw the use of nuclear weapons and destroy all nuclear bombs before detailed discussions about verification began.

Vannevar Bush and other ALC scientists hoped the Soviets would change their stance if the "facts" about nuclear weapons were presented at technical meetings. They also thought that inviting the Soviets to a scientific exchange would be a good test of their intentions, but American Unilateralists squelched this plan as too risky for U.S. security. Soviet leaders were also unwilling to let their top scientists interact freely with American experts. The main reason that the Soviet delegation to the U.N. Atomic Energy Commission included any scientists was to keep the West from using technical arguments as trump cards.[35]

The differences between U.S. and Soviet positions were so extreme that talks deadlocked.[36] Less than two weeks after the Soviets presented their proposal, the United States conducted its first postwar test of a nuclear weapon. The Soviets denounced the test as proof that the United States had never been serious about nuclear disarmament; the United States charged that the Soviets were being unreasonable about verification to avoid international constraints on their nuclear ambitions. Unilateralists on both sides perpetuated disagreements over inspection rights, the veto, and the transition sequence. But strategic use of verification arguments rested on serious substantive dilemmas. U.S. Unilateralists managed to exploit American ambivalence: few decision makers or citizens were willing to trust a nuclear arms control agreement without extensive verification or to share enough nuclear secrets to create a workable verification regime. Anything but the weakest verification would have been unacceptable even to Cautious Cooperators in the USSR, given the low value that they placed on cooperation with capitalists, the premium put on secrecy during Stalin's last years, and the concerted effort to end America's atomic monopoly.

McGeorge Bundy argues that the United States might have been able to negotiate limits on nuclear arms in the mid-1940s if the ALC had been more sensitive to "political realities."[37] He views their solution to the workable/tolerable dilemma as "technically excellent" but totally impractical, because the Soviets would never let the United States remain the only country that had developed nuclear weapons. Nevertheless, any treaty that allowed the great powers to make and keep a limited number of nuclear weapons would have exacerbated the verification problems that the ALC sought to minimize. It is more accurate to say that the ALC's most important substantive insight—that adversarial verification could not sustain significant cooperation—was correct, but that their strategic decision to downplay related dilemmas wasted an opportunity to educate Cautious Cooperators about verification trade-offs and let American Unilateralists change the ALC proposal in ways that stiffened Soviet resistance.

Verification Arguments for Extranegotiatory Objectives

As the Unilateralists hoped, failure to agree on international control of nuclear energy increased support for vigorous national programs. Nuclear negotiations were merged with talks on conventional arms in the new U.N. Disarmament Commission and continued purely for public relations reasons. Most contemporary Western accounts saw the rigid Soviet stance on verification as evidence that the USSR was not really interested in arms control, but the same could be said for the American position. The main goal of Truman's disarmament policy (as expressed in National Security Council Memorandum 112) was to ensure "sufficient US and allied military strength to meet, deter, and successfully oppose if necessary various types of Soviet armed aggression."[38] Therefore, U.S. verification policy was designed both to please different groups of Americans and to highlight the impossibility of U.S.-Soviet cooperation.

The Truman approach to verification stressed the ambitious goal of opening and democratizing the Soviet Union. This appealed to realists, who believed that the United States should use its nuclear advantage to coerce the USSR into changing its political system. In April 1945, for example, Secretary of War Henry Stimson wrote a memo arguing that the United States should not share nuclear secrets with the Soviets until they had adopted a liberalizing constitution, because a police state could never participate in the kind of verification regime that would be required for nuclear cooperation. The openness objective also appealed to idealists, who believed that sharing information needed for verification would help superpower leaders reason together on the basis of facts and recognize the benefits of mutual cooperation. This superficial consensus on the openness objective masked a deep split between those who saw political change as a prerequisite for arms control and those who saw nuclear cooperation as the engine for political change.[39] Using the openness objective to broaden the basis of domestic support for U.S. security policy also created a subtext to U.S. verification proposals that the Soviets found especially threatening.

The Truman administration compounded the problem by linking an absolutist stance on verification with an all-or-nothing approach to arms control. NSC 112 held that nuclear and conventional arms control were inseparably linked, that control of atomic energy required Soviet support for the Baruch plan or something equally effective, and that foolproof verification must be implemented before restrictions occurred. Because the United States insisted on solving verification problems before negotiating arms control and the USSR refused to discuss verification details before agreement on disarmament, talks about General and Complete Disarmament (GCD) continued only for extranegotiatory purposes. Ironically, both sides' willingness to perpetuate verification arguments for strategic purposes left a legacy of distrust that hindered later, more sincere, arms control efforts. Many Americans concluded that serious arms control efforts were pointless, because the USSR would never accept any reliable form of verification. Meanwhile, what the Soviets saw as a Western "obsession" with on-site inspection heightened their suspicions about that form of verification and "in that atmosphere of suspicion . . . distrust grew into a stable bias against on-site inspection."[40]

Competitive nuclear weapons development required the United States to watch for Soviet tests. In September 1947, the air force started sampling the atmosphere for radioactive particles. They soon added seismic and acoustic sensors to detect the shock waves generated by explosions. The United States assumed that the Soviets had similar capabilities, because it delayed a test in spring of 1948 to prevent the USSR from discovering its design by sampling fallout.[41] When the Soviets conducted their first atomic test in mid-1949, the rudimentary American air-sampling system could detect the explosion and determine that plutonium had been used but not pinpoint when the test had occurred.[42]

Some of Truman's advisers suggested that these unilateral verification capabilities might offer a way to break the disarmament deadlock. After the first

Soviet test, Edward Teller and other U.S. Unilateralists wanted a crash program to develop thermonuclear weapons that could be one thousand times more destructive than fission bombs. Most of the General Advisory Committee (GAC) for the Atomic Energy Commission (AEC) feared that this would hurt U.S. security, regardless of what the Soviets did. But two GAC members, Enrico Fermi and I. I. Rabi, saw a chance to rekindle popular support for arms control by inviting the Soviets to join a ban on thermonuclear weapons development. No agreement on verification would be necessary, because the United States already had methods for detecting a large explosion, as well as plenty of atomic weapons to punish the production or use of a hydrogen bomb.[43] This suggestion received little support. Unilateralists opposed any suggestion that the United States might restrict its nuclear options without inspections or conventional arms control. Moreover, the other Arms Control Advocates on the GAC did not want to condition U.S. restraint on Soviet reciprocation because they questioned the prospects for cooperation and feared that Unilateralists would use another negotiating failure as evidence that the United States must have thermonuclear weapons. They also doubted that Americans would accept any accord without full verification. As Oppenheimer (then GAC chairman) told George Kennan, "The notion of safeguards and of effective control have attained a kind of rigid and absolute quality" that could not be easily overcome.[44]

The NSC 112 strategy of using comprehensive arms control and verification demands to avoid serious negotiations also helps to explain why a similar proposal was ignored a few years later. In 1951, weapons scientists solved the main technical obstacles to thermonuclear weapons. Unilateralists wanted to test and produce a huge stockpile of thermonuclear weapons as quickly as possible. They were opposed by the State Department's Panel of Consultants on Disarmament, which included Oppenheimer and Bush. Benjamin Cohen, the U.S. representative to the U.N. disarmament talks, had suggested that the deadlock might be broken by agreement on an issue for which verification would not require a major breach of the Iron Curtain. Because an H-bomb test ban had the "unique characteristic that it separates the problem of limitation of armament from the problem of 'inspection,'" the consultants proposed using it as a "test case" to ascertain whether the Soviets would be seriously interested in cooperation if disagreements about verification could be avoided.[45]

The idea was quickly quashed again by the secretaries of state and defense, who believed that cooperation with the USSR was impossible and wanted the Soviets to shoulder the blame. An inspectionless H-bomb ban, opponents argued, would "essentially remove the flavor and the core of the U.S. argument on the absolute necessity for priority on disclosure and verification in any disarmament arrangement and would therefore lead many to believe that disclosure and verification [are] not essential."[46] Strong public support (68 percent) for proposing an H-bomb ban before accelerating the U.S. program may explain why Truman's top advisers feared an open discussion about verification without inspection.[47] Because the consultants had no independent standing within the Truman administration and would not violate the norms of secrecy by appealing to the public with their plan, they could not even postpone the first H-bomb test long enough for the next president to consider cooperation.

In short, although the politics of verification does not explain *why* Truman officials preferred unilateral deterrence and reassurance to serious negotiations, it does help explain *how* they were able to convince Cautious Cooperators that a vigorous military buildup was unfortunate but necessary, given Soviet resistance to U.S. verification demands. By insisting that arms control had to be comprehensive, that verification had to be foolproof, and that mutual agreement on verification was impossible, Truman Unilateralists short-circuited debates about arms control options and verification requirements. This blocking strategy worked, even though the United States had never conducted a comprehensive study of "what to inspect, how and where it would be inspected, and . . . what can and cannot be profitably inspected," because neither U.S. nor Soviet Unilateralists wanted answers to these questions.[48]

Internal Reviews and External Pressures for a More Cooperative Approach

Moving from the disarmament deadlock to serious consideration of a test ban as an independent measure involved convincing policy makers and attentive citizens to question whether arms control had to be comprehensive to be beneficial and whether verification had to be perfect to be acceptable. Internal policy reviews started first, prompted by leadership changes and growing concern about the long-term implications of unconstrained weapons development. Public debates following the BRAVO explosion in March 1954 informed citizens about the risks of nuclear testing and the possibility of using remote verification methods to avoid the workable/tolerable dilemma. Even though neither the internal reviews nor the external pressures produced an immediate agreement to start test ban negotiations, they weakened the Unilateralists' position that the only reason to talk about cooperation was to preserve support for military and political competition.

The Rapid Pace of the Arms Race Prompts Policy Reviews

The early success of the Unilateralists' strategy caused contextual changes that made their all-or-nothing approach to arms control and verification less sustainable. In January 1953, the consultants gave the new Eisenhower administration a fuller study of the impact of thermonuclear weapons on U.S. policy.[49] They argued that the Soviets had produced so much fissile material and nuclear bombs that inspectors could never be sure that they had found it all. Thus, even if the Soviets suddenly accepted the Baruch plan, America's verification proposals could not ensure total nuclear disarmament. Rather than continuing to advance disarmament proposals for propaganda purposes, the United States should think seriously about partial arms control measures that could enhance deterrence stability. Demands for "foolproof" verification were neither necessary to protect American security against possible violations of modest arms control measures, nor desirable if they caused the USSR to reject U.S. proposals out of hand. Henceforth, U.S. verification requirements should "do as little violence as possible to a principle [the Iron Curtain] which seems to stand near the center of the Soviet System."[50]

President Eisenhower was more receptive than Truman to arguments for obtainable arms control measures.[51] Eisenhower saw nuclear surprise attack as the greatest threat to U.S. security, because it would prevent the United States from utilizing its superior mobilization capacity.[52] He also worried that nuclear despair might lead to national paralysis and insufficient preparation for required deterrence and defense programs as long as the nuclear threat remained. These concerns prompted Eisenhower's Operation Candor education program and his Atoms for Peace proposal (a plan for the United States and the USSR to donate fissile material to an international organization dedicated to peaceful nuclear programs). Although the Soviets disliked many aspects of Atoms for Peace, it represented the first U.S. proposal for partial nuclear cooperation without inspection to "open up a new channel for peaceful discussions . . . to shake off the inertia imposed by fear, and . . . to make positive progress toward peace."[53]

Eisenhower also ordered a general review of U.S. disarmament and verification policy. The State and Defense Departments agreed that Baruch's plans for verification as control were no longer feasible or desirable, but they disagreed about what to do.[54] Defense Department policy held that the safest response was to continue using extreme verification demands to reap extranegotiatory benefits from futile disarmament talks. Some members of the State Department, by contrast, were increasingly worried that American intransigence and unrestrained nuclear weapons development were eroding international support for U.S. negotiating positions.[55] They wanted to offer a progressive arms control plan—starting with transparency measures but no arms restrictions—because Soviet acceptance would bring increased warning of a surprise attack, whereas rejection would be seen by the West as clear evidence of aggressive intentions. Because this position was unacceptable to DOD, arms control and verification policy continued to reflect NSC 112 by default.

Meanwhile, a parallel struggle to revise disarmament policy had begun in the Soviet Union.[56] In 1953, Stalin died and the Soviet armed forces received their first atomic bombs—two events that made it possible and necessary to evaluate the impact of nuclear weapons on national security. Opinions differed among top Party members as to what, if any, mix of confrontation and cooperation could lessen Western hostility. Vyacheslav Molotov, the foreign minister, perpetuated the Stalinist perspective that conflict with the West was inevitable and that steps to relax tensions would reduce Soviet vigilance and weaken the Socialist camp.[57] Georgy Malenkov, the new prime minister, maintained that military competition and confrontations in Korea and Berlin were ruining the Soviet economy and endangering security. Malenkov declared that both sides would lose in a nuclear war and suggested that the West would respond favorably to cuts in military spending, a minimal deterrence posture, and concessions on various regional issues.[58] His argument was inadvertently undercut, though, by the U.S. announcement in early 1954 of its "massive retaliation" strategy and other evidence that the United States hoped to "roll back" Communist victories.

Nikita Khrushchev replaced Malenkov as prime minister in February 1955. To satisfy conflicting factions, Khrushchev argued that it was possible to moderate Western hostility, but only from a position of strength. In February 1956, he announced that war was no longer inevitable now that the socialist countries had the material and moral means to prevent aggression by working with progressive forces in the West and threatening "a smashing rebuff" to any of the capitalists' "adventurist plans."[59]

The Soviet decision to take arms control negotiations more seriously reflected military, economic, and political considerations.[60] Because the USSR had a stockpile of fission bombs and a tested thermonuclear device, nuclear arms control would not necessarily leave it at a gross qualitative disadvantage. Unilateral efforts to match Western arsenals, however, would damage economic development. The Soviets emphasized the political side of deterrence and hoped to prevent war through diplomatic overtures backed by military might. If Western leaders responded positively, dangerous or expensive aspects of military competition could be restricted; if they rejected reasonable proposals, they would be constrained by domestic moderates and peace activists. But Western leaders knew little about the internal debates over disarmament policy after Stalin's death, and external signs of a Soviet policy shift were extremely subtle.

The Impact of BRAVO on Public Debates and Official Policies

The first U.S. explosion of a deliverable H-bomb on March 1, 1954, generated public pressure for limits on tests independent of other arms control measures. The BRAVO test had a yield comparable to 15 million tons (megatons, or mt) of dynamite—more than 100 times larger than the Hiroshima bomb.[61] The explosion dramatically demonstrated the destruction that would occur if deterrence failed. The radioactive fallout raised equally worrisome concerns about the ongoing health risks of nuclear testing. Prominent citizens and legislators in the United States and the U.K. called for an immediate ban on H-bomb tests and a renewed effort for nuclear disarmament. Some were so scared by BRAVO that they supported Prime Minister Jawaharlal Nehru of India's proposal for an unverified "standstill" while permanent arrangements to abolish nuclear weapons were devised. Others were intrigued after learning that long-range monitoring might make a test ban "self-enforcing."[62]

Many accounts of CTB negotiations credit the BRAVO explosion with swelling the ranks of Arms Control Advocates until they overwhelmed Unilateralist opposition.[63] But BRAVO did less to change alignments than to alter alliances among existing groups by increasing Cautious Cooperators' optimism about verification. Public opinion was consistently divided in the mid-1950s among a small group of Arms Control Advocates (approximately 15 percent to 30 percent) who wanted to end U.S. tests unconditionally, Cautious Cooperators (30 percent to 40 percent) who favored a CTB *if* other states reciprocated, and Unilateralists (20 percent to 30 percent) who opposed any test restrictions.[64] Total public support for a multilateral CTB after BRAVO was comparable to approval in 1946 for international control of all dangerous nuclear activities. BRAVO enabled Arms Control Advocates to appeal to Cautious Cooperators more effectively by showing that a low-risk measure could offer major benefits and by bringing information about remote monitoring methods into the public debate.

When the NSC debated Nehru's proposal, arguments reflected the struggle over U.S. disarmament policy.[65] Unilateralists, including the acting secretary of defense, Chairman of the Joint Chiefs of Staff (JCS) Admiral Arthur Radford, and Chairman of the AEC Lewis Strauss, insisted that anything hampering or stigmatizing nuclear weapons would damage the credibility of deterrence. They also feared that flexibility on verification would put the United States on a slippery slope toward nuclear disarmament. An unpoliced moratorium would contradict U.S. policies that conventional and nuclear forces must be reduced simultaneously, that atomic energy must be regulated, and that foolproof verification must be established—the Unilateralists' most effective brakes against pressures to "ban the Bomb."[66]

Secretary of State John Foster Dulles expected an international outcry if the United States simply rejected Nehru's proposal. The NSC briefly considered using verification uncertainties to justify a one-year moratorium on tests over 100 kilotons (kt). This would not hurt U.S. weapons development but would complicate the Soviets' test program if they agreed and make them look like foes of peace if they refused.[67] Dulles dropped that idea, though, after predicting that the Soviets would depict it as self-serving and put the United States "in an awkward propaganda position."[68]

Eisenhower was the only NSC member who seriously considered ending nuclear tests. He offered the most forceful arguments for cooperation because he "could perceive no final answer to the problem of nuclear warfare if both sides simply went ahead making bigger and better nuclear weapons."[69] The president's preferences hinged on verification. He declared that if there were "any way to abolish atomic weapons which would ensure the certainty that they would be abolished, he would be the very first to endorse it."[70] Without a "really foolproof" way to verify nuclear disarmament, the superpowers needed safe steps to initiate cooperation. U.S. monitoring capabilities made a moratorium attractive because "the minute we learned that the Soviets had not stopped testing these weapons, we would . . . start our own tests again."[71]

Lacking independent scientific advice and other strong voices for arms control on the NSC, Eisenhower reluctantly accepted the arguments of AEC and DOD specialists that U.S. monitoring capabilities were too weak, and its testing needs too pressing, for a moratorium. In public, Eisenhower dismissed calls for a test ban as a "vain hope that something less than secure safeguards could justify any curtailment of our power to defend ourselves, our allies, and the free world."[72] Behind the scenes, however, he sought to end the disarmament deadlock between the superpowers and among his own advisers. Eisenhower changed the Executive Branch decision-making structure by appointing Harold Stassen to the new Cabinet-rank position of special assistant to the president on disarmament, whose sole purpose was to promote domestic and international agreement on arms control and verification.

When Winston Churchill responded to Labour Party pleas for a test ban, he used verification arguments in several ways.[73] He invoked the workable/tolerable dilemma to claim that since limits on nuclear tests must be part of a comprehensive disarmament package, agreement on verification would be impossible until confidence among nations had increased. Churchill also maintained that test restrictions depended on U.S. willingness to share information needed for verification, because he knew that Congress was considering reducing the restrictions imposed by the Atomic Energy Act.[74] His comments made U.S. policy changes a prerequisite for arms control and implied that rash statements by Labour members could "set back the many favorable tendencies" toward nuclear cooperation. This also prepared legislators for a British thermonuclear program if technical exchanges and negotiated test limits were not forthcoming—a step Churchill secretly intended to take.

Soviet leaders faced less pressure to accept Nehru's proposal because domestic and allied support was less crucial to their nuclear program. They did try to use BRAVO to mobilize world opinion against the United States for "violating its trust" by exploding nuclear weapons in the Marshall Islands. Until Khrushchev's power was consolidated and the review of arms control policy was done, the Soviets largely ignored calls for test suspension and continued to demand elimination of all weapons of mass destruction under "strict" but unspecified forms of international control.[75]

Thus, BRAVO did not dramatically alter national policies or public opinion in the United States, but it did make the Unilateralists' rigid stance on arms control and verification less acceptable to Cautious Cooperators. Nuclear decision makers were thinking more seriously about partial arms control measures and verification trade-offs, both to achieve their own objectives and to preserve popular support for their negotiating positions. But arguments did not end about whether a test ban should be included in a package of partial measures and what kinds of verification should be required.

Three Plans for Coping with the Thermonuclear Dilemma

Barely a year after BRAVO, the Soviets included a test ban as low-risk, first step in their package proposal presented to the U.N. Disarmament Subcommittee on May 10, 1955. The proposal generated tremendous optimism among Western Arms Control Advocates because it suggested that the great powers had converged on similar ideas about nuclear vulnerability, arms control, and verification. The United States and the USSR were stockpiling everything from tactical nuclear weapons to multimegaton bombs, developing sophisticated delivery systems, and threatening to use nuclear weapons for a range of purposes. Proliferation was also a more urgent problem: the British had tested an atomic bomb (in October 1952) and were working on hydrogen weapons; the French nuclear research program was proceeding rapidly; and China wanted nuclear aid from the Soviet Union. Nuclear vulnerability multiplied the incentives for cooperation and the risks of exploitation. It increased the need for reliable verification yet made workable and tolerable arrangements more difficult to obtain. The subcommittee members all responded to this dilemma by trying to decompose disarmament into a series of increasingly significant cooperative steps. Nonetheless, crucial differences in the 1954 Anglo-French Memorandum, the Soviets' May 1955 proposal, and the U.S. January 1957 package revealed that verification preferences were still far apart.

The French government was the first to admit openly that the Western proposal for international control of all dangerous nuclear activities was unworkable, not just intolerable to the USSR.[76] No inspection system could guarantee that the Soviets had not hidden a softball-sized chunk of nuclear material for a clandestine bomb. As a "practical" alternative to pointless arguments about perfecting verification as control before or after total disarmament, the Anglo-French Memorandum proposed to alternate improvements in verification with advances in arms control. But the early steps involved cuts in areas of Soviet strength (conventional arms) and freezes where the West was ahead (weapons of mass destruction). The memorandum did not mention nuclear tests and specified that nuclear weapons would not be eliminated until conventional reductions had occurred *and* the control agency could "guarantee the effective observance" of nuclear disarmament.[77]

Much to everyone's surprise, the Soviets accepted the Anglo-French Memorandum as a starting point for negotiations. But the measures with the lowest risk and the greatest benefit for the Soviets proved very different. In the Soviets' first stage, the major powers would complete half their conventional reductions, begin the liquidation of foreign bases, convene a world conference on disarmament, and agree to use nuclear weapons only in self-defense. The USSR included a nuclear test ban in its first phase, to attract Western liberals concerned about fallout, sow dissension in NATO, and please developing world leaders. There was little risk that these public relations benefits would lead to limits on the Soviet program, given that the test ban was part of a package the West would reject.

On verification, the May 10 proposal mixed new thinking and old concerns.[78] Although the Soviets accepted the principle that stable cooperation required satisfactory verification and admitted that previous proposals for international control were inadequate, they argued that Cold War tensions increased incentives for espionage and that nuclear vulnerability raised its costs. The greater the distrust and the need for deterrence, the less willing they were to "trustingly provide other States with facilities of access to industrial and other resources which are vital to their security." The USSR argued that modest forms of indirect oversight, such as reviews of budgetary information, were enough for partial arms control. The only mention of test ban verification was a vague reference to an international commission that would submit reports to the Security Council and the General Assembly.

The proposal did include international observation posts to watch troop movements through major transportation centers—the first concrete sign that the Soviets would accept routine OSIs on their territory in areas of low military sensitivity for reductions that addressed Soviet concerns, such as German rearmament and a surprise NATO conventional attack.[79] Further discussion revealed that the USSR still wanted extensive control over verification.[80] For example, foreign observers would watch passively for suspicious activities, but the chief of each post would be a host national. Thus, the ground-control posts were mainly a way for states to trade reassuring information—far from perfect verification as control but better, the proposal stated, than the "false sense of security" produced by believing that inherently imperfect forms of international control could or should do too much.

The Americans rejected the European and the Soviet plans, preferring to revamp their verification-first approach in light of changes in the nuclear context. Stassen placed a reservation on all disarmament positions and declared, "If there is to be an agreed suit of armament for the major nations, the fabric of inspection must first be woven, out of which the suit may then be tailored. The nature and reliability and durability of the cloth of inspection will determine the type and descriptions and size of the agreed suit of armament."[81] He urged the Soviets to adopt Eisenhower's Open Skies proposal as a way to reduce concern about surprise attacks while gaining practical experience with inspection and reporting measures that could eventually be applied to arms limitations. The proposal involved exchanging blueprints of military facilities and allowing each side to take and independently analyze aerial photographs of military activities. Hence the Soviets dismissed the proposal as verification without disarmament that was especially dangerous because it would give the West the targeting information needed for a first strike. To the Soviets, the Open Skies proposal seemed less like a cooperative overture than an attempt to exploit their May 10 concession that some verification was necessary for arms control, which may explain why their stance on verification hardened again.[82]

The U.S. call for closer attention to verification was partly a delaying tactic, because Eisenhower's advisers still could not agree on a new disarmament policy. Alignments were changing, however, owing to Stassen's appointment and

Dulles' shift from seeing disarmament proposals as a propaganda exercise to thinking seriously about mutually beneficial arms control proposals. NSC members argued about the motives behind the USSR's May 10 proposal. Strauss, Radford, and Defense Secretary Charles E. Wilson assumed that it was a trick and demanded "concrete evidence of a revolutionary change in the ambitions and intentions of the Soviet regime," such as disavowing the Third International or lifting the Iron Curtain.[83] Stassen, Dulles, and Eisenhower, by contrast, thought that inviting "those Soviet villains" to talk about verification would be a more valid test of their reliability as a partner in low-level arms control.

If the Soviets were ready to negotiate in good faith, the United States had another problem: deciding what verification measures it (and the Western allies) could accept. Dulles noted that the United States still had not done a careful study of the number and type of inspections required or the security implications of inspections in the United States: "All of this confronts the United States with a serious problem when you actually got down into such disagreeable details. Nevertheless, we must admit some willingness to be policed by the Russians if we were to insist on policing them.[84]

Modest "try before you buy" verification proposals were the only arms control measures that Eisenhower's advisers would support sincerely. Stassen wanted to stop demanding that the Soviets implement foolproof verification before the United States would negotiate any arms control. Presenting "too tough and militaristic a front," he argued, would cost the United States essential "free world" support, might cause "friendly" governments to be replaced by neutral or pro-Soviet domestic opponents, and could even convince Soviet planners that war was inevitable.[85] Stassen suggested two interim innovations. He proposed a "technical exchange mission," a six-month period when teams of technical experts from each subcommittee would be granted managed access to members' territory and then report on lessons about workable and tolerable verification methods.[86] He also developed a plan for "test strips"—areas in the United States and the USSR with no especially sensitive sites, where inspection teams could freely verify exchanged data and inspect military forces.[87] The Joint Chiefs wanted to monitor conventional military activities to reduce the danger of a surprise attack. But when the NSC debated whether the United States should promise to negotiate conventional limits if the verification trials worked well, the Joint Chiefs were staunchly opposed.[88] Eisenhower and Dulles were ambivalent. They wanted "affirmative, saleable, understandable, and workable substitutes for such [Soviet] panaceas as 'ban the bomb,'" but they saw the failure of post–World War I arms control as evidence that trying to negotiate numerical limits on forces would not work and might tempt the Allies to "taper off" their defense preparation. Only Stassen argued strongly (and unsuccessfully) for a pledge to negotiate conventional limits if the inspection trials went well, to avoid the "upward trend" in armaments caused by the JCS' way of thinking.

The new U.S. package in January 1957 embodied a contradictory approach to verification.[89] The first stage was mostly monitoring without arms control, including notification and observations of nuclear tests. Contrary to the verification-first rhetoric, however, the initial stage also banned production of fissile material for military use, a measure that would be more difficult to verify than second-stage limits on nuclear tests and reductions in existing fissile material stockpiles. A total test ban and major conventional troop cuts depended on completing the first two stages and resolving political disputes; nuclear disarmament was not mentioned.

The offer to discuss "a secure manner" to monitor, limit, and potentially ban nuclear tests after a fissile materials cut-off represented only a tactical change in U.S. policy. Because a cut-off would freeze the Americans' quantitative nuclear superiority, the new negotiating position continued the strategy of using unacceptable demands to blame the Soviets for continued weapons development. It was also designed to preserve a united front among Western members of the Disarmament Subcommittee, because the British prime minister wanted to fend off Labour Party pressure for a unilateral test ban and the French were increasingly eager to preserve their nuclear option until the superpowers ended the arms race.[90]

Domestic pressure in the United States for an immediate end to nuclear tests was also becoming more vocal, organized, and influential. Congress was less willing to leave disarmament policy to the Executive Branch. Under the chairmanship of Hubert Humphrey, the newly formed Senate Committee on Foreign Relations (SCFR) had become an important forum for test ban debates. Grassroots organizations, such as the American Friends Service Committee and the Women's International League for Peace and Freedom, testified that an H-bomb ban would reduce fallout, demonstrate global leadership, and encourage progress toward universal nuclear disarmament. To counter these pressures, the Eisenhower administration tried to depict the United States as a "responsible tester" that released information about its program, whereas the Soviets kept their tests secret.

Verifiable test limits were a major issue in the 1956 presidential campaign.[91] Adlai Stevenson, the Democratic challenger, argued that a mutual moratorium on large H-bomb tests promised many benefits with few costs or risks. The Eisenhower administration tried to play down the health risks from nuclear tests and emphasize their "moral" objectives, such as developing "clean" bombs.[92] But because Cautious Cooperators no longer believed that test limits must be part of a comprehensive package to be beneficial, though, the Eisenhower administration's most effective response to Stevenson came from portraying him as a naïve outsider who overestimated U.S. monitoring capabilities, underestimated Soviet duplicity, and discounted the catastrophic consequences of undetected cheating. The "political kiss of death" for Stevenson's plan came after the State Department released a letter in which the Soviet premier offered to end tests immediately, noted that "certain prominent public figures in the United States" supported this proposal, and insisted that "the present state of scientific knowledge" could detect all explosions without inspections.[93]

Stevenson later charged that the NSC had voted unanimously in September 1956 to seek a test ban, only to have Eisenhower refuse to adopt his electoral opponent's suggestion. But nothing in the declassified NSC minutes suggests that Eisenhower's advisers were ready to propose terms that the Soviets might actually accept. During the 1956 campaign, the AEC had decided that U.S. officials should offer to discuss verifiable limits on the size, number, frequency, and location of explosions. The AEC insisted, however, that test limits could not be negotiated until verification problems were solved. Partial limits would be as hard or harder to verify than a total ban because they would involve complex problems of yield and fallout estimation. The AEC's "stunning concession"[94] was really just a more sophisticated way to use a verification-first approach to prenegotiation to get public relations benefits by discussing cooperation that would never come to pass.

In short, the Unilateralists' ability to retain absolutist disarmament and verification demands eroded as concern grew about the risks of competition and information spread about partial measures that might be verifiable through mutually acceptable means. By January 1957, each nuclear power was on record favoring some verified test limits—but not any type that all the others would accept. States could thus support proposals that brought public relations benefits despite internal disputes about the desirability of such an accord. Arms Control Advocates hoped to translate agreement in principle on the thermonuclear dilemma into agreement in practice on a test ban as a low-risk first step, but they had far to go.

The Prenegotiation Endgame

Before the major players would make a commitment to start serious test ban negotiations, they needed provisional answers to basic questions, many of which involved verification. The final attempt to reach agreement in the Disarmament Subcommittee involved a carefully orchestrated set of concessions that were reciprocated, then repudiated. Sometimes the endgame seemed less about learning to trust each other than about backing domestic and international opponents into a corner where cooperation was their only option. The success of these cornering strategies depended, however, on convincing key players that substantive questions about verification could be resolved.

The Final False Start

Stassen, who had spent nearly two years cobbling together a GCD package that could satisfy different NSC members, waited just two months to start modifying elements that the Soviets most disliked. As an Arms Control Advocate, Stassen played a complicated two-level game in which he unofficially mentioned forthcoming modifications in U.S. policy to Soviet negotiators, in hopes that they would respond with concessions that would convince U.S. decision makers to follow his recommendations. This strategy produced major changes in both sides' positions, but it also sparked distrust, resentment, and retrenchment within the NSC, among NATO members, and between the superpowers.

In March 1957, Stassen made a statement with three surprising shifts.[95] It dropped the link between nuclear and conventional arms control. It promised to limit and eventually stop tests once a fissile materials cut-off occurred. It also publicly raised the possibility that imperfect verification as deterrence might be adequate for partial measures: incentives to cheat and risks of exploitation would be minor because "those few weapons would be restrained, canceled out and deterred by the remaining capability in the hands of nations on various sides."

Because Stassen had been explicitly instructed to discuss only the January GCD package, these statements were probably a bureaucratic end run rather than a compromise reached within the NSC. Stassen's critics accused him of usurping the "authority to abandon effective inspection, the keystone to the American position."[96] Stassen defended his initiative by saying that the USSR had looked down the "barrel of atomic war" in recent crises and might be ready to cooperate if verification demands did not threaten their regime.[97] As Stassen hoped (and his critics feared), the Soviets reciprocated by offering a temporary moratorium on tests while verification questions were resolved.

The Soviet proposal changed the terms of debate in the NSC. Stassen wanted to revise the U.S. disarmament package so that a year-long unsupervised moratorium came before the fissile material cut-off.[98] Dulles was also willing to compromise because he thought that "the propaganda drubbings the United States was taking on the test ban issue were becoming too much of a handicap in the conduct of foreign policy."[99] The AEC and DOD were predictably opposed to test suspension.[100] Strauss brought prominent scientists from the weapons labs to warn Eisenhower that the Soviets might secretly develop "clean" weapons during a moratorium, whereas the United States could not.[101] It was hard to argue persuasively that a one-year hiatus posed a security risk, however, given that this was the normal preparation period between test series. Moreover, even without inspections, the CIA was "reasonably certain of detecting all Soviet tests greater than 20 kt."[102] Therefore, the AEC and DOD tried primarily to ensure that public pressure would not turn a one-year moratorium into a permanent ban with inadequate verification.[103]

During this internal debate, Stassen secured another crucial concession from the Soviet delegation.[104] On June 14, 1957, Valerian Zorin announced that the USSR would let an international commission establish verification posts on Soviet territory if the nuclear powers agreed to stop testing for two or three years. This resembled the 1955 Soviet proposal to monitor conventional troops, but it was the first time that the USSR had offered to permit in-country monitoring for a proposal with a chance of acceptance. The opportunity to set a precedent for OSIs inside the Soviet Union made a short moratorium more attractive to Cautious Cooperators like Eisenhower and Dulles. Although Zorin was vague about the details, Stassen's remark about imperfect verification for partial measures implied that the Soviets could keep the costs and risks of these stations tolerable.

For Westerners, this breakthrough brought test suspension "within the realm of possibility."[105] They called for a committee of technical experts to design a monitoring system, but the Soviets declined to discuss verification details until the subcommittee resolved remaining questions. Stassen indicated that a ten-month moratorium could start before the internal monitoring posts were operational and be extended if the participants were satisfied both by the test monitoring system and by progress toward agreement on verification for a future fissile material cut-off.[106]

U.S. Unilateralists countered with several strategies to complicate the prospects for agreement. In response to complaints from AEC scientists and conservative senators, Stassen promised that peaceful nuclear explosions (PNEs) could continue during the moratorium.[107] But it would be almost impossible to verify that experiments to reduce radiation so that PNEs did not kill civil engineers were not also providing information to make "clean" bombs. Stassen predicted that the Soviets would accept 8–10 internal stations, but the AEC and DOD insisted that the verification system must include 70–150 stations, overflight privileges, and unrestricted OSIs.[108] An air force study claimed that even such a system would have only a 50 percent chance of detecting tests below 1 kt, so DOD stressed the potential military significance of very low yield tests. Strauss warned that being vague about U.S. verification requirements to get a moratorium started would be like hanging up "a sign reading do not be afraid of our watchdog—he has no teeth."[109]

The AEC was also pushing to conduct tests underground, even at the risk of further complicating verification. Testing underground would reduce public concern about fallout, but the more the radioactive gases released by an underground blast are contained, the less likely atmospheric sampling is to detect an explosion. At this time, seismologists knew little about how to detect seismic signals generated by nuclear tests or differentiate between signals from tests and earthquakes. In a secret report, Harold Brown and Hans Bethe stated that "complete containment of test explosions underground may make it very difficult to gather effective proof that such tests have been carried out in violation of a suspension agreement."[110]

The AEC used questions about verification as an extra justification for an underground test. The yield of the RAINER test was kept small (1.7 kt) to minimize aftershocks and to determine whether low-yield tests could be detected from a distance.[111] The AEC claimed that RAINER was not detected by seismic stations more than 250 miles from the Nevada Test Site (NTS). When Senator Humphrey learned that seismic signals had been detected 2,300 miles away, he accused the AEC of suppressing scientific evidence "to prove a political point" about the unverifiability of a moratorium.[112]

The compromise that resulted from the NSC debates over the moratorium proposal came close to the Soviets' position. On August 21, 1957, Stassen announced that the West would suspend testing for twelve months and extend the moratorium for another year if all went well.[113] Stassen presented the plan as an independent measure that should begin "at the earliest feasible date" and explicitly stated that agreement on a fissile materials cut-off was not required to start or extend the test suspension.

When the West informally presented their full package of partial measures, Zorin rejected everything, including the two-stage test suspension. He complained that the subcommittee had "not advanced one inch" and accused the West of using "high-sounding statements about disarmament" to disguise its perpetuation of the arms race, proliferation of nuclear weapons in Europe, and preparation for aggressive war.[114] Two months later, the USSR announced that it would not participate in the Disarmament Commission or the subcommittee because it was the only communist country in either one.

Many Westerners mistakenly interpreted this behavior as evidence that the Soviet Union was not a reliable negotiating partner. The most common explanation was that the Soviets had feigned an interest in arms control to lull the West while they prepared to test their first ICBM (August 1957) and satellite (October 1957). If this was so, however, the USSR would not have agreed to technical talks and test ban negotiations less than a year later.[115] Another common explanation was that Khrushchev had sacrificed test suspension and other arms control efforts in return for military assistance during the June 1957 leadership challenge that led to Molotov and Malenkov's ouster. Although some members of Khrushchev's coalition were less enthusiastic about test suspension as an independent arms control measure, there are no signs that they demanded an end to disarmament talks as a quid pro quo for loyalty.[116]

From the Soviets' perspective, the West had retracted key concessions. The Western package formally presented on August 29 reverted to the position that all provisions were inseparable.[117] It required agreement on a fissile material cutoff *before* the moratorium started. It also legitimated the transfer of nuclear weapons to NATO countries, including West Germany, which contradicted one of the Soviets' main motivations for arms control.

Alliance politics explain the decision to relink test suspension to measures that the Soviet Union opposed. Relations among the United States, the U.K., and France had been strained ever since the Suez Crisis. France and West Germany were especially worried that the United States and the USSR might agree to partial measures that would restrict the allies' nuclear programs (France) or conventional rearmament (West Germany) without major cuts in superpower capabilities. This fear intensified in June, when Stassen let Zorin preview a proposal for inspections and conventional arms control in Europe that had not been cleared with NATO allies. Relinkage came as part of U.S. efforts to reassure NATO allies that subcommittee negotiations would not sacrifice their interests and help West Germany's Chancellor Adenauer win reelection.

The timing of the Soviet denouncement may have reflected a less effective attempt at multilevel gamesmanship. Adenauer had been trying to create the impression of improved relations with the USSR, and the Soviets may have believed that a dramatic signal of disharmony between East and West would hurt his re-election chances.[118] But the decision to stop subcommittee negotiations stemmed from the more general perception that the United States was less interested in arms control than in arming its allies. Stassen was demoted after he gave Zorin the sneak preview, and Dulles was given primary responsibility for negotiations. Because the Soviets believed that Stassen sincerely wanted to relax tensions but Dulles still saw arms control only as a propaganda exercise, they viewed Stassen's denigration as evidence that the West no longer wanted coop-eration.[119] Dulles announced that the United States would now clear any pro-posal related to conventional inspections and arms control with NATO allies.[120] The Soviets lost interest in the subcommittee once it ceased to provide private consultations and an expedited exchange of concessions.

The subcommittee's successes and failures hold valuable lessons about se-curing internal, allied, and international agreement on arms control. When some players are seriously interested in cooperation and others are more ambivalent or hostile to arms control, progress on individual items may occur because less enthusiastic players know that unresolved questions can still be used to stop a final deal. In the 1957 subcommittee sessions, questions about test ban verifica-tion got serious attention: some players had grown more interested in cooper-ation and others had made a tactical decision that verification concerns were not a plausible reason to block a brief test suspension. All the pieces for an agree-ment did not fall into place, partly due to conflicting U.S. objectives and partly to inept two-level gamesmanship. Increased flexibility on individual issues, how-ever, provided important evidence for Arms Control Advocates and Cautious Cooperators that agreement on test ban verification might be possible.

Countdown to a Commitment on Test Ban Verification Talks

In the West, support for test restrictions declined briefly after the Soviets launched Sputnik and left U.N. disarmament talks. Soon, though, extensive test series by both superpowers, coupled with the U.K.'s first thermonuclear explosions, led to a new round of protests and pleas for restraint. International opinion was sharply critical of the Soviets for storming away from the table but also of the West for restoring linkages and pressuring the U.N. General Assembly (UNGA) to endorse a disarmament package that the USSR opposed. When India spon-sored a resolution calling for the immediate suspension of nuclear tests, the so-cialist countries concurred with the majority of the Asian and African countries; most other nonaligned and moderately pro-Western states abstained. NATO leaders realized the need for more flexibility, but the Soviets refused to resume negotiations unless the West dropped its total linkage and agreed to a forum in which the East would have equal representation.

Eisenhower's advisers remained divided about how far the United States should go to regain international support for its nuclear policies. Stassen and Dulles favored renewed efforts to negotiate an independent two-year test sus-pension. The AEC also favored delinkage but took the position that the United States should unilaterally suspend all "dirty" tests aboveground and offer to continue this partial ban, if the Soviets reciprocated and permitted international inspections for nuclear tests in all environments.[121] The military was willing to accept a brief moratorium but argued that the United States should not consider test cessation unless it was linked to other disarmament measures because the United States needed to develop tactical nuclear weapons, better yield-to-weight ratios, and second-generation missile designs and defenses.[122]

Once again, Eisenhower responded to the disarmament deadlock by changing the decision-making structure to provide more independent arms control advice. After hearing the AEC and DOD plead for a multimegaton test despite his public pledge to stop testing very large weapons, Eisenhower complained that his "statecraft was becoming too much a prisoner of our (weapons) scientists."[123] He used post-Sputnik feelings of vulnerability and technical inferiority as an opportunity to appoint James Killian as science adviser and head of the new President's Science Advisory Committee (PSAC).

PSAC changed internal verification debates in important ways.[124] For many PSAC members, including Killian, Jerome Wiesner, and Herbert York, participation in the Gaither Committee's recent study of civil defense had been a major intellectual turning point that convinced them there was no technological solution to the nuclear threat.[125] Now scientists who shared the assumptions behind the ALC report and the Fermi-Rabi proposal had regular, direct access to the president. They encouraged Eisenhower and Dulles to think about detection probabilities, not "foolproof control," and to compare the risks of imperfect verification with those from unconstrained competition. When Unilateralists tried to exacerbate verification arguments, PSAC scientists countered that technical obstacles to test ban verification could be surmounted with sufficient political will.

The main conclusion of the Bethe Report, PSAC's initial study of test cessation, was that a "practical" system with seventy monitoring stations in the USSR and China, mobile inspection teams, and limited overflights could detect and identify almost all nuclear tests.[126] The report argued that perfect verification was not necessary if the detection probability was high enough that "the Soviets cannot afford to take the risk of being caught in a clandestine test." The authors disagreed about whether the United States or the USSR would reap more military benefits from a permanent test cessation, depending on whether they thought that it would perpetuate American nuclear superiority or prevent the United States from using its greater technical prowess to surge further ahead. All agreed, however, that it was neither desirable nor feasible to stop testing before the next series (HARDTACK) finished in the fall.

The Bethe Report provides interesting insights into early thinking about underground test verification. The authors proposed to discriminate between earthquakes and explosions based on differences in the first motion of their seismic signals. But because these differences would be hard to measure for small seismic events, 300 inspections might be needed in the USSR each year. The authors mention that decoupling a small explosion by detonating it inside a large cavity could reduce the magnitude of long-range seismic signals by a factor of ten. They also realized that explosions in soft rock around NTS would generate smaller seismic signals than would tests in hard rock—a distinction that received little attention but foreshadowed a debate two decades later over Soviet compliance with the TTBT.

Before Eisenhower's advisers had time to debate the implications for U.S. test ban policy, Khrushchev seized the initiative. He announced that the Supreme Soviet had abolished nuclear tests in the USSR but reserved the right to resume if others did not follow suit.[127] Americans quickly dismissed this move as self-serving, because the Soviets had just finished a major test series and the United States planned to start one soon. Still, U.S. leaders faced tremendous international pressure to reciprocate the Soviets' gesture.

The initial exchange between Eisenhower and Khrushchev followed the standard pattern. Eisenhower suggested that joint technical talks about verification would show more sincerity than a brief uninspected moratorium. His advisers could quickly agree on this response because it fit the verification-first approach to arms control, followed previous proposals for technical talks, and preserved the links between test limits and other disarmament measures. As expected, Khrushchev declined. He declared that technical experts could contribute nothing without political agreement on disarmament, and he accused the United States of proposing technical talks as a delaying tactic.

Eisenhower repeated his offer three weeks later, after he and Dulles had concluded that agreement on test ban verification might be possible. At the meeting to discuss the Bethe Report, Dulles had endorsed the concept of verification as deterrence by suggesting that the Soviets would not cheat if there was a 50-50 chance of detection.[128] Eisenhower's new letter included two changes that were not approved by the AEC or DOD. First, it mentioned a technical conference to discuss verification for test suspension but did not include a fissile materials cut-off, signaling a potential return to the pre-August 1957 position. Second, the letter strongly implied the West would enter negotiations if the technical experts could design a mutually acceptable verification system. Since precedents set in subcommittee meetings suggested that both sides could make concessions to satisfy each others' concerns, the prospects for agreement on *verified* test restrictions looked good. This trumped Khrushchev's uninspected moratorium, because even though the vast majority of world opinion wanted an end to nuclear tests, an equally large number did not trust the Russians.[129]

Khrushchev had little choice but to accept or undermine the plausibility of his own claims to favor a test ban. One of Khrushchev's main justifications for singling out testing as a good first measure was that existing technical methods could "record any explosions of atomic and hydrogen weapons, wherever they may be detonated."[130] This point was a key area of disagreement, so it was hard to refuse to discuss technical evidence with scientists from the West. Therefore, Khrushchev stated that although he still questioned the need for technical talks, he would acquiesce because the West attached such importance to the plan.[131]

With the invitation coming after the United States finished its preliminary analysis of data from RAINER, Soviet policy makers and some of the U.S. Unilateralists may have had more self-interested reasons for acquiescing in the plan. The Soviets could learn about Western testing and monitoring capabilities because the United States would need to share details about RAINER, such as tunnel design and estimated yield, in order to discuss underground test verification. Given Americans' reluctance to share nuclear information with their allies, it was remarkable that the AEC revealed details about RAINER to an adversary that had never tested underground. Gerald Johnson, field director of nuclear testing for Lawrence Livermore National Laboratory (LLNL) at this time, recalls that the AEC shared underground testing techniques because it wanted the Soviets to test underground.[132] Thus, the AEC may have agreed to a technical exchange less to enhance verification than to increase the chance the USSR would eventually accept an atmospheric ban without limits on underground testing.

The Conference of Experts

The Conference of Experts to Study the Possibility of Detecting Violations of a Possible Agreement on Suspension of Nuclear Tests opened in Geneva on July 1, 1958.[133] As the name indicated, the Western states still would not promise to start test ban negotiations if the scientists agreed on a verification system. The experts' consensus on the outlines of a CTB verification system did, however, provide the final push that American, Soviet, and British leaders needed to enter formal negotiations. But, the way that verification disputes were handled during the Conference of Experts left plenty of room for disagreements once tripartite talks began.

Western and Eastern participants had fundamentally different ideas about the nature and the objective of verification discussions. For Americans, the Conference of Experts rested on the premise that the technical capabilities of verification systems must determine political possibilities for arms control. To emphasize this, the U.S. delegation to the conference included no diplomats and only junior-level political advisers. Dulles told the delegates to "look upon their job as a purely scientific technical job" for which he did not anticipate "any need for political guidance."[134] In contrast, the Soviet Union saw verification talks as inherently political and sent a leading diplomat, Semyon Tsarapkin, with their delegation. One Soviet delegate declared that "science must not interfere with the task" of designing a test ban monitoring system.[135] According to the head of the U.S. delegation, though, the caliber of the Soviet team was high, their delegates were "technically sound," and they had "an element of objectivity" that enabled serious discussions.

Eisenhower's advisers continued to fight about how flexible the United States should be on verification. The AEC and DOD still wanted to maximize verification demands to "maintain our technical advantage as long as possible."[136] By directing delegates to "report on the evaluation of a less than complete detection system," Dulles authorized a risk-assessment approach. He also avoided acrimonious NSC debates by telling the delegates to "use their best judgement" about such crucial details as the desired detection probability or the yield threshold below which tests were insignificant. By selecting moderate scientists representing different schools of thought about a test ban, however, Dulles tacitly acknowledged that there was no such thing as completely objective advice on such a controversial policy issue.[137]

Discussions were plagued by information shortages. To avoid revealing military secrets, Eastern scientists presented calculations in theoretical terms, while Western delegates used empirical data that had already been publicized. Some problems, such as monitoring high-altitude tests, could not be resolved for lack of experience. Therefore, the experts discussed this problem only in theoretical terms and included no special high-altitude monitoring methods in their detection system.

The technical characteristics of explosions in the air and under water permitted nonintrusive monitoring of acoustic signals and air samples. But the United States wanted to set a precedent for aerial overflights near suspected test sites, whereas the USSR insisted that ground control stations would suffice. The experts compromised on air sampling over the ocean by weather planes. If this did not resolve the dispute, occasional territorial overflights could be permitted along prescribed routes by aircraft of the host country, with members of the accusing country acting as observers.

Underground tests posed the greatest difficulty. Decisions dealt with four interrelated parameters: (1) the detection threshold, (2) the detection probability,

(3) the number of monitoring stations, and (4) the extent to which OSIs would be needed to identify small seismic events as earthquakes or explosions. U.S. scientists associated with the AEC and the DOD initially pushed for a network of 650 stations and a 90 percent probability of detecting and identifying underground tests with a 1-kt yield. The Soviets, by contrast, maintained that a network of 100 stations could detect and identify most suspicious events, with little need for OSIs.

Some controversies reflected the immature state of seismology. The only data the experts had were declassified information about RAINER and evidence from Soviet chemical blasts. Eastern and Western scientists used different scales for measuring seismic activity. Delegates knew little about how differences in test-site geology affected signal size and were overoptimistic about using the direction of first motion to discriminate between earthquakes and explosions.

On August 21, the experts announced their consensus that "it is technically feasible to set up, with certain capabilities and limitations, a workable and effective control system for the detection of violations of a possible agreement on the world-wide cessation of nuclear weapons tests."[138] The "Geneva System" included 160–70 land-based control posts and ten ships with instruments for monitoring acoustic, seismic, and radio signals, as well as radioactive debris. The experts gave it a "good probability" of detecting yields above 1 kt and identifying tests above 5 kt.

The Geneva System's 170–80 control posts was an uncomfortable compromise for the superpowers. The USSR still wanted to reduce the number of international stations by using some existing national stations. The West, however, questioned the capabilities of existing stations and noted that the staff at nationally operated stations could falsify data on the first motion of seismic waves by reversing a few wires in the monitoring equipment. When the U.K. proposed a 170- to 180-station system, the United States wanted the experts to outline the capabilities and limitations of all three systems. The United States finally accepted the U.K. compromise, however, after the Eastern scientists argued that recommending a single system would have maximum political impact.

The Geneva Report ignored other controversial questions. It did not specify how many stations would be on Soviet soil or consider Chinese objections to a global monitoring system that they had not helped design. Nor did it mention criteria for choosing control-post staff and members of the central verification agency. The report sidestepped arguments about the frequency, criteria, and procedures for OSIs by saying that *if* seismic methods proved insufficient, the verification agency *could* send an OSI team.

Most observers paid less attention to these conspicuous silences and ambiguities than they did to the simple fact that the opposing sides had reached consensus on workable and tolerable test ban verification. Eugene Rabinowitch, a physicist and editor of the *Bulletin of Atomic Scientists*, rejoiced that the Conference of Experts had "confirmed the belief of scientists that once an international problem has been formulated in scientifically significant terms, scientists from all countries, despite their political or ideological backgrounds, will be able to find a common language and arrive at an agreed solution."[139]

Since the Eisenhower administration had repeatedly proposed technical talks about verification to avoid addressing conflicts among NSC members, it did not know how to react after the Soviets attended verification talks and agreed on the Geneva system. PSAC, the State Department, and the CIA favored negotiations based on the Geneva System. DOD and the AEC still opposed a test ban yet feared a public relations coup for the USSR.[140] Therefore, the AEC proposed a unilateral moratorium on atmospheric testing (knowing that the Soviets had not tested underground before). But DOD wanted to start negotiations, in the belief that the practical difficulties of implementing the Geneva System would prevent any test limits. Those who favored serious negotiations also wanted to postpone further U.S. testing to improve the climate for negotiations; the rest wanted to test until a treaty entered into force. In short, the popular perception that verification problems had been solved changed the political context but not policy makers' preferences.

Eisenhower's invitation to formal negotiations contained important qualifiers.[141] It called on states that had already tested nuclear weapons (France wanted no part of independent test limits) to negotiate the "suspension" of tests and the "actual establishment" of a verification system "on the basis of the experts' report." The United States would not test during the first year of talks, but it would rush to finish the HARDTACK II series before negotiations started on October 31, 1958. A reciprocal moratorium might be extended on a yearly basis if the monitoring system was installed and operating, PNEs were exempted, and progress on other arms control issues was satisfactory.

Khrushchev denounced these terms as proof that the West still sought "every possible loophole" to protect their nuclear testing programs.[142] He replied that negotiations should seek the permanent "cessation"—not just suspension—of testing, and he wanted the West to reciprocate his moratorium immediately. Khrushchev argued that the experts' consensus removed any legitimate reason to use dissatisfaction with verification as an excuse to resume testing. He also opposed any linkage to other disarmament measures. Khrushchev agreed to start test ban negotiations on October 31 but declared that the West's bad faith and intensified testing released the Soviets from their unilateral moratorium.[143]

Conclusion

Prenegotiation ended successfully in August 1958, when the three nuclear weapons states finally decided to start formal negotiations. This outcome cannot be explained without reference to the politics of verification. No consensus on arms control had been reached among policy makers or citizens. Although the arms race was an ongoing feature of the early Cold War years, nothing of an unprecedented nature happened in 1958 to convince political leaders that national nuclear weapons development must stop permanently or that the primary purpose of negotiations should be more than public relations. The consensus reached at the Conference of Experts showed that representatives of the East and West were capable of cooperative behavior, but the unprecedented rate of testing during 1958 was competitive in the extreme. Khrushchev's unilateral moratorium and Eisenhower's offers to talk about verification were more like challenges than friendly overtures. Superpower leaders were clearly not convinced that the other side seriously wanted cooperation or was worthy of much trust.

What did change between 1945 and 1958 were Cautious Cooperators' expectations about the possibility for agreement on verification. At the start of the nuclear era, Arms Control Advocates could not point to any successful examples of voluntary agreement on significant verification arrangements. Nor could they convince Cautious Cooperators that the new approach embodied in the ALC plan would be workable and tolerable, given Americans' ambivalence about sharing nuclear secrets and Stalin's hostility toward programs that would uncover military secrets or interfere with economic development. As long as U.S. and Soviet Unilateralists could plausibly maintain rigidly conflicting positions on the timing, type, and amount of verification, they could persuade Cautious Cooperators that unrestrained competition was an unfortunate necessity. This blocking strategy became harder to sustain after attention shifted from comprehensive disarmament to partial measures and information spread about monitoring methods that might satisfy both U.S. and Soviet verification concerns. Increased flexibility on verification in the Soviets' May 10 proposal and the 1957 subcommittee talks stemmed from a mixture of sincere and strategic motivations. But each concession set an important precedent that Arms Control Advocates could use to build a winning coalition for serious negotiations.

Invitations to discuss or implement verification during prenegotiations did not have the uniformly positive effect that Zartman predicted. Western participants favored a verification-first approach to arms control for divergent reasons. Verification-first proposals were often used to avoid domestic and interalliance conflict because the need for some verification was one issue on which Westerners could consistently agree. Since Arms Control Advocates could never conclusively prove that Soviet objections stemmed from legitimate concerns about spying, infringement of sovereignty, or other malign aspects of verification, verification-first proposals usually substantiated U.S. Unilateralists' accusations, increased Cautious Cooperators' suspicions, and exacerbated Soviet fears that the West was only interested in espionage.

It is impossible to say whether the agreement to hold the Conference of Experts stemmed more from a mutual recognition that verification questions were "ripe" for resolution or from an uncoordinated sequence of cornering moves with unanticipated results.[144] Political leaders on both sides clearly tried to structure verification discussions to promote their preferences in domestic debates and future negotiations. Technical experts necessarily made political judgments, whether or not they would admit it. The consensus report on the Geneva System was important in securing a commitment to negotiate test limits as the first independent nuclear arms control measure. But the scientists' decision to paper over a number of crucial political questions created overly optimistic expectations and the potential for serious disillusionment.

4

"Scientific" Approaches to Verification Decisions

WHEN TRIPARTITE TALKS STARTED ON October 31, 1958, many observers hoped that a scientific, step-by-step approach would prove more productive than the highly politicized GCD negotiations had been. Test ban negotiations were seen as a critical test of the superpowers' sincerity: since the Conference of Experts found no technical obstacles to agreement on verification, participants should be able to conclude a treaty quickly if they were Cautious Cooperators rather than Unilateralists in disguise. Arms Control Advocates also hoped that banning tests and implementing the Geneva System would lead to more significant cooperation by increasing confidence and providing practical experience with international verification arrangements.

Measured against these high hopes, negotiations were disappointingly slow and verification remained surprisingly controversial. Whenever talks deadlocked over verification, however, a bridging proposal restored public enthusiasm and raised the political costs of failure. Negotiators gradually narrowed their differences, and optimists hoped that the remaining obstacles to a phased CTB could be resolved at the Four-Power Summit in May 1960. These hopes were dashed when the Soviets shot down an American spy plane shortly before the summit, then terminated the meetings after Eisenhower refused to condemn the overflights. Arms Control Advocates have often seen the U-2 incident as an unfortunate historical accident that exacerbated misperceptions, blocked a breakthrough on CTB verification, and needlessly prolonged the arms race. Cautious Cooperators maintain that superpower attitudes toward inspection were still so far apart that agreement on the details of a workable and tolerable verification system would have proved impossible. Unilateralists typically claim that the U-2 incident was created or exploited as an excuse to avoid an agreement that neither side really wanted. Each explanation has some validity, but none is fully satisfactory.

A more complete picture comes from understanding how Arms Control Advocates, Cautious Cooperators, and Unilateralists interacted to shape verification decisions during an administration that approached verification as a technical problem. Because Eisenhower, Khrushchev, and Macmillan were Cautious Cooperators, their support for a CTB depended on satisfactory verification arrangements. Some of their frustration stemmed from the mistaken belief that technical experts had already resolved all the substantive verification questions prior to negotiations or could use their scientific expertise to find apolitical solutions as new disagreements arose.

The frustrating results also reflected important asymmetries on the strategic side of verification politics. Because tremendous uncertainty existed about the technical capabilities of seismic monitoring systems, Arms Control Advocates and Unilateralists interpreted ambiguous data to support their policy preferences. Soviet and American representatives used similar strategies in Geneva. Attempts to cast verification dilemmas as technical decisions to be solved according to scientific criteria gave undue weight to evasion scenarios that were technically possible but highly implausible. Moreover, each time that the East or the West refused to enter technical talks, resisted scientifically based verification proposals, or repudiated solutions that they once had deemed technically sound, doubts about their intentions increased. Arms Control Advocates countered such strategies by comparing the risks of imperfect verification as deterrence with those of unconstrained competition. But PSAC members saw themselves as technical advisers rather than policy advocates, so they were less vocal and more conservative analytically than were the Unilateralists.

Despite these substantive dilemmas and strategic asymmetries, negotiators made progress. They tried to depoliticize verification decisions by building a consensus on verification as deterrence and appointing technical working groups to augment the Geneva System. When these strategies failed to end verification arguments, negotiators sought to narrow the scope of cooperation by banning easily monitored tests at once, then extending the prohibitions as verification disputes were resolved. Domestic debates and international negotiations over such a phased approach laid the groundwork for potential agreement on CTB verification. If the U-2 incident had not occurred or had been handled differently, serious substantive disputes would have still complicated agreement on inspection procedures. But the likelihood that an explicitly political strategy could have forged a winning coalition for a step-by-step approach to agreement on CTB verification was higher in 1960 than at any other time during the Cold War.

Mixed Motives Cause Predictable Verification Arguments

The American, British, and Soviet delegations entered negotiations with leaders who favored mutual test restrictions but had little room to maneuver on verification.[1] Eisenhower, Macmillan, and Khrushchev wanted to explore the possibilities for cooperation but would not accept much risk of cheating or spying. They also knew that Unilateralists at home would fight any flexibility on verification. Thus, although the technical experts had reached consensus on the Geneva system, political indicators predicted controversies over test ban verification for both substantive and strategic reasons.

Internal Arguments, Ambivalence, and Avoidance Strategies

In the United States, responsibility for testing policy had shifted from the NSC to a smaller "Committee of Principals" composed of the secretary of state, the secretary of defense, the director of the CIA, the chairman of the AEC, and the president's science adviser. A CTB was the epitome of a mixed-motive issue, with some of Eisenhower's advisers firmly on one side and others personally conflicted. Table 4.1 summarizes their main arguments for and against nuclear testing.[2]

As usual, Eisenhower's advisers used arguments about verification to manage Cautious Cooperators' ambivalence and sidestep the conflict between Arms Control Advocates and Unilateralists. The principals agreed that any test ban treaty should only limit tests in environments and above yield thresholds that could be reliably verified. Expectations about verification correlated closely with attitudes toward a CTB. Arms Control Advocates liked the Geneva System; Cautious Cooperators wanted to know how negotiators would resolve open questions; and Unilateralists believed that the USSR would never accept satisfactory verification arrangements. U.S. policy makers decided that "the threshold problem" should be "advanced in connection with the discussion of inspection, and every effort should be made to force the USSR itself to open this issue."[3] Thus, the United States planned to confront the Soviet Union with a choice between partial limits on nuclear tests or unlimited inspection rights, but American leaders wanted the Soviets to take the political heat for suggesting something less than a total ban on nuclear tests.

British debates about nuclear testing involved a similar if less extreme mix of motives.[4] Government officials saw nuclear weapons development as a way to reduce reliance on conventional defense, preserve Western military superiority,

Table 4.1 Arguments for and against Nuclear Testing

Continue Testing	Ban Testing
Maximize U.S. nuclear capabilities to offset Soviet conventional strength	Prolong U S nuclear superiority
National security requires research into weapons development and defense	Obstacles to defensive systems could not be resolved through tests
Unanticipated evasion techniques might enable undetected tests	Workable and tolerable verification is possible
Delinking test limits from other disarmament measures might reduce Soviet incentives to accept broad Western package	Ease tensions and set verification precedents to facilitate more significant cooperation
Test ban might increase pressure for nuclear disarmament	U S could decide later how much arms control it wanted
Test ban would prevent PNEs	Stopping the arms race matters more than preventing PNEs, although latter could be exempted later
Underground tests would reduce public fear of fallout	Failure to negotiate in good faith would be seen by allies as warlike
Test suspension would hurt nuclear weapons laboratories	

induce the Soviets to negotiate on Western terms, and protect the U.K.'s great-power status. Since Britain was more vulnerable to nuclear devastation than the United States due to its size, proximity to the USSR, and weaker retaliatory capabilities, the opposition Labour Party rejected nuclear testing and the British nuclear deterrent. The popularity of nuclear disarmament in Britain and abroad finally convinced Macmillan to put his "full weight behind a sustained drive" for a test ban.[5] But as one British commentator observed, the U.K. was constrained because "not all the parts of the United States' choir were singing from the same score."[6]

The USSR also came to Geneva with mixed motives and internal divisions.[7] Soviet leaders had often used the fallout issue to stir up popular pressure for a CTB, but their decisions to resume atmospheric testing in 1958 and 1961 show that health and humanitarian concerns mattered less than military and political considerations. Nonproliferation provided a strong and enduring incentive for a CTB. Although the Soviets saw French entry into the nuclear club as inevitable, they wanted to keep West Germany from acquiring nuclear weapons and worried about the Chinese program. Soviet calculations about a CTB's impact on the military balance were complex. The West had a significant lead in nuclear weapons and delivery systems, but the Soviets were ahead in heavy weapons development.

Khrushchev had convinced the West of a "missile gap" in his favor, but arms control inspections might reveal the true extent of Soviet strategic weakness. Although the West had more experience with underground tests, the Soviets had less interest in tactical weapons for which small underground tests were appropriate. Soviet concerns about relative strength might be a reason to keep testing and catch up with the West or an incentive to ban tests and stop the United States from surging still further ahead. Moreover, even though a CTB could help Khrushchev shift spending from defense to consumer products by reducing international tensions and decreasing the number of areas for competitive weapons development, it would hamper efforts to get more "rubble for the ruble" by shifting resources from conventional defense to nuclear weapons. With these conflicting incentives, Khrushchev was a Cautious Cooperator and was seriously interested in a CTB *if* the costs and risks of verification were tolerable.[8]

Khrushchev's approach toward arms control gradually grew less coercive and more cooperative around the time that test ban talks started. In early 1958, Soviet foreign policy elites recognized only two types of diversity in the West: slight variations among groups of monopoly capitalists and a large split between the "peaceloving" people and their "militaristic" leaders.[9] Some Soviet policy makers hoped to coerce the West into arms control concessions by simultaneously increasing Soviet military power and using a "peace offensive" to mobilize popular opposition against the West's military programs. The Malenkovian idea that some Western leaders might respond favorably to Soviet moderation had been out of favor. Before CTB talks started, however, an article on internal divisions among U.S. policy makers developed the dichotomy between "madmen" (those committed to a suicidal conflict with the USSR) and "realists" (those who recognized a mutual interest in cooperation).[10] Some of Khrushchev's allies adopted this dichotomy, and by early 1959, Khrushchev himself opined that Eisenhower might reciprocate Soviet restraint because he was "not one of those military men who . . . would like to settle all problems by force of arms."[11]

Although Khrushchev's ability to determine policy was strongest between 1958 and 1960, important divisions among Soviet elites remained. Khrushchev and his "reformist" allies were opposed by more "orthodox" members of the Presidium (such as Frol Kozlov and Mikhail Suslov), the military, and the defense industry.[12] Opponents expressed displeasure in subtle ways, such as ignoring a CTB in their lists of Soviet foreign policy goals or mentioning it only as part of a GCD package. Soviet scientists were also split. Some, such as Andrei Sakharov (the "father" of the Soviet H-bomb), Igor Kurchotov (head of the Soviet nuclear testing program in 1958), and Yevgeni Federov (a geophysicist at the Conference of Experts) lobbied Khrushchev for a test ban. Other scientists reportedly pressured him to resume testing during the moratoria. Foreign affairs specialists' attitude toward test ban negotiations depended on their image of international relations. Orthodox intelligentsia still thought in terms of constant conflict between capitalist and socialist systems and assumed that the latter would inevitably win. Reformist scholars at the new international relations institutes were more worried about mutual destruction, sensitive to diversity among capitalist and socialist states, interested in using arms control concessions to strengthen peaceful elements in the West, and hopeful about liberalizing the USSR.[13]

U.S. decision makers knew little about these Soviet debates but received some clues from informal contacts between U.S. and Soviet scientists. Shortly before CTB negotiations started, Victor Weisskopf, a senior Manhattan Project scientist turned Arms Control Advocate, wrote Killian about conversations he had with Federov at a Pugwash conference.[14] Khrushchev had sent the Pugwash conference a telegram in which he accepted the Geneva System and urged the scientists to advocate test cessation. American scientists wanted the Pugwash statement to be "objective and cool" because they thought that the "test stop is essentially already 'in the bag'" and preferred not to "beat a dead dog."[15] Federov pled for a strong and explicit declaration, claiming that Soviet support for a CTB "hangs on a thread." He told Weisskopf that Soviet test ban supporters had worked hard to persuade the Presidium that the political gains from a test ban outweighed the military losses for the USSR. If the United States continued testing or Western arms control supporters seemed unenthusiastic about a CTB, however, Khrushchev's calculations could change. Thus, Weisskopf warned Killian that "there is a bitter fight within the USSR government between the test supporters and the test stoppers. . . . The stoppers have at present a slim lead which might break at any time."

Because neither side really understood the other's domestic divisions, both interpreted actions taken to placate hawkish factions as evidence of disinterest in mutual cooperation. As Federov predicted, the West's decision to continue testing until negotiations began convinced Khrushchev to conduct two tests immediately after talks opened.[16] These shots were unsophisticated weapons detonated to signal that the USSR was not bound by a moratorium declared unilaterally after the West had just finished a major test series. This political gesture provided no military advantage to the USSR but raised doubts in the West about Khrushchev's attitude toward negotiations. Such behavior by both sides replaced much of the goodwill created at the Conference of Experts with renewed suspicions, thus reducing the prospect for agreement on verification.

Negotiators Confront Verification Dilemmas

As soon as negotiations started, conflicts arose over issues that the technical experts had purposefully avoided. The talks had a deliberately ambiguous title—the Geneva Conference on the Discontinuance of Nuclear Tests—because participants could not agree on whether the goal was a temporary halt or a permanent end to testing. Semyon Tsarapkin, the head of the Soviet delegation, compared the West's desire to discuss verification details before agreeing in principle on a CTB to hunters arguing over which brand of mothballs they should use to preserve a bearskin while the bear was "in the woods, alive and well."[17] After three weeks of procedural arguments, such fundamental differences remained that talks proceeded without an agenda.

Many of the early disputes dealt with the type rather than the amount of verification. For example, negotiators agreed to establish a central control commission with one permanent member from each of the original three parties, in addition to several representatives of other signatories. Tsarapkin wanted the commission to make decisions by "mutual consent," which would let the Soviets veto OSI requests and violation reports.[18] The West argued that the Control Commission should act automatically when specific technical criteria were met on some issues (like initiating an OSI) and operate by majority rule the rest of the time. Comparable controversies occurred over the nationality of control post staff and on-site inspectors. The West sought to exclude all host country nationals from verification teams, whereas the Soviets wanted host country citizens to collect compliance data while foreign "control officers" observed their procedures.

Some American analysts have depicted Western proposals as "impartial" and the Soviet plans as "adversarial" verification.[19] But both approaches assumed that verifiers from the other side would try to distort verification for unilateral gain. The Soviets wanted maximum control over data gathering and decision making so that Western agents could not collect collateral information or make false accusations. The West expected the Soviets to hide evidence of violations and block international complaints about their compliance, so Americans derided Soviet proposals as ineffective and unacceptable "self-verification."[20] Western plans for tens of thousands of foreigners operating outside the host country's authority and automatic OSIs after every ambiguous event exacerbated Soviet fears of spying and meddling, however.[21] Thus, different but equally adversarial ideas about verification acted like a wedge that drove negotiating positions farther apart.

For Americans who viewed verification as a technical problem of detecting noncompliance, Soviet resistance to "reasonable" proposals seemed like incontrovertible evidence that they still saw arms control solely as political warfare. Two weeks after CTB talks started, Senator Albert Gore (a congressional adviser to the U.S. delegation) concluded that the Soviets were prolonging CTB negotiations and the moratorium to stop the West from developing tactical weapons but never intended to accept reliable CTB verification. He urged policy makers to refocus negotiations on an atmospheric ban monitored only by NTM that would be simpler to understand, easier to negotiate, and safer than the uninspected moratorium on underground tests.

The State Department, PSAC, and the CIA objected vigorously to avoiding verification arguments by narrowing the scope of cooperation. PSAC argued that if a CTB was to be "a first step toward disarmament, [Gore's proposal] simply is not logical."[22] A limited ban monitored by NTM would reduce fallout, but not slow the arms race, stop proliferation, provide practical experience with international verification, or open the USSR to inspection. Because Eisenhower's more hawkish advisers placed little weight on these goals, PSAC also pointed out that renouncing a CTB would cause "acute national embarrassment and a severe propaganda setback" for the United States. Such a "weak position" would provide the Soviets with a convenient excuse to end negotiations and blame the West. Eisenhower's advisers agreed for different reasons to continue CTB talks: some still hoped for an accord with the Geneva System; others expected verification disputes to prevent test restrictions.

New Strategies Exacerbate Substantive Conflicts

While CTB negotiators debated questions that the Conference of Experts had sidestepped, U.S. Unilateralists devised new reasons to reject the experts' recommendations. The Geneva System had been presented as a technical solution to the workable/tolerable dilemma, so opponents used scientific uncertainty to undermine Cautious Cooperators' confidence in the verification system. Nobody had much experience testing anywhere except in the atmosphere, so Unilateralists could exaggerate the dangers of hypothetical evasion scenarios and interpret small amounts of new data in ways that challenged the basic assumptions underlying the Geneva System. Such moves created a counterproductive dynamic in which American retrenchment increased Soviet suspicions and intensified their resistance to Western verification demands, thereby causing U.S. Cautious Cooperators to be even more skeptical about Soviet intentions. Arms Control Advocates tried to break the deadlock by proposing two new ideas—a quota of OSIs for a CTB or a ban on tests that the Geneva System could detect without inspections—but approaches remained too far apart for either bridging proposal to succeed.

Evasion in a "Gamesman's Paradise"

The Geneva System gave critics a specific set of arrangements to attack, so they devised cheating scenarios based on worst-case assumptions about Soviet intentions and the efficacy of evasion techniques. Since the Geneva System included no special means of monitoring high-altitude tests, for example, Edward Teller worked out a complicated scheme for testing in outer space. He postulated that the USSR could send a missile with a bomb and measuring instruments far from the earth, detonate the bomb by remote control, then send data back to earth using coded telemetry.[23] Even though his scheme was highly improbable, Teller assumed that the Soviets would be willing and able to implement it. He later charged that "testing in space provides a loophole through which one could drive a herd of wild elephants."[24]

The "Big Hole" theory had the greatest impact on the politics of verification. Although the Bethe Report had speculated that seismic signals of small tests could be decreased by a factor of ten, Bethe argued at the Conference of Experts that decoupling would not work. When Albert Latter of the RAND Corporation reworked Bethe's calculations, Latter reached the opposite conclusion: testing in extra-large cavities could reduce seismic signals by a factor of 100–300. Ignoring the size limits on natural or man-made underground cavities let test ban opponents claim that the Geneva System might not conclusively identify a 400-kt shot as a nuclear test![25]

Arms Control Advocates tried to counter these evasion scenarios by replacing the concept of foolproof verification with what came to be known as the adequacy standard. They argued that an imperfect verification system would deter most violations and detect the rest before they hurt U.S. security. For example, Bethe reassured senators that a potential cheater would have to conduct many explosions with low-yield weapons to learn when their seismic signals became detectable and that "somewhere on creeping up to the yield they would be detected."[26]

Unilateralists agreed that the United States should no longer seek foolproof arrangements, but they wanted more, not less, verification. One RAND analyst proposed a new standard: "smartproof" verification: "We don't need a system which works against a careless, uninformed, unimaginative opponents, but one that works well against an opponent who is smart, careful, and imaginative."[27]

Arms Control Advocates viewed these evasion scenarios as stall tactics. A PSAC member complained, "These men who don't want a test moratorium are like a kid you are trying to put to bed. First he wants a drink of water and then he wants to go to the bathroom, but what he really wants is not to go to bed."[28] Unilateralists planned to play this game endlessly. Albert Latter warned Killian that "whatever advances might be made in detection technology, the West Coast Group led by Teller would find a way to circumvent or discredit them."[29] These Unilateralists assumed that anything they could imagine, the USSR might do, and that it was inherently easier to be a "hider" than a "finder." Likening a nuclear test ban to Prohibition, Teller declared, "In the competition between the bootlegger and the police, the bootlegger has a great advantage."[30]

New Data on Verification Shakes the Geneva System's Foundations

Test ban opponents also attacked the Geneva System with data gathered in the spate of tests after the Conference of Experts. Project Argus had proven that high-altitude tests were possible at a reasonable cost.[31] HARDTACK II data also suggested that nuclear blasts generated smaller signals and that the direction of first seismic motion was a less reliable discriminant than previously believed.[32] Test ban skeptics, therefore, declared that the Geneva System's detection and identification threshold should be raised from 5 kt to approximately 20 kt, unless the numbers of control posts and OSIs were dramatically increased.

Eisenhower's advisers reacted to the new data in different ways, but no one opposed introducing it in Geneva. Unilateralists argued that a complete policy reversal would be the "most straightforward course of action consistent with the best technical data now available."[33] Instead of waiting for the Soviets to suggest a threshold ban, they argued, the United States should immediately confront them with a choice among (1) a low threshold on underground tests with a very larger number of adversarial inspections, (2) a higher threshold determined by new estimates of the Geneva System's capabilities, or (3) an immediate ban on atmospheric tests. PSAC's belief that scientists should always be open to new evidence convinced them that "no relevant data, whether favorable or unfavorable to a test should be held back."[34] But their confidence in scientific progress and technical experts' ability to transcend political differences reassured them that the Geneva System could be updated and its inadequacies repaired. Eisenhower felt betrayed by scientists who had used one data point (RAINER) to assure him that the Geneva System would work, then changed their minds when data from the next test series arrived.[35] He wanted to use the new data to test Soviet intentions, on the assumption that Soviet scientists would respond favorably if they were sincerely interested in stable arms control.[36] Dulles feared a diplomatic debacle because the technical experts had reached a unanimous conclusion, only to have the politicians revise the technical estimates on nuclear detection capabilities. "If the Russians did this," he cautioned, "we would object strenuously."[37]

Because Eisenhower's advisers were committed, some sincerely and others cynically, to a "scientific" approach to verification decisions, they could not ignore the new data for diplomatic reasons. The way in which they handled it, however, made it hard for the Soviets and other American policy makers to differentiate between substantive problems and strategic ploys. The United States introduced the new data immediately, rather than waiting for PSAC to ascertain that the Geneva System needed less revision than Unilateralists claimed. Moreover, U.S. officials did not talk openly about Latter's decoupling theory for many months, partly to avoid giving the Soviets any ideas. Thus, those who took decoupling seriously based public arguments on an exaggerated reading of the new data, whereas those who defended the Geneva System could not openly rebut a major concern.[38]

James Wadsworth, head of the U.S. delegation, recalls that presentation of the new data produced "the most violent reaction imaginable [from the Soviets]. It spread a pall over the negotiations from which they never fully recovered."[39] Having acquiesced to the West's desire to discuss verification before deciding about test limits, the Soviets were furious when the United States tried to change unilaterally the rules of the verification game. They insisted that the Geneva System was the agreed basis for negotiations. On the grounds that scientific progress must necessarily facilitate cooperation, they asserted that "new data and improved means of detection, far from weakening the conclusions of the Geneva Experts' conference tend rather to strengthen them!"[40] Soviet delegates accused the West of trying to derail negotiations or increase espionage opportunities. They also intensified their insistence on control over verification in case the Geneva System was expanded.

Since the West was using the new data to gauge Soviet intentions, this hostile reaction perpetuated a downward spiral. It reinforced U.S. Cautious Cooperators' fear that the USSR did not want workable verification for a CTB. Influential Senate moderates, such as Thomas Dodd and William Fulbright, shifted their support from a CTB to an atmospheric ban. This exacerbated Soviet suspicions that the new data was another excuse to avoid a CTB, intensified their resistance to redesigning the Geneva System, and thus confirmed American Cautious Cooperators' decision to back away from a CTB.

Bridging Proposals Fail to Break the Deadlock

With negotiations deadlocked over the new data, the West decided to dissociate itself from unpopular positions that "the Russians may use as a screen to evade accepting responsibility for failure in the negotiations or to evade facing up to the control problem."[41] Macmillan convinced the United States to stop linking test limits to other disarmament measures. American Unilateralists were willing to drop the linkage as long as the United States stood firm on automatic inspections, international staff at the internal control posts, and other intractable verification issues.[42] At this point, Eisenhower and Dulles believed that the Soviets had "no intention of allowing a true agreement." Since these Cautious Cooperators' support for a CTB depended on satisfactory verification, they thought that the Control Commission veto would be "a good issue to break on." For public relations purposes, therefore, the West changed its declared objective from temporary test suspension to permanent cessation. But in the event the Soviets unexpectedly accepted their verification demands, Eisenhower specified that a permanent treaty must include the right to withdraw if the verification system proved unsatisfactory.[43]

British and American leaders considered two ideas meant to break the verification deadlock rather than blame the Soviets for a negotiating failure. In a private discussion with a British negotiator, Federov had mentioned that the USSR might be more flexible on OSIs if it knew how many would occur each year.[44] The British delegation developed the idea of an OSI quota, and Macmillan suggested to Khrushchev that 3–15 annual inspections might satisfy the West without encouraging frivolous or abusive OSIs.[45] Soon thereafter, Senator Humphrey wrote to Eisenhower that an inspection quota would deter violations and reassure Khrushchev that the Control Commission would not inspect all "mines, quarries, woods, ravines, and the rest."[46]

Neither Khrushchev nor Eisenhower showed much overt interest in an OSI quota at first. Declassified documents indicate, however, that the Committee of

Principals already intended to accept an OSI quota as part of a threshold ban but still wanted the Soviets to raise the subject. For example, DOD responded to the new data by asserting that "either the yield limit for mandatory inspections of underground disturbances must be raised . . . with a corresponding reduction of required inspections below that limit, or the inspection system must be designed to provide for on-the-ground inspection of (number deleted) events per year."[47]

Eisenhower briefly considered proposing a threshold ban on underground tests that could be identified with NTM and in-country monitoring stations. Unlike Gore's proposal, a 10-kt ban would set some precedents for international verification and might be acceptable to the USSR if the West dropped its OSI demands. Eisenhower had decided that OSIs had been overemphasized because a PSAC panel led by Robert Bacher had concluded that inspectors were unlikely to find proof of small subsurface blasts, especially if the perpetrator tried to conceal them. Eisenhower's second science adviser later said that the Bacher panel had given an overly pessimistic assessment of OSIs because it "yielded to the aggressive arguments of one of its members"—Harold Brown, the deputy director of LLNL.[48] Still, Eisenhower feared that if the United States banned all nuclear tests on the basis of unreliable OSI provisions, "the tendency for suspicions will be very great and our whole nation will become more and more jittery."[49]

Before Eisenhower proposed a 10-kt threshold ban, however, PSAC's panel on seismic verification presented its first formal report on the new data.[50] This group, chaired by Lloyd Berkner, concluded that an explosion could be decoupled by "a factor of ten or more"—far less than Latter's estimate but still enough to complicate threshold verification, because a 90-kt shot might pass for a permissible explosion if a large enough cavity could be constructed.[51] The Berkner Panel anticipated that 300 annual earthquakes worldwide would generate seismic signals that could be confused with a small test. This number was lower than the 1,500 initially predicted from the new data, but larger than the 20–100 that the Conference of Experts expected. The report confirmed that the first motion of compressional waves was not a reliable discriminant but suggested that earthquakes and explosions would produce distinct patterns of different seismic waves.[52] It recommended a $55 million research program, including unmanned in-country monitoring stations to monitor regional seismic waves—what came to be known as "black boxes."[53]

The United States initiated several research programs on the Berkner Panel's recommendations. But the projects were assigned to the same agencies that opposed an underground test ban and so were treated differently depending on their implications for verification. Project Cowboy used chemical explosions in a salt mine to evaluate the decoupling theory. The AEC funded it; LLNL conducted it; and RAND joined the analysis. The project was finished in less than a year because experimental evidence of decoupling would undermine support for underground test restrictions. These organizations were slower to pursue recommendations for improving verification because this conflicted with their interests in further nuclear testing.[54] Authority for Project Vela (research on the monitoring of tests underground, at high altitude, and in outer space) was not assigned for six months, and initial funding was low compared with the panel's recommendations.

When negotiations resumed in April 1959, the West gave Khrushchev two unattractive choices.[55] CTB talks could continue if he changed his position on the veto, OSIs, and high-altitude detection. Alternatively, negotiators could "take the first and readily attainable step" by banning atmospheric tests under the Geneva System minus OSIs. Since the Soviets had rejected Gore's proposal for an atmospheric ban based solely on NTM, they were unlikely to accept one with more intrusive verification. Macmillan wanted to propose a mutual moratorium on tests in other environments so that the West would negotiate more seriously on CTB verification. (A "phased approach" that started with only an atmospheric ban would probably not go much further.) But the United States protested that this would "undercut our basic principle of effective [verification], and would be unlikely to increase Soviet interest in serious negotiation."[56] Since Eisenhower and Macmillan felt that "the indefinite prolongation of negotiations would be undesirable," they resolved to request an indefinite recess as soon as the Soviets rejected their two options.[57]

Disappointing Results from Depoliticization Attempts

Khrushchev refused the atmospheric ban, as predicted, but surprised the West by offering to negotiate a quota of veto-free OSIs and hold technical talks on high-altitude verification. This new flexibility on verification stemmed from several contextual factors, including the replacement of the dying John Foster Dulles as secretary of state by Christian Herter in March 1959, growing Soviet concerns about the Chinese nuclear program, and Khrushchev's desire for a summit to show the benefits of engagement with the West.[58] Since many Westerners used the Soviets' stance on verification as an indicator of their arms control intentions, these concessions increased popular pressure for a CTB. Attempts were made to depoliticize verification by getting a consensus on verification as deterrence and turning tough questions over to technical working groups. Without agreement on first principles from which technical experts should work, though, such strategies failed.

Deterring Violations with a Quota of Inspections

When Khrushchev expressed support for an OSI quota, he endorsed the concept of verification as deterrence. A small quota would be sufficient, he maintained, because the mere possibility of investigation "would deter governments or persons within governments who might wish to carry out explosions in violation of the obligations undertaken by them."[59] Using an OSI quota to deter violations played well in the U.K., where politicians took credit for finding a practical solution to a long-standing problem.[60] It also appealed to many Americans. Arms control negotiations had failed in the past, Senator Humphrey said, because of the military's insistence on "absolutely perfect, absolutely foolproof" control. Verification as deterrence was a reliable alternative because it was built on the "same principle" that had protected U.S. security since the beginning of the nuclear age.[61] Soon after Khrushchev's letter, the Senate unanimously adopted Humphrey's resolution in support of a CTB with an "adequate inspection and control system."[62]

Eisenhower's official response was carefully qualified.[63] An OSI quota was worth exploring, but verification as deterrence would not avoid disagreements about decision making, such as what evidence would support an OSI request, what voting procedures the Control Commission would use, and what arrangements would ensure timely access to suspicious sites. Since the East and the West undoubtedly had different ideas about the number of OSIs needed to deter violations, Eisenhower also wanted to know "the scientific basis upon which any such number of inspections would be determined and how it would be related to the detection capabilities of the control system."

In private, Eisenhower's advisers were more candid about their dilemma: should the United States sign a CTB if its current verification demands were met but some underground tests might still be concealed?[64] Eisenhower preferred an atmospheric ban but feared that "the world would not stand for it." He felt that if "our bluff were called by the Soviets dropping their veto demands we could accept [a CTB]." Killian did not argue strongly for a CTB because the decoupling scenario made him fear a "fatal error" on verification.[65] But he reminded the president that foolproof verification was neither necessary nor possible and urged him to estimate the "calculated risk" that the United States should run to breach the Iron Curtain. The AEC and DOD wanted to negotiate a mutual ban on atmospheric tests because public opinion would probably put them "out of the business" regardless of what the Soviets did. But DOD doubted that the United States "had a free choice in the matter at the present time," so it agreed to continue CTB talks if the United States insisted that the veto be dropped completely and the quota be determined "scientifically."

Eisenhower's advisers had various reasons for wanting decisions about verification to be based on scientific criteria.[66] This fit with the official depiction of verification as an objective process that determined the "truth" about Soviet compliance. It reflected U.S. fears that the British might be ready to accept insufficient verification just to get a CTB. It reinforced American demands that Soviet scientists work with them to revise the Geneva System. It played into the Eisenhower administration's plans to make the Soviets choose between many OSIs for a low-threshold ban or fewer OSIs for a treaty that allowed larger tests underground. It also had implications for domestic debates over verification requirements. Calculating the number of OSIs needed to deter noncompliance involved assumptions about the frequency of small seismic events, the Soviets' intentions, and the consequences of violations. The AEC wanted to define the OSI quota as a "technical matter" on which its views should prevail so that its pessimistic assumptions would produce a quota that the Soviets would never accept.

The idea that "effective international control" meant enough detection capabilities to deter violations soon became a shared assumption in Geneva, but this formula was too vague to end arguments over OSIs.[67] The USSR intimated that three OSIs would be acceptable, but Macmillan had talked with the United States about fifty OSIs for a CTB, and U.S. Unilateralists maintained that fifty would only be appropriate for a 25-kt threshold ban.[68] If the OSI quota was very small, the Soviets said, they would not require the right to veto requests. They did, however, want criteria for classifying an unidentified seismic event as a probable earthquake and thus ineligible for inspection. The United States tried to cast such questions as technical problems to be answered according to its proposed criteria; the Soviets insisted that the issues were political and had to be resolved through bargaining and compromise.

Technical Talks Surrounded by Political Controversies

Because the public expected convergence on verification as deterrence to promote CTB agreement, the three states sought to preserve the semblance of forward momentum. The West proposed technical talks about high-altitude monitoring to learn whether its proposed ban on atmospheric tests could be extended to other fallout-producing shots. The Soviets agreed to the proposal because the Conference of Experts had not dealt with this environment.

Technical Working Group I (TWG I) operated under difficult conditions. Before it convened, attempts to establish favorable terms of reference produced heated controversies, such as whether to mention the Conference of Experts (the West opposed and lost) or consider new data (the USSR opposed and lost). The Soviets saw technical talks as a symbolic act rather than as a serious attempt to grapple with substantive questions. Thus they wanted the delegations chosen and recommendations made within two weeks. TWG I had little reliable data; the United States argued that only two shots from the 1958 series were directly relevant, and the USSR withheld useful information from its testing program. The American delegation had no instructions about how much money the United States would spend to raise detection probabilities or how much risk it would tolerate to ban tests above 50 km, because the principals could not agree.[69]

The scientists reached consensus only because the U.S. delegation made political judgments about the benefits, costs, and risks of high-altitude test ban verification. Wolfgang Panofsky, head of the U.S. team, realized that a strictly technical approach would have ensured failure, because "given arbitrarily high incentives on the part of the violator, it will always be possible to devise an essentially undetectable means of carrying out the violation." Therefore, his recommendations reflected his judgment that there were insufficient incentives either for the violator to test under such extreme conditions or to expand the detection system to the maximum degree.[70]

TWG I's report gave specific recommendations on some issues and options on others. Of ten methods considered, only backscatter radar was excluded because it could provide intelligence on missile launches. TWG I also declined to recommend methods for determining who had caused a suspicious event, because the only technical solution would be to monitor all missile launches—a collateral information problem that bothered both sides. The report recommended an x-ray monitoring system to detect explosions at extremely high altitudes (e.g., Teller's space launch scenario). Delegates realized that the monitoring system could be degraded but concluded that shielding the blast would be too difficult, expensive, and time-consuming.

The USSR announced that the methods and instrumentation recommended by TWG I could be added to the Geneva System, but the West would only say that the report was a "correct technical assessment" of verification capabilities and limitations. Americans were unwilling to negotiate about a high-altitude/outer-space detection system for two years because the principals could not agree on a U.S. position. This interagency conflict left the United States in the position of arguing that the Geneva System's inadequacies at high altitudes were a major impediment to a CTB but not worth spending funds to fix. In 1961, after Vela provided more information about detection above 50 km, the United

States proposed a system that was more modest and less expensive than TWG I's recommendations—the reverse of what happened with the new data from the 1958 tests.

Uncertainty over Weapons Safety Leads to Hydronuclear "Experiments"

U.S. Unilateralists used their "unfavorable prognosis" for agreement on CTB verification to argue for test resumption when the U.S. moratorium expired in October 1959.[71] They suggested (with the support of George Kistiakowsky, the new science adviser) that the only way to resolve verification uncertainties was to conduct more nuclear tests at high altitudes and in diverse geological conditions.[72] They claimed that PNEs were not covered under the moratorium. They pled for permission to pursue ideas from Project Argus about electromagnetic pulse effects and ballistic missile defense. They also warned Eisenhower that some weapons might not be one-point safe.[73]

Eisenhower rejected arguments for open test resumption and announced that the United States would extend its moratorium until the end of the year. But he authorized secret, very-low-yield nuclear explosions to improve weapon safety. Since the U.S. moratorium declaration contained no explicit definition of a nuclear test, scientists from Los Alamos National Laboratory (LANL) argued that small nuclear explosions whose yield could be contained in fabricated vessels were "hydronuclear experiments," not violations. In so-called zero-yield tests, scientists slowly increase the fissile material until they detect a subcritical nuclear reaction with a yield up to one pound. More than forty such "creep-up series" were conducted until the end of the moratorium made clandestine safety checks unnecessary. Like PNEs, these small explosions had a dual purpose. LANL scientists credit them with letting the labs "maintain some small design and diagnostic capability that was to prove essential when nuclear weapons testing resumed."[74]

No Technical Solution to Arguments over Inspection

The superpower summit at Camp David in September 1959 improved the context for verification talks. Khrushchev came away convinced that Eisenhower was a Cautious Cooperator.[75] The summit strengthened Khrushchev's domestic standing and enabled him to make conciliatory gestures that might help Western "realists" prevail over "madmen" on questions like Berlin and peaceful coexistence.[76] To show that a constructive approach to negotiations could yield rapid results, the Soviets worked with scientists and diplomats from around the world to prevent the militarization of Antarctica, ban nuclear explosions there, and establish unlimited inspection rights in the region.[77] In January 1960, Khrushchev announced that he would unilaterally cut 1.2 million troops, partly to shift spending from defense to economic growth and partly to increase support in the West for arms control. Such moves threatened to cause a backlash from more orthodox Soviet elites, especially those who would be directly affected by conventional military reductions. Therefore, Khrushchev wanted evidence that Western leaders would reciprocate his overtures and agree on solutions to shared problems.

The improved context did not end controversies over the composition of the Control Commission, its method of decision making, the procedure for invoking OSIs (automatic or consultative), and other problems (such as French and Chinese participation, and a PNE exemption). Only after the United States threatened to present its own understanding of technical problems related to seismic verification did the Soviets suggest another technical working group (TWG II) to develop criteria for initiating OSIs. They were willing to discuss the new seismic data and supplemental instrumentation but would not consider fundamental revisions of the Geneva System.

TWG II was even more contentious than TWG I because the stakes were higher. American experts had no political instructions because the principals could not decide whether the goal was to accentuate problems or find solutions. Since the Soviets saw TWG II as a concession to the West, their delegates were told not to accept anything that made CTB verification seem more difficult than the Conference of Experts had concluded.[78] The Soviet delegates used a variety of technical arguments to protect the Geneva System's verification requirements and capabilities, such as charging that HARDTACK II data had been collected by stations without all the Geneva System instruments and analyzed with flawed statistical techniques. Although the West accused Soviet delegates of using pseudoscientific arguments for political reasons, data from Project Vela later showed that the Soviet delegates were more correct than the Americans.[79]

When Latter and Bethe presented some of their work on decoupling, the Soviets were "stunned."[80] They acknowledged that decoupling was possible in theory but doubted that it would work in practice. The West had some empirical evidence from British experiments with chemical explosives, but the first decoupling experiment in Project Cowboy was not detonated until the day before the conference recessed, and the results were not discussed.

Contrary to Soviet accusations, Western delegates recognized that this was not just a "congress of seismologists" pursuing knowledge for its own sake. Since the fate of a CTB depended on convincing Cautious Cooperators that underground test verification could be workable and tolerable, TWG II's conclusions were too important to let incomplete data and vague language serve as the basis for a consensual report. U.S. delegates were willing to recommend technical enhancements and research projects, such as joint nuclear tests to learn more about magnitude-yield relationships. But they would not compromise on criteria that would make more than a small fraction of unidentified seismic ineligible for OSIs.[81] Delegates could agree only to present divergent views in separate annexes, an outcome that hurt personal relationships between Eastern and Western scientists, underscored the limits of a technical approach to the politics of verification, and reinforced Soviet fears that the United States simply used technical talks to postpone a CTB.

The acrimonious outcome of TWG II marked the end of Eisenhower's efforts to negotiate a full CTB. He blamed the failure on the intransigence of "politically guided Soviet experts."[82] Domestic considerations were also important: Kistiakowsky, Herter, and others who had strongly favored a CTB were now warning Eisenhower that it would set a bad precedent to negotiate a "first step" treaty that could not be ratified.[83] Therefore, although most Americans wanted the moratorium extended for another year, Eisenhower would only say that the United States would continue "its active program of weapon research, development and laboratory-type experimentation" but would announce its plans before testing.[84] Khrushchev responded with a similar mix of temporary restraint and threats about what would happen if a CTB were not signed soon. He promised not to test unless the West did first, while warning that his scientists had a "fantastic" weapon in the "hatching stage."[85]

Progress through Compromise and Coalitions

Although neither the convergence on verification as deterrence nor the technical talks had solved the workable/tolerable dilemma, test ban negotiations had made too much progress to give up altogether. Instead, negotiators decomposed the CTB into more manageable pieces, compromised on some verification issues, and hoped to address the most intractable problems through two-level gamesmanship. The U-2 incident raised suspicions on both sides, seriously damaging the context for domestic and international agreement on verification. If this incident had not occurred, it might have been possible to assemble a winning coalition, but only if Eisenhower and arms control supporters in his administration had been willing to take an explicitly political approach to verification decisions.

A Phased Approach to a First-Step Treaty

In February 1960, the United States proposed to circumvent the "technical impasse" of TWG II by banning all tests that it considered verifiable and extending the limits as verification improved.[86] The proposal covered tests under water, in the atmosphere up to an unspecified altitude, and underground down to the yield that would produce a seismic signal of magnitude (m_b) 4.75 on the Richter scale.[87] This threshold formula avoided arguments about magnitude-yield relationships. (It corresponded to a tamped 19–20–kt explosion at NTS and reflected revised U.S. estimates of the Geneva System's capabilities.)[88] It also favored the West, since differences in test-site geology meant that a much smaller test in the USSR would generate a m_b 4.75 signal. If the Soviets accepted the American criteria, 30 percent of eligible events could be inspected; if not, 20 percent of all unidentified events could be inspected. Both formulas, Wadsworth noted, would produce approximately 20 annual inspections in the USSR, the number believed necessary for Senate approval. The proposal also specified that the three states would accept internal control posts and begin joint verification research to move toward a CTB as quickly as possible.

In a dramatic announcement on March 19, 1960, the Soviets offered to sign a phased treaty that included a moratorium on low-yield tests while scientists and diplomats worked on CTB verification. In practical terms, this would not be much different from a CTB based on the Geneva System, because public opinion would make it hard for the West to resume low-yield underground tests while the ban on other tests was working well. Still, it was the first time that the Soviets had acknowledged (however tacitly) a threshold below which technical monitoring methods were insufficient.

Eisenhower officials agonized over a response. A threshold ban with an OSI quota and internal monitoring stations had been the undeclared U.S. objective all along, but a formal moratorium on all nuclear tests seemed like the worst possible outcome to those who thought that only the United States would comply. U.S. negotiators sought clarification. How long would the moratorium last if verification problems could not be solved? The USSR wanted four or five years; the United States, one or two. What would the joint research program involve? The United States desired some nuclear tests; for the Soviet Union, chemical explosions would suffice.[89] What would the rules be for OSIs? The Soviets insisted that the quota be determined through political compromise but agreed that OSIs could be used to investigate events above or below the m_b 4.75 threshold. They also accepted a U.K. proposal to use temporary OSI eligibility criteria that could be modified after more experience. Although some Americans denounced the plan as "a pig in a poke," others viewed it as a promising path to a CTB.[90]

The U.S. decision to accept a two-year moratorium was affected by an important change in alignment. After decades of opposing any arms control without foolproof verification, the DOD representative to the Committee of Principals made the strongest case for an affirmative answer.[91] Deputy Secretary of Defense James Douglas argued that the Soviets' greatest strategic assets were secrecy and insularity, so "opening up" the USSR through CTB inspections would be more valuable than any gains from continued testing. This shift revealed a split between the uniformed military, who still wanted to develop new weapons, and DOD civilians, who were starting to think about finite deterrence requirements. Since the military had also supported Stassen's plan for trial inspections areas in 1956, when they were especially worried about surprise attack, it may also have reflected an interest in learning more about the "missile gap." Once Douglas agreed that the United States had little to lose from a two-year moratorium, AEC chair John McCone was alone in arguing that the United States should refuse arms control without inspections, as a matter of principle.[92]

Although Eisenhower thought that the United States should "give Khrushchev every chance" to prove that he wanted mutually acceptable solutions to CTB verification problems, he and Macmillan hedged their acceptance.[93] They stated that "coordinated" research programs should start before a phased treaty was signed so the West could conduct its own nuclear explosions for verification research if the Soviets would not join them. They also promised to refrain voluntarily from testing for an unspecified length of time after a treaty was signed but did not want this restriction in the treaty itself.

The step-by-step approach finally looked like it might succeed. Negotiators tried to "clear away as much underbrush as possible" so that political leaders could finalize a treaty at the Four-Power Summit in mid-May.[94] They reached agreement on some secondary issues, such as establishing a Seismic Research Program Advisory Group (SRPAG) and conducting a few joint nuclear explosions.[95] They also compromised on larger issues; for example, the administrator of the Control Commission would come from a neutral country and be approved by all three initial parties. Some core questions remained when negotiations recessed before the summit, including where the threshold of verifiability was, how many OSIs would be conducted, and how long the moratorium would last if agreement on CTB verification proved elusive. Kistiakowsky considered Eisenhower's willingness to keep the number of inspections an open question for the summit as an important acknowledgement that the issue was political rather than technical.[96] Many observers were optimistic that Eisenhower, Macmillan, and Khrushchev could find mutually acceptable solutions in Paris, then use their enhanced standing as successful arms control negotiators to secure domestic support.

The Backlash Builds

Not everybody liked the progress in Geneva. France and China indicated that they would not join a phased CTB. The JCAE held hearings on technical problems with test ban verification.[97] Witnesses concurred that the Geneva System's threshold was about m_b 4.75, but they disagreed about the possibilities for improving verification and the consequences of undetected tests. RAND's Richard Latter demonstrated how small changes in the technical parameters of a monitoring system could have major effects on the politics of verification. He calculated that there should be sixteen annual inspections in the USSR if the system had twenty-one stations on Soviet soil but that the OSI quota could drop to six with twenty-five internal stations. He also testified that Project Cowboy had confirmed that nuclear tests could be decoupled by a factor of 300, even though it involved chemical explosion whose decoupling factor was significantly lower.[98] Harold Brown's presentation about the uncertainties of on-site inspection convinced some senators that even with a large quota of OSIs, the probability of proving violations would be "close to zero."

Some analysts have claimed that American Unilateralists deliberately set up the U-2 shoot-down to wreck the Paris Summit, destroy détente, and block a test ban agreement.[99] Others have suggested that no solution on Berlin could have satisfied American, British, French, and Soviet leaders, so Khrushchev, under pressure from hardliners, seized a convenient pretext to end a "summit without substance."[100] The first position overstates how close the superpowers were to agreement on CTB verification before the U-2 incident occurred; the second underestimates the negative effects of the overflights and subsequent reactions on the politics of verification.

Khrushchev was in a delicate domestic position before the summit. He was strong enough to initiate unilateral troop reductions and other conciliatory gestures without the support of many Presidium members, but this left him personally accountable and vulnerable if the West did not reciprocate.[101] Opposition to Khrushchev's arms control initiatives intensified in early 1960 after Herter, his undersecretary, Douglas Dillon, and Vice President Nixon made hawkish speeches on Berlin. A U-2 overflight on April 9, 1960, further reduced Presidium support for defense reductions, although the Soviets did not openly denounce the intrusion into their airspace because they could not shoot the plane down. This, along with Francis Gary Power's overflight on May 1, decreased Khrushchev's willingness and ability to compromise on test ban verification by substantiating claims that the West was only interested in espionage, raising new doubts about Soviet defenses and Khrushchev's toughness, and contradicting claims about Eisenhower's peaceful intentions.[102]

Eisenhower knew that the USSR saw penetration of its airspace as belligerent and insulting, so he temporarily suspended overflights to preserve cordial relations after Camp David. Internal pressure to authorize new missions came from advisers who predicted that a failed summit would precipitate a military crisis in Europe, as well as those who wanted reassuring information about the Soviet ICBM program to counter calls for increased defense spending in response to inflated claims about a "missile gap." Eisenhower approved two overflights because he did not want to "oppose the combined opinion" of his advisers, doubted that the USSR could prove the flights were occurring, and underestimated their impact on Soviet policy.[103]

Two days after Powers was captured, the leadership struggle that started after Camp David was resolved by a reorganization that favored Khrushchev's critics, such as Kozlov and Suslov, at the expense of his allies.[104] But Khrushchev was still strong enough to determine how the issue should be handled.[105] He was furious that "the Americans had deliberately tried to place a time bomb . . . set to go off just as we were about to sit down with them at the negotiating table."[106] Eisenhower's description of the espionage missions as a "distasteful but vital necessity" given the closed nature of the USSR especially enraged the Soviet leader, because it implied that his country was not the sovereign equal of the United States.[107] Khrushchev tried repeatedly to disassociate Eisenhower from the incident by blaming "militarists from the Pentagon" who acted without the president's knowledge.[108] But he also demanded that Eisenhower publicly apologize for the overflights, punish those responsible, retract comments about America's "right" to conduct reconnaissance missions over the USSR, and promise to stop the intrusions. Khrushchev believed that Eisenhower would scapegoat one of his generals rather than sacrifice the summit, but even though the president canceled future overflights, he would not denounce the ones that had already taken place.[109] Some of Eisenhower's resistance can probably be explained by the American perception that the U-2 incident was actually evidence of Soviet deviousness and disinterest in arms control. Even the pro–arms control Kistiawkowsky thought that the Soviets had "virtually invited" the United States to conduct an overflight just before the summit by failing to protest the April 9 mission.[110]

The Geneva conference continued but accomplished little for the rest of the Eisenhower administration. The scientists in SRPAG made no progress because political leaders could not agree on safeguards to ensure that joint nuclear explosions for verification research did not help participants improve their own weapons or learn about the other side's weapons designs. Arguments over the numbers and locations of control stations revealed that the two sides remained far apart and that the United States was now offering to accept fewer stations on its territory than Richard Latter's JCAE testimony had assumed.[111] With prospects for any test ban treaty fading, Eisenhower decided that if a Republican won the presidential election, he would announce a new test series. If the Democrats won, he would leave the decision (and the blame) to them.[112]

A Lost Opportunity?

Eisenhower viewed his failure to negotiate a CTB as the biggest disappointment of his presidency.[113] But opinions vary widely about whether the U-2 incident actually destroyed a promising path toward agreement on test ban verification. Most speculation has focused on whether Khrushchev and Eisenhower could have compromised on an OSI quota at the summit or were too constrained by their own caution and conservative factions at home. Eisenhower's conclusion that OSIs were not reliable for verification (even if they were helpful in "opening" the USSR), Latter's calculation that six OSIs could be enough for a threshold ban, and DOD's new enthusiasm for a phased treaty suggest that Eisenhower could have come much closer to Khrushchev's position—as Kennedy did in 1961. There was strong Senate support for negotiations toward a CTB with adequate verification and tremendous popular confidence in Eisenhower's judgment on national security. One Senate CTB skeptic said that if the president put his weight behind a phased CTB, voting against the treaty would be "like voting for cancer."[114] Thus, a compromise on the annual number of OSIs could have been negotiated and ratified *if* treaty supporters had repudiated the idea that Soviet resistance to U.S. verification demands indicated an intention to cheat and countered Unilateralists' claims that a monitoring system must catch and prove every violation, regardless of how farfetched the evasion scenario.

Arms Control Advocates took a step in this direction by promoting the idea that imperfect verification could still deter violations. But the Eisenhower administration's emphasis on a technical approach to verification gave undue weight to treaty opponents, who used "new data" or "revised calculations" to suggest that any obtainable number of OSIs or monitoring stations was not enough to deter a highly motivated cheater. Killian came to regret that his narrow conception of the science adviser's role inadvertently assisted the Unilateralists' blocking strategies. PSAC, he wrote, should have tried harder to educate policy makers about scientific uncertainty because Americans were "too obsessed with the possibility rather than the probability of violations." It should also have revealed how treaty opponents were using technical arguments for political purposes. In short, "The expert advisers should have helped the policy makers to understand the primarily political character of the test ban negotiations and shown them how misleading it was to assume that the outcome of technical negotiations should be the deciding factor in their policy makers."[115]

A compromise on the OSI quota would not have been sufficient, however, because many of the most intractable disagreements dealt with the type rather than the amount of verification. Arguments about control-post staff and Control Commission decision making show how hard it is to reach agreement on verification when states worry that the other side might distort the process for unilateral gain. Such disputes reflected fundamentally different views of verification. Moreover, negotiators cared not only about how a compromise would affect the benefits, costs, and risks of test ban cooperation but also about the precedents it would set for more significant arms control. Negotiators found mutually acceptable compromises on many minor questions, but given the intensity of distrust and competition that characterized superpower relations in the late 1950s, it would have been hard to split the difference on core questions.

What overly pessimistic assessments forget, however, is that if tripartite talks had secured agreement on a phased treaty in 1960, the context for the politics of CTB verification would have changed in crucial ways. The West could have compromised on moratorium length by offering two or three years, and a promise to renew if it was pleased with progress on CTB verification.[116] The three countries might then have extended the expedient of "temporary" criteria for OSI eligibility to reach temporary agreement on other issues. Negotiating flexibility would be encouraged by the knowledge that provisional agreement could secure immediate arms control benefits without a permanent, precedent-setting commitment to ban all tests on the basis of untried verification arrangements. U.S. Unilateralists would have had difficulty convincing Cautious Cooperators that the value of ending atmospheric fallout and high-yield underground tests, implementing the Geneva System, and starting OSIs on Soviet soil was not worth some verification uncertainties during a two-year trial period.

Such an agreement would have postponed the toughest questions until the trial period was over. By then, the parties would have the practical experience needed to narrow their differences on technical problems, such as magnitude-yield relationships, and political issues, such as the rights and restrictions on foreign inspectors. If all went well, assumptions about the other side's intentions would have been improved by an arms control success after decades of negotiating failures. Unilateralists on both sides would have tried to discredit the provisional verification arrangements and to portray test resumption as essential to national security, but these groups would have been weaker and their arguments less plausible after successful cooperation than before anyone was willing to take the first step. Even if residual concerns about decoupling might have kept the threshold at 10–20 kt, this would still have been a great achievement as an independent arms control measure and a first step toward resolving more difficult verification issues.

Conclusion

The most important lesson from the Eisenhower-era CTB negotiations is that reaching agreement on verification was neither a technical solution to arms control dilemmas nor a total impossibility, given the high levels of Cold War suspicion and hostility. From the Conference of Experts to TWG II, attempts to depoliticize verification were singularly unsuccessful. Sometimes these attempts were cynical strategies employed to gain a stronger bargaining position; on other occasions, they were sincere attempts to show that scientists from both sides could agree on some verification questions. Without reliable political guidance, however, the technical experts had either to avoid core controversies or to propose solutions that made sense given their own assumptions but that lacked support from policy makers who thought differently about arms control and verification. The "can do" spirit of PSAC and other pro–arms control scientists helped sustain hopes for a CTB when the AEC, DOD, and the JCS preferred to conclude a quick atmospheric ban or leave test ban talks deadlocked forever. But scientists could not deliver what Cautious Cooperators like Eisenhower and Dulles wanted most—clear-cut answers to verification dilemmas.

Convergence on the idea of verification as deterrence seemed like another promising way to narrow domestic and international disagreements. For those who acknowledged trade-offs, it was an improvement over U.S. insistence on foolproof control and Soviet refusal to admit any inadequacies of remote monitoring. With no objective way to determine how much verification would deter or detect dangerous violations, however, groups continued to have divergent preferences. Moreover, the new way of thinking about verification reinforced a set of highly adversarial assumptions that exacerbated superpower arguments over verification authority.

The most progress occurred when political leaders tried to work with conflicting interests and ideas about verification. The failure of the phased approach was not overdetermined despite the intensity of military competition, the high level of distrust between the superpowers, the existence of domestic opposition to arms control inside the United States and the USSR, and the underdeveloped state of science and technology for test ban verification. These contextual conditions complicated the search for agreement, but Eisenhower, Khrushchev, and Macmillan could have gradually built a winning coalition if they had used their phased approach to create political and technical conditions more favorable for compromises on CTB verification.

5

The Corrosive Effects of
Coercive Diplomacy

A s a senator, John F. Kennedy had opposed test resumption and wanted "redoubled" efforts to achieve a CTB. As president, he was less ambivalent about arms control than Eisenhower had been, and his Committee of Principals was less internally divided about the value of verified test restrictions. Yet Kennedy never got as close as Eisenhower did to domestic and international agreement on CTB verification. In 1963, the United States, the U.K., and the USSR negotiated and ratified a treaty that banned explosions in the atmosphere, outer space, and underwater but placed no limits on underground tests and contained no verification provisions. The preamble depicts the LTBT as a first step toward a CTB and the "speediest possible achievement" of total disarmament "under strict international control."[1] But moves in the politics of verification helped change the LTBT from a first step into a final stop for more than a decade.

Arms Control Advocates, Cautious Cooperators, and Unilateralists explain this ambiguous outcome differently. Arms Control Advocates note that the LTBT was negotiated, signed, and ratified in less than three months. They contend that arguments over verification were easily resolved after events like the Cuban Missile Crisis dramatized the dangers of unilateral security. Cautious Cooperators assume that imperfect verification could support only modest cooperation: agreement on the LTBT occurred after reconnaissance satellites offered a new "win-win" way to watch for atmospheric explosions and underground testing minimized the risks of clandestine tests elsewhere. Unilateralists maintain that the superpowers perpetuated verification arguments to protect underground testing but not to preserve atmospheric tests whose fallout caused huge public relations problems for little military gain.

Once again, single-factor explanations are unsatisfactory. The Cuban Missile Crisis, like other frightening events in the early Cold War years, exacerbated the sense of nuclear vulnerability but did not end verification debates because Arms Control Advocates, Cautious Cooperators, and Unilateralists drew conflicting lessons about the mix of competition and cooperation needed to avoid catastrophe. Verification advances and concerns affected support for a CTB among American Cautious Cooperators, yet the LTBT bans high-altitude tests despite detection difficulties and ignores large underground explosions that could have been monitored without OSIs. Even the most cynical accounts are not complete, because they do not explain how the Unilateralists blocked all limits on underground tests when the heads of the United States, the U.K., and the USSR, the majority of American senators, and the bulk of Western public opinion favored negotiated restrictions on underground tests.

A more complete explanation combines these partial perspectives by showing how the concepts and strategies used in the politics of verification could only support limited cooperation. Many of the ideas developed during the Eisenhower years continued to shape Kennedy-era arguments over test ban verification. A crucial difference between the two administrations, however, changed the dynamics of domestic-international interactions in self-defeating ways. Because Eisenhower was personally ambivalent about a CTB, progress toward agreement was slow and easily disrupted by new doubts about verification capabilities. But as he and Khrushchev each grew increasingly confident that the other really was a Cautious Cooperator, they started to explore verification trade-offs. Kennedy was more firmly committed to a CTB than Eisenhower was and less susceptible to strategies that manipulated verification uncertainties. Yet his strong support for CTB was combined with a major increase in defense spending and a more confrontational approach toward the Soviet Union. His coercive diplomacy and "peace through strength" coalition-building strategies sent mixed signals about U.S. intentions that different Soviet factions interpreted according to their own beliefs. The more evidence orthodox elites had of American aggressiveness, the more Khrushchev relied on his own version of coercive diplomacy to satisfy competing domestic factions and militant Chinese communists. Such behavior increased American doubts about Soviet intentions and reinforced the Kennedy administration's reliance on coercive diplomacy. The desire to score propaganda points also tempted both leaders into strategies that exacerbated the workable/tolerable dilemma, such as casting all the blame for the "broken moratorium" on the other side. These counterproductive dynamics intensified after the Cuban Missile Crisis and during LTBT ratification debates. Thus, even though Kennedy, Khrushchev, and Macmillan wanted a CTB more than ever, the way they handled the politics of verification inadvertently assisted the Unilateralists' blocking strategies.

Coercive Diplomacy Erodes the Climate for Cooperation

From the Kennedy administration's opening moves at the CTB talks in spring 1961 until the superpowers resumed testing in September 1961, the Americans tried to narrow differences over verification while the Soviets backtracked on key issues. Arthur Dean, the new head of the U.S. negotiating team, characterized this period as one when the United States tried to go as low as it could without endangering national security or Senate support but constantly encountered a "solid wall of Soviet negatives" that Khrushchev used to hide his secret test preparations.[2] In actuality, the Kennedy administration combined minor concessions with rigid demands on the major points of disagreement and threatening actions outside the negotiations. This mix of conciliation and confrontation stemmed from divisions inside the Kennedy administration, and it had poorly understood effects on Soviet debates about testing and verification.

Complex Divisions in the Kennedy Administration

Senior members of the Kennedy administration concurred that the Soviets must be deterred, that peace was preferable to war, and that arms control could enhance security. But there were important divisions among and within the key agencies over deterrence requirements, Soviet intentions, bargaining strategies, and the importance of arms control relative to other goals, such as NATO relations.[3] These divisions created a constant tension between test restraint and resumption that was handled through carrot-and-stick policies whose minor concessions and threats of renewed testing would supposedly convince the Soviets to acquiesce on major verification issues.

The president wanted a CTB to avert proliferation, end fallout, and ease world tensions. But his election campaign had also attacked Eisenhower's refusal to close the mythical missile gap with a major U.S. nuclear modernization program, and his inaugural address had pledged to "pay any price, bear any burden, support any friend, oppose any foe" for U.S. security. Thus, Kennedy's approach to nuclear tests represented a contradictory combination of arms control advocacy and unilateralism. As a long-time politician with a weak electoral mandate, Kennedy was more disposed than Eisenhower to use active coalition-building strategies. Kennedy's youth and his relative lack of military leadership experience also made him more vulnerable than Eisenhower to charges of being "soft on security."

The administration had two strong institutional advocates for a CTB, but both had limited influence. The new Arms Control and Disarmament Agency, headed by William Foster, was an independent agency whose sole purpose was to promote domestic and international agreement on arms control. Congressional critics, however, had taken numerous steps to moderate ACDA's positions and constrain its effectiveness.[4] Jerome Wiesner, Kennedy's science adviser, was a weapons scientist who became an outspoken arms control enthusiast after serving on the Gaither Committee.[5] He was well versed in verification technology and convinced that the risks of a CTB were less than those of an unconstrained arms race. He was a more active player than Killian or Kistakoswy but may have had less influence because Kennedy did not believe that science could provide firm answers to arms control dilemmas.[6]

Top officials in the State Department were more ambivalent about a CTB. Secretary of State Dean Rusk, a Cautious Cooperator, was less optimistic about the prospects for arms control and more skeptical about Soviet intentions than were ACDA and Wiesner. Rusk's support for a test ban hinged on verification, and his confidence in verification changed with each new technical discovery. Some senior State officials, such as Paul Nitze, favored a confrontational approach toward the Soviets, whereas those concerned primarily with European affairs worried about the impact of negotiations on NATO relations.

Some organizations that had staunchly opposed a CTB in the past were internally divided. Strauss and McCone had used verification concerns to protect the AEC's test program, but Glenn Seaborg (the new AEC chair) was a Cautious Cooperator. He tried to be an "honest broker" between scientists who favored unconstrained nuclear weapons development (the perspective Teller fostered at LLNL) and those who saw both dangers and opportunities in competitive nuclear programs (the dominant view at LANL).[7] The divisions in the military pitted civilians who wanted to "rationalize" U.S. defense policy and arms procurement against members of the uniformed military who distrusted abstract analyses. They also involved rivalry between the air force (the main beneficiary of the massive retaliation strategy) and the army (which liked the increased role for conventional forces in Kennedy's "flexible response" policy). Robert McNamara, the secretary of defense, thought that the United States would gain more from a verified CTB than it would from continued testing. The JCS took the opposite view and now had a direct voice in test ban policy because Kennedy enlarged the Committee of Principals to include the chairman of the JCS.

Kennedy often used "peace through strength" arguments to broaden support for security policies. Unless the United States proved that it would never let the

Soviets win an arms race, prevail in a crisis, or break through containment, the argument went, Khrushchev would never agree to American conditions for verified arms control.[8] Therefore, Kennedy's 1962 defense appropriation was $46 billion, a nearly 10 percent increase over Eisenhower's last request. Between 1961 and 1963, the United States doubled its strategic alert forces and increased its operational ICBMs tenfold. By late 1963, the United States had five times as many strategic missiles and twice as many long-range bombers as did the USSR. CTB supporters hoped that such actions and the tough talk that went with them would convince the Soviets to bargain more seriously, increase domestic confidence in Kennedy's ability to secure favorable accords, and avoid the need to test again. Instead, this approach increased Soviet intransigence, pushed both sides to begin test preparations, and destroyed domestic support for a phased approach to test ban verification.[9]

A Downward Spiral in Negotiations

When the Geneva Conference resumed in March 1961, the Soviets adopted a more confrontational stance on nuclear tests and verification. Tsarapkin charged the United States and the U.K. with stalling negotiations so that France could test for NATO. He claimed that French testing gave the West "one-sided advantages," threatened chances for a CTB, and made any treaty that excluded France "pointless."[10] He also retracted support for a single administrator from a neutral country. The Soviets' "troika" proposal involved a collective executive that would "act as a single whole" in which "the three main groups of States would be equally represented and invested with equal rights."[11]

The West interpreted these moves in light of the overall decline in superpower relations following the U-2 incident. For example, it explained the troika proposal as a transparent attempt to block a CTB and a reaction against the "counter-revolutionary" role in the Congo Crisis that the Soviets attributed to Dag Hammarskjöld, the U.N. secretary general. Soviet internal politics, however, played a role that was not well understood in the West. Because Khrushchev was weaker after the U-2 incident, the easiest way to justify negotiations was to promise hardliners that he could coerce the West into major concessions. In January 1961, Soviet diplomats hinted that without a major arms control success, Khrushchev might be replaced by Kozlov.[12] Khrushchev may have also been given an ultimatum in February 1961 to resume testing in six months unless he got a breakthrough on Berlin.[13] The new U.S. administration, however, had just begun its test ban review and was not ready to make policy changes that might have mollified Khrushchev's critics. Instead, Kennedy's early actions strengthened orthodox arguments against accommodation with the West. For example, one Soviet commentator wrote that in the Bay of Pigs invasion, the Kennedy administration "threw off its mask of peacemaker for everyone to see."[14]

On April 18 (the day after the Bay of Pigs invasion), the United States and the U.K. formally tabled the first complete draft of a phased test ban treaty.[15] It contained concessions on secondary issues that might please the USSR without sparking too much domestic opposition. For example, the United States offered to use obsolete nuclear devices for seismological research so that the Soviets could inspect them without learning about current weapons designs. The West was prepared to ban high-altitude and outer space tests using TWG I's verification proposals. They also offered a three-year extendable moratorium on underground tests below m_b 4.75.

On the core questions, movement was minor. Kennedy would not lower U.S. inspection demands because "the number 20 had become a political fact of life and was almost sacrosanct to some members of Congress."[16] Thus, the draft contained a sliding scale formula that would still produce 20 OSIs if Western estimates of annual earthquakes were correct. Few concessions were made to Soviet demands for greater control over verification processes. The United States ridiculed the administrative troika with a Soviet veto but finally agreed to give Eastern and Western states equal representation on the Control Commission. The United States also said that the Soviets could veto the entire verification budget but not funds for OSIs or any other individual item.

Given the level of suspicion that characterized superpower relations, these minor concessions did not increase Soviet confidence in verification. Tsarapkin denounced the draft treaty as "the death knell of our Conference." He impugned the intent behind various provisions, such as using nuclear experiments to study evasion techniques (e.g., decoupling). He denounced the single administrator as a way for the West to use the verification organization for its own objectives. He denounced the possibility of "impartial" verification, stating that "every person must needs display sympathy for some particular country or some particular system. There is no person who would be completely impartial and neutral towards both the social and economic systems that now exist in this world."[17]

Khrushchev took another step backward at the Vienna Summit in June by declaring that a CTB would only be valuable as part of a GCD package. Soviet Unilateralists had always favored this all-or-nothing position. It now appealed to Cautious Cooperators in the USSR because it meant that test ban inspections would not occur until some future time when the level of tension had diminished. Americans dismissed suggestions that the U-2 incident, or anything else they had done, might have given the Soviets legitimate cause for concern about collateral information collection. Instead, Western policy makers blamed the closed, repressive nature of communism. For example, Western diplomats frequently explained Soviet resistance to OSIs with the "pair of shoes" theory—that is, communist leaders' fear that seeing well-made shoes on foreign personnel would give poor citizens subversive ideas.[18] Yet U-2 overflights had simultaneously shown that the Americans could penetrate Soviet air defenses and that any missile gap favored the United States. Thus, Soviet resistance to test ban inspections also reflected a fear that the West would learn about their weakness and vulnerability, as well as a desire to delay a test ban until the USSR was stronger.[19]

The Myth of the "Broken Moratorium"

Coercive diplomacy continued during the summer of 1961 in ways that worsened both short- and long-term prospects for agreement on verification. Khrushchev increased his defense budget by a third, postponed his unilateral troop cuts, and built the Berlin Wall. Kennedy responded by raising defense spending, mobilizing reserve forces, tripling the draft, and sending an army battle group to Berlin. Rumors in the USSR about secret American test preparations increased pressure on Khrushchev to end the moratorium.[20] In late July 1961, Khrushchev told John McCloy (Kennedy's disarmament adviser before ACDA was founded) that his scientists and military leaders wanted to test a 100-mt bomb but that he had told them to be patient and let the Americans test first. Ironically, because U.S. weapons designers were not interested in such huge bombs, these warnings were dismissed as more of Khrushchev's blustering with little basis in fact.[21]

Kennedy was also under tremendous pressure to test again, not only from Unilateralists but also from Cautious Cooperators, who were scared by Khrushchev's belligerence and skeptical of his arms control intentions. A PSAC panel reviewed justifications for test resumption and found neither solid evidence of secret Soviet explosions nor urgent technical reasons to test soon.[22] Nevertheless, Kennedy was convinced that the question was when, not if, he should announce new tests. DOD and the AEC had already prepared plans and tunnels at the NTS but needed three to six months for final arrangements.

The president preferred not to announce a new test series before the U.N. General Assembly (UNGA) met in the fall, so he adopted a two-track approach and quietly proceeded with test preparations while pressuring Khrushchev to prove that he was not doing likewise. Ambassador Dean invited the Soviets to tour NTS and assess the extent of American preparations—if the Soviets let the United States do the same.[23] This offer was purely symbolic and strategic, since the Soviets had never agreed to permit inspections before a treaty was signed. Kennedy himself was torn between depicting the United States as an open society where arms control violations would be quickly reported and hiding his preparations to test again in a few months' time.[24] The AEC had let reporters and photographers enter NTS to document U.S. compliance with the moratorium, but after visitors publicized the new test tunnels, Kennedy excluded the media from NTS, saying that "negotiations were in a sensitive stage."

To lay the political groundwork for renewed testing, Kennedy told Dean to make an offer that would be seen as a "decisive test of Russian intentions."[25] On August 28, the United States proposed to lower or abandon the m_b 4.75 threshold if the Soviets accepted more monitoring stations or OSIs. Far from a major concession, this simply restated past offers. As expected, Tsarapkin replied that international test ban verification must wait for comprehensive disarmament. With this evidence of Soviet intransigence in hand, Kennedy prepared to "make the appropriate decisions."[26]

When Radio Moscow declared two days later that the USSR would resume testing, U.S. policy makers took advantage of the "God-given" propaganda opportunity to blame the Soviets for something that the United States was preparing to do anyway. The White House immediately denounced the decision as "atomic blackmail, designed to substitute terror for reason."[27] Kennedy and Macmillan then resurrected Gore's idea of an immediate ban on atmospheric tests monitored solely by NTM. This was the first time that the United States had proposed a test ban agreement without international verification, but it was done as a tactical shift to embarrass the Soviets.[28] Ironically, this hurt the United States more than the USSR, because it acknowledged that the West had been demanding more verification than it really needed for partial limits but failed to convince the world that the Soviets alone were to blame for test resumption.[29] After two more Soviet blasts, Kennedy announced that the United States would resume underground testing. On September 9, Khrushchev formally rejected the atmospheric ban because stopping only one type of test "would be a disservice to the cause of peace."[30]

U.S. attempts to get maximum propaganda mileage out of Soviet test resumption killed domestic support for a phased CTB by convincing Cautious Cooperators that the West must not accept another "unpoliced" moratorium, because the Soviets would break it and catch the United States unprepared. The actual situation was much more ambiguous. When the West's unilaterally declared moratorium expired in December 1959, Eisenhower had stated that the United States would "consider itself free to resume nuclear testing" but would announce its plans in advance. The official Soviet response had been that the USSR would refrain from testing as long as the Western powers showed restraint. The Soviets claimed that French nuclear testing had released them from this obligation. It remains unclear, however, how much responsibility Khrushchev had for the decision to test first; sometimes he depicted it as his choice to promote agreement on Berlin and a CTB, but other indicators suggest that the final decision was made by orthodox elites while Khrushchev was on vacation.[31] Americans knew little about the struggle in the USSR between reformist and orthodox leaders; the CIA said that it saw no evidence of a division among Soviet elites about test resumption.[32] Nor did they understand how American attempts to keep its nuclear options open may have increased Soviet incentives to prepare for new tests. Regardless of whether the real story involved miscommunication, involuntary defection, a preemptive spiral, or outright exploitation, the "broken moratorium" became a potent weapon in the politics of verification.

The episode had the potential to stretch the scope of CTB verification beyond anything that either side would ever accept. Since few Americans knew about the "zero-yield" nuclear experiments and the U.S. test preparations during the moratorium, Unilateralists could persuade Cautious Cooperators that an open society like the United States would be at a gross disadvantage unless a CTB verification regime included ways to detect clandestine test preparations. National monitoring methods had not picked up hard evidence of Soviet test resumption plans until a few hours before the Radio Moscow announcement.[33] This new verification requirement might require "any time, any where" OSIs or a constant international presence at any potential test site.

For the rest of fall 1961, the politics of verification involved strategic maneuvering but no substantive progress. When the Soviets detonated a 57-mt explosion on October 30, Kennedy authorized preparations for atmospheric test in the spring.[34] After the Soviets finished their test series, they invited the West to sign an immediate ban on tests in the atmosphere, underwater, and in outer space that would be monitored by NTM. Tsarapkin pointed out that the West's atmospheric test ban offer in September had acknowledged that international verification was not needed for partial test limits. The United States and the U.K., however, were much less interested in such a treaty now than when they wanted to avert Soviet tests and expected the USSR to reject the offer. The Soviet proposal also had other unacceptable features, including a moratorium on underground tests while arrangements were made for international verification as a constituent part of a GCD agreement—that is, an indefinite, inspectionless moratorium. By January 1962, the two sides were so far apart that they could not even agree on a final communiqué when the Geneva Conference adjourned permanently.[35]

The Eighteen-Nation Disarmament Committee Fans the Embers

Test ban talks shifted to a different venue, where the pressure of world opinion kept negotiations going. The U.N.'s new Eighteen-Nation Disarmament Committee (ENDC) included the five Western and five Eastern states in the old Ten-Nation Disarmament Committee, plus eight new nonaligned members.[36] Moving from trilateral talks on separate test limits to a multilateral committee dealing with both a test ban and GCD had mixed implications for the politics of verification. It pleased those who believed that test restrictions or intrusive OSIs made sense only in a disarmed world and that negotiations were solely for public relations purposes. At the same time, it gave more countries a direct stake in test ban negotiations. This motivated them to learn about verification and think creatively about dilemmas that some groups in the United States and the USSR thought could not—or should not—be solved. The eight nonaligned members also emphasized a more fully international approach to test ban verification, a move that may have helped the superpowers recognize a shared interest in keeping control over verification in their own hands.

The Superpowers Jockey for Position

Shortly before the ENDC convened in mid-March 1962, Kennedy announced that the United States would begin atmospheric testing unless the Soviets accepted the Western CTB proposal by the end of April. This announcement reflected domestic and alliance bargaining more than a realistic hope of changing Soviet behavior. Americans were conflicted about conducting more atmospheric tests. The dividing concern was not fallout: the experts were more in accord now on scientific questions, while the public was better educated and less worried than in the mid-1950s.[37] Rather, the split was between those who favored unrestrained nuclear development and those who thought that atmospheric tests offered few benefits for the tension and criticism that they brought. Kennedy and Macmillan were firmly in the latter camp. At a meeting in Bermuda in December 1961, they expressed regret that the "Big Hole" scenario and American in-flexibility on OSIs had blocked a CTB in the 1950s.[38] Ironically, the head of ACDA gave the deciding argument for atmospheric testing: it would be easier to negotiate and ratify a CTB after the United States matched the Soviets' atmo-spheric test series.[39] Combining a "peace through strength" rationale for atmo-spheric tests with an offer to cooperate (on the West's terms) satisfied both fac-tions in the U.S. government, mollified Macmillan (who had pled for restraint), and convinced ambivalent Americans to support the president's decision.[40]

Since the United States had shown no flexibility on test ban verification, the arms control offer was only a propaganda ploy as far as the Soviets were con-cerned. Moreover, the tough talk about testing coincided with a *Saturday Evening Post* article that quoted Kennedy as saying that the United States might take the initiative in a nuclear conflict.[41] This article received much Soviet attention as evidence for orthodox claims that Western leaders were inherently aggressive.[42] When ENDC negotiations opened, therefore, the USSR insisted that a CTB should be monitored by remote means only, a position they had taken when all tests were conducted above ground but dropped by the Conference of Experts. Khrushchev claimed that he had "trapped" the United States into disproving the need for in-country monitoring and OSIs because the West had detected the Soviets' first underground test in February.[43] This 40- to 50-kt test, however, was well above the threshold where American doubts about NTM began.

The Kennedy administration wished neither to be totally unconstructive in the new negotiating forum nor to reward increasingly outrageous Soviet de-mands. Thus, most of the changes in the U.S. stance on verification were meant to reassure anxious Americans, not to address Soviet concerns. The United States offered to eliminate the threshold on underground tests, thus making the ban truly comprehensive, because it would not consider another uninspected mora-torium on low-yield tests and wanted to inspect suspicious events below the threshold. The one concession to Soviet sensitivities was a new sublimit on OSIs in areas with little seismic activity that would restrict most OSIs to peripheral parts of the USSR. The other two modifications—periodic inspections to verify the absence of preparations at declared test sites and provisions to ensure that OSIs could start soon after the treaty entered into force—addressed U.S. con-cerns in ways that increased Soviet opposition.

After one week of ENDC negotiations, the superpowers seemed as far apart on verification as they had been in the early 1950s. Western requirements were expanding again, and the Soviets had resumed alleging that the West wanted inspections only "for choosing the moment to attack the Soviet Union."[44] Test ban supporters deplored the deadlock, but since nobody expected that verification concessions would be reciprocated, they had little incentive to fight major domestic battles over minor policy changes.

Nonaligned States Make Modest Contributions

The eight nonaligned members of the ENDC tried to bring a fresh perspective to verification. They had to rely heavily on briefings by Wiesner and other American scientists, because few nonaligned countries had independent experience with nuclear research or test monitoring.[45] They saw themselves as neutral "referees" needed because the testers' "discoveries are beginning to frighten them. The immense investments required are all out of proportion to (the benefits). ... Our group knows that both East and West realize this, but each isn't sure that the other does."[46]

The nonaligned members presented a memorandum that sketched new ideas to facilitate agreement if the two sides were genuine Cautious Cooperators. The Eight Nation Memorandum suggested that test ban monitoring could be done "on a purely scientific and non-political basis" by collaborating with organizations, such as the World Meteorological Association and the IAEA.[47] A network of internationally supervised but nationally owned and operated stations would lower the cost and intrusiveness of the Geneva System. More important, as the ALC argued in 1946, the best scientists would also be more willing to participate if verification were combined with creative research than if it were pure police work.[48]

The Eight suggested a much larger verification decision-making role for nonaligned states than either superpower had ever envisioned. The memorandum proposed an international commission of highly qualified scientists who would process data from the verification network and identify nuclear explosions or suspicious events. Parties to the treaty "should accept the obligation" to provide the commission information and "could invite" the commission for a fact-finding visit. If the commission could not decide whether a test had occurred, it would consult with the state in question to determine what measures— "including verification *in loco*"—would facilitate assessment. The commission would inform all treaty signatories of the circumstances and its assessment, leaving them "free to determine their action with regard to the treaty on the basis of reports furnished by the International Commission."

The proposal was deliberately vague on key questions, such as whether OSIs were voluntary or obligatory. The Eight insisted that the nuclear weapons states must decide how the general proposals should work in practice. The memorandum's ambiguous language encompassed conflicting points of view and protected the Eight's neutrality on controversial questions. It also reflected splits inside the group. For example, since the Eight had relied heavily on U.S. scientists, they understood the limits of NTM but disagreed over the solution. Sweden questioned whether the value added by OSIs was worth the problems they caused in negotiations. India did not want a precedent for obligatory OSIs, partly from sympathy with the USSR but also from India's concerns about implications for the IAEA safeguard systems and its national nuclear program.

When the NWS met to discuss the Eight Nation Memorandum, each interpreted ambiguous points according to its own preferences, so "the schism grew in the fashion of medieval theological controversies."[49] For example, Zorin announced that the USSR would henceforth allow OSIs on a voluntary basis. The Eight saw this as a major concession, but the United States and the U.K. doubted that the USSR would ever invite foreigners to the site of a violation.[50]

Since nonaligned states were keenly aware of the political controversies connected with test ban verification, why did they emphasize "objective" criteria and "scientific" solutions for verification problems? This language may have reflected assumptions about verification absorbed during briefings by American scientists, as well as the general optimism in the early 1960s about a functional approach to international cooperation. Moreover, "impartiality" was the nonaligned states' main asset, because they were not testing nuclear weapons and could contribute little money and expertise for verification. "Objectivity" was an important watchword during debates over IAEA safeguards, because countries like India wanted to avoid being singled out for extra scrutiny. The hope that verification could be done on a purely scientific and nonpolitical basis probably also reflected an idealistic desire to escape from power politics to a world in which verification decisions were based on shared principles.

The 1962 Draft Treaties: Mixed Messages to Multiple Audiences

The Kennedy administration wanted to respond to the Eight's suggestions without being criticized at home for conceding too much to weak countries. It tried the familiar strategy of suggesting a technical meeting to discuss verification ideas in the Eight Nation proposal. Tsarapkin refused, claiming that American experts always represented agencies that opposed a CTB. He compared the proposal for another technical working group to "a demand that research into the effect of tobacco smoking in the origin of cancer of the lungs should be handed over to tobacco companies."[51]

When the United States and the U.K. tabled two treaty drafts in late August

1962, they emphasized the new aspects in international forums and stressed continuity with prior positions in domestic debates. Since both audiences had access to both sets of communication, this increased confusion on substantive questions and cynicism about the strategic use of verification arguments.

The first draft treaty banned nuclear tests in the atmosphere, under water, and in outer space, based solely on NTM. Several of the Eight had advocated such a proto-LTBT, but this was the first time that the United States and the U.K. had offered to ban tests in environments where they had doubts about the efficacy of NTM. The United States would not have Vela satellites that could monitor tests above 50 km for another year and had decided not to develop its own hydrophone system because the risk of underwater testing was too low to justify the expense. Thus, this proposal was an important change from the principle that the United States should only ban types of tests that could be monitored with high confidence, even though it simply expanded the proposal for an atmospheric ban to other environments where testing was unlikely.

The second draft was a CTB with a network of nationally owned stations and a quota of obligatory OSIs. On the surface, this draft sounded similar to past proposals, but the Kennedy administration had changed both the amount and type of verification. It was eager to avoid more atmospheric testing and confident that low-level cheating would not destabilize deterrence so long as the United States had an assured retaliatory capability.[52] Moreover, Vela had finally produced firm evidence that underground test verification was easier than the Conference of Experts had concluded and much less demanding than the United States had claimed on the basis of "new data" from the 1958 test series.[53] Finally, Dean had increased pressure on the Kennedy administration to make a new proposal by telling reporters that the United States had information that would support a reduction in Western OSI demands.[54]

The 1962 CTB draft was less intrusive but more international than the earlier Western versions.[55] The main decision-making body was the International Scientific Commission, composed of diplomats and scientists from four Western, four Eastern, and seven neutral states. The verification system would be smaller than the Geneva System.[56] Most stations would be nationally operated and internationally supervised, unless a poor country in a prime monitoring location could not maintain its own station. An unspecified number of obligatory OSIs would occur in the USSR each year, and the United States and the U.K. would decide which events to inspect. Inspection teams could be staffed by nationals from any country except the one being inspected and could have only neutrals if the commission's executive wished.

The treaty called for a single administrator who would be subordinate to the International Scientific Commission. The administrative staff would analyze data and prepare reports, but any signatory could request data and reach its own conclusions. There were no provisions to detect test preparations because the United States hoped that being ready to test on short notice would deter treaty breakout. Finally, the withdrawal procedure made it harder to use a vague dissatisfaction with verification as a justification. The only verification-related reason for withdrawal would be if a signatory failed to fulfill its obligations, including those related to on-site inspections, and this jeopardized another state's national security. If so, the latter could legally withdraw after presenting its case before a conference of signatories.

The 1962 draft CTB used ambiguity about the number of OSIs and monitoring stations to juggle international pressure for lower numbers and domestic demands for higher ones. Research by ACDA suggested that 25 nationally owned stations in the USSR and a reduced number of OSIs would provide the same detection capabilities originally attributed to the Geneva System's 180 international stations.[57] Foster believed that the United States would be safer with such a treaty than without, but he recommended against proposing specific numbers because ACDA had not yet found a position that it could defend against "both the neutrals who want it lower and the congressional critics who would say it is too low already." Foster saw no reason for the United States to reduce its demands as long as the Soviets opposed all obligatory OSIs. He also feared that "domestic opinion, particularly Congressional opinion, is not prepared for such a move," because the lower numbers reflected Vela data that had been available outside of DOD for less than a month. Therefore, he called for a "major campaign of domestic information and political preparation . . . as to the new data and its significance."

Test ban skeptics in the United States tolerated the shift to nationally operated monitoring stations and the vague hints about lower numbers because they expected Soviet rejection. Most members of the JCAE discounted the new proposals as a harmless "gesture to the neutralist bloc" and a safe way to "put the Soviet Union on the spot" as it prepared to renew atmospheric testing. But Representative Craig Hosmer, the ranking Republican on the JCAE, accused the Kennedy administration of "caving in and surrendering to Soviet demands for a one-sided treaty upon which it could cheat and gain overwhelming surprise nuclear weapons superiority while the United States and other free world nations basked in a false feeling of security."[58]

As predicted, the Soviets ridiculed the 1962 draft CTB as an "ugly old maid, whom the despairing parents every year deck out in a more fashionable dress."[59] Alongside the belligerent rhetoric, however, they offered to accept the proto-LTBT if the West added a moratorium on underground tests "while continuing negotiations on the final prohibitions of such explosions," without insisting that CTB verification occur in the context of GCD. Although the West had no interest in an uninspected moratorium, this change was significant, because Khrushchev had once called Western linkage demands the most "reliable means of frustrating" CTB negotiations.[60] Since the Soviets were secretly preparing to send nuclear missiles to Cuba, it is not clear whether the shift showed that they had already decided to be more flexible on arms control, or whether it stemmed from a compromise between reform and orthodox factions or reflected a calculated carrot-and-stick strategy.

The Cuban Missile Crisis Exacerbates Arguments over CTB Verification

Many analysts see the Cuban Missile Crisis as a turning point in the test ban negotiations. Yet it did not fundamentally alter the structure of verification arguments. After cooperating to avert nuclear catastrophe, Kennedy and Khrushchev were more willing to make verification concessions for a CTB, but both were constrained by domestic groups that had drawn different conclusions from the crisis. Because neither fully understood the other's domestic situation, they misread the mixed signals they received and responded in ways that further reduced the prospects for agreement on CTB verification.

Competing Responses to the Crisis

Different groups in the United States drew conflicting lessons from the Cuban Missile Crisis, just as they had from other episodes that underscored nuclear vulnerability. Kennedy was frightened by the extent of misperception on both sides and attributed the successful outcome not to nuclear brinksmanship but to a combination of diplomacy and contextual features (local U.S. conventional superiority, no direct impact on Soviet national security, and no "just cause" that the Soviets could plausibly plead before world opinion).[61] The episode strengthened Arms Control Advocates' fear that uncontrolled horizontal and vertical proliferation would cause deterrence failure due to miscommunication, command and control problems, or inadvertent escalation. Unilateralists drew the opposite conclusion: U.S. nuclear superiority stopped aggression this time and would always be the best guarantee of American safety.[62] They opposed any test restrictions that kept the United States from developing its nuclear arsenal as it saw fit, especially if imperfect verification let the Soviets match or surpass current U.S. capabilities. The Soviets' decision to sneak missiles into Cuba and lie about their intentions had increased Cautious Cooperators' mistrust and verification requirements.[63] But the peaceful outcome of the crisis helped Kennedy convince them to support low-risk arms control by enhancing his domestic standing on security issues, demonstrating that the superpowers could cooperate for mutual gain, and setting a precedent for agreement on U.N. aerial inspection to verify that the missiles had left Cuba.

Likewise, Soviet perceptions did not change, because elites interpreted the event according to their existing worldviews.[64] The successful resolution to the crisis reinforced Soviet reformers' confidence in Khrushchev and their belief that Kennedy would cooperate to reduce the risk of nuclear catastrophe and the cost of competitive security. Orthodox elites, by contrast, thought the gambit had failed because Khrushchev lacked the courage and the nuclear capability needed to face down the West. As Vasily Kuznetsov, the deputy foreign minister who negotiated the missiles' withdrawal, later explained, hardliners vowed that "the Soviet Union will never again face a 4-to-1 missile inferiority."[65] Chinese communists were harshly critical of both Khrushchev's "adventurism" and his "capitulationism." Even though the episode weakened Khrushchev domestically, it convinced him that using coercive strategies to push for arms control on terms that reformer and orthodox elites could both accept was ineffective and unacceptably risky.[66] Therefore, he used the brief "policy window" that opened after the crisis to argue for a more genuinely cooperative approach, but he had little room to maneuver or time to waste convincing domestic critics that the West would reciprocate rather than exploit Soviet concessions.[67]

Verification Overtures Are Out of Sync

In letters exchanged during the crisis, Kennedy and Khrushchev expressed their desire to conclude a CTB soon. This intention was reinforced by General Assembly resolutions calling for an end to nuclear tests by January 1, 1963; an urgent effort to negotiate a CTB; an atmospheric ban if a CTB remained out of reach; and a progress report by December 10, 1962. ACDA was still reviewing U.S. policy in light of the new Vela data but lacked interagency agreement on a new position. Consequently, Khrushchev's overtures on CTB verification received no rapid reciprocation from the United States.

At the next ENDC meetings, the Soviets offered to put unmanned seismic stations in areas with frequent earthquakes. When the Berkner panel first proposed the "black box" idea in 1959, the Soviets had refused because foreign personnel might spy while installing or servicing the stations. The concept was raised again by Soviet scientists at a Pugwash meeting shortly before the Cuban Missile Crisis. December 10, 1962, the day the test ban progress report was due, Tsarapkin announced that the USSR would accept two or three black boxes instead of OSIs and international stations. This was the first time in a year that the Soviets had offered to let foreigners in the USSR for routine verification activities. The West welcomed the move but wanted more stations (eight to ten) as a supplement to—not a replacement for—other monitoring methods.

A few days later, Khrushchev revived the possibility of two or three OSIs each year.[68] Instead of conceding the inadequacy of NTM, though, he referred to U.S. claims that the Senate would not ratify a CTB without any inspections. Miscommunications during an official conversation between Dean and Kuznetsov and an informal meeting between Wiesner and Federov had convinced Khrushchev that an annual quota of two to four OSIs in seismic areas of the USSR would meet this political requirement. Dean insisted that he had never mentioned any numbers below the official U.S. position of eight to ten OSIs. But he had a reputation for being vague, and Warren Heckrotte recalls that "most of us on the Geneva delegation felt that, irrespective of what Dean thought he said, Kuznetsov's report was a correct appraisal of what he thought he had been told."[69] Wiesner remembers suggesting that if Khrushchev revived his offer for three or four OSIs per year, the United States might counter with a quota of seven or eight OSIs and compromise on some number like five.[70]

Kennedy was not aware of these misunderstandings or the domestic opposition that Khrushchev had braved to revive the OSI offer. The president unintentionally confirmed orthodox suspicions that the West would pocket the concession and push for more by replying that he was pleased the Soviets could once again "accept the principle of onsite inspection" but that they should come up to the U.S. position, since the United States had already dropped down from twenty OSIs per year.[71] Since Khrushchev had promised the Council of Ministers that he could get a CTB for three inspections, he was extremely embarrassed. He later told Norman Cousins, editor of the *Saturday Review,* "Once again I was made to look foolish. But I can tell you this: it won't happen again."[72]

The Soviets agreed to private trilateral test ban talks in January only to see whether the West would accept their terms.[73] These talks collapsed quickly because the West would not lower its numbers unless it knew that the OSIs and black boxes would work effectively, and the Soviets would not discuss procedural or technical details until the West endorsed their numbers. In an early version of managed access inspections, the United States and the U.K. offered to balance concerns about cheating and spying by letting host countries exclude some sensitive installations and provide logistical support for OSI teams. The Soviet refusal to discuss how such inspections might work confirmed Dean's belief that Soviet officials still thought that "the only good inspection is a Soviet inspection."[74] The Soviets did agree to exchange data from national in-country seismic stations, thereby tacitly acknowledging that NTM was insufficient for a comprehensive ban. But the United States was so frustrated by Soviet intransigence on other issues that Kennedy authorized a new round of underground tests, even though the Soviets were still respecting UNGA's cut-off date for testing.

Proposed Compromise on "Reciprocal" Verification Adds New Complications

Soon after test ban negotiations resumed in the ENDC, the United States was ready to present its new verification approach. The basic idea was that reciprocal inspections would be faster and more reliable than OSIs conducted by an international agency, so fewer would be needed to deter noncompliance. This moved the superpowers closer on number of OSIs but apart on decision-making authority. It had the opposite effect on CTB critics in Congress.

The idea of purely reciprocal OSIs grew out of an ACDA-sponsored study group influenced by game-theoretic ideas about verification.[75] During the early 1960s, several books that became the classics of Cold War arms control theory had popularized the goal of enhancing deterrence stability and the standard of "adequate" verification as proportionate to the amount of risk and redundancy built into the system.[76] The study group formalized the idea that the main objectives of verification were to deter militarily significant violations, to detect noncompliance so that the United States could make a timely and appropriate response, and to build confidence by establishing a history of compliance. Trying to use verification for other purposes or insisting on inspections when other sources of compliance information were available, the study group warned, could hurt U.S. security by decreasing the chance of agreement on mutually beneficial arms control.[77] Since perfect verification was impossible, military and political leaders must decide how much and what type of verification they needed for formal and informal arms control. The study group argued that the United States could settle for less stringent verification if it planned to address violations unilaterally rather than mobilize an international response. Having adversaries verify each other's compliance avoided drawbacks that the United States now saw with international verification agencies, such as the difficulty of negotiating and funding them, concerns about the staff's competence and impartiality, and the fear that "neutral" agents would downplay compliance problems or act as "mediators rather than judges." The report added, however, that including some international personnel might give host countries more confidence in the verification arrangements and make the findings more useful as a basis for international action.

Foster was finally ready to push for a quota of six reciprocal OSIs.[78] ACDA proposed various techniques to reduce the annual number of ambiguous seismic events in the USSR to 25–30. Six OSIs would let the United States inspect 20 percent of the suspicious events—the same detection probability that the Eisenhower administration thought could deter cheating in a phased CTB.

The response to ACDA's proposal shows that the Kennedy administration was more divided than ever after Khrushchev's "take it or leave it" stand on black boxes and OSIs. Rusk and McNamara were willing to accept six OSIs if the Soviets agreed to reciprocal verification. Wiesner thought that five OSIs would suffice from a scientific standpoint, but he felt that the OSI number had obtained a kind of political "magic" in Congress, so that seven or eight might be necessary for ratification.[79] Maxwell Taylor (now chairman of the JCS), John McCone (the former AEC director who now headed the CIA), and Paul Nitze (assistant secretary of defense) opposed the plan. Kennedy finally resolved the dispute by authorizing Foster to offer seven reciprocal OSIs, with six as a "rock bottom" fallback number. He justified this decision in an Arms Control Advocate's terms by suggesting that any gains the Soviets might achieve through clandestine testing would be outweighed by the nonproliferation benefits of CTB.

The shift to reciprocal inspections was meant to ease the politics of verification, but it created new complications. The plan that Foster presented informally to Kuznetsov in mid-February 1963 let the United States and the U.K. choose events for inspection and prepare the final report.[80] They would also provide the OSI team leader and fourteen out of twenty staff members. (The rest would be chosen by the International Commission and could not be Soviet allies.) The USSR could observe OSIs and take some precautions, such as exempting certain facilities and flying inspectors to the suspect site in Soviet planes with covered windows. Despite these compromises, the USSR refused to raise its OSI number or discuss procedural details. These OSIs still seemed intolerably intrusive, even if they occurred infrequently.[81] Moreover, shifting to bilateral inspections meant that the key elements of verification would be controlled completely by hostile countries.[82] The International Commission would have neither the power nor the authority to act as a court of appeals if OSIs were abused or accusations disputed. The reciprocal approach also posed other problems. Since the United States and the U.K. had responded to the Eight Nation Memorandum by increasing the role for the International Scientific Commission, this reversal probably angered nonaligned members of the ENDC. It was also unclear how, if at all, this bilateral concept could be extended to France, China, and other states whose participation would be needed to fulfill nonproliferation objectives.

The new approach to verification had equally problematic effects in Congress. The idea of reciprocal verification was popular because many congressmen did not want to transfer any control over verification from the United States to an international organization.[83] But many congressmen thought that the United States should be increasing, not decreasing, its demands after the Cuban Missile Crisis. In January 1963, Hosmer and other influential Republicans panicked when they thought that Kennedy might accept Khrushchev's offer for a CTB with three OSIs and three black boxes, but no other international verification. They established a Republican Conference Committee on Nuclear Testing, which urged Kennedy to revert to the 1958 U.S. position on verification (twenty OSIs and nineteen internationally staffed monitoring stations on Soviet soil). In February, leading Democratic defense experts, such as Senators Dodd and Henry Jackson, declared that they could no longer support the 1962 draft treaty and that the United States should return to its "original Geneva formula."[84] The same month, twenty Senate conservatives sponsored a resolution urging the president to insist on "complete, on-the-spot" inspections of the USSR by teams that included members of Congress.[85] In early March, the JCAE heard testimony that the proposed U.S. system would not detect fully coupled explosions below 1 kt in granite and 20 kt in alluvium.[86]

CTB supporters in the Kennedy administration tried to defend the new plan by talking about other sources of verification information, arguing that a few reciprocal inspections could deter violations more effectively than a larger number of international ones and comparing the risk of one small undetected test with the dangers of horizontal and verification proliferation. This domestic criticism, combined with the lack of a favorable response from the USSR, probably explains why the United States never formally presented its draft treaty for a CTB with a network of national stations and seven reciprocal OSIs.

By the end of March, test ban negotiations were deadlocked again. The U.K. still hoped for progress, but the United States and the USSR actively discouraged nonaligned states from submitting a proposal in which each side would get a multiyear quota averaging four or five annual inspections.[87] Since CTB talks were going nowhere, the Kennedy administration considered a new atmospheric test series. This time, even Rusk (who had previously opposed atmospheric test resumption) supported test preparations in hopes that they might "do more to spur on the test ban negotiations than would any indication of concern about Soviet complaints."[88] As the Soviet ambassador later told Seaborg, however, signs that the West was planning another round of tests increased pressure on Khrushchev to do likewise.[89]

Convergence on the Limited Test Ban Treaty

What happened next is often seen as a textbook example of how a string of re-ciprocated initiatives can break a deadlock and produce a major cooperative accord.[90] Eager to end the CTB stalemate and avoid another round of atmo-spheric testing, Kennedy gave an impassioned speech at American University on June 10, 1963. He urged a fundamental reexamination of Cold War assumptions about arms and arms control, pledged to forego further atmospheric tests if the Soviets reciprocated, and announced that the United States and the U.K. would send senior officials to Moscow for high-level test ban talks. On July 2, Khrushchev offered to avoid arguments over OSIs by dropping his demand that a partial test ban include a moratorium on underground tests. The LTBT was initialed just ten days after the U.S. delegation went to Moscow, and it received overwhelming Senate support two months later.

Examining the politics of verification raises difficult questions, however. Since Kennedy, Khrushchev, and Macmillan all preferred a CTB to an LTBT, why did they not use the positive momentum to make one last try for agreement on CTB verification? Why did Khrushchev respond to Kennedy's friendly overtures by retracting his offer for an OSI quota, stating that the USSR would "never open its doors to NATO spies," and declaring that CTB inspections were "not a sub-ject for bargaining"?[91] Why did the partial ban neither include large under-ground tests that could have been monitored with NTM nor mention verifica-tion? Why did Kennedy feel compelled to adopt a ratification strategy, including a set of unilateral safeguards, that hurt his chances for extending the LTBT into a total ban during a second term in office?[92] The answers show how the "peace through strength" coalition-building strategies used throughout the Kennedy administration led to new verification roadblocks instead of ending the CTB deadlock.

A Partial Ban Avoids Verification Arguments

The Soviet decision to accept an independent LTBT stemmed from complicated interconnections among domestic debates, Sino-Soviet arguments, and East-West relations. The Soviets started calling for peaceful coexistence again in April after Chinese pressure for an ideological confrontation convinced even Orthodox elites like Suslov to stress the dangers of nuclear war and the need to reduce international tensions.[93] This group had never been interested in a total test ban and probably let Khrushchev revive the three-OSI offer in late 1962 only because they expected the West to reject it. More serious interest in an LTBT coupled with renewed resistance to OSIs in the July 2 speech suited their desire to avoid a CTB while still contrasting "peaceful" Soviet policies with "dangerous" Chinese militancy.

The mixed signals from Khrushchev about test ban verification suggest that he was not committed to this course of action until early July. Shortly after Kozlov had a heart attack in mid-April, Khrushchev asked Cousins to "tell the President I accept his explanation of an honest misunderstanding (about OSI quotas) and suggest we get moving. But the next move is up to him."[94] When Kennedy and Macmillan wrote Khrushchev about reviving CTB negotiations, his replies combined rude language with subtle signs of interest. For example, in response to the April 24 invitation to discuss CTB verification in the ENDC or in Moscow, the premier chose the latter, more serious option. Moreover, when Seaborg visited the USSR to discuss peaceful nuclear cooperation, Leonid Brezhnev (one of Khrushchev's few allies after the Cuban Missile Crisis) reassured him that Khrushchev's calls for peaceful coexistence were "not propaganda."[95]

On the day of the American University speech, Khrushchev told the leader of the British Labour Party that he might withdraw his offer for three OSIs, but the United States dismissed this as an attempt to "sell the same horse twice"—to extract new concessions for restoring a previous offer. As of June 14, the State Department still saw "no insuperable obstacle to Khrushchev's negotiating a test-ban agreement or a key element of one—the number of on-site inspections, if he chose to do so."[96] U.S. optimism increased further after the Soviets signed the Hot Line Agreement to enhance crisis communication and reversed their opposition to IAEA safeguards, including inspections in non-nuclear weapons states. Even after the July 2 speech, many Westerners hoped that talk about "NATO spies" was empty rhetoric meant to placate domestic hardliners and Chinese militants.

The U.S. delegation, led by Averell Harriman, was instructed to seek agreement on the 1962 draft CTB. An ACDA briefing paper maintained that the OSI disagreement "relates to what is solely a scientific question"—whether seismic signals alone could be used to distinguish between earthquakes and tests below 20 kt.[97] ACDA hoped that the high-level meeting would provide an opportunity "to point out to the Soviet political leaders the full political significance of the scientific facts." It recommended ways to acknowledge Soviet concerns, such as putting a sublimit on OSIs in aseismic areas and letting states "bank" unused OSIs, to avoid fostering a use-them-or-lose-them mentality. But at the first meeting, Khrushchev ruled out talk about CTB verification. When Harriman remonstrated that the West would not use OSIs to spy on the USSR, the premier retorted, "You're trying to tell me that if there's a piece of cheese in the room and a mouse comes into the room that the mouse won't go and take the cheese."[98]

American actions may have inadvertently contributed to Khrushchev's final repudiation of all OSIs. While Kennedy was making arms control overtures, he and other CTB supporters were also sending conflicting messages. From the Soviet standpoint, Kennedy's proposal for a mutual moratorium on atmospheric testing was hardly a major concession. The USSR had respected the U.N.'s testing cut-off, whereas the Americans had tested above ground that winter and needed a year to prepare before the round of atmospheric tests authorized for June 1964.[99] Shortly after the American University speech, McNamara announced the "no cities" nuclear policy for targeting military installations, which Khrushchev denounced as "rules for the waging of war" meant to legitimize "the demise of millions of people."[100] Kennedy made a highly emotional and confrontational speech in West Berlin that repudiated his own call for East-West cooperation.[101] These mixed messages probably raised Khrushchev's concerns about collateral information collection and reinforced orthodox opposition to significant arms control. They also help explain why Soviet ENDC delegates feared that if they offered four or five OSIs, the United States would again pocket the concessions and ask for more.[102]

Khrushchev may also have underestimated Kennedy's ability to secure domestic support for compromises on CTB verification. For years, U.S. negotiators had argued that the Senate would not ratify a CTB unless the Soviets accepted more OSIs and monitoring stations than pro–arms control experts such as Wiesner deemed essential. The Soviets undoubtedly knew that the Kennedy administration's flexibility on CTB verification was under attack in Congress and that the JCS had openly opposed the 1962 draft CTB once they realized that Kennedy was serious enough to send Harriman to Moscow.[103] Khrushchev may also have interpreted a Senate resolution for renewed attempts to end atmospheric testing as evidence that Congress favored an LTBT over a CTB, even though some sponsors were ardent CTB supporters and the net effect was to strengthen antitesting sentiment in Congress.[104] Soviet ENDC delegates worried that if the Kennedy administration agreed on four or five OSIs, the Senate would refuse to ratify the treaty, thus vindicating orthodox claims that the United States was not a reliable negotiating partner.[105]

Kennedy would have had to work hard for CTB ratification, but he wanted a test ban so much that he later said he would "gladly forfeit his re-election," if need be, just to win LTBT ratification.[106] Because Kennedy was reluctant to sign a first-step treaty that would not receive overwhelming support, he would not have given Harriman wide latitude to negotiate on the basis of the 1962 draft CTB if he did not think that he could overcome resistance by conservative congressmen and the JCS. ACDA had recently persuaded Dodd, a very Cautious Cooperator, that the United States would be safer with the 1962 draft CTB than with unconstrained testing and proliferation. Dodd's shift increased optimism that other congressional critics could be educated about the implications of the new Vela findings. Although a recent private survey by Senator Joseph Clark (a strong CTB supporter) concluded that only fifty-seven senators supported the current CTB proposals, it also showed that most senators were so consumed with civil rights and other domestic concerns that they did not feel strongly about disarmament issues. Unqualified popular support for a limited test ban increased from 52 percent in early July, to 63 percent after the LTBT was signed, and to 81 percent after the Kennedy administration made its case before Congress.[107] This suggests that many senators would have become CTB supporters if the president had signed a treaty and made a strong case for ratification. In short, Khrushchev may have believed that there was no point in talking about a CTB again because he thought that Kennedy's hands were tied more tightly than they really were.[108]

This is not to say that the superpowers could have reached agreement in Moscow on CTB verification, if they had tried. Khrushchev had signaled repeatedly that the West must make further concessions, but Kennedy went the other way by choosing the 1962 draft over the seven reciprocal OSIs discussed in the ENDC that spring. Even though the Cuban Missile Crisis had strengthened domestic and international pressure for a CTB from Arms Control Advocates, it had also intensified American and Soviet Unilateralists' opposition to constraints on nuclear weapons development and verification compromises. Moreover, years of using "peace through strength" rhetoric to finesse the contradictions between test ban negotiations and nuclear weapons development had generated so much distrust on both sides that neither new seismological data nor bold political initiatives could completely satisfy Cautious Cooperators' verification concerns.

If Khrushchev had been willing to discuss verification, though, negotiators might have found intermediate measures that would have facilitated progress toward more significant test limitations. ACDA's preparatory paper suggested that if Harriman could not secure agreement on OSIs, he should propose a threshold ban with an annual quota of twelve underground tests below the m_b 4.75 limit. ACDA argued that a threshold/quota treaty would prolong the U.S. lead in such areas as tactical weapons and permit the United States to "relax its insistence on compulsory on-site inspections, . . . [since] a violation would be much less critical" than if the United States was not testing at all. Even without a low-yield quota (that might have caused Congress to demand some OSIs), a threshold treaty would have capitalized on U.S. seismic monitoring capabilities and Soviet support for less intrusive forms of international verification, such as the exchange of data from national seismic stations and foreign involvement with "black box" monitoring. It also would have done more than an LTBT to slow the arms race, reduce spending on nuclear weapons development, and show that the superpowers could jointly foreclose some avenues for competition. The JCS derailed this discussion, however, by questioning whether any test limits served U.S. interests, so Harriman was not instructed to pursue intermediate options.[109]

The LTBT makes no mention of verification because the United States, the U.K., and the USSR were satisfied with national monitoring systems. Moreover, they had not yet developed the practice of prohibiting interference with NTM or prescribing procedures for consultation and clarification of ambiguous events. The treaty's main impact on the politics of verification was to set precedents for tacit acceptance of arms control without inspection (for the United States) and satellite surveillance (for the USSR).[110] Since it offered no role for an international agency, the LTBT embodied the notion of reciprocal adversarial verification that came to dominate superpower arms control.

The Continued Costs of Kennedy's Coalition-Building Strategy

Verification issues played an important, if indirect, role in ratification decisions. Kennedy wanted to emphasize the treaty's political benefits as a first step toward superpower cooperation, an obstacle to proliferation, and an answer to popular fears of fallout. But Senate committee hearings and floor debate focused primarily on security issues, such as the implications for ABM development and the wisdom of any cooperative measure that might reduce vigilance. No consensus had developed about arms control; opinions differed among a small group of senators who were Arms Control Advocates and larger groups of Cautious Cooperators and Unilateralists.[111] Although some Unilateralists asserted that the Soviets could get away with militarily significant violations by testing in deep space or doing atmospheric tests near Chinese territory, both they and Cautious Cooperators worried more about general deviousness than about specific evasion scenarios. The broken moratorium affected ratification decisions by strengthening opposition to arms control in general, reinforcing doubts about Soviet intentions, and raising concerns that the USSR had made a major discovery during its high-yield tests in fall 1962 that it hoped to keep the United States from replicating.[112]

The Kennedy administration decided that the way to build the biggest margin of support for the LTBT was to "agree with and even reinforce the common view of Soviet perfidiousness" while noting that the Soviets did keep agreements that suited their interests and depicting the LTBT as "self-policing."[113] Rusk reassured Cautious Cooperators that the United States was not "relying upon the good faith of the Soviet Union, or upon Soviet respect for treaties and international law." Instead, U.S. security would be protected by "its own ability to detect Soviet violations and to maintain a military and scientific posture that will deny to the Soviet Union any gains that might accrue from a violation of the treaty." As the hearings progressed, arguments about the LTBT's favorable impact on the military balance overshadowed depictions of the treaty as a first step toward superpower cooperation. Senator Humphrey protested (to no avail) that "this treaty gives people an opportunity to give some thoughtful consideration to ... the processes of peace. ... I would not want the whole world to think that all we were primarily concerned about was whether or not we had enough leeway within this treaty to create bigger and better weapons.[114]

The LTBT safeguards are the clearest example of this self-help response to uncertainties about Soviet compliance. Since the LTBT had tremendous popular support, arms control opponents did not try to block ratification.[115] Instead, they used worst-case scenarios to argue for measures that would keep the LTBT from becoming a first step toward more significant test constraints. The JCS chairman, Maxwell Taylor, recommended four safeguards as unilateral insurance against clandestine tests, unexpected treaty abrogation, or unknown advances made by the Soviets' last test series:

1. The conduct of comprehensive, aggressive, and continuing underground nuclear test programs . . . .

2. The maintenance of modern nuclear laboratory facilities and programs . . . .

3. The maintenance of the facilities and resources necessary to institute promptly nuclear tests in the atmosphere . . . .

4. The improvement of our capability . . . to monitor the terms of the treaty, to detect violations, and to maintain our knowledge of Sino-Soviet nuclear activity, capabilities, and achievements.[116]

Through its long-standing emphasis on peace through strength, its accusations about the broken moratorium, and its tactical decision to work with the Unilateralists' characterization of the USSR, the Kennedy administration created a situation in which it had no choice but to accept Taylor's safeguards in order to obtain a JCS endorsement and convince Cautious Cooperators that the treaty was relatively risk-free. But these commitments made it much harder to build upon the LTBT. The United States should not even consider further test ban negotiations, Hosmer declared two years later, because "a CTB would destroy three of those safeguards and without adequate means of verification, including OSIs, would make a mockery of the fourth safeguard."[117]

The safeguards also locked the administration into actions that severely eroded the arms control significance of the LTBT. U.S. spending on underground tests quadrupled between 1964 and 1969.[118] Both superpowers' rate of testing was three times higher in the seven years after the LTBT was signed than in the seven years before the 1958 moratorium.[119] Both countries' nuclear arsenals continued to expand at stupefying rates: from 1962 to 1972, the number of American ICBMs and submarine-launched ballistic missiles (SLBMs) went from 22 to 1,710; the corresponding Soviet total grew from 60 to 1,950.[120] In short, by reinforcing American suspicions about Soviet intentions and addressing these anxieties through unilateral monitoring and safeguards rather than cooperative verification measures, the Kennedy administration reduced the value of the LTBT as an independent arms control measure and a first step toward more significant cooperation.

Treaty opponents made one last effort to use the principle of arms control inspections to gut the LTBT. In his attack on the Kennedy administration's OSI concessions after the Cuban Missile Crisis, Dodd had charged that the United States had a "record of consistent and continuing retreat from the basic principle of inspection."[121] Unilateralists tried to convince Cautious Cooperators like Dodd that although NTM could monitor compliance with the LTBT, "it would be a serious lapse from a previously held, and a strongly held, position if the

United States were to lose interest . . . in international inspection and control as an essential condition of disarmament."[122] The Senate rejected an amendment that would have kept the LTBT from entering into force until the United States, the U.K., and the USSR negotiated provisions for on-site inspections. It voted overwhelmingly for ratification on September 25, 1963, and the Soviet Presidium ratified the LTBT the following day.

Arms Control Advocates hoped to build on the LTBT, but as one commentator noted, "A treaty smothered in a blanket of fear and distrust represents a poor foundation for further progress."[123] Five days after Kennedy's assassination, the General Assembly directed that CTB negotiations proceed in the ENDC "with a sense of urgency."[124] Both the United States and the USSR voted for the resolution, then reiterated their incompatible positions on OSIs. Neither supported Brazil's compromise proposal to extend the LTBT by adding a ban on underground tests above the m_b 4.75 threshold and a moratorium on low-yield tests while further work on verification was done. Seaborg notes that their refusal to endorse "this eminently practical idea was considered an indication that each wanted to continue testing, and that the verification issue was to some extent a smoke screen."[125]

An internal exchange of letters about the extension idea shows how the assumptions that were reinforced during the LTBT ratification debate hurt the prospects for near-term agreement on a CTB. Donald Brennan, who had testified on behalf of the LTBT for the Federation of American Scientists, argued against extension. He felt that the marginal benefits for nonproliferation were not worth the costly "political flap" that would be caused by fears about clandestine tests, hidden U.S. vulnerabilities, and lost military options, even if such perceptions were "100% mistaken."[126] Herbert Scoville Jr., an Arms Control Advocate serving as ACDA's assistant director for science and technology, responded that Brennan was being "too narrow and defeatist" by contrasting the immediate difficulties of a seeking a CTB with its value as an isolated nonproliferation measure rather than its long-term value as a first step toward a less nuclearized world.[127] Brennan's main argument was that the cost of a nuclear program was high enough that few potential proliferants would care about the small added disincentive posed by a CTB rather than an LTBT alone. Scoville countered that a CTB would demonstrate an American commitment to slowing the arms race, not just keep other countries from acquiring nuclear weapons, and that this might have an important impact on domestic debates about the nuclear weapons option in countries of concern. It is little wonder, though, that Brennan's view of further test restrictions prevailed over Scoville's, because the

Kennedy administration's ratification strategy had been to accept many of the skeptics' worst-case assumptions and argue that the LTBT was so narrowly drawn that it avoided all verification dilemmas, preserved U.S. military advantages, and placed no significant constraints on American nuclear weapons development.

Conclusion

The politics of verification during the Kennedy administration highlight the problems that stemmed from Kennedy and Khrushchev's use of peace through strength justifications to enlarge arms control coalitions. Such policy justifications appealed to policy makers whose immediate interest was military preparedness, as well as those who thought that arms control was essential for long-term security. Yet tough talk, test resumption, increased defense expenditures, and arms build-ups never frightened either side into verification concessions. Instead, coercive diplomacy increased Cautious Cooperators' anxieties about the other side's intentions and exacerbated Unilateralists' opposition to significant test restrictions. Moves that increased the likelihood of international agreement on CTB verification lowered the level of domestic support for arms control, and vice versa. The Cuban Missile Crisis intensified this dynamic, as did the confusing mix of accommodationist and aggressive gestures that both superpowers made in the following months. Neither leader fully understood the effect of his moves on the other side's internal debates or the domestic constraints on his counterpart's ability to make verification compromises. There was room to maneuver—sometimes more than either side realized. But neither leader was in a position to make major verification accommodations when the other could, thus reinforcing the perception that concessions would be pocketed rather than reciprocated. Kennedy and Khrushchev finally settled on a lowest-common-denominator treaty that did little to increase the likelihood of future agreement on CTB verification. The same counterproductive dynamic continued during ratification hearings, when the Kennedy administration reinforced doubts about Soviet intentions, depicted the LTBT as a modest measure that placed no real constraints on nuclear weapons development, and accepted unilateral safeguards that obstructed progress toward a CTB.

6

The Politics of Verification during Détente

FOR ALMOST A GENERATION after the ratification of the LTBT, the politics of test ban verification were driven by debates about whether competition, cosmetic arms control, or significant cooperation should characterize superpower relations. U.S. security policy was shaped by increasingly public arguments over the best response to Soviet strategic parity. Arms Control Advocates believed that the superpowers could safely pursue a wide range of common arms control interests as long as both sides had secure nuclear retaliatory systems. Unilateralists, in contrast, still thought that the United States needed offensive and defensive superiority at each stage of the escalation ladder. These two groups competed for the support of Cautious Cooperators, who were often distracted by domestic problems, the war in Vietnam, or the ramifications of growing global economic interdependence.

After Khrushchev's ouster in 1964, the Soviet leadership united around the goal of matching American military capabilities. By the late 1960s, however, they too were struggling to decide whether offensive and defensive superiority was possible, preservable, and useful or if the USSR could gain more security at less cost through serious arms control. In the mid-1970s, Brezhnev decided that a CTB would serve Soviet interests, but his ability to move the USSR toward verification positions that the West would accept was constrained by institutionalized opposition to intrusive inspection and orthodox doubts about American reliability as a negotiating partner.

U.S. and Soviet leaders initially tried to manage conflicting pressures for cooperation and competition by expressing support for an "adequately" verified CTB while perpetuating disputes about whether this included OSIs. This avoidance strategy prolonged the lull in test ban negotiations, but the more mature state of verification knowledge made extreme positions harder to sustain than they had been in the 1950s. This avoidance strategy also left a legacy that hindered more serious efforts to get agreement on test ban verification. The 1974 TTBT and the 1976 PNET were lowest-common-denominator treaties meant to symbolize superpower cooperation without triggering verification dilemmas or domestic opposition. But superpower agreement on test restrictions well above the current verification threshold had the unexpected effect of igniting a domestic debate about whether the United States really wanted a CTB. After trilateral CTB talks resumed in 1977, negotiations made unprecedented progress until Unilateralists once again used rigid and adversarial ideas about verification to stymie CTB negotiations and build a domestic backlash against arms control.

Critics of détente often depict Soviet resistance to verification as the critical obstacle to meaningful arms control.[1] This chapter paints a different picture by showing how Unilateralists on both sides worked to preserve verification deadlocks despite advances in monitoring technology and widespread support for test ban cooperation. It also demonstrates that the Soviets did accept data exchanges, in-country monitoring, and managed-access inspections in the mid-1970s when they wanted more test restrictions and believed that the United States would reciprocate. As Chapter Seven shows in more detail, President Reagan's anti–arms control coalition took great pains to ignore cooperative precedents set in these negotiations, belittle and retard the capabilities of remote monitoring systems, and devise new verification requirements that the Soviets would not (and could not) satisfy. Yet only by grossly distorting the politics of test ban verification during the rise and fall of détente could the Reagan administration claim that a more confrontational approach was necessary to secure Soviet support for reliable test ban verification measures.

Perpetuating the Lull after the LTBT

Despite their promise to negotiate a CTB with "greatest urgency," the superpowers made no further progress during the 1960s. The LTBT offered ambiguous precedents: the Soviets claimed that it signified the sufficiency of NTM, whereas the Americans insisted that it underscored the need for appropriate verification. The LTBT reduced incentives to compromise on verification by ending concern about fallout, hiding a potent symbol of the arms race, and reassuring Cautious Cooperators that the superpowers could control the risks of nuclear competition. Because the treaty had not stopped China from conducting its first nuclear test in 1964, the new superpower leaders wanted to negotiate nonproliferation measures for other states while developing new offensive and defensive systems themselves. The countries whose nuclear ambitions most concerned the superpowers rejected a "naked" nonproliferation treaty and considered a CTB crucial to the package of equitable mutual obligations around which an NPT should be built. Therefore, the superpowers spent the next decade proclaiming support for an adequately verifiable CTB while exacerbating verification conflicts and ignoring avenues for compromise.

Arguments over "Adequate" Verification as an Avoidance Strategy

When Leonid Brezhnev and Aleksei Kosygin replaced Khrushchev in 1964, they were less interested than Brezhnev in using arms control to strengthen moderate factions in the West and less concerned about the economic costs of defense. According to one senior Brezhnev official, policy makers suffered from the "Cuban Missile Crisis syndrome"—the belief that the USSR could gain military and political advantages by matching and potentially even surpassing U.S. nuclear capabilities.[2] Rather than offering to compromise on verification, they resumed trying to coerce concessions from the West by strengthening Soviet strategic capabilities, by using "divisive détente" to weaken NATO, and by exploiting Americans' growing preoccupation with internal unrest and conflict in Vietnam.[3] The USSR supported U.N. resolutions for a CTB but retracted its OSI offer and stopped supporting an extension of the LTBT to ban all tests. It also refused to discuss the technical limits of NTM on the grounds that OSIs were a purely political issue.

U.S. leaders were equally obstinate but were more concerned than the Soviets about appearing to be constructive on verification. Although the Gilpatric Committee, a task force on nonproliferation appointed after China's first test, recommended that a CTB should be "a prime objective" of U.S. policy, Lyndon Johnson did not share Kennedy's personal desire for a CTB.[4] When his Committee of Principals pondered test ban policy, they tried to reconcile the nonproliferation value of a CTB with the JCS' desire to test missiles with multiple independently targetable re-entry vehicles (MIRVs) and ABM components. Some of the principals would have reciprocated Soviet interest in underground test limits but would not expend energy kick-starting negotiations. Others, such as Seaborg, had come to privately share the JCS' desire for continued testing but saw no need to publicize their preferences while the OSI deadlock persisted.

This mix of apathy and antipathy led the Johnson administration to show symbolic support for a CTB by funding verification research, then perpetuating verification conflicts despite technological advances.[5] For example, at a principals' meeting in August 1965, a DOD representative estimated that American NTM could identify all but thirty seismic events in the USSR each year—a 50 percent reduction in unidentified events since ACDA's 1962 estimate. But the JCS wanted to protect the U.S. position on OSIs by downplaying these improvements. ACDA, in contrast, wanted to reduce U.S. inspection requirements but recognized that the bureaucracy and key members of Congress were unlikely to approve a policy change before the ENDC adjourned. McNamara, Bundy, and Rusk deemed it "better to stay with a sound policy than to change for the sake of change," especially since the Soviets were not likely to reciprocate.

As Seaborg acknowledges, "The United States found itself locked into a position . . . that was increasingly difficult to defend on technical grounds but that could not be easily changed for reasons of domestic and international politics."[6] It continued to argue in Geneva that forty-five unidentified seismic events would occur in the USSR each year and that seven OSIs were necessary. Because the United States wanted to publicize the progress being made by Vela, Foster changed U.S. verification requirements to match new monitoring capabilities and stressed identification problems for seismic events below m_b 4.[7]

Although the nonaligned members of the ENDC devised new bridging proposals, neither superpower wanted to discuss partial measures that would avoid—but not resolve—arguments over OSIs for a total ban. The nonaligned states were less deferential, however, than when the Kennedy and Khrushchev governments had persuaded them to drop embarrassing proposals. Sweden was especially bold about questioning the scientific basis for American insistence on mandatory OSIs and Soviet claims that NTM could resolve all compliance concerns. It tabled its own draft CTB in 1969, the first time that a nonaligned state had offered a "vision text" showing how key disputes could be resolved. Such actions kept a CTB on the international agenda, indicated that the representatives of world opinion rejected both superpowers' rigidity on CTB verification, and developed compromise options that proved useful when serious CTB negotiations resumed in the late 1970s.

The most important ENDC innovation was Sweden's attempt to design a self-help verification system to enhance confidence in compliance without eroding national sovereignty.[8] Since negotiators no longer talked about a huge international organization to assess compliance, Alva Myrdal assumed that a CTB would be verified through national efforts. To equalize information and reduce transaction costs, she proposed a "detection club" whose members would share seismological data but reach their own conclusions about potential violations. Myrdal maintained that advances in seismology had greatly reduced the number of unidentified seismic events but still could not always distinguish between small earthquakes and low-yield tests. If the seismic data seemed highly suspicious, Myrdal argued, "the standing of the suspected party in the international community would . . . make it imperative for him to vindicate his veracity if he claimed to be innocent," possibly through an invitational OSI. Placing the burden of proof on the accused was unusual, but it was appropriate in the test ban case, Myrdal argued, because "it is technically so much easier to prove one's own innocence than to prove somebody else's guilt."

If doubts about compliance remained, the Swedish proposal suggested that "challenge" OSIs would be as useful as mandatory inspections because a pattern of repeated refusals would be clearer evidence of guilt than a mandatory inspection was likely to find. Myrdal recognized the need for a neutral jury and hoped that scientifically informed international opinion would "act as a corrective, both on unwarranted accusations and on inconclusive denials." She stopped short of endorsing reciprocal OSIs, though, because "without an element of international participation or checking of results, it might be difficult to get a consensus from all the many parties concerned as to whether a nuclear weapon test had been proven."

Myrdal's proposal for "verification by challenge" assumed that states were committed to mutual test ban cooperation, were willing to pay a high price to demonstrate their own compliance, and were predisposed to be reassured by invitational inspections and consultations. Since the superpowers did not feel this way about a CTB in the mid-1960s, neither saw much merit in her suggestions (although they did express interest in seismic data exchanges). The United States doubted that the Soviets would behave cooperatively if a suspicious event occurred on their soil and predicted that the climate of distrust between the superpowers would be worsened by a verification system based on "accusations" and assumptions of guilt.[9] Since the United States did not want to inspect every unidentified seismic event—only those it deemed most suspicious—the American plan for mandatory OSIs also involved accusations but lacked a right of refusal. The Soviets were not willing to discuss any OSI procedures because "states and peoples, especially those which . . . have borne the heavy consequences of foreign aggression . . . will certainly not assume an obligation to open their territories to inspection, for which there is no necessity."[10]

The superpowers played different roles and favored different types of verification arrangements in the ongoing NPT negotiations than they did in CTB discussions. The United States and the USSR wanted to maximize the number of non-nuclear weapons states (NNWSs) who would sign and comply with the NPT treaty, and so they weighed verification trade-offs carefully. Although their own civilian nuclear programs would not be subject to mandatory safeguards, their non-nuclear allies would be. Therefore, the NPT safeguards system involved relatively inexpensive, routine, and unintrusive procedures to reassure signatories that material from civilian nuclear plants had not been diverted for military purposes. The system could flag a sudden serious discrepancy between the amount of fissile material that should be at a facility and the amount actually there, but it could not detect or deter many plausible evasion schemes. Since members of the European Atomic Energy Community (EURATOM) wanted to use their own safeguard system, the United States initially proposed that even the weak, managerial IAEA safeguards should be voluntary—a far cry from its inspection demands for a CTB.[11] In this case, Soviet fears about West German proliferation caused it to reject the EURATOM alternative as unacceptable "self-verification" and to insist that all NNWSs permit mandatory IAEA safeguards.[12] The superpowers finally compromised, insisting that NNWSs accept arrangements the IAEA deemed effective but keeping confidential the details of each country's safeguards agreement.

The tension between American arms control and weapons development objectives intensified shortly before the NPT was signed. Evidence that the Soviets were deploying an ABM system around Moscow convinced President Johnson and Congress that the United States needed a new generation of offensive nuclear weapons and an accelerated defensive program. This required a vigorous testing program, but ACDA did not want to withdraw support for a CTB shortly before the NPT was ready to be signed. Therefore, Foster explicitly outlined a strategy for using the politics of verification to avoid a direct conflict between U.S. nuclear development and nonproliferation policies:

1. The U.S. will attempt to focus attention on other measures . . . to deflect attention from the comprehensive test ban.

2. In commenting on the comprehensive test ban, the U.S. delegation will reiterate that . . . a comprehensive test ban cannot be adequately verified without some onsite inspections. If we are pressed on this point, the U.S. will reiterate our willingness to undertake technical discussions on test ban verification problems, provided the Soviet Union would also participate.

3. The Soviets probably have their own nuclear weapons testing requirements which tend to diminish their interest in a comprehensive test ban. If the U.S. continues to stipulate that we would not accept a comprehensive test ban without onsite inspections and the Soviet Union continues to maintain that such inspections are not necessary, pressure from other countries to reach an agreement can probably be kept within manageable proportions for the time being. If the Soviets ever do agree to onsite inspections of some sort, we would have to enter into negotiations, but these negotiations could be quite protracted.[13]

The United States followed this avoidance strategy until the NPT was signed on July 1, 1968. Thereafter, it had less incentive to express support for a CTB that would hinder nuclear modernization programs, so Johnson's midsummer message to the ENDC omitted a CTB from its arms control goals. Yet the nonproliferation benefits of symbolic support for a CTB did not disappear, because Article VI of the NPT committed signatories to negotiate in good faith on measures to end the arms race—a provision widely understood to include a CTB.

Failure to do so would give potential proliferators such as India a politically potent justification for rejecting the NPT as discriminatory. Furthermore, since the original agreement called for a 25-year treaty with review conferences held every five years (starting in 1975) and a decision in 1995 on the future of the accord, dropping a CTB from the list of U.S. arms control goals could undermine the NPT regime.

Verification Research Challenges the OSI Deadlock

The strategy of symbolizing support for a CTB by funding verification research while ignoring the results was too contradictory to sustain. The United States spent about $270 million on underground test ban verification research and development in the 1960s, a major increase over previous seismological spending.[14] When pressure for an agreement was high, however, more than one third of the Vela budget went to study evasion rather than detection, location, and identification.[15] Vela seismologist Jack Evernden recalls that funding control was also used to forestall advances in test ban verification.[16] Still, Vela paid for some projects that threatened the bureaucratic interests of lead agencies, such as the Air Force Technical Applications Center (AFTAC) and DOD's Advanced Research Projects Agency (ARPA, later known as DARPA). Much of their work was classified, so test ban supporters outside the U.S. government did not know where the United States had seismic monitoring stations, what their capabilities were, or how well the United States could supplement seismological data with other intelligence. Some projects were entirely open, though, including the Worldwide Standardized Seismograph Network (WWSSN) of national stations with state-of-the-art equipment.[17]

The most important breakthrough involved a positive way to identify most nuclear tests without on-site inspections. During the 1960s, seismologists showed that for a given amount of energy released (m_b), explosions typically generate smaller surface Rayleigh waves (M_s) than do earthquakes. According to Bruce Bolt, the "spectacular" plots of m_b against M_s showing a clear difference between most earthquakes and nuclear explosions "set in motion renewed drives for a CTB on the part of many seismologists."[18]

The Stockholm International Peace Research Institute (SIPRI) hosted a conference on the new research with senior seismologists from ten Western, Eastern, and nonaligned countries. Like the Conference of Experts, this group reached consensus on crucial technical issues.[19] Participants agreed that data from the current WWSSN could identify 20- to 60-kt explosions in hard rock

(m_b 4.75–5.0, depending on location), although the identification threshold would be higher for decoupled blasts and tests in porous materials. The conference also confirmed the validity of the m_b:M_s discriminant and provided the first public signs of Soviet research on this method. Most participants doubted that other criteria could positively identify a seismic event as an explosion, but many thought that statistical techniques could combine multiple diagnostic aids into a powerful but unintrusive identification method.

Once again, technical unanimity was achieved by avoiding key issues (the SIPRI report makes no mention of OSIs) and couching conclusions in ambiguous language. Therefore, the superpowers could respond predictably to the report. The Soviet delegate described it as a global consensus that underground explosions could be identified through NTM alone; U.S. officials emphasized the inadequacies of individual seismological identification techniques rather than possibilities to combine and enhance them.

When Richard Nixon became president, he and top advisers, such as Henry Kissinger (national security adviser) and James Schlesinger (chairman of the AEC), continued the previous administration's disinterest in a CTB. Their preferences were reinforced by scientific advice that now came primarily from the Pentagon and weapons laboratories rather than PSAC. ACDA, the other traditional advocate for test ban cooperation, had to go along with official policy if it wanted any influence. For example, ACDA director Gerard Smith and his deputy, Philip Farley, argued publicly that a reliable CTB required OSIs, although this was not their personal belief. ACDA became even less of a counterweight to pro-testing agencies after Smith resigned and other Arms Control Advocates were driven out in 1973.[20]

Since the Nixon administration did not formally withdraw support for an "adequately verifiable CTB," Evernden tried to relax American OSI demands by holding an ARPA conference on seismological discrimination. Scientists at the 1970 Woods Hole conference concluded that the m_b:M_s discriminant worked as well at m_b 4 as it did at m_b 5. They discussed lowering the identification threshold further by using a fuller characterization of seismic signals from earthquakes and explosions. They noted that earthquakes occasionally produce m_b:M_s patterns similar to those of explosions but that such events were caused by geological and geophysical conditions that could be addressed by the verification system. Their conclusion was stronger and less ambiguous than the SIPRI report: "Tectonic stress release associated with some or most explosions is, in a surveillance context, no real problem."[21] It removed the last shreds of technical plausibility from continued U.S. insistence on seven OSIs for a CTB.

ARPA officials responded to this inconvenient conclusion by rewriting the public conference summary and classifying the original version.[22] The new summary stressed the theoretical nature of the research, emphasized potential problems with seismic discrimination, and implied that unidentifiable seismic events would be frequent without OSIs. Instead of the unambiguously positive conclusion of the initial report, the revised version stated that the "major result of the meeting was a clear impression that much research has yet to be done."[23] Carl Romney, assistant technical director of AFTAC, called the revisions "more balanced."[24] Yet six participants reported that ARPA had not consulted them and that the initial summary was more accurate. The deception outraged members of Congress who had grown increasingly distrustful of the Executive Branch. Senator Clifford Case fumed, "It is not an uncommon occurrence for scientific findings to be strongly resisted by government bureaucracies. . . . When such bureaucratic resistance is translated into overt manipulation or suppression of the frank opinion of scientists, however, it becomes an abuse of authority which cannot be tolerated."[25]

Senator Case called for an SCFR subcommittee hearing, whose dominant theme became dissatisfaction that the Nixon administration would fund verification research but not make negotiating initiatives based on verification improvements. Most of the senators' questions reflected Arms Control Advocates' assumptions about CTB verification. Administration witnesses repeatedly endorsed, then contradicted, these assumptions. For example, Farley agreed that "100-percent risk-free arms control" was impossible, but when asked how the administration calculated the "balance of risks" with and without an imperfectly verifiable CTB, Farley emphasized the possibility of minor cheating over its probability and military significance. He admitted that the United States had never formally reviewed its request for seven mandatory OSIs in light of Sweden's proposals or seismological advances. Farley tried to reassure the senators: "We don't view onsite inspection as . . . an albatross around our neck . . . [but as] something that has a very important function."[26] His vague justifications, however, seemed to substantiate suspicions that this function was to preclude a CTB agreement.

Senator Case tried to use Congress' budgetary power to ensure that money spent on test ban verification research would promote rather than obstruct agreement on a CTB. In mid-1972, he offered an amendment to the Arms Control and Disarmament Act that would have transferred control over Vela from ARPA to ACDA. Both DOD and ACDA opposed this legislation, but the amendment still had strong support among those who questioned the logic of letting an agency with a vested interest in nuclear testing have control over test ban verification research.[27] Although the Case amendment was defeated, it sent another signal that Arms Control Advocates were impatient with the strategic prolongation of arguments over OSIs.

Cosmetic Accords or Cooperative Breakthroughs?

The 1974 TTBT and the 1976 PNET represent a return to the strategy of satisfying conflicting domestic and international preferences by negotiating narrow restrictions on nuclear explosions. They reflected the assumptions that shaped superpower arms control negotiations from 1969 to 1980: (1) neither side could gain a lasting advantage from unconstrained development of offensive or defensive systems; (2) nuclear deterrence would be stable if both sides had secure retaliatory capabilities; (3) both sides could benefit from incremental steps to lower the costs and risks of deterrence; and (4) verification was adequate if it could detect violations that would threaten the stability of deterrence.

The twin treaties are often dismissed as the kind of cosmetic cooperation that Arms Control Advocates and Unilateralists dislike intensely, for different reasons.[28] They were meant as a low-cost, low-risk way to keep the spirit of détente alive after agreement on SALT I in 1972. By setting the 150-kt threshold far above the monitoring capabilities of the 1958 Geneva system and ignoring subsequent advances in seismic monitoring, though, superpower leaders angered those who sincerely wanted to ban tests as quickly as verification problems could be solved, as well as those who had been cynically exploiting the OSI deadlock to protect underground tests. Often lost in the controversy was a recognition of how far the USSR came to agree on cooperative verification measures appropriate to the substance of the accords.

The Threshold Test Ban Treaty

In February 1974, Soviet diplomats proposed negotiating a CTB that would not take effect until all five NWSs had signed. Brezhnev's desire to revive test ban talks reflected ongoing concerns about proliferation and increasing fears about the economic impact of the arms race. The USSR had achieved strategic parity, but political leaders realized that attempts to obtain offensive superiority and end defensive vulnerability would bankrupt their country, with little chance of success.[29] The 1972 SALT I ceilings on strategic launch vehicles and ABM defenses were part of a Soviet strategy to codify their status as equal to the United

States and dissuade Americans from using military means to interfere with the inevitable spread of socialism.[30] Soviet leaders still disagreed over whether military doctrine, force structure, and arms control proposals should give priority to decreasing the chance of nuclear war or minimizing the damage to the USSR should such a war occur.[31] The more emphasis that they put on peaceful coexistence, deterrence stability, and diplomatic moves to "make the world safe for political change," the more they wished to solve the workable/tolerable dilemma for CTB verification.[32] Because SALT I would be verified by NTM alone, the Soviets may have also expected that the United States was ready to drop its demands for CTB inspections.

The United States refused to negotiate a CTB with entry-into-force conditions that could be used to coerce French and Chinese participation and would not have been interested in a total test ban, even without such a provision. Kissinger and Nixon were more receptive, however, when Brezhnev suggested a bilateral threshold ban verified by NTM because they needed something to sign at an upcoming summit, and they probably also wanted some evidence of test ban progress before the first NPT review conference in 1975. Representatives from the two sides held technical talks in Geneva without the knowledge of interested agencies in Washington, thus avoiding domestic criticism from CTB supporters and opponents until the two leaders had made a political commitment to negotiate a TTBT.

Nixon and Kissinger's decision to circumvent the regular American policy-making process reflected the growing controversy over arms control in the United States. SALT I had not ended U.S. arguments about nuclear testing. Arms Control Advocates, most of whom were outside the Nixon administration, saw a CTB as the next logical step, now that the superpowers had acknowledged their mutual vulnerability and the disutility of further nuclear weapons development. Cautious Cooperators, like Nixon and Kissinger, viewed détente as a way to moderate Soviet behavior and devise shared rules for competition but still believed that the credibility of American threats depended on the continued refinement of U.S. nuclear capabilities. Unilateralists feared that the United States had sacrificed too much for SALT I and questioned the basic premises of détente. Some, such as James Schlesinger (then secretary of defense) believed that limits on delivery systems increased the value of improvements in warhead technology; others wanted to keep testing because they had not given up hope for ballistic missile defense.[33]

A high-threshold TTBT had the potential to please many different domestic constituencies. Arms Control Advocates might view it as a step in the right direction. Cautious Cooperators would have little to fear from limits that could be easily monitored by NTM. Moreover, the treaty banned only very large tests that were increasingly irrelevant, because the trend was toward improved accuracy and MIRVed missiles with smaller warheads. Since the Soviets still relied more on high-yield weapons, Unilateralists might see the treaty as a relative gain for the United States.

The TTBT committed the superpowers to limit underground nuclear tests to 150 kt, minimize their annual number of tests, and continue working toward a CTB.[34] The United States never considered a yield limit close to the seismic monitoring threshold: ACDA argued for 75 kt, and Nixon initially suggested 100 kt, but Kissinger raised the U.S. proposal to 150 because Schlesinger would support nothing lower.[35] Nevertheless, U.S. officials tried to depict the 150-kt threshold as the result of U.S. verification research. When asked if current capabilities could support a lower yield threshold, ACDA director Fred Iklé answered misleadingly: "Precisely how much you could verify, whether it's 140, 150 or 160 . . . even the expert seismologists disagree. . . . Rather than trying to explore precisely how far down you could push the threshold, it seemed valuable to reach an agreement on this threshold now."[36]

Article II specifies that "each Party shall use national technical means of verification at its disposal in a manner consistent with the generally recognized principles of international law," a formula designed to legitimate remote monitoring for cooperative purposes without sanctioning military surveillance or noncompliance accusations based on espionage, defectors' reports, or press rumors. Each party promised to refrain from interfering with the other's NTM and to consult on compliance concerns. Since tests of new designs can have larger than expected yields, the chief negotiators also reached an understanding that "one or two slight, unintended breaches per year would not be considered a violation of the Treaty."[37] The treaty did not expressly prohibit concealment measures because there were no plausible scenarios for hiding the signals from very-high-yield underground tests.

The TTBT threshold was defined in terms of explosive yield rather than signal magnitude because an explosion in porous rock at NTS would generate much smaller signals than would the same-sized blast in hard rock around Soviet test sites. Seismic signals also attenuate more quickly as they pass through the hot, tectonically active upper mantle under NTS than when they pass through the cooler, less active geological formations under the Soviet Union. American policy makers had known since the Bethe report that a threshold defined in terms of seismic magnitude would favor the United States.[38] A yield-based threshold would be fairer but more complicated to verify.

U.S. scientists had data about magnitude-yield relationships for American and French test sites, but they needed data about Soviet tests and test site geology to calibrate yield estimation formulas. The Soviets agreed to furnish this information so that both sides would have the same yield limits. They also wanted to set the precedent that seismic monitoring was sufficient for underground test ban verification. Therefore, the TTBT had a separate protocol in which the parties promised to test only at declared locations; report on the geological characteristics of their test sites; and exchange yield, date, time, depth, and location information for two tests in each geologically distinct testing area. This was the first time that Soviet negotiators had agreed to reveal detailed information about an ongoing military activity. The protocol stipulates, however, that the data exchange would occur "simultaneously with the exchange of instruments of ratification" because the Soviets did not want to share sensitive information if the treaty lacked sufficient domestic support in the United States.

The Peaceful Nuclear Explosions Treaty

The TTBT was negotiated in five weeks, but it took eighteen months to work out arrangements for verifying that PNEs with high individual or aggregate yields were not used to evade TTBT limitations. Because seismographs or satellite photos cannot reveal whether a "peaceful" explosion is providing weapons-related information, both sides agreed that the only way to conduct high-yield PNEs without concerns about TTBT compliance would be to permit OSIs; the question was whether such OSIs could be both workable and tolerable, or if all questionable PNEs should be stopped.

The tension between promoting peaceful uses of atomic energy and preventing military applications had been a lurking problem during all test ban deliberations. At first, the Soviets wanted to ban all nuclear explosions while some Americans argued for a PNE exemption because they were genuinely interested in the economic benefits, saw a PNE program as a politically acceptable avenue for research relevant to "clean" bombs, or hoped that test ban negotiations would deadlock over PNE inspections. When the LTBT was negotiated, the United States reluctantly dropped demands for a PNE exemption in return for the explicit right to withdraw if continued compliance would jeopardize national security. U.S. interest in PNEs decreased significantly after independent scientists reviewed the AEC's program and found "no single use that stands out as obviously a great thing."[39] Once the noneconomic costs of PNEs, such as radioactivity and seismic damage were taken into account, the U.S. program was virtually ended. India's claim that its 1974 explosion was peaceful made nonproliferation experts even more eager to close the PNE loophole. The USSR, however, had not yet reached an internal decision about its program; since high-yield PNEs would be possible only if verification problems could be solved, Minatom (the Soviet counterpart to the AEC) and others who wished to keep this option open were unusually motivated to facilitate agreement on verification.

PNE verification has some unusual features that eased the OSI deadlock. PNEs are not conducted at weapon test sites, so foreigners need not visit sensitive facilities and have fewer opportunities for collateral information collection. Because the U.S. government had already ended its PNE program and the Soviets were unlikely to conduct high-yield PNEs often, if ever, inspections would only occur when the Soviets decided that the benefits of a large PNE outweighed the costs and risks of an OSI. PNE inspections would also be used routinely to demonstrate compliance, not implemented after accusations about noncompliance had been made. Still, PNE negotiators paid close attention to the precedents that their verification provisions might set for future arms control.[40]

Instead of staking out conflicting positions on verification details, PNE negotiators spent the first three rounds discussing general principles, developing a common language, understanding one another's concerns, and cultivating the personal relationships.[41] The term *designated personnel* was devised to refer to OSI teams without saying *inspectors*, a word that the Soviets felt carried invidious implications. Both sides also agreed that any nuclear blast conducted at a declared test site would be subject to the TTBT limitations. Detonations elsewhere would be governed by the stricter verification provisions of the PNET.

Early in the preliminary phase, the Soviets suggested American participation in their PNE program as a substitute for rigid restrictions and formal inspections.[42] This resembled the ALC premise that active participation is necessary to ensure peaceful intentions—a major departure from previous Soviet efforts to keep foreigners in passive oversight roles. The proposal may have been a last-ditch effort to conduct individual PNEs with yields above 150 kt. It also may have been less cooperative than it sounds. The USSR separated its PNE staff, who decided where and when they needed a particular type of explosion, from the explosion experts who conducted the blast. The Soviets might have been willing to include a few Americans on their PNE teams because they would not have been directly involved in the detonations, had access to diagnostic equipment, or known if militarily relevant data was being collected. This explains why the Soviet PNE staff at the talks later complained that the United States wanted "more of a presence than our PNE people have."[43] American officials never pursued this proposal because they questioned its verification value, wished to avoid involvement in projects that might cause accidents or violate the LTBT, and wanted a precedent that "peaceful" and "military" explosions should be subject to similar legal restrictions.

PNET negotiators found no workable and tolerable way to ensure that individual PNEs with yields over 150 kt did not provide military information or expertise. They banned all such explosions and concentrated on two easier verification problems—improving yield estimation for PNEs in unfamiliar geographical locations and ensuring that a group of permitted PNEs whose aggregate yield surpassed 150 kt was not mistaken for a treaty violation. The solution was to rely primarily on NTM and to increase data exchanges and on-site monitoring as the aggregate yield rose. Like the TTBT, the PNET forbid interference with NTM and provided for consultation and clarification of ambiguous events. But the Joint Consultative Commission would also discuss changes in PNE technology, consider possible PNET amendments, and recommend avenues for cooperation.[44]

The sliding scale for PNET verification fit well with the Soviet principle of proportionality between the significance of a treaty provision and the applicable verification measures. The signatories had no special obligations for PNEs with expected aggregate yields below 100 kt, other than to provide advance notice and follow-up information. If the aggregate yield was between 100 and 150 kt, data requirements increased. The state conducting the PNE could also invite designated personnel to visit the project, confirm the data exchanged, and observe the PNE's emplacement and explosion. If the PNE's aggregate yield exceeded the 150-kt limit of the TTBT, OSIs became obligatory. Moreover, designated personnel could request photographs and use electrical equipment to measure the yield of individual explosions.[45] They could also add a local seismic network if the aggregate yield was over 500 kt.

Once political leaders had made a commitment to cooperation and negotiators had reached agreement on the principles of PNE verification, the Soviets were ready to discuss the details of managed access inspections. They still wanted to minimize intrusiveness but would compromise if Americans convinced them that a provision was needed to protect the integrity of verification.[46] Negotiators had few precedents because this was the first arms control accord to grant designated personnel access to either superpower's territory. They had to allocate verification rights and responsibilities, establish privileges and immunities for foreign inspectors, and even specify intellectual property rights to information obtained during the verification process.

Some of the data collection procedures in the PNET were genuinely cooperative, something downplayed by the few Americans who later looked to the PNET for lessons about OSIs. For example, Heckrotte maintained that the host's role was to facilitate the logistics of data collection but that anything which "entailed Soviet personnel working alongside U.S. personnel carrying out verification procedures . . . could be used to thwart the purpose of verification. . . . Verification that was not solely the responsibility of the verifying side would amount to self-inspection."[47] In actuality, however, host nationals were sometimes assigned to do sensitive verification procedures while designated personnel ensured that they followed agreed procedures. For example, host nationals would take all requested pictures so that no unauthorized photographs were taken, but designated personnel could request an immediate reshoot if they were not satisfied. The party conducting the PNE was also responsible for installing the electrical yield-estimation equipment and filling the emplacement hole—important steps, because yield estimates can vary depending on the location of the cable and the surrounding material. Thus, PNE data collection was more cooperative than Heckrotte's rejection of self-verification would imply, even if assessments of compliance remained each country's responsibility.

Negotiators found creative compromises on numerous questions, such as whose monitoring equipment to use. The challenge was to ensure that the seismic network and the electrical equipment allowed the designated personnel to estimate PNE yields accurately without learning about the design of the explosive devices. The United States proposed a complicated plan to share the risk. If the designated personnel used their own equipment, they would provide two sets. The other side would select one set to be examined and the other to be used for verification. Each set would include two data recorders. After detonation, a coin toss would determine which side received which recorder. Presumably, the designated personnel would not tamper with the equipment if they stood a 75 percent chance of discovery. This duplication strategy would be expensive, so the Soviets added a provision allowing designated personnel to use the other side's equipment if they wished, thus shifting some of the cost to the side seeking extra reassurances that the equipment did only what it was supposed to do.

In short, the TTBT and PNET negotiations served as a dry run in which the superpowers first made a political commitment to limit underground tests and then worked out the details of a cooperative verification system that balanced the risks of cheating and spying, and allocated the costs of verification in an equitable fashion. Although the Soviets maintained an active PNE program, they never conducted large group blasts that would trigger an OSI. When the United States later suggested lowering the TTBT and PNET thresholds, Timerbayev replied that the OSI provisions would have to be renegotiated, because the inspections might occur more frequently.[48] The Soviets also insisted that agreement on PNET inspections did not change their position that NTM and data exchanges were adequate for a total ban on tests.[49] These negotiations were extremely important nonetheless, because the superpowers finally worked through a set of substantive dilemmas without the usual strategic distortions. In retrospect, Timerbayev sees the PNET negotiations as crucial to the development of Soviet thinking about verification. They "put to test the willingness of both sides, and above all of the Soviet Union, to accept highly intrusive verification procedures. . . . Many other aspects (legal, organizational, financial, etc.) were worked out as well, which may have laid at least some of the groundwork for subsequent verification schemes."[50]

Inadequate Support for Ratification

The TTBT and PNET never received as much attention as SALT II, but they became entangled in the same domestic controversies and suffered a similar fate. President Ford transmitted the treaties to the Senate in July 1976, but he did not urge the SCFR to consider them quickly because Ronald Reagan was attacking his stance on arms control as they competed for the presidential nomination. When President Carter resubmitted the treaties in a renewed effort to secure a CTB, the SCFR gave an unenthusiastically positive recommendation, until Carter decided in mid-1978 that the ratification process could jeopardize a CTB. The SCFR withdrew its recommendation and the treaties languished unratified for more than a decade. This outcome had less to do with the treaties than with their symbolism for domestic groups with different ideas about official support for an "adequately verifiable CTB."

The Ford administration tried to build popular support for accords with "marginal" arms control utility by depicting them as a "historical milestone" in the politics of verification. Kissinger also argued that "all serious students of arms control" should welcome the TTBT and the PNET, because the Soviets had never accepted the principle of on-site inspection or agreed to provide detailed information about their military testing program.[51] This exaggerated the novelty factor: the Soviets had accepted the principle of test ban inspections twice and agreed to OSIs in practice, not only for NNWS parties to the NPT but also for their own ships, stations, and cargoes in Antarctica. Comments like Kissinger's obscured the extent to which these treaties fit traditional Soviet verification principles and detracted from the truly novel achievement—the development of detailed procedures to enhance verification through cooperative measures. Each of these points became a serious problem in the anti–arms control backlash that prevented TTBT and PNET ratification until new verification measures were negotiated in 1990.

The more immediate problem was the domestic political fallout caused by depicting these treaties as a major verification breakthrough after years of supporting an "adequately verifiable CTB" while exaggerating verification problems. The official definition of "adequately verifiable" meant radically different things to different groups. As long as the U.S. government could convince Cautious Cooperators that the Soviets would not acquiesce to necessary verification measures, the phrase "adequately verifiable CTB" served as a "fraudulent umbrella" to cover a range of conflicting policy preferences.[52] Once negotiators concurred that NTM was adequate to monitor some limits on underground tests and reached agreement on some OSIs in Soviet territory, however, American leaders could no longer avoid tough questions.

Unilateralists followed the same approach during the SCFR hearings on the TTBT and PNET that they had with the LTBT. They did not attack the treaties' verifiability because the 150-kt limit was far above acknowledged monitoring capabilities. Instead, they used various tactics to prevent further test restrictions. Harold Agnew, then director of LANL, stressed the uncertainties of seismic yield estimation. He testified that "we can guarantee that we will know their yields within a factor of two . . . that is, [a test which appeared to be 150 kt could actually be] from 75 to 300."[53] He failed, however, to mention steps to improve the accuracy of seismic yield estimation, such as the TTBT data exchanges. Roger Batzel, then director of LLNL, was even blunter, insisting that "these verification provisions would clearly not be adequate for a lower threshold, or for a CTB."[54]

The lab directors and the JCS also wanted TTBT safeguards, including an explicit commitment to keep testing up to the treaty limits and to remain ready to resume very high yield tests on short notice. Some of their arguments resembled those used to paint the LTBT safeguards as insurance against undetected violations or unexpected breakout by the Soviets. They also used the (exaggerated) uncertainties of seismic yield estimation to argue that the United States would be at a relative disadvantage, because Congress might mandate that American tests be unilaterally restricted to yield levels that could not possibly be mistaken for TTBT violations.

Unilateralists in the Ford administration mounted an undercover campaign to convince Cautious Cooperators that the Soviets could not be trusted to comply with test ban treaties. In October 1976, for example, an anonymous Ford official told reporters that the Soviets had been "chiseling" on the TTBT by conducting tests near the 150-kt limit. He charged that the Soviets had violated the spirit of the treaty by doing the same thing that the lab directors sought as a legislated safeguard. He also challenged the Soviets' respect for international law by claiming that "if they wanted to be punctilious (about their treaty obligations) they wouldn't be doing it."[55]

CTB opponents outside the administration were even more critical of the treaties and U.S. test ban policy in general. Two LANL scientists argued that agreement on "cooperative" PNET inspections is "totally different in principle from an 'adversary' inspection procedure of the type still considered essential by the United States under a CTBT."[56] They maintained that the TTBT had "permanently finessed a CTB" by firmly establishing the precedent that yield thresholds must be fully verifiable regardless of the low military significance of undetected violations or the cooperative benefits that could be gained despite imperfect verification. Still, they feared that the United States might have "opened a 'Pandora's box' of arguments leading to further threshold reductions."[57] Therefore, they urged U.S. leaders to abandon the fiction that adequate verification was necessary and sufficient for test ban cooperation.

Cautious Cooperators on the SCFR asked probing questions about verification, primarily to determine how much lower American NTM could go. Senator John Glenn, the most vocal spokesperson for this point of view, insisted that "I do not trust the people with whom we are dealing any more than anyone else does." Yet he saw a 150-kt limit as irrelevant to the nuclear dilemma, noting that a ban on tests ten times larger than the Hiroshima explosion did not reduce his anxieties.[58] He joked that TTBT should stand for "timid test ban treaty" and suggested that the "threshold" image was apt because there was a "long walk ahead ... to get where we ought to be." He tried repeatedly to determine the lower limit of U.S. verification capabilities, only to receive evasive responses or hear that the information was classified. Not until the third day did witnesses refer to a monitoring threshold of m_b 4.0, but this was done to emphasize the inadequacies of seismic monitoring for a CTB. When Agnew declared that "at yields of perhaps between 5 and 10 kt, a country that can control its population could evade detection, at least by seismic means and could test pretty much at will," Glenn asked why the threshold was not that low, only to be told that 150 kt was a "negotiated figure."[59]

The Arms Control Advocates who testified before the SCFR were the most overtly negative witnesses. George Rathjens, who spoke on behalf of the Federation of American Scientists (FAS), and Herbert Scoville Jr., who represented the Arms Control Association (ACA), argued that the 150-kt threshold made a mockery of U.S. claims to want a CTB as soon as verification problems could be solved. They worried that the United States had set a dangerous precedent by limiting only military explosions in the TTBT and had sent the wrong signal by negotiating complicated procedures to permit high-yield group PNEs. Scoville agreed with the Unilateralists that the PNE inspections were irrelevant to a CTB, in his case because he doubted the need for any CTB inspections. "I look upon those on-site inspections with great amazement, wonder, and admiration for those who must have had to negotiate those kind of arrangements with the Soviet Union," he said. "My only regret is that this great talent was wasted on such an unimportant project."[60] Since the Nixon administration had seen the TTBT as a substitute for serious CTB negotiations, both the FAS and the ACA had initially urged the Senate to reject the twin treaties and demand more significant test restrictions. After the Carter administration decided that ratification would be a useful step toward rapid agreement on a CTB, the FAS decided to withhold judgment. The ACA, by contrast, still considered the treaties to be "worse than nothing." Scoville wanted the SCFR to recommend that the TTBT and the PNET be put "on the back burner" while the president negotiated an end to all nuclear tests.[61]

The SCFR followed the advice of the person who would lead the U.S. team in the second generation of CTB negotiations. Paul Warnke, the new head of ACDA, depicted the treaties as a "hedge" against the possibility that CTB negotiations would go slowly or collapse completely again. He warned that failure to ratify might raise doubts about the reliability of the United States as a negotiating partner and thus lessen the likelihood of early agreement on a CTB. After this lukewarm endorsement, the SCFR decided to recommend ratification but delayed writing its report while it dealt with more important business (the Panama Canal). In mid-1978, the Carter administration decided that the minor benefits from ratification were not worth the risk that CTB opponents would mobilize opinion against underground test restrictions or block a CTB by attaching restrictive conditions to the resolution of ratification. The SCFR agreed to reconsider its vote of approval, which left the superpowers obligated by the Vienna Convention on the Law of Treaties to observe the 150-kt limit but not to exchange the calibration data called for in the TTBT protocol until they formally ratified or rejected the treaties.[62]

Could More Have Been Accomplished?

Failure to ratify the TTBT and the PNET shows that it is not necessarily easier to build a winning coalition on verification for treaties with little military significance than it is for more consequential accords. When the general level of interest in an agreement is low, the ratification process can be delayed by a few treaty opponents and even by supporters who are distracted or want a more ambitious accord. Although most Unilateralists were not highly motivated to block limits on high-yield tests, most Arms Control Advocates were either indifferent or hostile to the TTBT and the PNET. The result was an "ends against the middle" alliance in which a small group of active Unilateralists and Arms Control Advocates used similar arguments (e.g., PNET inspections do not set useful precedents for a CTB) and had the same objective (prevent ratification), even though they preferred diametrically different policy alternatives. Even Cautious Cooperators, the group that would be most likely to favor low-risk measures and verification "overkill," did not believe that these treaties addressed their security dilemmas and would not fight for the accords on their own merits.

In his postmortem for the TTBT and PNET, Kissinger suggests that "nothing could better symbolize the fact that the policy of détente and arms control was losing its domestic base in the United States."[63] A more accurate assessment would be that few Americans liked the type of cosmetic cooperation that the treaties seemed to symbolize. The strongest voices against ratification were those of Arms Control Advocates, who viewed the treaties as a huge step backward from the official U.S. position that nuclear tests should be banned as quickly as verification problems could be solved. Cautious Cooperators saw little value added from ratifying these treaties because they did not believe that it would help solve remaining differences over CTB verification. The 150-kt threshold was 10–20 times higher than the yield limits at which arguments about the efficacy of NTM began. Moreover, the utility of the TTBT data exchanges was not appreciated by nonspecialists. In the testimony about whether the right to inspect large PNEs was a useful precedent for CTB talks, little attention went to the more important precedents for a joint problem-solving approach to negotiations and to cooperative verification compromises that balanced concerns about cheating and spying. Ironically, some players who were most eager to ratify the treaties were less interested in promoting détente than in protecting against further test restrictions by setting obstructive precedents or attaching restrictive amendments. In short, after years of using official support for an "adequately verifiable CTB" to avoid an open conflict between arms control and weapons development, U.S. leaders' inability to get Senate approval for the TTBT and PNET said less about popular support for significant arms control (75 percent of Americans favored a CTB in 1978) than about disagreements over the next step.[64]

A threshold closer to current NTM capabilities would have had stronger domestic support (and more intense opposition) than did these minor accords, but would it have blocked a breakthrough on cooperative verification? Suppose, for example, that the Nixon administration had been willing to propose a 50-kt limit—still safely above the NTM threshold, even with cautious assumptions about evasion opportunities and seismic yield estimation uncertainties. The Soviets would have had even more incentive to share calibration data, since both sides knew that the unadjusted yield-to-magnitude formula from the NTS would exaggerate the size of Soviet blasts. The real question is whether the USSR would have agreed to managed-access provisions for PNE inspections that could have been triggered more often or let designated personnel use on-site equipment or a local seismic network to verify the accuracy of calibration data. The Soviet principle of proportionality and their decisions to suspend PNEs and allow challenge OSIs during the Carter-era CTB negotiations suggest that they would have, if they had thought that Americans wanted to move quickly from a lower threshold to a CTB. But, the strategic manipulation of the OSI deadlock and the tendency during the early years of détente to focus on superpower agreements that could be verified by NTM reinforced Soviet resistance to rethinking their extreme caution about collateral information collection, even after they had obtained strategic parity. Thus, if the only way to get a breakthrough on cooperative verification really was to negotiate treaties whose military significance was too low to garner much domestic support, the problem was a product of the way in which the politics of test ban verification had been played to date.

Second-Generation CTB Talks: Substantive Successes, Strategic Disputes

One of Jimmy Carter's chief CTB negotiators characterized him as the president who tried the hardest but accomplished the least in arms control.[65] The president's ability to achieve his arms control goals was severely constrained by conservative critics, whose arguments gained plausibility each time the Soviets violated American expectations about détente. Yet, the contradictions in Carter's own beliefs, plus the conflicts over these questions among his top advisers, created vulnerabilities that arms control opponents could easily exploit, as they did during the Kennedy administration.

Unilateralists could no longer count on an overblown construction of the workable/tolerable dilemma to block cooperation. Knowledge about test ban verification was more highly developed and diffused in the 1970s than during the first generation of CTB talks. Moreover, the Soviets were ready to work out detailed arrangements for cooperative solutions to the inadequacies of NTM. Almost a decade before Mikhail Gorbachev formally announced his policy of glasnost, the USSR agreed to data exchanges, in-country monitoring, and managed-access inspections for a major arms control accord. Delegations still had different ideas about some verification dilemmas, but chief negotiators all thought that these substantive disagreements were surmountable.

CTB opponents responded to progress in the politics of verification with a double-pronged attack. They increased their emphasis on the need to test for stockpile reliability and expressed more openly their opposition to a CTB, even if verification problems could be solved. At the same time, however, they took steps to complicate international agreement on verification and ensure a vicious ratification battle if a CTB were signed. They convinced U.S. and British leaders to take positions that lowered the benefits of cooperation, raised the costs and risks of verification, and increased Soviet doubts about American intentions—moves that revived Soviet resistance and restored the verification deadlock.

Many observers maintain that domestic debates about verification did not begin until the mid-1970s.[66] The test ban case, however, shows adaptations rather than dramatic alterations in domestic debates. Arguments among Americans became more obvious early in the second generation of CTB negotiations because there were fewer points of stark disagreement between U.S. and Soviet negotiators. Moreover, the higher level of congressional and public scrutiny of security policy generated by the Vietnam War increased popular awareness of verification controversies that had previously occurred mainly inside the Executive Branch. The particular way in which the Executive Branch portrayed verification also contributed to the problem. Policy makers who specialized in arms control knew that issues of verification and compliance were complicated, fragile, ambiguous, and imperfect. To build public support for NTM-based accords, such as the LTBT and SALT I, however, subsequent administrations had created a public impression that "political problems at the negotiating table could be overcome through a judicious combination of science and engineering. There was a tendency to view verification largely as a cut-and-dried process, based on routine actuarial calculations of detection [probability] . . . , with a 'cops and robbers' plot, and simple determinations of guilt or innocence."[67] This myth let arms control opponents use a relatively small amount of ambiguous evidence about Soviet compliance to generate strong feelings of disillusionment and betrayal among American Cautious Cooperators.

Arms Control Advocates Win the Early Rounds

One of Carter's major campaign promises was to end nuclear testing.[68] As a nuclear engineer who had worked on U.S. submarines, Carter had first-hand knowledge about nuclear weapons and could understand the technical side of arms control. But as a former governor of Georgia, he knew little about working with the U.S. foreign policy bureaucracies or negotiating with Soviet diplomats. His own thinking about arms control and verification also included basic contradictions. He wanted a CTB and deep cuts in strategic arms (possibly down to a small submarine-based force for minimal deterrence), yet he saw no conflict between his "unequivocal commitment" to nuclear arms control and his support for "a quiet, steady, and well-planned strengthening of our military capability."[69] Nor did he recognize a tension between his support for significant superpower security cooperation and his view of verification as a technical yet adversarial process.[70]

These contradictions in Carter's thinking resulted in an administration filled by people with conflicting views about test bans and verification. Secretary of State Cyrus Vance, ACDA director Paul Warnke, and Science Adviser Frank Press strongly supported a CTB to promote nonproliferation and prevent future weapons developments from disrupting nuclear parity or destabilizing deterrence. They were optimistic about agreement on verification because they doubted the military significance of tests that were small and infrequent enough to escape detection. JCS chairman David Jones and Secretary of Energy James Schlesinger openly opposed a CTB on the grounds that deterrence required U.S. nuclear superiority. They argued that the United States must test to develop new counterforce weapons, ensure the reliability of existing stockpiles, and preserve the technical expertise and facilities needed for future military requirements.[71] They also maintained that the difficulties of detecting and identifying small tests could place the United States at a serious disadvantage. An open society would never cheat, they claimed, whereas a closed society could use very-low-yield tamped or larger decoupled blasts to check reliability, preserve design skills, and maybe even make significant improvements in tactical weapons or primaries for strategic warheads.[72] Secretary of Defense Harold Brown kept a low profile, despite his long history of involvement with test ban verification. National Security Adviser Zbigniew Brzezinski deemed the CTB a "non-starter," but given Carter's strong feelings, Brzezinski sought to "move the bureaucratic machinery toward meaningful proposals—yet ones which would not jeopardize our ability to continue the minimum number of tests necessary for our weapons program."[73]

These splits caused brutal bureaucratic battles over whether the U.S. should start serious CTB negotiations and what would constitute adequate verification. Carter intervened personally to settle the first question, but neither he nor his administration ever reached a firm decision on the second because they could not define a "militarily significant violation" without deciding whether U.S. security should rest on minimal deterrence, mutual assured destruction, or a renewed quest for nuclear superiority.

Carter's decision to start CTB negotiations was influenced by signs that the Soviets were ready for serious verification discussions. Just days after his election, the USSR reiterated its willingness to consider invitational inspections.[74] Once again, the Soviets did not concede a technical need for OSIs but offered them as a political concession. The Soviets also agreed to participate in the Ad Hoc Group of Scientific Experts to Consider Cooperative Measures to Detect and Identify Seismic Events (GSE) established by the ENDC's successor, the Conference of the Committee on Disarmament (CCD). This was a major step for the Soviet Union, which had previously refused to join the WWSSN or provide seismograms from their stations for Soviet test dates.

Signs of internal opposition appeared among Soviet security elites. A CTB would probably end their PNE program; hamper improvements in yield-to-weight ratios, warhead accuracy, and weapons miniaturization; and involve unprecedented verification measures. Political leaders emphasized that a CTB could strengthen the nonproliferation regime, enhance détente, and preserve deterrence stability. Military leaders questioned its net effect on Soviet security, Carter's willingness to agree on tolerable terms, and his ability to secure Senate support for CTB ratification. The major agencies agreed to seek a temporary test ban treaty: the Foreign Ministry assumed that it would be hard for the superpowers to resume testing after successful short-term CTB cooperation, while the Ministry of Defense hoped for a different outcome.[75]

The British were more internally divided about a CTB than they had been for decades. The U.K. only conducted two tests in the twelve years from 1966 to 1977, a self-imposed moratorium that reflected the minimal requirements for their independent deterrent, the Labour Party's unease with British nuclear weapons, and the strong public opposition to nuclear testing. When the superpowers decided to start CTB negotiations, Labour prime minister James Callaghan wanted to join. His enthusiasm for a CTB, however, was not shared by the Ministry of Defence or the British Atomic Weapons Research Establishment. York describes the internal U.K. politics as "a microcosm of the situation in Washington with only irrelevant differences in the details."[76]

Formal trilateral negotiations began well in October 1977. Once again, negotiators started by talking about general principles rather than staking out conflicting positions. Many of them had worked on the TTBT and the PNET, so they had friendly relationships, a common language, and a nuanced understanding of relevant precedents. Several major concessions by the USSR also provided momentum. In November, Brezhnev offered to halt PNEs for the duration of a CTB.[77] The Soviets also moved closer to the U.S. position on duration. They had initially suggested an 18-month treaty that would expire if the other NWS did not sign, but the United States preferred an indefinite ban without restrictive renewal conditions. The Soviets shifted to a three-year ban that could be renewed if world conditions were favorable, then tacitly accepted a U.S. proposal in May 1978 for a five-year initial accord that could be extended indefinitely without French or Chinese participation.

The USSR also made major concessions on verification. It offered to join an international seismic data exchange so that signatories without sophisticated seismic monitoring capabilities could make their own verification decisions. It also agreed to negotiate special verification agreements (SVAs) detailing arrangements whereby the United States, the U.K., and the USSR would install automatic in-country seismic monitoring stations and conduct reciprocal challenge inspections. According to John Edmonds, the second head of the U.K. delegation, "The first few months of these Comprehensive Test Ban negotiations had cleared away all the traditional differences of principle, almost entirely in directions preferred by the West."[78]

Because the idea of challenge inspections had originally been devised to bridge the gulf between voluntary OSIs and obligatory inspections, the superpowers stressed the part of the concept that fit their preferences. The Soviets claimed that signatories would gladly host an inspection if consultations failed to dispel doubts about the peaceful nature of an unidentified seismic event. The Americans agreed to drop their demands for mandatory inspections if a refusal to grant an OSI request was seen as tantamount to thwarting an obligatory OSI. The Soviets accepted these conditions, even though the United States was not yet willing to acknowledge that a "frivolous" OSI request would also be a serious matter. This reinforced a guilty-until-proven-innocent mentality and could have caused serious problems if a signatory refused an OSI request in a highly seismic area where no violations had occurred but other military activities were underway.

The PNET offered a valuable but incomplete model for CTB inspections. Several major new substantive issues had to be addressed, because determining the nature of a suspicious event after it has occurred is more difficult than observing a permitted activity as it happens. For example, the Americans initially argued that any type of evidence could be used to request an OSI. The Soviets wanted to avoid requests based on soft data, such as defectors' reports or newspaper stories, so they countered that seismic evidence meeting specific criteria should be required. The Americans responded that any type of physical evidence should be sufficient but declined to develop a list in order to avoid excluding future developments in monitoring technology.

The superpowers also disagreed about inspection procedures. The Americans wanted the right to request additional procedures after an OSI challenge had been accepted if, for example, an aerial survey would help indicate where in the inspection area to concentrate. But because the OSIs might be occurring in a sensitive location, the Soviets wanted to know exactly what would be involved before they agreed to an inspection.[79] The Soviets also wanted host and challenger nationals to prepare a joint report so that the Soviets would know what information the United States had collected and could advance their own interpretation of any ambiguous evidence. The United States was willing to share data and provide a preliminary report drafted by the designated personnel but insisted that this factual report should not include judgments about compliance— that was for each government to decide.[80]

Negotiators spent much time on OSI details even though the West saw the right to request OSIs primarily as a deterrent to be invoked infrequently, if at all. The logistics would be daunting.[81] Approximately thirty designated personnel with computers, metal detectors, seismic monitors, drilling devices, and equipment for chemical and physical analysis would have to be transported quickly from the point of entry to the area where a suspicious event had occurred. A joint aerial survey might cover hundreds of square kilometers, and the area chosen for intensive ground inspection could be tens of square kilometers. The OSI team would need several weeks to do a systematic search for signs of suspicious activity and still might not find unambiguous evidence if a very small test had occurred in or near the search area.

The United States never developed an official position about conducting a few inspections despite the low probability of uncovering a nuclear test. Alan Neidle, a delegate from ACDA, thought that OSIs would rarely be worth the expense and tension they might cause. Heckrotte and Warnke believed that the United States should plan to investigate a few ambiguous events each year to gain experience with on-site inspection, increase confidence in cooperation, and make OSIs seem so routine that it would not be "a big deal" to request one if real concerns arose.[82] Had the United States chosen to challenge the Soviets two or three times a year for these benign-sounding political purposes, however, it would have reinforced Soviet fears that unnecessary OSIs were a cover for intelligence activities. It would have also lent credence to U.S. Unilateralists' claims that the Soviets were cheaters but that U.S. monitoring capabilities were unable to provide the proof required to repudiate the accord.

New Strategies Revive the Verification Deadlock

Members of all three delegations maintain that substantive disagreements about verification could have been resolved if political leaders had continued to place a high priority on a CTB.[83] Yet every step toward agreement increased resistance from Unilateralists in the United States, the U.K., and the USSR. These groups formed a tacit transnational alliance whose members maneuvered their governments into rigidly conflicting positions on a range of issues. The politics of verification was not the only venue for this blocking strategy, but it worked particularly well because many arms control supporters still were not comfortable with trade-offs and compromise on compliance evaluation. When talks bogged down over verification issues, Cautious Cooperators were quicker to blame the other side than to recognize how key players in their own country might have contributed to the problems.[84]

Efforts to undermine CTB talks and discredit the unratified TTBT were part of a larger attack against Carter's arms control and defense policies. Traditional Cold Warriors from both parties joined neoconservative Democrats to form antidétente organizations, such as the Committee on the Present Danger and the Coalition for Peace through Strength.[85] Their core message was that arms control placed disadvantageous constraints on the United States without reducing the threat posed by the USSR. They questioned the wisdom of arms control with a country whose behavior in other spheres conflicted with U.S. interests. They also warned that cosmetic cooperation could "lull" American vigilance, thus limiting public support for an increase in defense spending.[86]

Unilateralists focused on verification problems, to garner support from the majority of Americans who supported arms control but did not trust the Soviets. For example, a 1977 amendment to the Arms Control and Disarmament Act mandated a regular report to Congress about U.S. capabilities to verify compliance with each provision of proposed and current arms control accords. It was initiated by SALT opponents but gained support from Senators Claiborne Pell, Clifford Case, Alan Cranston, and other long-time arms control proponents. The final legislation replaced the call for "effective verification" in the House version with language about "adequate verification" from the Senate version. Yet the legislation institutionalized a highly adversarial, worst-case approach by specifying that ACDA's assessment should "assume that all measures of concealment not expressly prohibited could be employed and that standard practices could be altered so as to impede verification."[87]

As part of their anti-CTB campaign, Unilateralists amplified accusations of Soviet TTBT violations. Both sides had agreed to honor the 150-kt limit after March 31, 1976, even though the treaty was unratified. AFTAC soon began reporting seismic signals that could correspond to Soviet tests well above 150 kt, but the Soviets denied any wrongdoing.[88] AFTAC's scientific review panel unanimously concluded that its yield estimation formula needed a bias correction to account for differences in test site geology. To minimize the likelihood of underestimating Soviet yields, however, the panel recommended a correction factor that was only about half as large as the most likely value indicated by the seismic data.[89] After an intense interagency study, the Carter administration concluded that "the balance of evidence" suggested Soviet compliance, but CTB opponents inside and outside the government were not convinced.[90] Had the TTBT been ratified and its protocol implemented, the United States would have had better information about the appropriate bias correction. Still, this would not have satisfied American Unilateralists, who maintained that reliable calibration data could only be collected by U.S. agents making on-site measurements during Soviet nuclear tests.

Unilateralists used the TTBT compliance controversy to increase popular anxiety about test ban cooperation. They asserted that new yield estimation procedures let the Soviets test much larger bombs than the Americans could while still appearing to be in compliance.[91] For example, a *New York Times* article reported that the Soviets had violated the TTBT with a test that seemed to be at least 160 kt by the new estimation procedures but that might have been as large as 650 kt if the old methods were used.[92] Of course, the lower estimate was well within the compliance range, given the random fluctuation of seismic signals. The higher estimate both ignored the need for a bias correction and assumed that the true yield was at the very top of the range defined by a factor of 2 uncertainty. But when test ban supporters pointed this out, opponents used it as evidence that seismology was inherently imprecise and thus an unreliable basis for CTB verification.

American Unilateralists also used the stockpile reliability issue to convince Carter that the domestic battle to ratify a CTB would jeopardize his other arms control goals. Since scientists with extensive nuclear weapons experience challenged the technical merits of the stockpile reliability argument, Harold Brown asked York to evaluate the competing claims. York concluded that a CTB would not actually reduce stockpile reliability but that "the U.S. national security establishment is too high strung and nervous to live contentedly with a CTBT."[93] York did not think that Carter was persuaded that potential reliability problems could not be detected and fixed without nuclear tests, only that the domestic costs of CTB ratification would be higher than he had expected.[94] Thus, even though Carter did not realign his own preferences (as Agnew claims), he began to search for new ways to avoid a conflict between his desire for a CTB and others' interest in testing.[95]

The more that Cautious Cooperators worried about stockpile reliability, the easier it was for Unilateralists to ratchet up U.S. verification demands. Donald Kerr, one of DOE's most outspoken test ban opponents, testified that the Soviets could conduct secret reliability tests if the CTB verification system could not detect and identify subcritical explosions—an impossible task without granting inspectors access to nuclear laboratories.[96] A report produced by the House Armed Services Committee claimed that a CTB "would amount to a policy of U.S. self-denial of scientific and technical information about existing and new weapons. ... To the extent that the United States would be unable to *prove* whether a nuclear test has taken place, a CTBT would depend upon faith and trust in the leaders of the U.S.S.R."[97]

Carter did not question whether it was realistic or necessary to insist that CTBT verification provide incontrovertible proof of any violation. Instead, he tried to calm critics by shrinking the duration and scope of test ban cooperation. In September 1978, the president moved from supporting a five-year ban with easy conditions for renewal to a treaty that would have to be renegotiated and reratified after three years. The United States also announced that small nuclear explosions should be permitted during the brief ban on larger tests, although negotiators never clearly defined the difference between a "permitted nuclear experiment" and a small banned explosion.[98] Carter remained committed to a CTB but thought that his arms control agenda would have a better chance of success if SALT II were ratified before he brought a less ambitious test ban treaty to the Senate. These modifications failed to satisfy domestic critics, who argued more openly that test limits would destabilize deterrence, especially now that the United States lacked across-the-board nuclear superiority.

Once the president indicated that a complete and permanent test ban was no longer a high-priority objective, individuals and agencies who had never shared that goal felt free to be more obstructive. Negotiators had trouble getting timely instructions from Washington and when directives arrived, they often changed the U.S. position in counterproductive ways.[99] For example, the United States shifted from saying that instruments for in-country seismic stations could be manufactured anywhere as along as they met agreed specifications to insisting that equipment for the National Seismic Stations (NSSs) in the Soviet Union must be made in America (which deprecated Soviet technical capabilities).[100] After the Soviets accepted an American invitation to visit a prototype NSS built in the United States, months of bureaucratic infighting were required to arrange the visit.[101] Similarly, when the Soviets agreed to let the Americans place a U.S. seismic station near the reactor center at Obninsk, the project was blocked by new U.S. rules restricting the transfer of technology to the USSR.

Such shifts convinced the Soviets that the United States was not a reliable negotiating partner. Carter and Gromyko had reached a private agreement in late September 1978 to slow CTB negotiations until SALT II was complete.[102] Whereas Carter hoped to keep the CTB in a holding pattern until circumstances seemed more favorable, the Soviets apparently concluded that he was losing at home and might have already given up the fight. Senior Soviet officials told Warnke that changes in the American position on scope and duration convinced them that the United States was "not serious" about seeking a CTB.[103] Carter's decision to withdraw the TTBT and PNET from the ratification process increased Soviet skepticism about his desire for a CTB and his ability to ratify an accord, even if they continued to make verification concessions. The Soviet government also interpreted the resignation of Paul Warnke in October 1978 as "a clear indication . . . that anti-CTB forces were gaining the upper hand."[104] This suspicion was strengthened when Warnke was replaced at ACDA by Lieutenant General George Seignous, a retired military officer who belonged to the Peace through Strength Coalition. Warnke's role as ambassador to the CTB negotiations went to York, a former LLNL director with a strong commitment to arms control but serious doubts about the ratifiability of a CTB at that time.

The NSS issue best illustrates how test ban opponents convinced their governments to take positions that increased the substantive and strategic obstacles to cooperation. Regional seismic signals are useful for detecting decoupled explosions, as well as for discriminating between low-yield tests and small earthquakes. The United States had initially asked for 15 tamper-proof in-country monitoring stations inside the USSR. When it shifted to a finite three-year ban, it still wanted at least ten NSSs on Soviet soil. Andronik Petrosyants, head of the Soviet delegation, objected that the Soviets were "not prepared to incur heavy expenditures of resources on verification measures for this brief period."[105] Each station could cost $5 million to $6 million to install, plus another $1 million in annual operating costs.[106] Construction would take several years, so the treaty would expire soon after the NSSs were operational. Nevertheless, Gerald Johnson, the deputy delegation head, told the Soviets that he would not ask the Senate to ratify a CTB without ten NSSs. He trivialized the Soviets' cost concerns by asking, "Why should superpowers be discussing such minor expenses?"[107]

Test ban opponents and skeptics among Soviet elites seized on this issue as evidence of dubious American intentions. According to Neidle, the rigid American position "stimulated primordial Soviet fears regarding arms control as a means of collecting intelligence" and strengthened the position of those who expected the United States to improve its monitoring techniques in the three-year term of the treaty and then resume underground testing.[108] The NSS issue was "fought hard" in the Politburo.[109] The compromise announced in late November was to accept ten NSSs if both the United States and the U.K. agreed to bear an equal burden. The Soviets also wanted the stations scattered throughout the former British empire. York thought that the sites "seemed to have been selected by someone in Moscow using an old atlas or a child's stamp album as a guide. They made little sense in the modern world . . . seven out of ten sites were inappropriate, and five were even illegal."[110]

Soviet CTB proponents and opponents had different reasons for demanding that the British accept ten NSSs. The official justification was that the U.K. had tested in its territories before and might again, but Timerbayev admits that this was extremely unlikely.[111] For him, the real purpose was to gauge the West's intentions and keep a potential point of discord in reserve should Soviet leaders come to regret their earlier concessions. Since the United States justified its demand for ten NSSs on political grounds (persuading skeptical senators to ratify the treaty), the USSR replied in kind by insisting on British stations that would contribute little to verification and were in politically sensitive locations.[112] This move foreshadowed Gorbachev's decision to call the West's bluff on intrusive verification by asking for more of a presence than others would accept. It undoubtedly also appealed to Soviet Unilateralists as an opportunity to do what their American counterparts had been doing for years—use an unreasonably extensive verification demand to block cooperation.

The U.K. categorically rejected the Soviet list. One NSS inside British territorial limits was as far as the U.K. would go. Its justifications echoed Soviet complaints: ten stations were technically unnecessary for verification; they would be politically and logistically difficult to install; and they would increase the economic costs of CTB cooperation beyond what the government was ready to spend. Those who might have been willing to accept some extra NSSs for a CTB expected future arms control accords to be more expensive and complicated, so they wanted to set a precedent for agreement on the "minimum technically sound" verification.[113] Many British bureaucrats had less benign motives, however. Callaghan was heavily influenced by opposition stirred up by Victor Macklen, the deputy chief scientist in the Ministry of Defence, in conjunction with American test ban opponents, such as Kerr and Richard Perle (a member of Senator Jackson's staff).[114]

The NSS dispute could easily have been resolved if national leaders had still believed that their concessions would be reciprocated and the resulting agreement ratified. For example, the British could have embraced a Soviet suggestion to verify a three-year ban through NTM, data exchanges, and invitational OSIs, then add an NSS network after signatories had concluded a more permanent

CTB.[115] Likewise, the Soviets could have invoked their principle of proportionality as a face-saving way to justify having only one NSS in a country whose testing program was less than a tenth the size of the superpowers'. The Soviets had a fallback position on NSSs but were only prepared to use it if the West began taking a more constructive approach to the negotiations.[116] York later learned that Carter and David Owen (Callaghan's foreign minister) had tentatively agreed to offer three NSSs on British territory. Neither York nor Edmonds knew this during the negotiations, however. Hope for a compromise disappeared after Margaret Thatcher's Conservative government replaced Callaghan's Labour government in May 1979. By the time that SALT II was signed in June 1979, negotiators were so pessimistic about the prospects for a CTB that no one attempted to settle the NSSs numbers dispute, although they did resolve some technical details.

Shortly before the second NPT Review Conference in 1980, the United States, the U.K., and the USSR presented a progress report to an enlarged version of the CCD, now called the Conference on Disarmament (CD). Since negotiations recessed indefinitely after Carter's defeat in November, this progress report became the final formal statement of the tripartite talk's accomplishments.[117] The report indicates that negotiators had reached agreement in the late 1970s on each component of the CTB verification regime adopted in the 1990s: NTM; an international exchange of data from national seismic stations; challenge inspections; and a consultative commission. Some substantive verification questions remained, including what type of information should be used to trigger OSIs, how "permitted nuclear explosions" would be defined, and how large chemical explosions could be conducted without raising compliance concerns. Unfortunately, both the accomplishments and the remaining substantive dilemmas were often forgotten in the mounting attacks by domestic critics of test ban cooperation. In the words of one participant, adversarial positions taken on issues such as NSS "consumed, rather than built, goodwill . . . [and] contributed to the further decline . . . of détente."[118]

Conclusion

The superpowers' official support for an "adequately verifiable CTB" and their uneven progress toward that goal from 1963 to 1980 were a function of the way that the politics of verification fit into domestic and international struggles over security in a world with two roughly equivalent nuclear powers. The slow progress at the negotiating table did not correlate with advances in test ban verification technology. Instead, national representatives and domestic groups argued constantly about current verification capabilities, the purpose of new research projects, and the policy implications of technical advances. The development and diffusion of test ban monitoring methods made superpower claims to support an "adequately verifiable CTB" sound increasingly implausible as long as they refused to reconsider rigidly conflicting OSI demands or negotiate a limit on underground tests that was close to the verification threshold. Still, it took a series of political decisions in the USSR and the United States before negotiators began to explore whether improvements in NTM offered win-win ways to address most verification concerns.

Technical advances had brought the superpowers closer together, but a range of substantive questions remained that could only be answered through political bargaining and compromise. Some moves, such as the Soviet's PNE moratorium and the superpowers' convergence on the principle of challenge inspections, offered cooperative ways to cope with the shortcomings of NTM. Others, such as Carter's decision to address the stockpile reliability issue by unilaterally narrowing the scope and duration of a test ban, kept national leaders who sincerely wanted a CTB and had extensive monitoring capabilities from reaching agreement on verification.

Most analyses of arms control during the 1960s and 1970 examine how strategic parity affected superpower agreement on significant arms control. This chapter offered a different perspective by exploring the ways in which the politics of verification influenced how the superpowers responded to strategic parity. U.S. security groups had conflicting reactions to Soviet nuclear parity, as they had to other major developments in the nuclear arms race. Arms Control Advocates believed that secure nuclear retaliatory capabilities on both sides increased the value of a CTB, decreased the risks of cooperation, and reduced the requirements for verification. Unilateralists thought that the rapid growth in Soviet nuclear capabilities and the loss of U.S. nuclear superiority made test restrictions more dangerous and effective verification more difficult than ever before. The astounding expansion of the superpowers' arsenals increased Cautious Cooperators' anxieties and their ambivalence about arms control, for a mistake in either direction could have catastrophic consequences. Soviet leaders were less overtly divided than were Americans; nevertheless, once they reached rough parity there were many signs of internal disagreement over the value of arms control, the risks of verification, and the reliability of the United States as a negotiating partner. The challenge is to explain why superpower leaders responded to these debates with rhetorical support for an adequately verifiable CTB, followed by two modest test ban treaties, then a major push for a CTB, and why none of these approaches had enough domestic support to be stable.

Because both superpowers had repeatedly used verification deadlocks as a way to express support for test restraint while avoiding new restrictions in the past, it is little wonder that they tried first to revive their traditional avoidance strategy. Calling for an "adequately verifiable CTB" while perpetuating the OSI deadlock worked temporarily, because most Arms Control Advocates and Cautious Cooperators still assumed that support for verification research was a reliable indication of cooperative intentions. As seismic monitoring capabilities improved and interest in nuclear arms control increased, this avoidance strategy collapsed. Nixon and Kissinger tried to gain domestic support for a pair of "first step" treaties that bypassed most verification arguments and placed few significant constraints on nuclear testing programs. But American opponents and proponents of a CTB both saw the TTBT and the PNET as steps away from their preferred interpretations of official support for an "adequately verifiable CTB." Moreover, a decade of Soviet refusal to consider any cooperative test ban verification had created a paradoxical situation wherein international agreements for data exchanges and PNE inspections were first reached for minor accords that lacked the domestic constituency needed for ratification. Given this legacy, the second generation of CTB negotiations started with a mix of optimism about solving verification problems and skepticism about domestic support for arms control. Over time, Unilateralists were able to exploit divisions in the Carter administration to alter U.S. policy in ways that decreased the significance of test ban cooperation, increased Soviet resistance to Western verification demands, and exacerbated doubts about superpower arms control.

Still, the superpowers made major progress on verification at a time when their rivalry remained strong and decision makers lacked a clear consensus on arms control policy. Once Brezhnev became seriously interested in a CTB, the Soviets were willing to negotiate verification measures that would have been both workable and tolerable without using "sinkers" (a PNE exemption or insistence on French and Chinese participation) to preclude final agreement. Soviet willingness to compromise depended on their assessment that a provision was necessary for verification and sufficient for ratification. The stronger their doubts about either of these conditions, the harder it was to reach agreement. If President Carter had had a clearer understanding of the politics of verification, perhaps he would have handled questions about stockpile reliability, Soviet TTBT compliance, treaty duration, and NSS differently, thus reducing the counterproductive two-level dynamics that killed the second generation of CTB negotiations.

7

Cooperative Verification at the Cold War's Conclusion

WHEN PRESIDENT REAGAN ASSUMED OFFICE in January 1981, the prospects for arms control seemed worse than they had since the disarmament deadlock of the early 1950s. The new administration argued that arms control could only enhance American security if the United States regained military superiority, then used coercive diplomacy to secure intrusive verification of asymmetrical reductions in the most threatening Soviet systems. By the end of Reagan's second term, the USSR had agreed to routine observation and challenge inspections of conventional military activities for the 1986 Stockholm Accord, and it granted unprecedented OSI rights for the 1987 INF Treaty. The pattern of increasingly extensive verification for more significant accords continued as the Bush administration negotiated quantitative and qualitative constraints specified by START I (1991) and CFE (1990). With these accords came a dramatic improvement in superpower relations, growing liberalization in the USSR, democratization in Eastern Europe, the dissolution of the Warsaw Pact, and the disintegration of the USSR in December 1991. Were the unprecedented verification accords of the 1980s a cause or a consequence of the Cold War's conclusion?

Once again, theorists and practitioners answer this question differently depending on their assumptions about international relations. Unilateralists maintain that Reagan's "peace through strength" policies forced the USSR to accept verified arms control on U.S. terms because continued competition would be worse. Arms Control Advocates, on the other hand, maintain that domestic changes in the USSR caused a convergence in superpower interests and attitudes toward verification. These explanations assume that agreement resulted from shifts in the balance of power or a harmonization of interests. Cautious Cooperators, by contrast, see agreement on verification (due to technological advances or political concessions) as enabling more significant arms control and improved political relations.

This chapter evaluates the politics of test ban verification from the anti–arms control backlash of the early 1980s through the 1992 passage of U.S. legislation mandating a moratorium and serious CTB negotiations. The test ban case does not provide a complete picture of verification politics in the 1980s because the most dramatic breakthroughs occurred on other arms control issues. Yet the 1986 in-country seismic monitoring project by the Natural Resources Defense Council (NRDC) and the Soviet Academy of Sciences (SAS) represents the first actual implementation of a cooperative verification accord in the USSR. The test ban case is also valuable for other reasons. Detailed knowledge of past arguments and agreements contradicts claims that Gorbachev suddenly and completely transformed Soviet thinking about verification to match U.S. policy preferences. Evidence that coercive diplomacy has historically complicated the politics of verification challenges Reagan administration assertions that this strategy was necessary or even intended to facilitate agreement on test ban verification. Contrasting the NRDC-SAS project with the 1987 JVE assesses the extent to which transnational groups can use verification achievements to promote arms control, as well as the degree to which governmental actors can manipulate technical information to block cooperation. Finally, the roundabout route to the 1992 revival of serious CTB negotiations reveals the complicated relationship between the substantive and strategic sides of verification politics.

Verification disputes and coalition-building strategies continued to have an independent but often counter-cooperative effect on arms control decisions at the end of the Cold War. Contrary to claims of broad-based domestic support for their "trust but verify" policies, Reagan Unilateralists failed to institutionalize their test ban preferences (no new limits) because they found it increasingly difficult to convince Cautious Cooperators that restrictions could not be reliably verified through mutually acceptable means. Similarly, even though Gorbachev could make major changes in Soviet verification policy, his use of verification concessions to increase pressure for CTB negotiations was constrained by Soviet hardliners, doubts about his motives among Western Cautious Cooperators, and his own calculations about the benefits, costs, and risks of test ban verification. The ideas about verification that dominated U.S. domestic debates delayed serious test ban negotiations much longer than one would predict from the changing political, military, and technical context. The superpowers could not agree on a TTBT verification protocol until 1990, and then the Bush administration declared that the United States needed ten years of experience with the new verification arrangements before considering further test restrictions. The legislative defeat of this blocking strategy was possible only because Gorbachev had called American Unilateralists' bluff on verification enough times to erode the plausibility of this claim for Cautious Cooperators in Congress.

Test Ban Verification as a Weapon in Reagan's Attack on Arms Control

The Reagan administration was less divided over and less favorable toward arms control than any administration since Truman's.[1] The new president opposed negotiated constraints on U.S. defenses because he believed that American technological prowess was a more reliable source of security than were Soviet promises. Détente-era arms control was fundamentally flawed, his administration argued, because the Soviets preferred exploitation to cooperation and thought that "promises are like pie crusts, made to be broken."[2] They charged that verification based primarily on NTM neither deterred all significant cheating nor provided the unambiguous proof needed to repudiate bad bargains. As two Reagan associates wrote, verification for future arms control accords must be "so airtight that we can have no doubt whether or not the Soviets are living up to the spirit as well as the letter of the agreement."[3] Even when the USSR complied with treaty limits, arms control still hurt U.S. security if it codified Soviet strategic advantages or lulled American vigilance. Instead of thinking that deterrence was stable if both sides had secure retaliatory capabilities, the Reagan administration argued that U.S. nuclear neglect had created a "window of vulnerability," a time when ruthless Soviet leaders might use their strategic superiority to attack or blackmail the United States.[4] Rectifying this dangerous situation required a five-year, $180 billion effort to modernize each leg of the nuclear triad and develop strategic defenses.[5] To achieve this goal, the administration needed to sustain domestic support for defense spending; minimize popular pressure for meaningful arms control; and prepare to repudiate SALT II, the TTBT, the ABM treaty, and maybe even the LTBT should they block progress toward a nuclear warfighting capability.

"Peace through strength" and verification-first policies appealed to both Unilateralists and extremely Cautious Cooperators in the Reagan administration. The more ideological and confrontational group included Defense Secretary Caspar Weinberger and his assistants, Fred Iklé and Richard Perle. The roles that had been occupied by the strongest test ban supporters in previous administrations—the director of ACDA and the science adviser—had also been given to proponents of nuclear self-reliance.[6] They approached arms control negotiations in the same way that Truman-era Unilateralists had: as a "propaganda war" fought to increase support for U.S. defense spending and military policies.[7] Alexander Haig and George Shultz, Reagan's secretaries of state, led the more pragmatic faction that wanted "hardheaded détente."[8] They saw arms control discussions as necessary for alliance relations and potentially useful for managing the superpower competition but believed that arms control agreements would not serve American interests unless the United States negotiated from a position of strength and solved verification problems before accepting arms restrictions.

The new administration entered office with a brief window of domestic support for confrontation. The 1979 invasion of Afghanistan had coalesced public anxieties about Soviet belligerence and dramatically increased support for defense spending.[9] Soon after his inauguration, Reagan requested and received a $32.6 billion addition to the defense budget. This, plus the $20 billion that Carter added before leaving office represented a 12.5 percent real growth in budget authority for 1981 and a 12 percent increase for 1982.[10]

The new administration used this hawkish honeymoon to break the tradition of symbolic support for an "adequately verifiable CTB." It suspended, then ended, trilateral negotiations because "international conditions are . . . not now propitious," even if verification problems could be solved.[11] As long as the United States depended on deterrence, Reagan officials argued, it must test to ensure the safety and reliability of nuclear stockpiles, learn more about weapons effects, and develop optimal warheads for new delivery systems. After the administration made the development of strategic defenses a top priority in 1983, it had another strong reason to reject a CTB. U.S. representatives offered to talk about test ban verification problems in the Conference on Disarmament (CD) but never mentioned the progress that had been made toward agreement on test ban verification in détente-era negotiations.

The negative domestic reaction to Reagan's withdrawal from CTB negotiations was symptomatic of growing doubts about nuclear deterrence. Only 42 percent of poll respondents supported his decision to end CTB negotiations—a large increase over the 17 percent who opposed a CTB in 1978 but well below the 54 percent who wanted talks to continue.[12] Such reactions reflected worrisome trends for the administration, including a forty-point drop in support for defense spending and rapidly growing pressure for an immediate freeze on all nuclear weapons testing, production, and deployment.[13]

Reagan officials tried to dissipate pressure for arms control by stressing verification problems, because most Americans assumed that the Soviets would cheat if they had the chance.[14] In May 1982, for example, 20 percent of respondents were Arms Control Advocates who favored a freeze even if violations could escape detection, 67 percent were Cautious Cooperators whose support depended on verification, and 13 percent were pure Unilateralists who opposed a freeze under any circumstances.[15] Therefore, Reagan officials used doubts about test ban verification to woo Cautious Cooperators, although this was not their primary reason for ending CTB negotiations.

The Unilateralists' blocking strategy had four interlocked components: (1) intensify noncompliance accusations to reinforce doubts about Soviet intentions; (2) develop a tougher U.S. standard for treaty verifiability; (3) ensure that the Soviets will be unable or unwilling to meet the new verification demands; and (4) use Soviet resistance to American verification demands as further evidence that they are unreliable arms control partners. The Reagan approach to TTBT ratification shows how this worked in practice.

U.S. officials charged the Soviets with "likely violations" of the TTBT as part of a larger campaign to convince Americans that there was a "systematic pattern" of Soviet arms control violations.[16] References to classified research by Heckrotte and Peter Moulthrop (another LLNL scientist) were used to support these accusations. This work, begun during the Carter administration, actually showed that the pattern of Soviet testing was compatible with TTBT compliance. Uncertainties in seismic yield determination made it impossible to rule out minor violations, however.[17] CTB opponents focused only on the second part of this analysis, even though many of the government's own seismic experts thought that the evidence was equivocal. The deputy manager of LLNL's seismic monitoring program maintained that "the Administration and the military just want to believe the worst."[18] Scientists at LANL were more skeptical about the Soviets' TTBT compliance. According to Heckrotte, though, the LANL analysis rested on an unrealistic assumption.[19] It may have also reflected LANL's parochial interest in presenting its own on-site yield estimation techniques as preferable to the seismic methods emphasized at LLNL.

Since seismic evidence was "not inconsistent" with these charges, but also not conclusive, the Reagan administration announced that it would not submit the TTBT and PNET for ratification or consider further test restrictions without negotiating a new TTBT verification protocol. They did not initially specify what effective verification involved, other than to say that NTM must be supplemented with "cooperative" measures, including OSIs. To buttress this position, Reagan officials downplayed the improvements in seismic monitoring by switching from a 90- to a 95-percent confidence level and insisting that seismology still had a factor of 2 uncertainty under this more demanding standard.[20] They also presented verification statistics in a misleading manner. One official testified that "a Soviet test for which we estimate a yield of 150 kt may have, with 95% probability, an actual yield as high as 300 kt."[21] There was, however, there was only a 1 in 40 chance that a single test with a central yield value of 150 kt was actually 300 kt, and a 1 in 1,600 chance that two 300-kt blasts would appear compliant.

To anyone who did not understand the intricacies of seismic yield estimation, such testimony strongly implied that the Soviets were almost certainly cheating in a major way but that the seismology could not provide the proof required to stop violations or abrogate the TTBT.

The accusations about TTBT noncompliance illustrate how powerful players can manipulate technical arguments for strategic purposes. Pro-CTB seismologists tried to educate citizens and policy makers about more accurate yield estimation procedures but had trouble getting a hearing and had their arguments dismissed as self-serving.[22] When Charles Archambeau circulated a draft article describing how DARPA had corrupted the peer-review process to bury evidence about a more realistic yield estimation procedure, DOD quickly classified the article.[23] In response to an air force study contradicting claims of likely TTBT violations, Perle attacked the intelligence community for "undermining" the administration's position and insisted that his department should "control this area."[24] After two noncompliance reports using the old methods, the CIA updated its procedures in 1986 and reduced estimates of past Soviet yields by 20 to 30 percent.[25] ACDA and DOD, however, retained the old method and altered or deleted sections of public hearings that mentioned the revised compliance record.[26] Officials who used the old method claimed that nonseismic intelligence validated their position but were unable or unwilling to support this claim. Perle finally admitted, "I didn't particularly care much what the (correct) answer was. It doesn't have any profound bearing on our policy."[27]

Reagan officials also purposefully perpetuated problems with seismic yield estimation. Arms Control Advocates argued that uncertainty could be reduced to 1.5 by exchanging calibration data or using information from more types of seismic waves. Instead, DOE declared that since "a test ban or moratorium is not now in the security interests of this country," it would not "support or fund any effort that is contrary to Administration policy."[28]

After intense interagency debate, the Reagan administration decided that the new TTBT verification protocol should permit an on-site hydrodynamic yield estimation method, CORRTEX, for all Soviet tests over 75 kt.[29] Shock waves from large explosions expand more quickly than those from smaller shots. CORRTEX uses an electrical cable in a vertical hole (the test shaft or one near it) to measure shock front expansion by seeing how quickly the point where the front crushes the cable moves upward.[30] U.S. officials claimed that CORRTEX could lower uncertainty to 1.3, although small location errors raise uncertainty to the factor of 2 associated with basic seismological methods.[31] They also asserted that CORRTEX was inherently better because hydrodynamic verification is "direct" and seismic monitoring is "indirect," although both procedures measure a signal that has traveled some distance from its source.[32]

Reagan officials doubted that the Soviets would include CORRTEX in a new TTBT verification protocol, even though (or perhaps because) the USSR continued to support an immediate CTB. Anyone who sincerely believed that the Soviets were violating the TTBT assumed that the USSR would resist steps to tighten verification. Those who knew that the Soviets probably were in compliance should have realized that they would have legitimate reasons for opposing CORRTEX. On-site yield estimation would multiply the costs and risks of an accord that offered only minor arms control benefits. Personnel using CORRTEX must be present for ten weeks before and during each test, but seismologists can work outside national boundaries or at internal locations far from test facilities. To achieve 1.3 uncertainty, CORRTEX requires information that might reveal the purpose or performance of the test.[33] The Soviets might still have been willing to pay this price if they had believed that ratifying the TTBT and PNET would promote near-term agreement on a CTB. Making domestic support for the TTBT contingent on CORRTEX would have the opposite effect. Seismic networks can detect extremely small tests around the world, but CORRTEX is increasingly impractical for yields below 50 kt and useless for unannounced tests. Thus, the Soviets had little incentive to set a precedent that would complicate lower test limits and obstruct a CTB.[34]

As part of an election-year attempt to tone down his bellicose image, Reagan made a proposal in September 1984 for superpower scientists to try hydrodynamic yield estimation at each other's test sites.[35] This fit the Reagan administration's strategy of using the Soviet response to unacceptable U.S. verification demands as the litmus test of their arms control intentions. Few members of Congress or attentive citizens understood the technical basis for arguments about Soviet TTBT compliance or alternative yield estimation procedures, so it was easy to convince them that Soviet support for "cooperative" verification was politically important to increase American confidence in arms control, regardless of whether more intrusive monitoring methods were technically necessary.[36] With public debate in the United States focused on the benign functions of verification, the Soviets' negative response to Reagan's invitation was easily depicted as evidence of their unwillingness to resolve TTBT compliance disputes or improve verification.[37]

Reagan officials also hoped that their CORRTEX proposal would decrease pressure for test ban negotiations in other ways. Privileging a government-controlled mode of verification would trump seismic evidence from open sources. Arguing about the relative merits of seismic and hydrodynamic monitoring would also make Arms Control Advocates fight a two-front battle for intermediate limits and a total ban. Frank Gaffney, Perle's deputy, later admitted his rea-

son for pushing CORRTEX: "The more time wasted on discussions and experimentation of monitoring techniques irrelevant to the verification of an environment in which there are no legal tests, the easier it will be to stave off demands for the more constraining comprehensive test ban."[38]

In short, because the Reagan administration was more hawkish than most
Americans, it tried to use the politics of verification to institutionalize its test
ban preferences before support for its nuclear modernization program ebbed
away. Cautious Cooperators favored arms negotiations but distrusted the Soviets, so Reagan officials sought to convince them that the Soviets had violated
previous test restrictions and opposed effective verification even for the relatively insignificant TTBT. The short-term success of this strategy reflected the
Reagan administration's ability to manipulate technical information about monitoring capabilities and depict support for verification-first proposals as a reliable
indictor of arms control sincerity.

Challenges to the Reagan Administration's Blocking Strategy

The blocking strategy also assumed that Soviet leaders would always react neg-
atively to coercive pressures for intrusive verification and that this hostile reaction would reduce domestic pressure for arms control. Even before Gorbachev
came to power, however, both of these assumptions had been contradicted. In
an effort to restore détente, Brezhnev and his heirs continued to show increased
flexibility on verification, but their overtures attracted little attention in the West.
American distrust of the USSR had not decreased much by the start of Reagan's
second term, but fear of nuclear war had grown so great that the dangers of unconstrained competition began to outweigh the risks of imperfect verification.
Gorbachev's main innovation on the test ban issue had less to do with changing
Soviet ideas about verification than with finding a strategy to channel American
anxieties into effective pressure for CTB negotiations.

Initial Efforts Accomplish Little

In the early 1980s, the Soviets neither matched Reagan's Unilateralism nor
launched an effective counter-response. The USSR was led by a series of men
who were old, tired, and ill: Brezhnev until November 1982, Yury Andropov until
February 1984, and Konstantin Chernenko until March 1985. They were alarmed
by Reagan's military buildup and afraid that he was using a "myth of a Soviet
threat" to justify aggressive preparations. Instead of increasing its military effort,
though, the USSR kept the lower level of defense spending that it had adopted

in the mid-1970s.[39] It continued to take an incremental approach in START and INF negotiations, and saved its bolder proposals for issues the United States opposed, such as a ban on space weapons.

The Soviet Union made several important but largely unacknowledged changes in its verification policy during this period. After decades of suspicion toward international monitoring agencies, the USSR started to speak approvingly of the IAEA in 1982, offered to put some nuclear power plants and research reactors under IAEA safeguards, and suggested that the IAEA's vast experience might be relevant to other arms control problems.[40] In 1984, the Soviets modified their stance on verification for a chemical weapons ban to include not only NTM and challenge inspections but also permanent oversight by international agents at CW destruction facilities.[41] Yet most Americans knew too little about Soviet verification policy to spot these signs of increased openness.

East bloc negotiators tried unsuccessfully to convince Soviet leaders to alter other verification positions that were difficult to defend and detrimental to the Soviet image, such as the claim that NTM alone could determine whether the warheads on a particular ICBM were fully MIRVed.[42] On core security issues such as strategic arms control, old-guard leaders were unwilling to make major shifts that would not be reciprocated. Instead, they fell back into their old pattern of hoping that belligerent statements would frighten domestic groups in the West and increase popular pressure for arms control concessions. But once the NATO deployment of INF was imminent in fall 1983, Soviet leaders concluded that Western citizens were too satisfied with their improving standard of living to rise up against their leaders and reverse the decision.[43] In frustration, the USSR played into the Reagan administration's blocking strategy by walking out of the INF talks and suspending START negotiations.

U.S. officials depicted the Soviets' refusal to negotiate as further evidence of their evil intentions. By 1984, however, the Reagan administration's military buildup and one-dimensional anti-Soviet rhetoric had caused an unexpected counter-reaction in public opinion.[44] Popular attitudes toward the USSR were more complex and ambivalent than during the immediate post-détente backlash. Sixty percent of Americans still thought that the Soviets "have cheated on just about every treaty and agreement they've ever signed," yet 88 percent believed that Russians and Americans could be friends if Soviet leaders had a different attitude. Ninety-three percent felt that "picking a fight with the Soviet Union is too dangerous in a nuclear world," whereas more than two thirds of respondents preferred "live-and-let-live pragmatism" over ideological anticommunism. A majority, moreover, was ready to take some risks for peace. Sixty-one percent favored declaring a unilateral freeze on nuclear weapons development to see if the Soviets would follow suit; 56 percent wanted arms control "even if foolproof verification cannot be guaranteed." Support for a CTB had rebounded to 69 percent.[45] In short, instead of institutionalizing broad support for confrontation, Reagan's Unilateralism pushed many Cautious Cooperators in the opposite direction.

The Reagan administration's manipulation of verification politics to prevent further test restrictions also alienated many nonaligned states. The CD's Group of Scientific Experts continued to meet regularly, and their 1984 trial run of a prototype data exchange network was a "qualified success."[46] The neutral members of the CD rebelled, however, against further discussion of test ban verification without a mandate to begin serious negotiations. In May 1984, the leaders of Argentina, Greece, India, Mexico, Sweden, and Tanzania called for a complete freeze on the testing, production, and deployment of nuclear weapons.[47] When the United States pointedly ignored this "Five Continent Peace Initiative," the Soviets proposed using the Reagan administration's attitude toward immediate CTB negotiations as the litmus test of its intentions.[48]

Gorbachev's New Thinking about the Politics of Verification

Gorbachev came to power in March 1985 with a strong desire to revitalize the Soviet economy by gaining control over the military budget and minimizing pressures to match the American buildup. He had few fixed ideas about security other than that previous policies (invading Afghanistan) and attempts at coercive diplomacy (ending INF negotiations) had been counterproductive.[49] Searching for new ways to moderate the Cold War, Gorbachev changed the structure of security decision making in ways that increased flexibility and brought new people into the process. In the Brezhnev era, arms control decisions were made by consensus among a small group of policy makers dominated by the Ministry of Defense; Gorbachev, in contrast, simultaneously exerted more control from the top and expanded the circle of debate to include civilians from the Ministry of Foreign Affairs, the Soviet Academy of Sciences, and reform-oriented international relations institutions. The new decision-making structure allowed access for a range of indigenous ideas and transnational proposals.[50] It also enabled Gorbachev to implement policy changes relatively quickly. Yet debates over Soviet security never produced a complete consensus. Instead, Gorbachev had to build arms control coalitions in a political environment in which critics could challenge his authority.

Many ideas associated with Gorbachev's new thinking, such as mutual security and reasonable military sufficiency, had been discussed by Soviet intellectuals for decades. During the mid-1980s, however, these ideas entered the political mainstream and dramatically altered arms control policy. Debates tended to be about implementation more than the concepts' validity.[51] For example, Soviet leaders had always believed that diplomatic initiatives could enhance security. But Gorbachev wanted to give priority to political approaches rather than military methods, whereas traditional thinkers still questioned whether the West was a reliable negotiating partner. Mutual security and defensive defense were especially uncomfortable concepts for military leaders, because they contradicted traditional assumptions about the inherent aggressiveness of capitalist countries, the zero-sum nature of power, and the desirability of protecting the USSR by repelling an attack, then defeating and occupying hostile countries. Implementing these general principles was even more controversial because major arms control threatened vested interests. Reconfiguring the Soviet military to be purely defensive would also be difficult and expensive, especially if the West did not make comparable changes. How far and how fast Gorbachev could go on arms control depended, in part, on how U.S. responses affected domestic coalitions in the USSR.[52]

Gorbachev's earliest moves on verification—including his promise at the November 1985 Geneva Summit that the Soviets would be reasonable about CTB verification if the United States agreed to stop testing—occurred in areas in which the Soviets had already decided that they could be more open if the West became serious about arms control again. By 1986, the Soviets were routinely declaring that they favored "the strictest possible verification in any form."[53] After Gorbachev announced an array of arms control initiatives on January 15, 1986, for example, Foreign Minister Edward Shevardnadze announced that the problem of verification "is non-existent now" because the USSR was ready for international monitoring and bilateral inspections, as well as NTM.[54] Such unconditional statements were part of an effort to call the Reagan administration's bluff and discredit verification-based blocking strategies. Soviet officials across the security spectrum could support such moves because those who favored a rapid, radical implementation of the new thinking saw transparency as a key component of mutual security; those who were more skeptical did not expect that the Reagan administration would sign major arms control accords, regardless of their verification provisions.[55]

When it came to practical proposals in serious negotiations, the Soviets still weighed verification trade-offs. Increased flexibility came from changes in their cost-benefit calculations due to the broader vision of arms control, the realization that OSIs would provide little collateral information not available from other intelligence sources, the desire to avoid embarrassment caused by implausible verification claims, and the recognition by key institutions that fears of verification abuse had been exaggerated.[56] The biggest departures, such as the Soviet decision to permit intrusive monitoring of retained systems covered by START limits, occurred in the late 1980s, after the Reagan administration had signed some accords, thereby demonstrating that its verification demands were not always an excuse to avoid arms control. Internal Soviet resistance to U.S. verification demands also decreased as the negotiation and implementation of the Stockholm Accord, the INF treaty, and the CFE treaty forced the West to design verification provisions that it could live with and to demonstrate that it would conduct OSIs in a reasonable manner.[57]

Western observers have often overstated the novelty of Gorbachev's approach to verification. Few Americans knew enough about the history of arms control negotiations to recognize the range of verification options that the Soviets had already proposed or accepted under appropriate circumstances. Moreover, without a detailed knowledge of the politics of verification, few foreigners could judge which previous Soviet verification offers were pure propaganda, made when the prospects of agreement were low, and which were sincere efforts to reach a mutually acceptable accord. Reagan officials compounded the confusion by routinely ignoring all instances of Soviet support for cooperative verification before Reagan's peace through strength policies. Even some Arms Control Advocates exaggerated the unprecedented nature of Gorbachev's verification policy in an attempt to convince Cautious Cooperators that he had a radically new attitude toward arms control.

To increase popular pressure for serious CTB negotiations, Gorbachev declared a moratorium on Soviet nuclear tests from August 6, 1985 (the fortieth anniversary of the Hiroshima bombing), until the end of the year. A five-month moratorium was a purely symbolic gesture. Still, this was one of more than twenty-five arms control initiatives that Gorbachev undertook during his first two years in office to reassure Western Cautious Cooperators and force Western leaders to take responsibility for the absence of new accords.[58]

Reagan responded predictably to Gorbachev's initiative: joint efforts to improve verification would be safer and more meaningful than another unmonitored moratorium. The day that Gorbachev announced his halt, the United States repeated its offer for Soviet scientists to observe a CORRTEX display.[59] It did not require reciprocal rights to take hydrodynamic measurements of a Soviet test, since none were occurring. This ruled out collateral information collection by the United States, as well as any possibility that a CORRTEX experiment in the USSR could resolve the TTBT compliance controversy or enhance seismic monitoring for a CTB. The USSR, therefore, replied that further TTBT monitoring measures should be discussed only if verification proved inadequate after the twin treaties were ratified and calibration data exchanged.[60]

In a third-party maneuver to magnify the political impact of the moratorium, the leaders of the Five Continent Peace Initiative offered to place monitoring devices on their own territory and help the superpowers set up in-country seismic stations.[61] Several American scientists most opposed to Reagan's test ban policy had developed this proposal so that scientists could see how new seismic techniques functioned in the field and diplomats need not negotiate and implement a full-blown system based on unproven technology. In an unprecedented show of Soviet support for implementing verification before agreement on arms control, Gorbachev endorsed the plan. The United States, however, refused to join even a monitored moratorium.

Reagan Unilateralists tried to depict the moratorium as further evidence of Soviet duplicity: Gorbachev was not serious about arms control but hoped to put the burden of noncooperation on the United States. The national security adviser, Robert McFarlane, accused the Soviets of conducting a "flurry" of tests before the moratorium, although the number of Soviet tests in 1985 was about half their annual average for the last decade.[62] Adelman invoked the broken moratorium myth from the 1960s as evidence that a closed society could conduct clandestine tests or secret preparations for a breakout. A moratorium would also halt vital U.S. research on strategic defense, accurate warheads, and communication during nuclear war, thus undermining "the safety, reliability, effectiveness, and credibility of our nuclear deterrent which keeps the peace."[63]

The moratorium created a public relations problem for the Reagan officials but did not convince Congress to demand CTB negotiations.[64] Even though the Senate had passed a nonbinding resolution for TTBT and PNET ratification and CTB negotiation before the moratorium started, the House decided not to vote on a similar measure in October 1985, after the moratorium was under way. The administration warned that voting would present a dangerous "image of internal discord on arms control matters" before the superpower summit. Arms Control Advocates agreed to hold back because they sensed that many of their supporters were "losing interest in the fight." They also feared that their resolution might be replaced by an alternative that would have called for delaying TTBT ratification until the Soviets accepted CORRTEX and postponing CTB talks until deep cuts in nuclear arsenals had been achieved.[65]

In short, by the end of 1985, American and Soviet Arms Control Advocates had broken old patterns in the politics of verification but not found a winning strategy. Gorbachev and Reagan were offering competing proposals for verification-first projects in hopes of convincing American Cautious Cooperators that they were sincerely interested in stable mutual cooperation. The target audience in Congress was conflicted and responded by withdrawing support for both Reagan's Unilateralism and test ban activism. Therefore, test ban supporters needed a new strategy to change policy in the United States before pro-testing factions in the USSR rebelled against the moratorium.

An Appeal to Congress via Nongovernmental Verification Collaboration

The NRDC-SAS in-country seismic monitoring project was a novel attempt to use a nongovernmental demonstration of verification capabilities to challenge official U.S. policy on nuclear testing. Whereas previous Soviet attempts at two-level gamesmanship in the politics of verification had aimed primarily at strengthening moderates in the U.S. Executive Branch, the main purpose of this project was to convince Cautious Cooperators in Congress to cut off funds for U.S. nuclear testing, regardless of what the Reagan administration wanted. The project proceeded despite vigorous attempts by Reagan Unilateralists to derail or discredit it. But it could not have happened without assistance from State Department officials who favored a return to serious arms control negotiations. Its effects on U.S. test ban policy were mixed. It helped to reenergize Arms Control Advocates and increase Cautious Cooperators' interest in test ban verification as a way to "open" the USSR. Many Cautious Cooperators and most Unilateralists were uneasy, however, about an alliance between the president's critics and the head of a foreign country. Thus, the Reagan administration did not have to move far to restore support for its step-by-step approach to test ban negotiations.

Transnational Collaboration to Circumvent the Reagan Administration

The NRDC-SAS project grew out of parallel proposals by different groups of Arms Control Advocates around the world. Shortly before the Five Continent Peace Initiative proposal for third-country monitoring of a mutual moratorium, Evgeny Velikhov (vice president of the Soviet Academy of Sciences and Gorbachev's unofficial science adviser) told Frank Von Hippel (an FAS physicist at Princeton) that the Soviet government might let foreigners set up a seismic monitoring system near the Soviet test site.[66] Meanwhile, Evernden was trying to gain data for a 1-kt threshold monitoring system by expanding a seismic monitoring agreement between the United States Geological Survey (USGS) and the SAS. Members of the NRDC, a large American environmental advocacy group of scientists and lawyers, wanted more information about United States and Soviet testing practices to educate Americans about the technical aspects of weapons development and arms control. In February 1986, therefore, Thomas Cochran, a senior NRDC scientist, devised a plan for independent superpower scientists to monitor the presence or absence of tests in both countries.

In an attempt to "change U.S. and world opinion about the sincerity of Soviet nuclear disarmament proposals," Velikhov invited representatives from these organizations to a seismic verification symposium in May 1986.[67] He chose the NRDC proposal for three seismic stations around NTS and Semipalatinsk because it required the least support from the U.S. government yet could have the greatest political impact by putting American scientists near the main Soviet test site. Since Evernden's efforts seemed to have support from the USGS and DARPA, and the NRDC had received a green light from the State Department, conference participants were optimistic.[68]

Velikhov wanted the NRDC-SAS project to start by the end of June, because he hoped that a quick and visible test ban breakthrough would have favorable effects on domestic debates in the United States and the USSR.[69] The U.S. House of Representatives was scheduled to vote in August on a 1-kt moratorium as part of the FY87 defense authorization bill. Gorbachev had managed to extend the Soviet moratorium over the objections of pro-testing groups in the USSR by presenting evidence that U.S. and international Arms Control Advocates were working hard for a CTB.[70] He needed proof that Soviet restraint could change U.S. testing policy, however, to secure another extension before the moratorium expired in August.

American participants in the NRDC project wanted to attack the technical and political components of Reagan's blocking strategy. Seismologists who agreed to operate the stations in the USSR were eager to "do good science." Measuring waves that have traveled from U.S. tests to seismic stations in Kazakhstan provides data about signal attenuation. If the stations could record when the USSR resumed testing, scientists could also compare regional waves with signals measured at teleseismic distances. Cochran also saw the project as hypothesis testing: since Gorbachev maintained that access would not be a problem for CTB verification and Reagan insisted that verification remained a major obstacle, requesting permission for in-country monitoring stations provided an "opportunity to make a liar out of one of them."[71] For Jacob Scherr, the NRDC lawyer who led the project with Cochran, the primary purpose was to change public perceptions of the Soviet Union. If Gorbachev was willing to let the project go forward, a dramatic demonstration of his new openness would reassure Cautious Cooperators in a way words never could.[72] Therefore, the stations were located "right on the doorstep" of the main Soviet test facility, ready to detect tiny explosions should the USSR violate its own moratorium.[73]

To start the monitoring project by the end of June, the NRDC needed official allies who shared their objectives and would facilitate their efforts. They had barely a month in which to raise more than a million dollars, select equipment, secure export licenses, and recruit seismologists.[74] Some State Department officials saw the NRDC project as a way to end the TTBT compliance controversy, set useful verification precedents, learn about short-range seismic monitoring, and refine U.S. negotiating positions.[75] John Whitehead, the deputy secretary of state, quietly assigned a liaison and expedited export licenses for the project. He did not, however, want his agency publicly associated with efforts to reverse U.S. policy. State officials were told to answer questions about the NRDC project by applauding Soviet willingness to share verification data yet questioning the merits of an asymmetrical arrangement between scientists sponsored by the Soviet government and a private organization opposed to official U.S. policy.[76]

Despite Gorbachev's support, Velikhov faced resistance from the Soviet Foreign Ministry, which disliked the idea of a diplomatic initiative directed by scientists, and from the Ministry of Defense, which opposed Americans near the Soviet test site.[77] When the NRDC team arrived in July, they had to wait in Moscow for four days while Velikhov argued that sending them home would create a major public embarrassment. Since the military's main concern involved monitoring once the test moratorium was over, the stand-off was resolved when the NRDC representatives signed a document stating that monitoring a Soviet nuclear test would not be essential to their project.

The onset of in-country monitoring produced an upsurge of American interest in arms control. This was the first time that an agreement on intrusive verification inside the USSR had ever been implemented. Once the NRDC took *New York Times* reporters, television crews, and *National Geographic* photographers to Semipalatinsk, U.S. Unilateralists could not easily ignore or dismiss the moratorium.[78] Nor could they insist that the Soviets would never open their borders to American inspectors. On August 8, 1986, the House voted 234–155 to withhold funds for nuclear tests above 1 kt from January 1987 until September 1987 if the USSR reciprocated and allowed in-country seismic verification.[79]

Chris Paine, the staffer for Senator Edward Kennedy who led the push for a 1-kt moratorium, believes that a well-orchestrated series of briefings about the NRDC project and a striking visual display in the lobby on the day of the House vote helped the measure pass by the largest margin of any arms control vote in Congress. According the Paine, the key to victory was that supporters made openness and verification, not test limitations per se, the focus of the vote.[80]

Closing the Window of Public Diplomacy

Since U.S. officials routinely depicted the inadequacies of seismic verification as a major obstacle to a CTB, those who had no interest in new test restrictions attacked the NRDC project. One of Perle's assistants admitted that "the NRDC's goals were totally the opposite of our own." They wanted to prove that a CTB is verifiable, while we'd made verification into the main public objection to a CTB because "verification is such a show stopper."[81] Even an agency like DARPA, which sought to improve its seismic monitoring capabilities, did not want independent scientists and arms control activists using a high profile project to challenge official claims about Soviet compliance and CTB verification requirements.[82]

A DARPA memorandum about the NRDC-SAS agreement illustrates the administration's dilemma.[83] Any response, the memo declared, should promote current U.S. testing policy and reduce the influence, propaganda value, or political gains for the USSR. The authors alleged that a nongovernmental project would provide unreliable information because the USSR could locate the seismic stations in noisy or unrepresentative locations. Nevertheless, they expected that Arms Control Advocates would use the ambiguous data to support their claims for seismic monitoring capabilities. This could "divert attention from, or claim to be a substitute for, the standing U.S. proposal to make CORRTEX measurements on nuclear tests. It will be hard for the public to distinguish between an essentially irrelevant and a highly valuable measurement program." Thus, the administration sought to blunt the political impact of the NRDC project without seeming intransigent on verification.

The fight between Cautious Cooperators and Unilateralists in the Reagan administration focused on visas for SAS members. The State Department wanted to reciprocate Soviet openness by granting unconditional visas. DOD, however, insisted that SAS members come only as government officials and solely to observe a CORRTEX demonstration. Rather than debate the real issue, the NSC staff announced that SAS members could make an official visit, watch CORRTEX, and go wherever else they wished. Alternatively, they could come to the

United States as guests of the NRDC on visas that would not let them to visit potential monitoring sites in the United States. The Soviets chose the second option and agreed to select their sites based on geological maps, photos, and rock samples, and then analyze data sent to the USSR.

Whereas the Reagan administration had initially depicted Soviet support for cooperative verification as the true test of their arms control intentions, it now portrayed Gorbachev's sponsorship of the NRDC-SAS project as a cynical attempt to "confuse the domestic debate about the need for American nuclear testing" and to "promote an inequitable and unverifiable ban on nuclear testing."[84] The Senate's reaction to the project was more ambivalent than the House's, especially since the Reagan administration vowed to veto the defense authorization bill if it included a 1-kt moratorium. Still, Arms Control Advocates hoped that the House and Senate conference committee could reach a compromise. This hope was dashed in early October, when Reagan suddenly announced that he and Gorbachev would meet soon in Reykjavik, Iceland. Senate moderates then argued more strongly against legislated test restrictions to protect the president's bargaining leverage, and the House agreed to remove the 1-kt moratorium from the defense authorization bill.

In return for the House decision, Reagan promised to submit the TTBT and the PNET for ratification once effective verification provisions had been negotiated, and then start a "step-by-step" program to limit and ultimately end nuclear testing. Some analysts have seen this as a policy change "of great sharpness" caused by transnational collaboration.[85] But, the pledge was consistent with the previous policy that the Soviets must accept CORRTEX before the TTBT could be ratified and that a CTB was a "long term goal" for a time when the United States no longer relied on deterrence. The superpowers started holding expert-level discussions on test ban verification, but they only underscored how far apart the two governments were about the need for CORRTEX and the speed with which they should move toward a CTB.

Congress' failure to force even a partial pause in U.S. testing increased Soviet criticisms of the moratorium. At a press conference in late August 1986, the chief of the Soviet General Staff declared that the military would not continue to tolerate the damage done by unreciprocated restraint.[86] Each new U.S. test intensified the opposition.[87] After Congress dropped test restrictions from the defense authorization bill and the Reykjavik summit floundered over the Strategic Defense Initiative (SDI), Gorbachev bowed to hardline pressure: the moratorium would end after the first U.S. nuclear blast in 1987. In February 1987, the NSC again made visas for the SAS team contingent on their observation of a CORRTEX demonstration. (This time, they declined to visit the United States.) Even some

of the moratorium's initial supporters in the USSR came to see it as a "humil-
iating failure because the United States flaunted its continued testing while Soviet nuclear test sites were dormant."[88] Since the monitored moratorium had not
brought the USSR any tangible benefits, opponents were unwilling to let the
NRDC stations collect data when the USSR resumed testing at the end of February. U.S. officials used the shutdown as evidence that Gorbachev had never
been serious about in-country monitoring for anything but a total ban, while the
NRDC claimed credit for the first public notification of an impending Soviet test.

The renegotiation of the NRDC-SAS agreement in June 1987 suggests that
mixed messages from the United States convinced Gorbachev to follow a two-
track strategy. Shortly before the NRDC-SAS agreement was due to expire, the
House voted again for a 1-kt moratorium. But continued U.S. refusal to grant
SAS members reciprocal access to NRDC monitoring stations near NTS had increased Soviet resistance to a continuous U.S. presence in Semipalatinsk.[89]
Therefore, Soviet policy makers decided to extend the NRDC-SAS project for
fourteen months and allow them to monitor during tests, but require that the
three existing stations (and two new ones) be moved 600 miles away from the
test site and be operated by Soviet nationals. Off-site monitoring set important
precedents for in-country monitoring of an active testing program in the USSR.
It also signaled a shift in Soviet test ban strategy, because monitoring an active
test program would provide the facilities and the practical experience needed to
negotiate a low-yield threshold treaty if Congress did not end all funds for nuclear testing.[90]

In September 1987, three days before the Senate reconsidered a 1-kt moratorium, an NRDC-SAS team detonated three 10- to 20-ton chemical blasts near
Semipalatinsk to show that regional monitoring could detect a decoupled 1-kt
explosion. When a fortuitous earthquake shook the seismometers, participants
obtained striking evidence against the "hide in an earthquake" cheating scenario
because the big earthquake and the small explosion generated very different signals.[91] The USSR also invited U.S. congressmen and NRDC experts to visit the
Krasnoyarsk radar installation, site of an alleged violation of the ABM treaty.
Neither the verification breakthroughs nor the Krasnoyarsk visit changed Senate Unilateralists' attitude toward a short moratorium or decreased Cautious
Cooperator's concerns about Gorbachev's motives. By nearly two thirds, the Senate rejected the Kennedy-Hatfield amendment for a mutual two-year, 1-kt moratorium with in-country monitoring.

Ironically, Gorbachev's decision to supplement public diplomacy with official talks on nuclear testing may have cost him the Senate vote. As Soviet scien-

tists learned that seismic collaboration could not overcome U.S. insistence on CORRTEX as the price for TTBT ratification, they began to ask more detailed questions in the experts' meetings and consider the trade-offs more carefully at home.[92] Rather than renew an unreciprocated moratorium, Gorbachev agreed to step-by-step negotiations but insisted that a CTB should be a near-term goal, not a by-product of nuclear obsolescence. The two countries argued for nearly a year about the name and agenda for the meetings. Finally, in September 1987, they agreed to start official "nuclear testing talks" (NTT) to draft new verification protocols for the TTBT and PNET, as well as to pursue intermediate limits and progress toward a CTB. Senator Mark Hatfield feared that this agreement, reached a week before the vote on his amendment, "handed the opposition . . . some good rhetoric." Indeed, many moderates who had favored some type of legislated test restrictions in 1986 voted against a ban in 1987, because official efforts now seemed more promising.[93] In Scherr's words, the "window of public diplomacy" closed in September 1987. The Reagan administration had moved just enough to mollify Cautious Cooperators in Congress but not enough to sustain Gorbachev's grassroots strategy against internal critics.

Soviet willingness to discuss testing on the Reagan administration's terms gave U.S. Unilateralists a new incentive to obstruct the NRDC-SAS project. The day after the INF treaty was signed in December 1987, Gorbachev and Reagan agreed to conduct the JVE by using hydrodynamic methods to measure the yield of a blast at each other's main test site. The United States planned to showcase CORRTEX; the USSR hoped to demonstrate that seismology could outperform hydrodynamic methods with less intrusion and expense. Because advance visits by SAS scientists to seismic stations around NTS could improve the accuracy of in-country monitoring for the JVE, the NSC denied a third visa request, even though the Soviets had now met the CORRTEX condition. SAS members were not allowed to visit NTS until spring 1988, after the resignations of Perle, Gaffney, and Weinberger left DOD less inclined to fight the issue.

The pattern repeated itself one more time before Gorbachev gave up on transnational collaboration as a shortcut to test restrictions. In April 1988, the SAS team established the first Soviet-equipped and -operated seismic stations in the United States and recorded three small chemical blasts in Nevada. One optimistic observer declared, "The world had changed. No more could governments pretend that a Comprehensive Test Ban Treaty would be unverifiable. . . . The NRDC has given hope . . . by showing that determined private citizens can lead even superpower governments out of the deadly traps they fashion for themselves.[94] A few days later, the House voted again for a 1-kt amendment. But even though Kennedy and Hatfield's version raised the threshold to 5 kt and permitted two 15-kt "reliability" tests each year, the Senate tabled and thus killed the amendment in mid-May.

Translating Transnational Collaboration into Policy Changes

The NRDC-SAS joint monitoring project was the most innovative move in the politics of test ban verification. Yet it failed to have an immediate impact on U.S. policy because the American belief that verification should be apolitical left many Cautious Cooperators uncomfortable about an explicitly political collaboration between the president's critics and the leaders of a traditionally hostile state. Popular perceptions of U.S.-Soviet relations brightened dramatically during the NRDC-SAS project. But even after NRDC scientists were allowed to monitor simulated nuclear blasts at Semipalatinsk, 68 percent of Americans still believed that "we cannot trust what Soviet leaders say."[95] Ironically, transnational collaboration may have fed their skepticism by intensifying fears that "on-site inspections are a new weapon in the Soviet arsenal of propaganda and deception."[96]

The NRDC-SAS project brought verification to the forefront of congressional deliberations in ways that perpetuated the conflict between those who wanted to ban nuclear tests and those who supported the president's position. Arms Control Advocates saw the project as evidence that the Soviets would cooperate to improve verification, but most of them had rejected each component of the Reagan administration's blocking strategy before the NRDC project began.[97] A more ambivalent Congressional Research Service report praised the project but doubted its relevance: "Welcoming a private group that advocated negotiations toward a CTB does not necessarily imply readiness to welcome an official group that may be perceived as adversarial and primarily interested in detecting violations."[98] Most Republicans resented the NRDC's attempt to do an end run around the administration. For example, House Republican Leader Robert Michel denounced the 1986 1-kt amendment as the "first step of a radical and unprecedented attack by the President's critics to capture and dominate arms control policy."[99] Given these divisions and widespread reluctance to appear unpatriotic by tying Reagan's hand shortly before a superpower summit, the few binding measures that were passed into law involved relatively uncontroversial issues, such as increased funds for seismic research and studies about stockpile reliability.[100]

Technical data from the NRDC project had to be brought into the policymaking process indirectly to minimize accusations that evidence contradicting current policy lacked objectivity. When the Office of Technology Assessment

(OTA) proposed a major study to evaluate seismic verification, it was told that this subject would be too "political" for a technical agency. Board members approved the project only after the OTA director promised not to focus on the NRDC data.[101] Participants included a range of independent scientists and representatives from DOE, DOD, and the intelligence community, but nobody directly involved in the NRDC project. The OTA report concurred with the NRDC's main technical conclusions: it found no evidence of TTBT violations; it determined that CORRTEX offered little, if any, advantage over sophisticated seismology; and it concluded that high-quality internal seismic systems could detect and identify tests above 5 kt.[102] Despite these careful attempts at consensus-building, the OTA report still encountered harsh criticism from test ban opponents when it was released in May 1988. Robert Barker, the first head of the American NTT delegation, testified that it "homogenized fact with fiction," but when invited to prepare a line-by-line critique of the report, neither Barker's staff nor other scientist obliged.[103] Instead, they ignored the inconvenient technical analysis and simply asserted that the "totality of evidence strengthens the previous findings of likely TTBT violations."[104]

The project's clearest success was to increase technical collaboration inside and between the superpowers. Gorbachev's endorsement encouraged links between SAS scientists and Soviet military seismologists.[105] Excitement generated by the project led to a "blossoming" of interest in seismic verification among independent scientists in the West.[106] U.S. government scientists were warned to "keep their hands off" the project because it was a "political hot potato."[107] By making their data public, though, NRDC seismologists fostered tacit collaboration with like-minded government scientists. Some LLNL seismologists were so excited by the NRDC data that they quietly processed it into a user-friendly format, even though it might be used to challenge U.S. policy.[108] Archambeau and Paine also devised a complicated plan for DARPA to fund the in-country network's operation and expansion without openly undercutting the Reagan administration stance on seismic verification.[109] Such efforts broadened the verification knowledge base without altering policy makers' preferences, at least in the short run.

Besting Test Ban Opponents at Their Own Game

Gorbachev's decision to participate in the JVE was the logical extension of his public diplomacy strategy. After he realized that American Cautious Cooperators were uncomfortable with the political symbolism and technical findings from a nongovernmental project that challenged official policy, he tried to appeal to

them through a governmental project that worked with the Reagan administration's purported preference for CORRTEX and a step-by-step approach to a
CTB. Again, the point was to call the Reagan administration's bluff by demonstrating that American disinterest, not Soviet resistance to reasonable verification requests, was the primary obstacle to a CTB. When the results of the JVE
contradicted each component of the Reagan blocking strategy, U.S. officials
sought new ways to restore the verification deadlock. Yet these strategies had lost
their plausibility, due partly to contextual changes and partly to congressional
frustration with the Reagan and Bush administrations' manipulation of verification to protect the nuclear testing.

The Joint Verification Experiment

The Soviets explained their decision to conduct the JVE in terms that fit American Cautious Cooperators' benign, technical view of verification. Given the
"deficit of mutual trust," the Soviets declared, arms control must be based on the
"most stringent mutual verification."[110] Henceforth, when the West asked for
"double verification," they would respond "with readiness for triple verification"—
national technical methods, obligatory bilateral measures, and international
monitoring.[111] In the past, real or alleged verification problems had blocked a
CTB and thus perpetuated the arms race.[112] The JVE, however, would show that
these issues could be settled through "businesslike deliberations" rather than
ideological confrontations.[113] The Soviets still disagreed with the United States
about the need for routine on-site measurements of all tests over 50 kt but were
ready to exchange the data specified by the original TTBT protocol and use
hydrodynamic measurements to calibrate seismic yield estimation formulas.
Now, they said, "everything revolves around the political will and responsible attitude of Washington. The ball is in the American court."[114]

The Reagan administration suddenly tried to downplay the JVE's significance
after years of using the Soviets' refusal to watch a CORRTEX demonstration to
question their motives, fuel the TTBT compliance controversy, and cast asper-
sions on seismology. Because the Soviets had passed the litmus test by responding favorably to cooperative verification, Reagan officials told Congress that defense policies should be based on "facts" about Soviet military capabilities rather
than "theories" about their intentions.[115] The JVE announcement explicitly
stated that the experiment "will not be designed to produce statistically significant results."[116] U.S. officials also tried to minimize chances that the JVE would
strengthen the case for seismic monitoring by declining a Soviet invitation to
take local and regional data along with hydrodynamic measurements. An ad-

ministration official defended the decision to forego useful information by saying that the purpose of the JVE was to "demonstrate the practicality and effectiveness of CORRTEX and not other less effective systems."[117]

The American JVE team almost invalidated its own claims that on-site monitoring would not compromise military secrets.[118] In January 1988, twenty experts visited each other's site to learn about testing practices. Negotiators hammered out a hundred-page protocol meant to ensure that 140 Americans could live and work at the Soviet test range for several months without incident. In July, though, three members of the U.S. preparation team were caught secretly shipping home soil samples, rocks, and other prohibited material. U.S. officials called the situation "embarrassing" but portrayed it as "unauthorized souvenir collecting" rather than espionage.[119] Although the incident did not derail the JVE, it undoubtedly substantiated Soviet fears that CORRTEX was an excuse for collateral information collection. It also demonstrated that meticulous treaty language could not prevent friction and ambiguity during the verification process.

The U.S. approach to the JVE proved less cooperative than the Soviets'. The first JVE explosion occurred at NTS on August 17, 1988, and the second transpired at Semipalatinsk four weeks later. Both sides took hydrodynamic measurements, while the NRDC-SAS stations monitored regional waves and international seismologists watched for teleseismic signals. Participants prepared a joint report about agreed data and technical disputes, but the U.S. side was instructed not to sign.[120] Although both governments pronounced the JVE a success, only the USSR wanted to publicize the results. Because neither could release data unless both agreed, the United States was able to block revelations that might "limit the range of options and tactics" for NTT negotiators.[121]

Data leaks explain why the U.S. government refused to provide its own citizens with information given to the USSR.[122] The New York Times reported that the true yield at the NTS was in the mid-140-kt range. NRDC-SAS seismologists judged the yield to be 139 kt; the three hydrodynamic estimates put the size at 155, 163, and 170 kt.[123] These figures suggested that in-country seismic monitoring was more accurate than any hydrodynamic method and cost much less than the $28 million spent by the United States on the JVE. They also illustrated the fallacy of noncompliance accusations that ignore the uncertainty associated with all forms of yield estimation—a point that Tass gleefully made with an article entitled "American CORRTEX Registers American Violation."[124] An unsophisticated reading of the hydrodynamic results would suggest that the blast violated the TTBT, but all four estimates fell well within the 1.3 uncertainty range for a 145-kt test.[125] The JVE at the Soviet test site further undermined the Reagan administration's noncompliance charges.[126] In short, the JVE results contradicted each component of the Reagan administration's blocking strategy and confirmed Arms Control Advocates' conviction that CORRTEX was a "needlessly complex and circuitous assault on a largely manufactured problem."[127]

C. Paul Robinson, head of the American NTT delegation during the JVE, tried to portray it as a "trial run" showing that the superpowers could use hydrodynamic equipment at each other's test sites and thus should routinely do so. Asked to compare seismic and hydrodynamic methods, he spoke only of early teleseismic estimates that the NTS shot was 80–100 kt and claimed that the USSR was rethinking its reliance on seismology. Despite the OTA's conclusion that CORRTEX offered little over sophisticated seismic methods, Robinson continued to assert that seismology had an uncertainty of 1.7 or 1.75, far greater than the 1.3 claimed for CORRTEX. Rather than discuss what the JVE said about past TTBT compliance, he insisted on CORRTEX to avoid future false alarms.[128] Finally, he predicted that the new TTBT protocol could be drafted quickly and precisely because the detailed JVE provisions had been field-tested and potential problems corrected.[129]

Defeat of the Reagan-Bush Blocking Strategy

The two-year delay between the JVE and agreement on a new TTBT protocol shows that the experiment did little to end verification arguments because every party involved in the negotiations interpreted the results to support its preferred position.[130] Yet, the political symbolism and scientific evidence of the JVE helped undercut the Reagan-Bush blocking strategy by convincing American Cautious Cooperators that superpower agreement on reliable test ban verification measures would be possible. As vague allegations about verification problems lost their plausibility, test ban opponents had to emphasize other objections that did not resonate as deeply with Cautious Cooperators. In the final year of the Bush administration, therefore, Arms Control Advocates and Cautious Cooperators in Congress finally forged an alliance that forced the United States to resume serious CTB negotiations.

The Soviets' continued refusal to permit routine use of CORRTEX just to placate the Reagan administration shows that they still thought carefully about verification trade-offs. They had little interest in accepting the costs, risks, or dangerous precedents associated with an on-site technique that was not demonstrably better than less intrusive means. They may also have hoped that the JVE results would renew congressional pressure for TTBT ratification and CTB negotiation without a CORRTEX accord—unlikely during an election year and the transition into the Bush administration.[131]

Reactions to the JVE in the United States revealed splits over CORRTEX within the administration. Some testing proponents allied openly with Arms Control Advocates in arguing that routine use of CORRTEX would be overly expensive, intrusive, and inconvenient. Before the JVE, the CIA had warned that "if the Soviets said 'yes' to our initial proposals, we would be in trouble" because the United States had not considered the costs and risks of admitting foreign inspectors to NTS.[132] Afterward, one of LLNL's testing experts told the SCFR that CORRTEX should only be used for calibration purposes, because "the JVE demonstrated that the dollar and the resource costs associated with such measurements will be substantial."[133]

Despite these concerns, the Bush administration refused to reduce U.S. CORRTEX demands because it had no desire to take the next step toward a CTB. American officials also devised other strategies to dissipate pressure for progress on test restrictions. Shortly before the first JVE explosion, Reagan had tried to create a double bind by linking further test limits to a parallel program of weapons cuts while claiming that weapons reductions might require more tests to ensure the safety, reliability, and survivability of the remaining arsenal.[134] Once it looked like the Soviets might call the Americans' bluff by accepting its conditions for TTBT verification, Bush repudiated Reagan's pledge to follow ratification with immediate talks on intermediate limits. Instead, he called for a "period of observation . . . to assess the verification lessons learned" by implementing the TTBT protocol and reiterated that a CTB was a long-term objective possible only when the United States no longer depended on deterrence.[135] This was followed by a report to Congress in which DOE announced that it needed ten more years of nuclear testing at the current rate to determine if the U.S. deterrent could be maintained with lower yield limits.[136] Since the lab directors were currently fighting with Congress to protect the budget for nuclear testing, this linked future test restrictions to present support for a vigorous testing program.[137]

The Soviets finally acquiesced to U.S. demands for a TTBT verification triad in June 1990, after contextual changes decreased the costs and risks associated with the new protocol.[138] Budgetary pressures made it unlikely that the United States would routinely spend $10 million on CORRTEX when compliance could be confirmed by less expensive means. Moreover, popular protests in the USSR had reduced the number of Soviet tests to be monitored. In March 1990, the Soviets decided to close the Semipalatinsk site and test only at Novaya Zemlya, where inhospitable conditions, difficult logistics, and opposition from Nordic neighbors constrained operations.[139] The only Soviet test covered by the new protocol occurred in October 1990—too soon after ratification to prepare for CORRTEX. Moscow sent personnel to tests at NTS in September 1991 and

March 1992. One cannot, however, evaluate how the TTBT protocol worked in practice because the signatories never released such information.

During Senate ratification hearings on the TTBT and the PNET, representatives from the JCS, DOE, and DOD tried unsuccessfully to condition support on unilateral safeguards that would protect the current testing program. They wanted Senate pledges to test up to treaty yield limits, maintain modern nuclear laboratories, preserve the ability to test in prohibited environments and yield ranges, and fund strong verification and intelligence programs. These "insurance policies" were not presented as protection against Soviet cheating or verification uncertainties but as a "hedge against unexpected political or technical events, affecting the military balance."[140] The SCFR refused to make recommendations based on unspecified worst-case assumptions, because "unexpected political or technical events can have positive, as well as negative, effects." They modified the safeguards to fit lower yield limits and urged superpower leaders to "make every effort to achieve . . . a verifiable comprehensive test ban."[141]

On September 25, 1990, the Senate gave its unanimous advice and consent for ratification with little debate and few illusions. Largely despite the JVE rather than because of it, the Soviets had finally accepted on-site yield estimation for monitoring TTBT compliance. Instead of building on this breakthrough to achieve more meaningful test restraints, however, the Bush administration planned to spend tens of millions of dollars and unknown years practicing cooperative verification of very high yield tests. Cautious Cooperators could see that the step-by-step approach was leading nowhere fast. As Congressman Jim Leach (R-Iowa) put it, the JVE was "rather interesting enormous progress on step back aspects of verification."[142]

During the next year and a half, international pressure for a CTB rose. The 1990 NPT Review Conference ended in acrimony because the United States and the U.K. refused to resume serious CTB negotiations. In January 1991, the backers of the Five Continent Peace Initiative organized a conference to amend the LTBT into a CTBT—a symbolic gesture because the original three signatories could veto any amendments.[143] The Soviet Union and France both announced moratoria on nuclear testing. The CD's Group of Scientific Experts conducted its second full-scale test of a prototype global seismic network based on existing seismic stations and the communication system of the World Meteorological Organization. According to Australia and New Zealand, this trial network had a 90 percent chance of detecting 10-kt tests in most environments and could detect smaller tests in the more heavily monitored northern hemisphere.[144] A system designed specifically for a CTB, therefore, could presumably do even better.

Congress finally lost patience after the Bush administration announced that despite TTBT ratification, the collapse of the Soviet Union, the Russian moratorium, and the verification demonstrations, it still must conduct at least six tests a year. In June 1992, the House approved an amendment to the FY93 defense authorization bill that prohibited testing for a year if the Soviets exercised similar restraint. Two months later, the Senate overwhelmingly approved (68–26) the Hatfield Amendment to the FY93 energy and water appropriations bill.[145] This amendment banned U.S. tests for nine months, permitted no more than five carefully regulated safety and reliability tests for the next three years, required the president to submit a plan for achieving a multilateral CTB by September 30, 1996, and mandated a permanent ban on U.S. tests thereafter even without a formal accord, as long as Russia reciprocated. Arguments over verifiability did not play much of a role in the debate. Instead, supporters stressed the need to strengthen Yeltsin's domestic standing by reciprocating his moratorium and the importance of a CTB for the 1995 NPT extension decision, while opponents complained that the ban would hurt U.S. stockpile reliability without stopping proliferation. Because the amendment was attached to a bill that Bush saw as critical for his reelection, he reluctantly signed it into law. Still, he was defeated by Bill Clinton, whose campaign included the pledge to begin serious CTB negotiations.

Conclusion

Arms Control Advocates who survived the test ban verification battles of the 1980s refer to a refrigerator magnet that says, "Don't wrestle with pigs because you both get dirty and the pigs enjoy it." Test ban opponents, such as Perle and Gaffney, were remarkably candid about the ways in which they used trumped-up noncompliance charges and manufactured verification arguments to mire the arms control movement. Although the administration's position was technically weak, it was politically potent because the public was not interested in "an arcane debate among technical wizards . . . that few people can understand, much less judge."[146] Congress shifted from supporting Reagan's arms buildup to mandating a test moratorium because U.S. and Soviet Arms Control Advocates spent a decade in the mud, pinning each new pig sent into the arena, and making allegations about test ban verification problems seem increasingly implausible even to those who did not understand the technical issues.

It is not surprising that first-wave authors saw verification arguments primarily as surrogates and stall tactics because the politics of verification were primarily strategic in the 1980s. In the test ban case, little of substance changed in the technical capabilities of test ban monitoring systems or the types of cooperative measures that Moscow would permit for a CTB. In the second-generation CTB negotiations, the Soviets had already accepted international data exchanges, challenge inspections, and bilateral in-country monitoring (in the form of the NSS). CORRTEX was irrelevant to a CTB, and the geological information gained through the JVE could have been obtained a decade earlier by ratifying the TTBT. The Reagan administration's "peace through strength" policies did not bring the superpowers closer to agreement on CTB verification, nor were they meant to. Ironically, the clearest effect of the massive arms buildup and virulent anticommunist rhetoric was to frighten many Americans enough that the dangers of unconstrained competition outweighed their doubts about Soviet intentions. Fear of nuclear war and distrust of Soviet intentions both declined with the end of the Cold War, democratization in the USSR, and the collapse of the Soviet empire. After decades of being the Unilateralists' most effective "show stopper," allegations of unverifiability became the dog that did not bark in congressional debates, because Cautious Cooperators no longer believed strategic assertions that substantive concerns about CTB verification could not be resolved through serious negotiation.

Gorbachev's desire to stop the arms race increased Soviet flexibility on verification, yet there is little evidence that a sudden convergence in U.S. and Soviet approaches ended superpower arguments over test ban verification. Gorbachev accelerated a trend in Soviet policy of accepting more cooperative forms of verification when the USSR was interested in measures that could not be reliably monitored with less intrusive means. His words, however, changed more sharply than his actions, while his reasons for endorsing the NRDC-SAS project and the JVE were more political than technical. Moreover, Gorbachev's decisions about how to manage the NRDC-SAS project and when to accept CORRTEX indicate that he still weighed trade-offs rather than assumed that verification was purely benign and would always promote cooperation.

Although contextual changes affected U.S. and Soviet verification preferences, the politics of verification had independent effects on test ban outcomes at the end of the Cold War. At first, the effects were primarily negative: the verification-based blocking strategy explains how Reagan officials avoided new test restrictions despite strong domestic and international pressure for progress toward a CTB. During the mid-1980s, Gorbachev's new thinking on arms control and verification, dramatically demonstrated by the NRDC-SAS collaboration, reenergized Arms Control Advocates as enthusiasm for a nuclear freeze waned. Yet, transnational collaboration had little immediate impact on policy because

American Cautious Cooperators drew mixed messages about Gorbachev's motives for collaborating with Reagan's critics, while Soviet conservatives withdrew their support when the moratorium and flexibility on verification were not reciprocated. The JVE represents an even bolder attempt by Gorbachev to beat the Reagan administration at its own game: the political symbolism of the project sent a clear message that the superpowers could cooperate on verification; the scientific results increased confidence in Soviet compliance and seismic monitoring. Both the NRDC-SAS project and the JVE also provided professional contacts and practical experience with in-country monitoring and on-site inspections that helped allay unfounded suspicions, increase sensitivity to the other sides' verification concerns, and educate Cautious Cooperators about verification trade-offs. Progress was not smooth, nor was there an immediate correlation between greater transparency and more significant test ban cooperation. Nevertheless, Gorbachev's approach of targeting verification initiatives to Cautious Cooperators in Congress ultimately forged an alliance for a resumption of serious test ban negotiations.

8

Working with the Politics of Verification

THE HISTORY OF COLD WAR TEST BAN verification arguments and agreements contradicts the common conception of verification as a technical process that determines the "truth" about compliance. At the same time, it underscores the inadequacy of first-wave studies in which the politics of verification is a second-order problem of calculating "how much is enough," based on assumptions about other policy issues. The test ban case demonstrates that decisions about verification are both inherently political and inevitably politicized. It substantiates the utility of a two-level analytical framework in which arguments among domestic groups with divergent first principles are linked to disagreements between states with different dominant conceptions of verification. It also indicates that verification decisions cannot be completely "depoliticized"; domestic and international agreement depend on strategies to build blocking and winning coalitions.

The unexpected intensity of verification arguments during the final generation of CTB negotiations and the bittersweet success of agreement on a treaty with improbable entry-into-force conditions suggest that the end of the Cold War changed the arms control context without resolving basic verification dilemmas. Since efforts to ratify and implement a CTB are still in progress, one cannot do the kind of detailed decision-making analysis presented in Chapters Three through Seven. One can, however, easily identify parallels between the structure of verification arguments and the strategies used to exacerbate or resolve them during and after the Cold War. Moreover, similar problems are threatening the significance and stability of cooperation over other issues. Thus, a broader understanding of verification politics in general and the specific lessons of the test ban case remain relevant and valuable for post–Cold War theorists and policy makers.

Reconceptualizing Verification Politics:
Lessons from the Test Ban Case

From the earliest arms control efforts, negotiations over verification were intensely controversial, because states had different material interests and conflicting conceptions of security. Since the international system lacks both an overarching power to impose a verification regime and an authoritative body of shared knowledge from which optimal arrangements can be derived, verification decisions had to be reached through political processes of persuasion, bargaining, compromise, and coalition formation. They were always contested for substantive reasons, because alternative approaches reflect divergent principles; set alternative precedents; and allocate the benefits, costs, and risks of cooperation in different ways. Arguments about verification also had a strategic side, for their resolution or perpetuation had important implications for the start of serious negotiations, the significance of potential arms restrictions, the likelihood of agreement, and the stability of the resulting accord.

Throughout the Cold War, American and Soviet diplomats advanced proposals based on contradictory myths about the nature, scope, function, and forms of test ban verification. Americans depicted verification as technical and benign, whereas the Soviets viewed it as highly political and potentially malign. Both approached verification as an adversarial process, yet the Americans were primarily concerned that Soviet involvement would make verification an unreliable indicator of cooperation, and the Soviets worried that Americans would use verification for competitive purposes. These conflicting conceptions led to predictable arguments about maximizing monitoring capabilities to prevent cheating or constraining them to prevent spying and other verification abuse. They produced equally common and consequential arguments about the allocation of responsibility for monitoring and assessment among the states whose compliance was being verified, its main adversaries, and third parties. Countless workable/tolerable trade-offs precluded anyone from arguing persuasively that their solutions to such dilemmas were objectively correct. Although the superpowers often took polarized stands on verification rights and responsibilities, sometimes they switched places (the NPT safeguards) or repudiated their own extreme positions when they became more serious about cooperation.

The politics of test ban verification also had a domestic dimension, with a predictable structure that corresponded to competing conceptions of international relations. Contrary to notions of a Cold War consensus destroyed by the Vietnam War, domestic verification decisions were no less contentious when policy debates occurred primarily inside the Executive Branch than when Congress became more engaged in the mid-1950s or when public interest groups opened verification debates still further in the 1970s. The relative strength and influence of Arms Control Advocates, Cautious Cooperators, and Unilateralists varied among administrations, but even when Arms Control Advocates were excluded from top policy-making positions, they participated indirectly as experts (the ALC and the Panel of Consultants) and pressure groups (the Nuclear Freeze and the NRDC).

Divisions in Congress and public opinion were deep, enduring, and important to policy makers who hoped the politics of test ban verification would increase support for U.S. defense policies. Aside from temporary aberrations caused by contextual factors (e.g., Sputnik or the invasion of Afghanistan), seemingly wild swings in public opinion resulted from the juxtaposition of questions that described arms control in terms that only Arms Control Advocates would accept, with questions worded in ways that also appealed to Cautious Cooperators. Whether the issue was international control of atomic weapons in 1946, limits on nuclear tests in the 1950s, or a nuclear freeze in the early 1980s, approximately 20–30 percent of the population favored arms control under any circumstances; 40–60 percent wanted reciprocal, verified restrictions; and 20–30 percent opposed any restrictions on U.S. military programs.

Given these divisions, the net effect of democratic pressures made U.S. negotiating positions neither more nor less cooperative. Popular concern about the arms race and knowledge of nonintrusive monitoring techniques motivated the Eisenhower administration to start CTB talks and stay at the negotiating table despite countless frustrations. By contrast, congressional objections to verification compromises complicated Kennedy's attempts to secure a CTB. Well-organized and vocal opponents of détente pressured Carter into moves that restored the CTB verification deadlock by decreasing Soviet expectations about the benefits of an accord and the prospects for ratification. Yet arms control activists in Congress and groups such as the NRDC kept interest in a CTB alive despite Reagan administration attempts to erase it from the arms control agenda. Thus, the most consistent effect of democratic pressures was to prevent any administration from institutionalizing policies that violated the first principles of Arms Control Advocates, Cautious Cooperators, or Unilateralists.

Although policy making in the USSR was more insulated from public opinion and less open to foreign view, divisions among elites did affect Soviet test ban preferences, verification proposals, and negotiating strategies. Debates and power struggles among "orthodox" and "reformist" decision makers influenced when Khrushchev made test ban overtures, whether the objective was to coerce one-sided concessions or encourage mutually beneficial agreements, and what verification compromises were possible. During the Brezhnev years, internal divisions were narrower and muted by a more consensual decision-making style, yet arguments over issues such as national seismic stations indicate continued disagreement about the benefits, costs, and risks of détente-era arms control. Although much of Gorbachev's "new thinking" had roots in minority arguments made during these earlier debates, even after the principles of common security, significant arms control, and "triple verification" were endorsed at the highest level, leaders still disagreed about their value and practical implications for test ban policy.

Since verification preferences depended on the conceptual lenses that decision makers used to interpret observable facts about international politics, failure to agree on CTB verification was not overdetermined by the political or military context. The level of tension in superpower relations, the vertical and horizontal proliferation of nuclear capabilities, and the crises that exacerbated concerns about nuclear vulnerability affected specific verification preferences but did not determine outcomes, because different groups understood and responded to contextual developments in divergent ways. When superpower relations warmed after the 1959 Geneva Summit or during the early years of détente, Arms Control Advocates and Cautious Cooperators became more optimistic about cooperation, while Unilateralists in the United States and the USSR redoubled efforts to reveal the other side as an unreliable arms control partner. Terrifying events, such as the Cuban Missile Crisis, reinforced test ban supporters' belief that the risks of imperfect verification were less than those of unconstrained competition; they also exacerbated Cautious Cooperators' ambivalence and increased Unilateralists' opposition to any accord that might enable low-level cheating or spying. On the one hand, the development of superpower strategic parity eased the workable/tolerable dilemma for those who thought that low-level cheating or collateral information collection could no longer destabilize deterrence. On the other, it increased resistance to verification compromises among those who thought that a small advantage for the other side might tip the scales decisively in their favor. And as the next section shows, the massive contextual changes brought by the end of the Cold War have had far less impact on verification arguments than would be expected if the politics of verification were a purely derivative problem.

Fundamental disagreements over first principles also made it impossible to depoliticize test ban verification decisions. In American policy debates and superpower negotiations, calls to depoliticize verification were often strategies to determine which first principles would be used as the basis for decisions, or to present a favored verification solution as objectively correct and thus nonnegotiable. Of course, the Soviets were equally disingenuous when they refused to discuss the technical limitations of seismic monitoring on the grounds that OSIs were a purely political issue. Even when Gorbachev proclaimed that verification regimes should be designed by scientific experts working together in a businesslike manner, his motivations—to discredit Reagan administration claims about test ban verification and reassure American Cautious Cooperators by using their language—were primarily political.

Many arms control supporters did sincerely hope that Western and Eastern technical experts could transcend national loyalties to devise fair and effective verification arrangements. The Conference of Experts and the technical working groups, however, could not answer tough questions without political instructions or personal judgment calls. Pugwash meetings, the CD's Group of Scientific Experts, and other scientific contacts offered informal channels of communication and a stockpile of verification suggestions that political leaders could use when it suited their objectives. But a tension existed between scientists' search for technically excellent solutions and negotiators' need for advice that acknowledged the messy political problems of negotiating and ratifying arms control accords. Superpower agreement in the 1970s on most verification measures for the TTBT, PNET, and CTB suggests that "businesslike" discussions took place not when technical deliberations were divorced from political considerations but when they were preceded by a genuine desire for arms control and informed by mutual respect for each other's verification dilemmas.

American test ban verification policy was never shaped by a unified epistemic community. Scientists always split over technical questions, such as the capabilities of monitoring systems or the plausibility of evasion scenarios. They were equally divided on political issues, such as the amount of uncertainty that the United States should tolerate for a test ban or the appropriate way for scientists to engage in policy debates. Research from Vela and other projects gradually narrowed the range of "responsible" opinion about detection, identification, location, and yield estimation capabilities, until Reagan officials such as Perle and Gaffney redefined the term to mean responsive to their policy objectives. Despite valiant attempts to find areas of consensus among scientists with diverse affiliations and test ban preferences, the 1988 OTA seismic verification report was a compromise document that many pro-CTB seismologists considered too conservative and opponents attacked for "homogenizing fact with fiction."

Instead of technical knowledge having independent effects on test ban policy, political factors shaped the development, dissemination, evaluation, and utilization of verification technology. Funding and interest in seismology increased dramatically once a verified CTB became a policy goal, but money and time were spent differently depending on whether agencies in charge wanted to identify verification weaknesses or solve monitoring problems. Government officials often deliberately played down the capabilities of classified monitoring systems and related intelligence assets, allegedly to prevent the Soviets from knowing what could escape detection, but also to protect U.S. negotiating positions. Agencies opposed to a CTB used their positions and powers of classification to mislead policy makers about the 1970 Woods Hole Conference and the CIA's 1986 correction of its yield estimation techniques. Presidents Johnson and Nixon ignored research that should have reduced U.S. inspection requirements; Reagan officials repudiated the judgment of their own scientists when it contradicted official policy.

Interactions between politics and technology had some unintended effects on test ban verification. The dual-use nature of monitoring technology meant that Unilateralists' need for intelligence on Soviet nuclear weapons development created the capability to monitor most test restrictions without intrusive inspections. American attempts to symbolize support for a CTB by funding verification research while perpetuating verification arguments were inherently unstable because test ban supporters would only await further research if they believed that better data would promote agreement. By depicting the OSI deadlock as the sole obstacle to a CTB in the 1960s and 1970s, the superpowers inadvertently encouraged independent scientists to pay more attention to verification. When the Reagan administration attacked seismology and Soviet TTBT compliance, these alternative sources of technical expertise eventually convinced all but the most ideological agencies to modify their positions. Leaks about the JVE results are perhaps the clearest evidence of limits on powerful players' ability to control scientific information and use technical collaboration for counter-cooperative purposes.

Outcomes in the politics of test ban verification are best explained by focusing on the processes through which winning or blocking coalitions formed. Here, the key insight from the test ban case is that ideas influenced not only the initial preferences of states and domestic groups but also the selection of coalition-building strategies and their impact on verification decisions. Although arguments about verification were often framed as disputes over detection probabilities and other numerical issues, test ban negotiators never tailored a threshold ban on underground tests to a specified level of confidence in detection, identification, and yield estimation capabilities. Coalitions did not form on the basis of precise rational choice calculations. Rather, decisions about the acceptability of particular verification arrangements depended on whether arguments advanced for or against them made sense, given decision makers' unquantifiable beliefs about national security, nuclear weapons, state motivations, and verification.

For long stretches of time, national leaders' primary goal in the politics of verification was not to reach agreement but to avoid making a clear-cut choice between cooperation and competition. During the three CTB prenegotiation phases—1945–55, 1963–73, and 1981–92—one or both superpowers professed support for arms control yet used rigidly conflicting positions on verification to deflect pressure for significant arms control from domestic constituents and non-nuclear weapons states. These avoidance strategies only worked while the underlying justifications sounded plausible to Cautious Cooperators. When debates following the BRAVO explosion convinced Western Cautious Cooperators that a test ban would be a mutually beneficial first-step measure that could be verified without intrusive inspections, the plausibility of all-or-nothing disarmament positions and demands for foolproof verification decreased. But because verification is a complex and esoteric subject, strategic arguments based on faulty technical information often remained politically potent long after they had been scientifically discredited. Witness the persistence of U.S. demands for seven OSIs despite the seismic monitoring advances of the 1960s, as well as the continued allegations of Soviet TTBT violations after even most of the Reagan administration's experts had revised their yield estimates.

Failure to start serious test ban negotiations often resulted from misguided identification efforts and deliberate misidentification strategies. The three prenegotiation phases did not end with a commitment to start CTB negotiations until Cautious Cooperators believed (rightly or wrongly) that the other side was sincerely interested in mutual test restrictions and that agreement on verification would be relatively easy. Americans often saw invitations to technical conferences and proposals to increase transparency prior to arms control as a low-risk way to determine whether the Soviets were Cautious Cooperators or Unilateralists in disguise. These were highly unreliable indicators, however, because the Soviets did not share the underlying assumptions—that verification dilemmas have technical solutions and that increases in verification necessarily enhance cooperation. Thus, American Unilateralists could take advantage of these assumptions to increase doubts about Soviet intentions and misidentify themselves as Cautious Cooperators. Arms control supporters in the United States and the USSR were also often tempted to downplay verification disagreements in the hope that consensus recommendations from technical experts would push political leaders into serious negotiations. This was a risky strategy, however, because it enabled arms control opponents to raise new doubts about the other side's motives when inevitable arguments arose over ambiguous recommendations and controversial questions that the technical experts had avoided.

Although political leaders never achieved consensus on the first principles from which test ban verification decisions should be made, some noteworthy changes in alignment affected policy coalitions. Verification research and experience with arms control negotiations contributed to incremental changes in the content of verification preferences and the tactics used to forge winning or blocking coalitions, but new knowledge never caused widespread convergence on a single worldview or approach to verification. Conversions were rare, but not nonexistent. During the Eisenhower administration, support for serious CTB negotiations increased when Dulles slowly moved from the Unilateralists' view of arms control as a propaganda exercise to the Cautious Cooperators' position that agreement on modest first-step measures might be mutually beneficial. Another important shift occurred when some civilians in the Eisenhower Defense Department argued for a phased CTB on the grounds that the value of increased transparency outweighed advantages that the United States might gain from further tests.

Abrupt changes in the structure of test ban verification arguments often reflected high-level personnel changes. Sometimes the balance of power among groups was altered by the introduction of new players, such as the special assistant for disarmament, the science adviser, PSAC, and ACDA. At other times, individuals in key positions were replaced by people representing different perspectives, due to the transition between administrations or the reorientation of a presidency (Carter's replacement of Warnke by Seginous or Reagan's decision to tone down his bellicose image). Such shifts in alignment did not end arguments over test ban verification, but they did influence the speed of internal agreement on negotiating proposals, the substance of U.S. verification offers, and the prospects for ratification.

Comparable changes in alignment affected Soviet positions on test ban verification. Khrushchev shifted between coercive and more conciliatory bargaining strategies depending partly on objective factors, such as the strategic balance and the relative strength of orthodox and revisionist factions, and partly on whether he was thinking about arms control more like a Unilateralist or a Cautious Cooperator. Brezhnev came to power with the assumption that achieving strategic parity was more important than bilateral arms control but then decided that an unconstrained nuclear arms race would ruin the Soviet economy without furthering its political or military objectives. Gorbachev changed the structure of Soviet test ban verification debates in several ways. He did so most dramatically by rethinking the nature of Soviet security, becoming more personally involved in arms control decision making, and choosing advisers who strongly favored cooperation with the West. By inviting civilian scientists and reform-oriented international relations specialists into policy debates, he also reduced the influence of arms control opponents.

Most alliance strategies involved competition between Arms Control Advocates and Unilateralists to build domestic support for negotiating positions that other states would be more or less likely to accept. Test ban supporters constantly searched for bridging concepts, such as verification as deterrence and managed-access inspections, that would simultaneously appeal to Cautious Cooperators at home and bring the superpowers closer together. Convergence on these vague concepts, however, often masked major domestic and international disagreements about the probability of detection that would deter violations or the types of inspection procedures that would increase access to compliance information, yet protect sensitive sites and preserve what were considered legitimate military secrets. Arms Control Advocates tried to build domestic support for compromise positions by convincing Cautious Cooperators that the benefits of an "adequately verifiable CTB" outweighed the potential costs and risks. Yet anyone who sought to modify U.S. verification demands was vulnerable to politically potent accusations of being "soft on communism." Moreover, the dominant conception of verification as a purely benign self-help process meant that Unilateralists could always trump Arms Control Advocates by calling for a little more compliance information and more U.S. control over the verification process than the Soviets would accept—just to be safe.

Test ban opponents routinely used evasion scenarios and noncompliance accusations to widen the gap between the significance of an arms control proposal and the scope of U.S. verification demands. The "Big Hole" theory became a virtual show-stopper, partly from ignorance about the technical constraints on decoupling but mostly because few policy makers would dismiss the possibility as too remote to justify extravagant verification measures. Reagan's requirement for on-site yield estimation was calculated to ensure Soviet rejection because it was grossly disproportionate to the arms control benefits, substituted the more intrusive CORRTEX for seismic methods that the Soviets deemed equally accurate, and set precedents that decreased the prospects for near-term agreement on a CTB. When the Soviets were not seriously interested in a CTB, they used the same strategy in reverse by rigidly insisting that NTM could answer all CTB compliance questions or by refusing to consider test ban inspections until after comprehensive disarmament had been achieved.

Test ban outcomes were also affected by strategies to alter the domestic determinants of verification decisions on the other side. Soviet leaders frequently tried to move the West toward more congenial positions. Those who perceived few meaningful divisions among American elites hoped that a combination of threats and arms control promises would divide NATO members and multiply popular pressure for concessions. Those who drew a distinction between "realists" and "madmen" among Western policy makers sometimes used conciliatory gestures to strengthen the domestic position of leaders who might negotiate mutually satisfactory solutions to security problems. The complexity of verification politics, however, often undermined such two-level strategies. For example, Kennedy wanted to reciprocate Khrushchev's black box and OSI offers after the Cuban Missile Crisis, but the slow interagency process delayed American concessions until Khrushchev had been humiliated and the Soviet position had hardened again. Gorbachev's attempts to circumvent the Reagan administration by convincing Congress to legislate test restrictions were foiled for years, because many moderate senators who favored a CTB thought it should be sought through normal negotiating channels.

American policy makers rarely considered the impact of their actions on Soviet arms control and verification decisions because they were barely aware of domestic divisions in the USSR. Some information came through unofficial channels, such as Weisskopf's warning about the bitter fight between test supporters and test stoppers in the Khrushchev government, but there is little evidence that it influenced American actions. Americans typically interpreted Soviet moves on verification issues as calculated attempts to gain a negotiating advantage rather than as outcomes of internal struggles. For example, the Kennedy administration viewed Khrushchev's July 1963 retraction of his OSI offer as an attempt to sell the same horse twice rather than as an indication that he no longer had the domestic support needed for any CTB inspections. U.S. leaders rarely worried about the counter-cooperative effects on Soviet policy debates caused by increased U.S. defense spending, espionage activities, confrontational strategic doctrines, and test-related activities during Soviet moratoria. Even after *glasnost* provided clear evidence that Gorbachev needed progress toward a CTB to shore up domestic support for arms control and verification overtures, Reagan made no meaningful concessions. Although Americans had frequently argued that agreement on intrusive inspections would "open" the USSR, not until the 1992 Hatfield amendment did the hope of using arms control concessions to strengthen pro-democracy factions in Russia actually affect test ban policy decisions.

The test ban case clearly contradicts the notion that winning coalitions are easiest to build for lowest-common-denominator accords. On several occasions, political leaders did try to minimize verification arguments by negotiating partial measures in which the probability and significance of violations would be low. Such attempts, whether intended as the first step toward more significant test restrictions (the LTBT) or as a quick and uncontroversial cosmetic accord (the TTBT and the PNET), became a battleground where domestic groups fought to set precedents that would move policy in their preferred direction.

Arms control supporters were not willing to fight hard for partial measures that neither significantly constrained weapons development nor contributed much to resolving core disagreements about CTB verification. Agreement on partial measures did not reduce Cautious Cooperators' ambivalence much either, because the benefits of cooperation were lowered along with the risks. In the 1977 Senate hearings on the TTBT and the PNET, for example, Arms Control Advocates and Cautious Cooperators pushed administration witnesses to disclose the lowest limits of U.S. monitoring capabilities and explain why the TTBT yield threshold was more than ten times higher. Some participants supported the twin treaties because they set precedents for cooperative measures that might facilitate CTB negotiations. Others opposed ratification because they did not want to legitimize PNEs and doubted that the inspection provisions were relevant or necessary for a CTB. Yet failure to ratify these modest measures hurt CTB negotiations by exacerbating Soviet doubts about whether more significant verification concessions would secure Senate approval. Even efforts to generate forward momentum by maximizing domestic support for a first-step treaty sometimes backfired. For example, the Kennedy administration's attempts to assuage Cautious Cooperators' anxieties by reinforcing worst-case assumptions about Soviet intentions eroded the goodwill that might have induced both sides to be more flexible on OSIs.

Unilateralists responded to partial accords by seeking precedents and safeguards that would obstruct further test restrictions. In 1963, they used the myth of the broken moratorium to secure commitments from Kennedy that increased the rate of testing, gave opponents a new argument against underground test restrictions, and positioned the United States to resume atmospheric testing quickly if either superpower abrogated the accord. They derailed TTBT ratification in 1978, in part, because CTB supporters feared that opponents would attach restrictive amendments to the resolution of ratification and complicate efforts to achieve a comprehensive ban. Only after the Cold War was clearly over did the Senate reject the notion that low-risk test restrictions required unilateral safeguards based on worst-case assumptions about future political and military developments.

Despite the intensity and complexity of arguments over CTB verification, more progress toward agreement occurred during the Cold War than is often recognized. The process was highly iterative: no state or domestic group could ever achieve its most desired outcome in the politics of verification, so every player was motivated both to find more effective strategies and to change the structure of the game.

Both the political-military context and the rigidly contradictory nature of superpower ideas about verification gave Unilateralists some systematic advantages. Yet the outcome they preferred—no serious negotiations and no significant test restrictions—never remained stable for long. Sometimes Unilateralists undermined their own blocking strategies, either through disingenuous moves in the politics of verification that did not elicit the negative response expected from the other side or through competitive policies that changed contextual factors in ways that increased Cautious Cooperators' hopes for agreement on verification. Test ban supporters spent immense amounts of energy attacking each component of Unilateralists' blocking strategies, both by suggesting win-win solutions to specific verification problems and by challenging the basic assumptions that made agreement on CTB verification seem impossible. Each advance was countered by new allegations that U.S. monitoring capabilities could not detect all significant cheating and that the Soviets would never accept the cooperative measures required for reliable verification.

Technical advances and diplomatic breakthroughs gradually made such claims less plausible, thus forcing Unilateralists to place more emphasis on other issues, such as stockpile reliability. But they always tied these issues back into the politics of verification by claiming that no obtainable verification system could provide proof of very small tests that might give an enemy some strategic advantage.

When national leaders were seriously interested in test restrictions, negotiators sought to understand the other side's concerns, weigh verification trade-offs, and find mutually acceptable arrangements. Progress toward agreement on a phased test ban treaty before the U-2 incident, negotiation of cooperative verification for the TTBT and the PNET, and the Soviet acceptance of challenge OSIs and in-country monitoring in the second generation of CTB talks all contradict claims that the USSR would never have tolerated reliable verification prior to Reagan's "peace through strength" policies or the Gorbachev revolution. Yet little attempt was made to educate Congress or other attentive Americans about verification dilemmas and appropriate compromises. Arms Control Advocates often hesitated to talk about trade-offs because they did not want to decrease Cautious Cooperators' confidence in verification arrangements. Unilateralists had little incentive to endorse verification compromises unless arms control seemed inevitable and their own mission (e.g., weapons testing or counterintelligence) would suffer from overly expensive or intrusive verification demands. Even then, Unilateralists used adversarial assumptions about evasion or breakout scenarios to gain Cautious Cooperators' support for self-help safeguards. Gorbachev eventually convinced Congress to mandate serious CTB negotiations by calling for technical solutions to test ban verification arguments and offering to accept triple verification. In doing so, though, Gorbachev inadvertently reinforced a way of thinking about verification that would reproduce Cold War arguments in post–Cold War negotiations and ratification debates.

Change and Continuity in the Post–Cold War Context

A brief analysis of the arguments, dynamics, and outcome of multilateral CTB negotiations shows that the politics of verification are more complicated but not fundamentally different in the post–Cold War context than they were in the first two generations of CTB negotiations. Predictions that a CTB could be signed before the 1995 NPT Extension Conference proved wrong, partly because verification dilemmas were more problematic than expected. Verification debates involved the same arguments about amount and type that had plagued trilateral negotiations. The search for mutually acceptable arrangements was complicated by the large number of participants; asymmetries in national intelligence assets, technical expertise, and security situation (own nuclear status and concerns about rival states); and conflicting views of verification trade-offs. When others resisted U.S. attempts to maximize compliance information and control over verification, Americans attacked their motives, hardening positions all around. In the final frantic months of negotiation, a compromise package was assembled that secured a CTBT. It was a mixed success, though, because these compromises lowered the treaty's significance, lessened the likelihood of ratification, and may prevent the CTBT from ever entering into force.

Reasons for Initial Optimism

The CD's Ad Hoc Committee on a Nuclear Test Ban (NTBC) was instructed to "negotiate intensively a universal and multilaterally and effectively verifiable comprehensive nuclear test ban treaty."[1] In the past, such an ambitious mandate would have ensured years of fruitless discussions. When talks started in January 1994, however, even seasoned negotiators thought that the end of the Cold War had reduced strategic and substantive obstacles to agreement on test ban verification. The committee chair maintained that a treaty was "doable and doable in a relatively short time"—by early to mid-1995.[2]

Part of the optimism stemmed from the Clinton administration's promise to be "out front pulling (for a CTB), rather than in the back dragging our heels."[3] After a difficult interagency battle, most policy makers concluded that the nonproliferation value of a CTB outweighed the potential gains from further testing, even if they disagreed about the type of treaty that the United States should seek.[4] Military requirements for testing had decreased over the decades as the superpowers accumulated different types of warheads, concentrated on improving delivery and guidance systems, and gained experience with nonexplosive techniques to design and maintain nuclear weapons. Clinton had extended the moratorium mandated by the Hatfield amendment because he did not believe that further tests were warranted for safety and reliability reasons or as an appropriate response to China's occasional blasts. A CTB would foreclose certain projects, such as third-generation weapons (e.g., x-ray lasers) and very-low-yield tactical weapons, but neither the United States nor Russia currently considered these attractive options.[5] As Israel and South Africa had shown, states outside the NPT could obtain a small stockpile of simple uranium bombs without testing, but they could not confidently develop plutonium bombs or thermonuclear weapons. An international CTB verification system would provide the global coverage needed to complicate evasion attempts and detect most low-yield tests anywhere in the world. It would also greatly strengthen the international norm against weapons testing, which would assist domestic groups opposed to overt weaponization in countries like India and cause a strong international response if pro-weaponization groups prevailed.

Not everyone in the Clinton administration found this logic equally persuasive. Hazel O'Leary, the secretary of energy, became a surprisingly strong CTB supporter, but military leaders and weapons designers were more skeptical. Because most Unilateralists assumed that Congress had put the United States "out of the nuclear testing business" for the foreseeable future, however, few sought to block an accord putting other countries under similar constraints.[6] Instead, they tried to condition a CTB on an ambitious "stockpile stewardship" program and include an "easy exit" clause that would let states withdraw from a CTB without explanation at a ten-year review conference.[7]

Russian political leaders strongly favored a CTB because they had no pressing need for nuclear tests, no convenient test site, and no money to spare when the price of one test could pay a year's salary for ten thousand workers.[8] Some military leaders and weapons designers revived familiar arguments about the need for more tests to ensure stockpile safety and reliability, as well as to improve verification capabilities.[9] They also claimed that the collapse of the Soviet Union, the prospect of NATO expansion, and the high cost of conventional forces meant that Russia should increase its reliance on nuclear deterrence. Despite these objections, President Boris Yeltsin seemed firmly committed to achieving a CTB before the NPT conference.

The other NWSs also professed support for a CTB, some less enthusiastically than others. Although France and the U.K. were not currently testing, France was engaged in modernization efforts that might require more tests and the U.K. was worried about the CTB's long-term implications for its independent nuclear deterrent.[10] Neither country had as much expertise as the Americans with computer simulations and other techniques for operating in a no-test environment, although the British could rely on American research, since their warheads were based on U.S. designs. Contrary to the superpower's call for a CTB before the NPT extension decision, the U.K. and France argued for "reverse linkage" because they would have less need for new weapons if the nonproliferation regime remained strong.

China had the most ambiguous position of the five NWSs due to an internal struggle between political and military leaders. It had conducted the fewest nuclear tests and wanted to increase missile accuracy, improve safety and reliability, reduce vulnerability, and achieve a MIRV capability.[11] China claimed that a no-first-use agreement would reduce horizontal and vertical proliferation as well as a CTB could. It promised to sign a CTB "no later than 1996," yet it wanted to exempt PNEs and link a CTB to nuclear disarmament—positions that other NWSs had advocated in the past but strongly opposed now.

The "threshold states" (India, Pakistan, and Israel) had maintained an ambiguous nuclear posture without testing (aside from India's one "PNE" in 1974) and stood to gain little from becoming overt nuclear weapons states. India had been closely associated with the international drive for a CTB ever since Nehru proposed a testing "standstill" after the BRAVO explosion, and Pakistan routinely said that it would sign a CTB or an NPT if India did. Israel was not among the thirty-seven members of the CD, so it could only work informally on a treaty text. There were strong pressures to expand the CD so that Israel, North and South Korea, Iraq, South Africa, and other countries of special interest could have a direct voice in negotiations and thus be more likely to sign an accord. But the United States blocked expansion until the NTB negotiations were nearly done, on the grounds that a country under U.N. sanctions (Iraq) should not be admitted to the CD.

In short, Arms Control Advocates and Unilateralists who believed that past arguments about CTB verification had been strategic maneuvers to sabotage negotiations now assumed that the superpowers would not play this game. They also hoped the other NWSs would behave themselves if negotiations occurred in the CD, where the threshold states would be constantly reminded of international support for a CTB.[12] Since the United States and Russia had already voluntarily ended nuclear testing, they had strong incentives to agree on reasonable verification measures to reassure each other and get other countries on board. Many arms control supporters felt that previous accords had exhibited "a gross excess of verification per kiloton of disarmament. This is because verification in the past was part of the traditional Cold War exercise to keep the other side from gaining some hypothetical advantage. . . . Today, verification measures need only be added to disarmament steps that have already been adopted . . . [which could be done] in a matter of months."[13]

Cautious Cooperators' optimism stemmed from the perception that CTB verification problems had finally been solved. Nobody argued that CTB monitoring capabilities would be perfect, only that they were good enough for a world where the Cold War "obsession with 100% verifiability" was gone.[14] During the Cold War, the superpowers had focused most of their monitoring assets on each other's test sites. Now the monitoring system needed to pay more attention to other parts of the world. In most instances, this was not expected to be a problem. If a proliferator wanted to test a home-grown nuclear weapon, the likely yield would be 10 kt or more, and the new testers would lack the expertise required for successful decoupling.[15] More challenging problems arose if a new nuclear nation wanted to test a tactical weapon obtained from someone else or if an advanced NWS wished to decouple a very-low-yield explosion. Experts argued about whether existing monitoring systems would have a high probability of identifying very small nuclear tests (1 kt), but the GSE was confident that a "system could be designed to meet any specified political requirements."[16] Moreover, the international monitoring system (IMS) would be supplemented by classified national intelligence assets focused on areas of special concern, as well as several thousand high-quality seismic stations used primarily for earthquake research. Cheaters would be surrounded by "uniformed police" (the IMS), "plainclothes police" (NTM), and a "neighborhood watch" (other open seismic stations), so militarily significant tests were likely to be noticed.[17] Negotiators now also had numerous precedents for obligatory OSIs if concerns about a potential violation could not be resolved through consultation and clarification. Thus, many observers saw "no scientific reason why verification procedures should be an obstacle to a rapid conclusion of a CTBT."[18]

Verification Arguments Slow the Pace of Negotiations

Contrary to expectations, negotiations made little progress before the NPT Extension Conference.[19] When members finally agreed in September 1994 to use a "rolling text," more than a thousand brackets indicated alternative proposals and disputed wording. Clinton tried to generate momentum by dropping the "easy exit" idea in January 1995. Although this required a major interagency battle, the move had little effect on negotiations because other states had always considered the proposal to be a "non-starter."[20] Two weeks before the NPT Extension Conference began, Britain (with tacit support from France) dropped another non-starter—a proposal to permit periodic safety tests. These gestures may have helped secure the indefinite and unconditional extension of the NPT. The statement on objectives and principles adopted at the conference, however, stressed the NWS' disarmament obligations and specified that a CTB should be signed by 1996. This deadline, plus the international outcry when France resumed testing soon after the NPT extension decision, revitalized negotiations without resolving the key disagreements.

By early 1996, a thousand brackets remained in the rolling text. The root cause of many disputes involved the purpose of negotiations, as it had during the first generation of CTB talks.[21] The NWSs saw a CTB primarily as a nonproliferation bargain in which they accepted constraints on future weapons development in return for pledges that NNWSs would not test even if they had not signed the NPT. Many of the NNWSs, however, valued a CTB as a step toward nuclear disarmament; they sought strong language on disarmament in the preamble and opposed stockpile stewardship programs meant to preserve confidence in nuclear weapons capabilities. Australia and Iran offered alternative vision texts that were less extreme than some positions but still leaned clearly toward the preferences of the advanced industrialized countries and the nonaligned states, respectively. When the last NTBC chair (Jaap Raamaker of the Netherlands) finally presented his own draft text in late March 1996 (barely three months before the deadline for a treaty that could be signed at the UNGA in September 1996), it still indicated numerous unresolved issues—a clear sign that key decisions had not been depoliticized. Almost all of the thorniest issues either involved verification directly or had major implications for verification decisions.

CD members had radically different interpretations of a universal and multilaterally and effectively verifiable CTB. The negotiating mandate did not specify how to weigh the benefits of verification measures that would make the regime more workable but less tolerable for some countries, and thus less likely to have universal participation. Nor did it say what to do when measures to make verification more truly multilateral, such as distributing IMS stations and seats on the Executive Council equitably across regions, would be less effective than locating more stations in areas of extra concern and granting permanent seats on the Executive Council to states with special expertise or funding responsibilities. Numerous debates also occurred about the criteria for a "cost-effective" system when some countries had few concerns about compliance and wanted low-cost reassurance, while others sought the most efficient means to detect and deter potential violators. CD members had faced similar questions during CWC negotiations, but they disagreed about the lessons and their relevance to a CTB. Some were eager to build on precedents for cooperative security and joint verification set by the CWC; others thought that post–Cold War euphoria had produced a verification regime that was too ambitious, intrusive, expensive, and internationalized.

In the early NTBC sessions, tensions also developed between scientists and diplomats. The seismic experts had done an admirable job of insulating their discussions from the political turmoil that undermined CTB negotiations in the 1970s and prevented their resumption during the 1980s. Now that the NTBC had a negotiating mandate and a time deadline, however, some diplomats criticized GSE members for continuing to operate as if they were in a political vacuum. Frictions developed when the seismologists were asked to incorporate other types of remote-sensing equipment into their network. Frustrations also arose because diplomats wanted results from the GSE's third test of a prototype network more quickly than the scientists could deliver them.[22] Another source of difficulty was the uneven level of technical expertise among the delegations. Small delegations that lacked their own scientists but did not want to rely on briefings by GSE members came to depend on independent analysts, such as Rebecca Johnson, for help in understanding the political implications of technical arguments.

These problems paled beside the difficulties posed by diplomats' inability to agree on the political criteria that the IMS should meet. Since assumptions differed widely about the probability and significance of very small clandestine tests, participants argued about whether a system that could detect and identify 1-kt tamped tests in hard rock constituted effective verification.[23] They fought about technologies that should comprise the international network. Russia and most nonaligned countries favored a "bare bones" system composed solely of seismic and radionuclide detectors, whereas the United States preferred a more elaborate system with hydroacoustic monitors and infrasound detectors. China and Pakistan also wanted the IMS to include satellites and electromagnetic pulse (EMP) sensors, to avoid reliance on technologically advanced states or commercial suppliers for such data.[24]

Difficulties resolving these questions led to familiar arguments about whether the details of verification should be determined before or after arms control began. Many countries endorsed Australia and Russia's call for an "evolutionary approach," whereby agreement in principle on the basic components of verification would be elaborated by a preparatory commission and refined or expanded after CTB signatories learned how the system worked in practice.[25] The United States took a much more contractual approach and wanted to nail down the verification details when it had maximum bargaining leverage, before an agreement was signed. The French initially embraced an even more restrictive "try before you buy" position by arguing that the entire verification system should be operational before a treaty was signed, something that could not occur before they finished testing.

The American position that judgments about compliance should be each country's responsibility caused heated controversies about the role of the data center. The United States wanted the IDC to resemble the "detection club" proposed by Alva Myrdal—that is, an organization whose purpose was to reduce transaction costs by minimizing duplication of monitoring efforts. Since the IDC would receive about 5 billion bytes of raw data each day, most countries wanted bulletins containing preliminary analysis and identification of suspicious events. The United States, however, feared that attempts to present data in a user-friendly format might bias judgments by highlighting some ambiguous events and ignoring others. The Group of 21 (G-21) nonaligned states accused the United States of "superpower arrogance" in promoting a discriminatory regime within which most countries would lack the time, money, and technical expertise to benefit fully from the IMS. Some American negotiators belittled these equity concerns by arguing that countries wanting to be "serious, credible players" on CTB verification must make the necessary investments; otherwise, they should "buddy up" with someone who had and accept their judgments.[26] The United States finally agreed that the IDC could do preliminary analysis, but only if each country could also access and analyze the raw data as it saw fit.

Arguments over inspections mirrored OSI debates in earlier test ban negotiations. Knowledge about the strengths and limitations of remote monitoring was too widespread for credible claims that IMS data could resolve all compliance concerns, but states still disagreed about making OSIs voluntary or mandatory. NTBC members concurred on the principle of managed access but not on the details of differentiating between sensitive locations that could be excluded from inspections and suspicious sites that should be open to view. Precedents from the Chemical Weapons Convention were not particularly helpful: most CWC inspections would be routine observations at declared facilities, whereas CTB inspections would necessarily be ad hoc events after accusations of a potential violation.

Negotiators had fundamentally different preferences about designing OSIs to maximize detection and deterrence or to minimize verification abuse. Most Western states wanted OSIs to be easy to obtain, quick to start, and comprehensive in coverage. They favored "red light" procedures whereby an inspection would start automatically upon a request from a member state unless the Executive Council voted against it. Countries with serious regional security concerns, such as China, India, Israel, and Pakistan, worried about frivolous OSIs, so they argued that states should first try to resolve their concerns through consultation and clarification—a process that could take weeks and preclude uncovering time-sensitive evidence of nuclear blast. They called for a "green light" decision-making procedure, which required approval by a large majority of Executive Council members. They also sought and secured an acknowledgment that frivolous OSI requests would be regarded as a serious matter and that states making such requests should be punished, perhaps by bearing the full cost of the inspection. Russia preferred conservative procedures for triggering an OSI but agreed with the West that managed-access inspections could be both workable and tolerable. This response led several participants to speculate that years of negotiating and implementing OSIs had made Russia more comfortable with the concept than were arms control newcomers.

As during the second generation of CTB negotiations, those countries favoring maximalist OSI procedures did not expect that they would be used often, if at all. American policy makers recognized that OSIs should only be used as a last resort. Calling for an OSI would be a confrontational act that could hamper attempts to address concerns in a more cooperative manner and would erode confidence in arms control, even if a satisfactory explanation was provided. Had a test actually occurred, the chance of finding a "smoking gun" would be small. Without unambiguous proof of a violation, however, the United States could be criticized and potentially penalized for a frivolous OSI request. U.S. policy makers also feared that a hostile country might retaliate for an American OSI request by using an ambiguous event on an earthquake fault near San Francisco as an excuse to call an inspection at Livermore Laboratory.

When asked why inspections should be easy to trigger if they were really so unlikely, Western policy makers responded that the threat of an inspection would be more likely to deter violations if OSIs were swift, sure, and highly intrusive. Yet proponents of green-light procedures saw no reason why Western proposals would make OSIs a more credible deterrent if they would only be invoked when the evidence was so overwhelming that most Executive Council members would give their approval. The perceived illogic of the deterrence argument intensified suspicions that the United States (or particular U.S. agencies) had ulterior motives for insisting on maximalist OSI procedures. Some American policy makers acknowledged domestic reasons for rigidity on OSIs, such as the continued Cold War mindset of influential agencies and individuals or the belief that the Senate would require maximalist OSI procedures as a symbol of effective verification. Unilateralists who opposed compromising on OSIs accused Clinton of "trying too hard" for an agreement, however, and insisted that the United States hold out for maximal verification rights as a hedge against unforeseen future developments.

Debates about the IMS and OSIs were connected in complicated ways. For example, Israel wanted to supplement the IMS with data from other seismic stations that had been certified by the IDC, so that the nature of an ambiguous event might be determined without an on-site inspection. By contrast, other countries worried that making more seismic data available would increase the number of very small events that could be detected but not identified without an inspection.[27]

Another interesting issue involved the extent to which IMS data should be made public and nongovernmental organizations encouraged to participate in the monitoring process. One way to sustain interest and resources for verification would be to encourage advocacy groups and scientists to watch for suspicious events while conducting their regular research on earthquakes, weather patterns, or whale migrations. A potential problem with the "neighborhood watch" concept, though, is that the operational style of such individuals and organizations might clash with the diplomatic requirements for international verification. Confidence might be eroded unnecessarily if a confrontational environmental organization such as Greenpeace or an anti–arms control descendent of the Committee on the Present Danger publicized ambiguous evidence of a possible nuclear test and pressured national leaders to request an inspection before there had been time for consultation and clarification. For example, shortly before Senate hearings on the CTBT started in October 1997, the conservative *Washington Times* reported that American officials had expressed concerns to Russian leaders about a possible underground nuclear test at Novaya Zemlya. After independent seismologists and the CIA concluded that the August 16 event had occurred under the ocean 130 kilometers away from the test site and was not a nuclear test, CTB supporters accused the Clinton administration of "acting too hastily," before it had time to analyze evidence from the IMS and other seismic stations. Clinton's top CTB adviser on the NSC justified the initial U.S. reaction, which caused lingering problems for U.S.-Russian relations and ratification efforts, by saying that the rapid availability of seismic data on the Internet put the administration in a "countdown situation" where it must act before public debate began.[28]

One of the thorniest arguments involved the use of national intelligence sources to request an OSI, determine the area for an inspection, or conclude that a violation had occurred. This paralleled unresolved arguments in the second test ban negotiations about whether OSI requests must be based solely on seismic evidence, could be backed with a combination of seismic and other types of NTM, or could rest solely on nonseismic intelligence. Declassified estimates suggest that the United States can detect and identify a 2- to 3-kt decoupled explosion or few-hundred-ton tamped blast in regions of particular concern.[29] Americans argued that it would be irrational to sign a treaty that prevented full use of their monitoring capabilities, but policy makers recognized that the real issue was not whether the United States would pay attention to suspicious evidence from NTM and other nationally controlled sources (e.g., spies or defector debriefings) but how that evidence would be brought into the multilateral decision-making process. One American response to arguments that the only admissible evidence should come from the monitoring system that everyone had accepted and could access equally was that small countries could concentrate their limited intelligence resources on neighbors whose behavior worried them most. Another was a variant of Cold War justifications for maximalist verification demands: the United States was an open society, so poor countries did not need expensive satellites to know if activity at NTS had suddenly increased.

Opposition to the use of national intelligence also stemmed from G-21 concerns that the United States would manipulate the verification process with accusations based on evidence that other countries could not evaluate because the United States would not reveal its "sources and methods." Americans tended to dismiss such allegations as ideologically motivated paranoia or evidence of a guilty conscience. But the allegations were not groundless. Even close American allies believed that Reagan administration accusations about Soviet TTBT violations rested on a politically motivated refusal to analyze data correctly. The Chinese ambassador to the CD had been personally involved in a 1993 incident in which the United States accused China of shipping chemical weapons components to Iran but found nothing after a week-long inspection of the ship.[30] Concerns about the irresponsible use of national intelligence were reinforced in

December 1995, after the *New York Times* printed leaked information that India might be preparing for a nuclear test. The story stirred up a nationalist fervor in India as evidence of an American attempt to perpetuate the "nuclear apartheid regime" by pressuring India into signing a CTBT without guarantees of nuclear disarmament by the NWSs.[31] It also prompted Pakistan to publicize its own test preparations so that it would be perceived as India's equal.[32] Such incidents led most NTBC members to favor some limits on the type of information that could be introduced (e.g., a distinction between NTM and human sources), as well as procedures for independent evaluation of national intelligence. But the United States objected until the last minute that Congress would not ratify a treaty that restricted or revealed American intelligence capabilities.

Two of the most hotly contested endgame issues, scope and entry-into-force, had important implications for test ban verification. Previous negotiators had never precisely defined a comprehensive test ban, because they could not agree on the line between dangerous weapons tests and beneficial nuclear experiments. In the third generation of CTB negotiations, China argued vigorously for a PNE exemption, although it had never conducted a PNE and did not have an active PNE program. Since the PNET negotiators had found no way to ensure that PNEs were not providing weapons-relevant information or expertise, the Chinese proposal would have created intractable verification problems. It was finally dropped in the endgame, with the face-saving understanding that the treaty could be amended if PNEs became economically attractive and verification problems had been solved.

The other NWSs favored the next most permissive approach: a treaty that would allow hydronuclear experiments (HNE) with yields up to 200 tons.[33] Despite pressure from the DOD and the JCS for higher-yield HNEs, the original U.S. position called for a definition of zero yield that would permit HNEs whose fission yield was less than their high explosive yield (under four pounds). A four-pound yield limit would have caused numerous verification problems. For example, since HNEs can produce a much higher yield than expected, the United States planned to do them underground at NTS. This could have caused concerns that the Americans were actually doing slightly-higher-yield tests or preparing to "break out" of the treaty. It would have also raised questions about whether an accidental overshoot should be considered a violation or excused by a "whoops clause" similar to the understanding associated with the TTBT.

In August 1995, France and the United States suddenly endorsed a "true zero yield" treaty that prohibited "any nuclear weapon test explosion or any other nuclear explosion" (the Australian scope formula).[34] The U.K. and Russia grudgingly acquiesced, because this scope delineation would permit "subcritical experiments" (hydrodynamic tests) and other forms of stockpile stewardship. Of course, if subcritical experiments are conducted at former test sites, signs of unusual activity may be used as evidence of a small decoupled test, as occurred with noncompliance accusations after the August 1997 event near Novaya Zemlya. The NWSs could negotiate transparency measures for their subcritical experiments but in doing so would create concern that a potential proliferant could learn something useful by serving as an observer.[35] A related complication developed in early 1996, when Russia suddenly insisted that seismic and radionuclide stations be placed at each test site to ensure "equal transparency" under a true zero ban.[36] This gesture threatened to reopen old disputes about the location of IMS stations, because China objected that its test site was already monitored more closely than the global average. Russian diplomats resurrected an old American two-level strategy and claimed that this demand, while not necessary from a technical standpoint, was a political requirement for ratification. Still, one senior Russian official confessed that the move was motivated less by genuine verification concerns than by anger that Russia had not been consulted before the United States reached its "true zero" decision.[37]

Sweden, Germany, and many of the G-21 states initially sought an even more restrictive treaty. They thought that a CTB should prohibit certain substitutes for nuclear testing (e.g., hydrodynamic explosions, inertial confinement fusion, or computer simulations), prevent preparations for nuclear testing, and possibly mandate the permanent closure of test facilities. These prohibitions would have complicated verification in some ways and simplified it in others. For example, the only way to verify a ban on simulations would be to grant inspectors full access to high-powered computers. By contrast, closing former test sites would prevent a potential cheater from using existing tunnels or equipment for decoupled explosions and forbidden HNEs. Regardless of these verification issues, proponents realized that the NWSs would never accept such measures. Therefore, most of them eventually endorsed the Australian scope formula but still hoped the preamble would stress the objective of ending all nuclear weapons development.[38]

Entry into force (EIF) became the most intractable issue in the CTB negotiations. The trade-off was between making the treaty fully binding as quickly as possible and ensuring that all five declared NWSs, or eight testing-capable states, accepted the treaty's restrictions. The U.K., Russia, and Pakistan argued that requiring ratification by all eight testing-capable states would maximize pressure on potential holdouts, but India objected vehemently to such arm-twisting. The U.K. made matters worse when it justified its EIF conditions by saying that the CTB was really only for the eight testing-capable states and that the NNWSs had only been asked to participate so that they would share the financial burden of verification.[39] When the chair of the NTBC proposed that EIF depend on participation by all states with primary monitoring stations on their territory (a way to capture the threshold states without according them special status), India withdrew its station from the IMS. Given increasingly clear signals that India would not sign the CTB, the United States objected to EIF conditions that would leave the treaty hostage to countries whose participation was not essential. It preferred an EIF formula that included ratification by all five NWSs, plus forty to sixty additional countries. The Americans did not want to pursue this issue too strenuously, however, because doing so could cost support for their maximalist OSI positions.

India's growing opposition to the CTB was only indirectly related to verification. India had been a constructive participant in the first two years of negotiations but became increasingly insistent during 1996 that a CTB must be linked to other disarmament commitments. Many American policy makers concluded that India had not been serious about a CTB for a long time (if ever) but had adopted a holier-than-thou attitude as long as it was sure that the NWSs would never agree to stop testing. An alternative explanation is that some Indian security elites still sincerely supported nuclear disarmament, or preferred a world where they retained their ambiguous deterrent without testing, but that domestic decision-making dynamics led these two groups to join the pro-testing faction's outcry against "nuclear apartheid."[40] In either case, the indefinite extension of the NPT and the NWS's convergence on a "zero yield" formula that permitted simulations and subcritical tests provoked a heated debate in India. The longer the United States clung to adversarial positions on the weak role of the IDC, the maximalist nature of OSIs, and the full use of national intelligence, the easier it was for Indian CTB opponents to depict the treaty as another tool of great power domination. A counter-cooperative spiral developed in which perceived pressures from the West led to India threatening to refuse to sign the treaty. Its recalcitrance fueled demands for rigid EIF conditions, which in turn convinced India to block consensus in the CD on the chair's CTB text.

The text prepared by the chair involves numerous compromises rather than convergence on key issues. It allows OSIs if they are approved by three fifths of the Executive Council—a weak green-light procedure with a strict timeline.[41] National intelligence can be brought to the Executive Council but only if it is based on objective information, deals solely with the CTBT's subject matter, was collected in the least intrusive manner possible, and respects national sovereignty—wording open to countless interpretations. The treaty cannot enter into force until all forty-four states on the IAEA's list of nuclear-capable CD members have ratified it; this formula requires Indian participation even though it no longer had an IMS station on its soil. If EIF has not occurred by the third anniversary of the treaty's signing, those states that have ratified can hold a conference to discuss measures "consistent with international law" that might accelerate ratification and EIF—a formulation that avoids the contentious question of amending the EIF conditions. These compromises seemed to satisfy most major players. Yet they created an anomalous situation whereby signatories would be obligated to refrain from testing, even though neither the inspection procedures nor the collective oversight by an Executive Council could actually be implemented until some unknown time when the treaty entered into force.

The CTBT was saved through a series of unprecedented maneuvers. Australia organized some "friends of the treaty" who took the chair's text to the UNGA, where majority voting is allowed. After a bilateral deal in which the United States basically accepted China's position on OSI initiation procedures in return for China's agreement that NTM could be used in an OSI request, the five NWSs declared their support for the chair's text. Given the rigid EIF conditions and the weak language on disarmament in the preamble, though, it was uncertain whether a majority of NNWSs would endorse the treaty. The UNGA vote on September 10, 1996, was surprisingly strong: 158 states supported the treaty; only India, Bhutan, and Libya opposed it. The CTBT was opened for signature on September 24, 1996, and India, Pakistan, and North Korea were the only members of the "magic 44" that did not sign within the next few months.

At the signing ceremony, President Clinton lauded the CTBT as the "longest-sought, hardest-fought prize in arms control history."[42] But it is hard to know whether the compromises made to secure a CTBT have laid the groundwork for a permanent end to nuclear testing and weapons development, or whether they will turn out to be a post–Cold War variant of the Unilateralists' blocking strategy. By the end of 1997, few signatories had ratified the CTB, in part because even strong supporters have been reluctant to pay for an expensive verification system if the treaty may not enter into force. In the United States, the two most controversial issues in preliminary ratification hearings have been the sufficiency of a yearly $4.5 billion stockpile stewardship program and the effectiveness of verification. Witnesses for the Clinton administration have stressed the wide array of "overlapping and complementary" monitoring resources, including U.S. intelligence, the IMS, the OSIs, bilateral transparency measures, and such open sources as universities, laboratories, and even oil exploration teams. They argue that even if verification is not perfect, "The odds are favorable, and the benefits [of the accord] are legion."[43] Nevertheless, skeptical senators have used the August 1997 earthquake as evidence that remote monitoring methods cannot identify all suspicious events and questioned why the United States traded away stricter rules on OSI initiation for the right to base requests on NTM. Witnesses against the CTBT have pronounced it "unverifiable" (often without supporting evidence) and insisted that U.S. security requires both a full-fledged stockpile stewardship program and a minimum of six nuclear tests a year.[44]

Optimists maintain that even if ratification and entry into force take time, by signing the CTBT, the five NWSs and the vast majority of NNWSs have strengthened the norm against testing, committed themselves to an extensive cooperative verification regime, and ensured that domestic support for expensive stockpile stewardship programs will decline over time. They hope that work in the Preparatory Commission will proceed in a businesslike fashion and that quiet diplomacy will convince India to join or persuade other signatories to relax the EIF requirements. Pessimists predict that doubts about EIF and verifiability will erode support for ratification and encourage the NWSs to hedge their bets by taking full advantage of the research and design opportunities permitted under the CTBT. They fear that concerns about compliance will increase, yet none of the procedures for consultation, clarification, inspection, and assessment by the Executive Council will be in place, so eventually the entire CTB regime will collapse. The history of the test ban case suggests that neither scenario will prove entirely correct. Instead, the fate of the CTB regime will depend on the ideas and strategies that shape arguments over these issues among Arms Control Advocates, Cautious Cooperators, and Unilateralists in the United States and around the world.

Enhancing the Prospects for Agreement on Verification

The test ban case shows that the end of the Cold War has changed the context but not the basic structure or dynamics of the politics of verification. Multilateral negotiations involved many of the same arguments about the amount and type of verification that arose in bilateral and trilateral test ban talks. American policy makers paid more attention to the costs and risks of verification than they had in the earliest nuclear negotiations. As usual, however, Arms Control Advocates were willing to be flexible about these trade-offs, while Unilateralists used them to create anticooperative Catch-22s (i.e., arms control is acceptable only if high confidence in compliance can be obtained with little expense, intrusion, or inconvenience for the United States). Verification disputes—such as arguments about disarmament commitments, stockpile stewardship requirements, or EIF conditions—had a strategic dimension. Their political potency, however, depended on the plausibility of positions from a Cautious Cooperator's perspective.

The process of policy formation and negotiation involved complex coalitions with cross-cutting cleavages on different issues. Increased complexity, however, was neither an a priori help nor a hindrance to the prospects for cooperation. Sometimes test ban supporters found bridging concepts and coalition-building strategies that let them use large numbers and issue linkages to increase support for cooperation. But at other times, those who wanted to minimize constraints on their national nuclear programs used complexity, uncertainty, and heterogeneity among NTBC members to delay negotiations, increase suspicions, and secure provisions that threatened the significance and stability of the CTBT.

The tremendous complexity of arguments over test ban verification makes the metaphor of a Rubik's Cube seem more appropriate than that of a standard two-level game. In contrast to the image of a single chief of government choosing moves on two interconnected chess boards where the pieces are visible, the rules are known, and the consequences of a move are fairly easy to predict, multiple players in the politics of verification struggle to get control of the cube and make policy twists that can have numerous planned or unintended consequences for other parts of the puzzle. In the multilateral CTB negotiations, for example, positions taken on OSI were related, openly or not, to numerous other matters, among them (1) such verification issues as the IMS and NTM; (2) other types of test ban decisions, such as scope and EIF; (3) preferences about nuclear testing and stockpile stewardship; (4) other arms control concerns, such as the NPT extension and pressure for time-bound disarmament measures; (5) interagency turf battles; and (6) bilateral relations with the other NWSs. Test ban supporters tried to find bridging proposals. Yet it was hard to know whether moves that increased the chances of agreement on one problem would make it easier or harder to solve others. When players offered verification concessions, moreover, it was sometimes difficult to tell whether they were seriously interested in cooperation or simply making a strategic calculation that another problem (such as EIF) would prevent all the pieces from falling into place for stable arms control.

The complex interconnections in the politics of verification defy simple explanations, reliable predictions, and clear-cut prescriptions. But this does not limit social scientists to pure description. The analytical framework offered here is valuable, not only for organizing complicated information and identifying important aspects of continuity and change over time but also for understanding the specific processes through which two-level agreement has been promoted or obstructed. Scholars and policy makers often claim that test ban outcomes can be explained by a simple story in which the politics of verification plays a minor, derivative role at best. Nonetheless, detailed historical analysis has shown that these simple explanations say more about the speaker's own worldview than they do about what actually happened. Greater awareness that moves in the politics of verification often have unforeseen effects should help arms control supporters avoid strategies that increase support at one level while making problems more intractable at another. Realizing how unpredictable the politics of verification can be should also decrease temptations to manipulate verification arguments for unrelated purposes.

Although a CTB was once considered an easy problem for the politics of verification, the arguments and strategies present in this case are typical of those that arise on other arms control issues, environmental accords, economic bargains, and human rights agreements. For example, the 1997 Kyoto agreement on specific targets for greenhouse gas emission reductions will intensify debates about whether the associated verification measures should embody an enforcement or a regulatory management approach to compliance assessment. In the same manner, the 1997 announcement by American apparel manufacturers of a code of conduct to combat global sweatshop labor has sparked arguments about whether human rights organizations should work alongside monitors hired by the firms themselves, and whether any violations should be made public or quietly corrected to avoid bad press.[45]

Each mixed-motive problem has unique features that facilitate or complicate two-level agreement on verification. The strength of different domestic groups or the structure of decision making may promote more flexible or rigid verification preferences. The subject matter of a potential accord may lend itself to clear-cut distinctions between prohibited and harmless behavior or involve dual-use items that are dangerous in some contexts and beneficial in others. There may be a menu of well-developed monitoring methods to choose from or tremendous uncertainty about how a limited number of options would work in practice. These possibilities are all variations on themes that have characterized the politics of test ban verification.

A senior policy maker who has worked on numerous verification issues once commented that the Arms Control Advocate, Cautious Cooperator, and Unilateralist ideal types were analytically useful but that many practitioners "have our feet in all three camps at times." This points to two basic features of the politics of verification. First, the best way to promote domestic and international agreement on the politics of verification is to understand the perspectives of all three domestic groups, as well as the differences between dominant American ideas about verification and those prevailing in other countries. Second, intellectual contortions are necessary not only because the world is full of people with different ideas about verification but also because no one way of thinking about the politics of verification can provide a complete explanation or reliable prescriptions. What are the implications of these points for international relations theory and arms control policy?

Hobbesian, Grotian, and Kantian theorists each have a piece of the truth about the politics of verification. Hobbesians are right that the superpowers never completely achieved domestic and international agreement on verification for an accord restricting types of tests that either side wished to continue. But this reflected the Unilateralists' skill at using rigidly conflicting and highly adversarial ideas about verification to build blocking coalitions; it was not the inevitable result of the political, military, or technological context in which arms control decisions were made. Grotians accurately depict the Cautious Cooperators' way of thinking about verification—a crucial perspective, because Cautious Cooperators are the swing voters who determine whether more competitive or cooperative responses to security problems are adopted. Yet the more tightly the Cautious Cooperators cling to the Grotian ideas that increased transparency always enhances cooperation and that verification is a self-help substitute for centralized judgment and enforcement systems, the harder it will be to reach agreement with other countries in which different views of verification prevail. Kantians are correct that adversarial, law-enforcement models of verification cannot sustain significant cooperation, especially given the complexity of most modern agreements, the ambiguity required to encompass multiple points of view, and the uncertainties created by rapid changes in the post–Cold War context. Their proposals for cooperative security and managerial verification, however, assume a basic harmony of interests on core issues, a shared set of norms with which to judge right and wrong, and a common commitment to resolve disputes using fair procedures in a spirit of good will. These conditions may be more common than Hobbesians and Grotians realize, but until they are more fully developed and recognized by policy makers, it is unrealistic to expect a revolutionary change in ideas about verification.

There are no easy answers to arguments about verification. No consensus exists on first principles, and none is likely to develop. These are fundamentally contested questions with an ideological component that defies logical persuasion, especially since ambiguous evidence can be interpreted to fit conflicting beliefs about international politics. The relative strength of different schools of thought can shift over time through a combination of educational trends and contextual changes that make one worldview more attractive than another to uncommitted thinkers. The generation of scholars and policy makers who are coming of age intellectually in the post–Cold War world may be more comfortable with managerial verification than were previous decision makers. Yet the intensity of debates about arms control and security in the twenty-first century are evidence that arguments among Unilateralists, Cautious Cooperators, and Arms Control Advocates will persist into the foreseeable future.

No verification solution will be stable if it is fundamentally at odds with the ideas and interests of any country or domestic group whose approval is required to avoid negotiations, design an agreement, or ratify and implement an accord. This leaves little choice but to change how theorists and policy makers work with the politics of verification so that dominant ideas and strategies begin to favor winning coalitions over blocking ones. The first step is to understand the structure of the problem—to recognize that there are legitimate reasons for disagreement about verification among Arms Control Advocates, Cautious Cooperators, and Unilateralists, as well as between the United States and other countries. American policy makers and noncognitively oriented social scientists have often had a difficult time accepting that one view of reality is not necessarily more correct than another, but the problem is particularly acute on verification issues because of the myth that verification uncovers the "truth" about cooperation. Looking at verification decisions from each perspective will not make conflicts disappear. It will, however, minimize the chance of misidentifying potential allies and adversaries by assuming that anyone who shares concerns about verification is serious about cooperation and that anyone who expresses different concerns is not. It will also aid in the design of verification solutions that can appeal to different groups for different reasons.

Arms control supporters also must think more carefully about verification dilemmas. Perhaps the two most difficult challenges involve transparency and sovereignty. Academics have tended to take extreme positions on transparency. Some argue the liberal position that openness and the free exchange of information increase the general good; others embrace the realist view that relative advantages come from keeping secrets, spreading lies, and defeating others' attempts to do the same. Only by keeping both possibilities in mind is it possible to design verification regimes that maximize the beneficial uses of compliance information and minimize opportunities for abuse. Perfect verification is impossible. All too frequently, however, each provision of a verification agreement is evaluated against an extreme, such as total transparency or the most ruthless and resourceful evader. A better way to increase Cautious Cooperators' support for verification compromises is to stress the synergies among numerous ways of evaluating compliance and to contrast the benefits and risks of imperfectly verified cooperation with the costs and uncertainties of unconstrained competition.

Over the past decade, the proliferation of arms control proposals and accords that cannot be monitored solely by NTM has forced more Americans to think more carefully about trade-offs involving the amount of verification. Much less progress has occurred in confronting dilemmas associated with the type of decision making. Even though negotiators know that verification almost always involves some reduction in sovereignty, the myth persists in the United States that verification is ultimately a self-help activity. Americans may be comfortable with the international monitoring system as a supplement to national intelligence capabilities, but not as a source of information that could ever trump evidence that the United States has collected and analyzed on its own. Similarly, Americans may accept the practical need for some type of collective decision-making body, but only if the rules are designed so that multilateral decisions do not conflict with U.S. preferences. Yet the more significant an accord is, the less likely other countries are to accept data collection and decision-making procedures that seem unfair or manipulable by the most powerful states.

Thinking about the politics of verification as a process of coalition formation among groups with conflicting ideas about international politics leaves one cautiously optimistic about the prospects for cooperation. A universally signed and ratified accord has not yet been achieved for a total ban on nuclear testing. But the failures, frustrations, and low-significance successes were not overdetermined by inescapable features of international politics; instead, they were a function of the particular ideas and coalition-building strategies used in the politics of test ban verification. The optimism stems from the recognition that provisional agreement has been reached on numerous issues, even under very difficult circumstances. Although not every piece of the Rubik's cube has fallen into place for domestic and international agreement on CTB verification, each partial solution and provisional accord provides precedents and lessons that enable the next round to go further. The caution comes from recognizing that major dilemmas are only beginning to be addressed and that the complexity of cooperative problems continues to increase. Whether complexity works for or against cooperation depends very much on the ideas and strategies used to play the game.

Notes

Chapter One   Verification: The Key to Cooperation?

1. U.S. Arms Control and Disarmament Agency (hereinafter cited as ACDA), *Verification.*

2. The breakup of the USSR creates semantic difficulties. I will use such terms as *Soviets, USSR,* and *East bloc,* except when analyzing events after December 1991 or lessons for post–Cold War arms control. When a sentence bridges the two eras, I will use *Moscow* to indicate the political leadership of the USSR before December 1991 and *Russia* thereafter.

3. Enforcement involves problems of response after someone has been judged to be in violation. It is analytically distinct from verification because a state or international organization could have proof of noncompliance yet be unable to decide on or implement an effective response. Therefore, this book will address enforcement only as it relates to theoretical or historical arguments over verification.

4. For a comprehensive analysis of objectives sought through arms control before, during, and after the Cold War, see Croft, *Strategies of Arms Control.*

5. Game theory provides a shorthand for strategic interactions in which players choose between "cooperation" and "defection." The four possible outcomes from player A's perspective are mutual cooperation; A exploits B by defecting while B cooperates; B exploits A, who gets the "sucker's payoff"; and mutual defection (deadlock).

6. Young, *Compliance and Public Authority.*

7. Although nonrational factors such as organizational imperatives, bureaucratic bargains, and domestic political pressures can contribute to arms buildups, they can also help sustain arms control. See Chayes, "An Inquiry into the Workings of Arms Control Agreements."

8. The labels refer to the intellectual descendants of three early international relations theorists: Thomas Hobbes, best known for *Leviathan* (1651); Hugo Grotius, often considered the father of modern international law and the author of *The Law of War and Peace* (1625); and Immanuel Kant, most commonly associated with *Perpetual Peace* (1795). On the three traditions, see Bull, *The Anarchical Society,* 24–27.

9. There is a rich literature on cognitive factors that influence foreign policy decisions. For example, see George, *Bridging the Gap*; Holsti, "Foreign Policy Viewed Cognitively"; Jervis, *Perception and Misperception in International Politics*; and Larson, *Origins of Containment*.

10. Levy, "Learning and Foreign Policy," 283.

11. For the argument that cooperation is rare because states fear both cheating and relative gains, see Grieco, "Anarchy and the Limits of Cooperation."

12. See Blaker, "On-Site Inspections."

13. Adelman, "Why Verification Is More Difficult."

14. The Reagan administration routinely called for "cooperative verification" but defined this as Soviet willingness to let U.S. verification teams have complete access and control over information gathering and assessment, something the United States knew the Soviets would refuse.

15. On arms control paradoxes, see Gray, *House of Cards*.

16. Buzan, "From International System to International Society," and Rosenau and Czempiel, *Governance without Government*.

17. For examples, see Oye, ed., *Cooperation under Anarchy*; Keohane, *After Hegemony*; and Stein, *Why Nations Cooperate*.

18. Bull, "The Grotian Conception of International Society."

19. Young, *Compliance and Public Authority*, 65.

20. Oelrich, "The Changing Rules of Arms Control Verification."

21. NTM refers to remote-sensing devices like satellites and seismic monitors that are owned and used by a verifier from outside of the target country's territory. The term explicitly excludes human intelligence collection through on-site inspection or espionage.

22. Dunn, "Arms Control Verification: Living with Uncertainty." Dunn served as assistant director of ACDA in the 1980s.

23. Passive cooperation includes bans on encrypting the telemetry data from missile tests and covering new missiles so that the other side cannot see from satellite photos whether the missles' size exceeds permissible dimensions.

24. Even perfect verification could not substitute completely for trust because potential cooperators must also weigh the risks that an adversary will exploit a relaxation in tensions to make strategic gains elsewhere and the costs associated with responding once violations have been discovered. See Larson, *Anatomy of Mistrust*, 8–11.

25. When actors with mixed motives seek to secure a collective good, individuals may be tempted to enjoy the benefits without paying the costs if such "free-riding" cannot be recognized or punished. Several theorists have suggested that the difficulty of solving different types of cooperative problems depends on the number of second-order dilemmas involved. See Hasenclever et al., "Interests, Power, and Knowledge," 189–90.

26. Ostrom, *Governing the Commons*, 94–100.

27. Interview with author, Washington, D.C., June 7, 1989.

28. This process includes defining cooperation, collecting relevant information, processing the data, identifying suspicious events or activities, seeking clarification, and making judgments about compliance.

29. Nolan, ed., *Global Engagement*, 4–5.

30. For early Kantian analyses of arms control and verification, see Barnet and Falk, eds., *Security in Disarmament*.

31. Florini, "The Evolution of International Norms."

32. Chayes and Chayes, *The New Sovereignty*.

33. Chayes and Chayes, "From Law Enforcement." Antonia Handler Chayes served as undersecretary of the air force during the Carter administration; Abram Chayes was legal adviser to the State Department during the Kennedy administration.

34. Ibid., 161–62.

35. Downs et al., "Is the Good News about Compliance Good News about Cooperation?" critiques the managerial thesis by using a rational choice model to argue that the need for enforcement grows along with the significance of cooperation in mixed motive games. Managerialists would question not only the nature of the underlying game (a question that Downs et al. explicitly sidestep) but also the methodology. They would do so on the grounds that decision makers do not constantly compare the benefits of compliance and defection but instead show bounded rationality in their instrumental calculations and care about the intrinsic value of membership in good standing of various global regimes. See Chayes and Chayes, *The New Sovereignty*, 3–9, 26–28.

36. W. B. Gallie and Richard Little, quoted in Buzan, *People, States, and Fear*, 7.

37. By 1995, the bibliography on verification published by the Canadian Department of Foreign Affairs and International Trade had 3,700 entries.

38. For example, see Brams, *Superpower Games*; Meyer, "Verification and the ICBM Shell-Game"; and Wittman, "Arms Control Verification and Other Games Involving Imperfect Detection."

39. Representative writings of this group include Krass, *Verification: How Much Is Enough?* and "The Politics of Verification"; Krepon, "The Political Dynamics"; Lowenthal and Witt, "The Politics of Verification," 153–68; and Schear, "Verification, Compliance, and Arms Control."

40. Meyer, "Verification and Risk in Arms Control," 113.

41. Eden, "Contours of the Nuclear Controversy," 3.

42. See Kokeyev and Androsov, *Verification: The Soviet Stance*, 5, and Slocombe, "Verification and Negotiation," 87.

43. Myrdal, *The Game of Disarmament*, 293–94.

44. For an example of this "double bind" argument, see testimony by Harold Brown in *The SALT II Treaty: Report of the Senate Committee on Foreign Relations* (Washington, D.C.: G.P.O., 1979), 221.

45. Eugene Rostow, quoted in Schear, "Verifying Arms Control Agreements," 77.

46. For a concise discussion of arguments over nuclear strategy, see Glaser, "Why Do Strategists Disagree about the Requirements of Nuclear Deterrence?"

47. The term *NUTS* (for Nuclear Utilization Target Selection) was coined by Wolfgang Panofsky and Spurgeon Keeny Jr., in "MAD versus NUTS."

48. Seay, "What Are the Soviets' Objectives in Their Foreign, Military, and Arms Control Policies?"

49. Gordon, "All or Nothing," 730.

50. Krass, "The Politics of Verification," 751.

51. Gray, "Does Verification Really Matter?"

52. Lowenthal and Witt, "The Politics of Verification," 168.

53. See Meyer, "Verification and Risk in Arms Control," 126.

54. See Liftin, *Ozone Discourses*, 7, and Levy, "Learning and Foreign Policy," 312.

55. George, "Case Studies and Theory Development," 51–52.

56. Fetter, *Toward a Comprehensive Test Ban*, and Findlay, "A Comprehensive Nuclear Test Ban: Post–Cold War Prospects."

Chapter Two   Substance, Structure, and Strategy in Verification Politics

1. See Cheon and Fraser, "Arms Control Verification," 38–40.

2. Krass, *Verification*, 6.

3. Scribner and Luongo, *Strategic Nuclear Arms Control Verification*, 38.

4. Lowenthal and Witt, "The Politics of Verification," 153.

5. Timerbayev, *Verification of Arms Limitation and Disarmament*, 4.

6. To contrast this with domestic politics, imagine what would happen if prohibitions against abortion would take effect if, and only if, all Americans could agree on ways to monitor doctors and women without excessive expense, interference with legal medical activities, or invasions of privacy.

7. Statement by the Soviet representative (Issraelyan), March 31, 1981, U.S. Department of State, *Documents on Disarmament 1981*, 127–28. Hereinafter cited as *DoD/Year*. Some Sovietologists have found fluctuation and pragmatism in Soviet verification positions. Thus, Issraelyan's principles should be seen not as absolutes but as ideas that informed how Soviet leaders calculated the benefits, costs, and risks of cooperation: the more uncomfortable they were with the principles or procedures embodied in a verification proposal, the more compensation would be required for assent. See Potter, "The Evolution of Soviet Attitudes toward One-Site Inspection," and Scherr, *The Other Side of Arms Control*, 242–76.

8. Lord, "Verification: Reforming a Theology."

9. Typical was Walter Slocombe's claim that verification is "for all practical purposes . . . strictly an American concern." See "Verification and Negotiation," 87.

10. The U.S. intelligence community assigned each treaty provision a confidence level based on its estimate of American detection capabilities, current Soviet practices, and potential evasion scenarios.

11. Walter Pincus, "U.S. Devising New Verification Terms for Talks on Missiles," *International Herald Tribune*, July 28, 1983, p. 2.

12. Sims, "Arms Control Process: The U.S. Domestic Context," 56–59.

13. Some official publications recognized that political pressures could distort compliance evaluation but expressed confidence that democracy and professionalism ensured U.S. objectivity. See ACDA, *Verification*, 29.

14. Soviet military dictionaries contained no definitions of the term *verification*. By

the late 1980s, however, some Soviet commentators did use the anglicized word *veri-fikatsiya*. See Cohen, "The Evolution of Soviet Views on Verification," 68n.

15. Timerbayev, *Verification*, 30. Even this assessment had a political purpose, since one of Timerbayev's main points was that excessive American verification demands undermined Soviet efforts to control the arms race.

16. Timerbayev (as Zheleznov), "Monitoring Arms Limitations Measures," 82.

17. Soviet skepticism about the neutrality of organizations like the United Nations stemmed in part from the fact that their supporters were initially outnumbered by pro-Western states, but it also fits E. H. Carr's argument that states will not submit vital disputes to international judgment so long as they disagree about the principles and procedures that should be applied. See *The Twenty Years' Crisis*, 195–99.

18. McFate and Graybeal, "The Price for Effective Verification," 73–90; and U.S. Congressional Budget Office, "U.S. Costs of Verification and Compliance under Pending Arms Treaties."

19. William C. Foster, Hearings before the Senate Committee on Foreign Relations, *Disarmament and Foreign Policy*, 86th Congress, 1st Session (Washington, D.C.: G.P.O., 1959), 61–63.

20. Timerbayev (as Zheleznov), "Monitoring Arms Limitation Measures," 75.

21. Richard Lugar, "Verify, and Then Trust," *New York Times,* June 28, 1989, p. 23.

22. Morrocco, "Verification Raises Cost, Technology Concerns."

23. The September 1991 initiatives included mutual pledges to hasten the deactivation of strategic systems covered by START I, cancel the development of new mobile ICBMS, and eliminate ground- and sea-based tactical nuclear weapons—measures that previous administrations would never have negotiated without detailed verification provisions.

24. The USSR agreed that disarmament required international "control," but the Russian cognate means "oversight," not direct restraint or operational involvement by international agents.

25. See Molander, "The United Nations and the Elimination of Iraq's Weapons of Mass Destruction," and Towle, *Enforced Disarmament*, 183–201.

26. Chayes, "Inquiry," 946.

27. Eugene Rostow, Hearings before the Senate Committee on Armed Services, *Arms Control Policy, Planning, and Negotiation*, July 24, 1981 (Washington, D.C.: G.P.O., 1983), 58. See also Graybeal and Krepon, "The Limitations of On-Site Inspection."

28. Pool, "Public Opinion and the Control of Armament."

29. Lehman, "Lehman's Lessons: The Arms Control Agenda," 9.

30. Cohen, "The Evolution of Soviet Views," 68n.

31. Karkoszka, *Strategic Disarmament, Verification and National Security*, 3; and Timerbayev, *Verification*, 25.

32. Timerbayev insisted that "verification must be carried out so that no nation or group of nations . . . could impose its will." *Verification*, 20.

33. Bohn, "Non-Physical Inspection Techniques"; Gupta, "Remote Sensing and Photogrammetry in Treaty Verification." Jeremy Leggett even proposed a verified reassignment of anyone with expertise on nuclear testing to ensure compliance with a CTB. He ad-

mitted that an orchestrated brain drain seemed idealistic but predicted that if environmental problems erode national sovereignty, "the idea of checking the academic output of several dozen physics professors who once ran a nuclear testing programme will come to seem less utopian than it does today." In Leggett, "Recent Developments and Outlook for the Verification of a Nuclear Test Ban," 96.

34. See Towle, *Enforced Disarmament*, 80–81, 190.

35. Timerbayev, *Verification*, 135–36.

36. Jayantha Dhanapala, Preface to Sur, ed., *Verification of Current Disarmament and Arms Limitation Agreements*, vii.

37. Adelman, "Why Verification Is More Difficult," 143.

38. Grier, "Poking and Prying for Peace," 25; Algoni, "Verification and Congress?"; and Rose, "Nuclear Test Ban and Verification," 20.

39. Interviews by author with UNSCOM and IAEA officials, summer 1993.

40. See Wendt, "The Agent-Structure Problem in International Relations."

41. See Kapstein, "Is Realism Dead?"

42. Waltz, *Theory of International Politics*, is the classic example. Yet even Waltz recognizes that policy makers have some freedom in their response to systemic imperatives.

43. For an analysis using domestic factors to explain deviations from game-theoretic predictions, see Weber, *Cooperation and Discord in U.S.-Soviet Arms Control*.

44. Meyer, "Verification and the ICBM Shell-Game."

45. Buzan, "From International System to International Society"; Milner, "The Assumption of Anarchy"; and Stein, *Why Nations Cooperate*.

46. For constructivist treatments of security, see Katzenstein, ed., *The Culture of National Security*. A more general but highly readable analysis is Finnemore, *National Interests in International Society*.

47. Wendt, "Anarchy Is What States Make of It."

48. Florini, "The Evolution of International Norms," 381.

49. Domestic-level analyses of arms control include Solingen, "The Domestic Sources of Regional Regimes"; Clarke, *Politics of Arms Control*; Miller, "Politics over Promise"; Shimko, *Images and Arms Control*; Sims, *Icarus Restrained*; and Wirls, *Build-up*.

50. Snyder, *Myths of Empire*.

51. Lavoy, "Nuclear Myths and the Causes of Nuclear Proliferation."

52. Gourevitch, "The Second Image Reversed."

53. On crisis-induced learning, see Lebow, *Between Peace and War*.

54. Snyder and Diesing, *Conflict among Nations*.

55. The two-level games model is developed and applied to a range of cases in Evans et al., eds., *Double-Edged Diplomacy*.

56. A country's win-set includes all accords that would get the necessary domestic support when compared with "no agreement." An involuntary defection occurs when national leaders lack the capability to implement an agreement.

57. See Keohane, "International Institutions," and Goldstein and Keohane, eds., *Ideas and Foreign Policy*.

58. See Nisbett and Wilson, "Telling More Than We Can Know."

59. This is consistent with Snyder and Diesing's finding that hard- and soft-line bargaining approaches are more a function of personal beliefs than of governmental role. See *Conflict Among Nations*, 297–310.

60. Knopf, "Beyond Two-Level Games."

61. Risse-Kappen, ed., *Bringing Transnational Relations Back In*.

62. Eichenberg, "Dual Track and Double Trouble."

63. Eichenberg, "On Public Support," 168.

64. This was a particular problem in bloc-to-bloc negotiations over the 1990 Conventional Forces in Europe Treaty. See Bühl, "Verification," 58; and R. Jeffrey Smith, "U.S., Allies Ease Terms on Arms Verification," *Washington Post*, March 14, 1990, p. A24.

65. Moodie, "Ratifying the Chemical Weapons Convention."

66. For an overview of this approach and its applications, see Haas, "Introduction: Epistemic Communities and International Policy Coordination."

67. Adler, "The Emergence of Cooperation."

68. Levy, "Learning and Foreign Policy," provides a valuable survey of the reciprocal interactions among learning, domestic politics, and external context.

69. By this, Hampson means that people fear an impending catastrophe, feel personally vulnerable, believe that experts can avert or manage the risks, but do not understand the issue well themselves. See Hampson, *Multilateral Negotiations*, 38–39.

70. See Litfin, *Ozone Discourses*, for a critique of the apolitical bent of most epistemic community research and the argument that receptivity to technical information is often a function of perceived interests.

71. Krepon and Caldwell, eds., *The Politics of Arms Control Treaty Ratification*.

72. Snyder argues that this was misguided, because the broad concessions angered many of Gorbachev's domestic constituents and failed to produce specific economic benefits that might have increased internal support for reform. It fits well, however, with Charles Osgood's recommendations for safely de-escalating an arms race that neither side really wants to continue. See Snyder, "East-West," 121; and Osgood, *An Alternative to War or Surrender*.

73. Everett Carll Ladd found a forty-year tradition of support for arms control and distrust toward the Soviet Union. See "The Freeze Framework."

74. Haas, *Saving the Mediterranean*, 214–47.

75. Weber, "Interactive Learning in U.S.-Soviet Arms Control."

76. Snyder, "East-West," 104–5, 115–16.

Chapter Three   How the Politics of Verification Shape Prenegotiation

1. Stein, ed., *Getting to the Table*.

2. Zartman and Berman, *The Practical Negotiator*, 36.

3. See Higgins, *The Hague Peace Conferences and Other International Conferences Concerning the Laws and Usages of War*.

4. Towle, *Arms Control in East-West Relations*, 138.

5. The Russians wanted a weak inquiry organization as a safety valve to reduce public pressure for retribution. Other countries argued that refusal to permit an impartial investigation would be tantamount to an admission of guilt. Holls, *The Peace Conferences at the Hague*, 207, 213.

6. Carroll, "Germany Disarmed and Rearming, 1925–1935," 114–24.

7. Roddie, *Peace Patrol*, 317.

8. Gumbel, "Disarmament and Clandestine Rearmament under the Weimar Republic," 203–19.

9. Roddie, *Peace Patrol*, 35–36.

10. Towle, *Enforced Disarmament*, 73–87.

11. *Foreign Relations of the United States* (General) 1926, vol. 1 (Washington D.C.: G.P.O., 1941), 88, hereinafter cited as FRUS. As concern about German rearmament grew, U.S. and British officials called for intrusive verification—contingent on others' willingness to do the same—but many viewed this as a public relations ploy. See Towle, *Arms Control*, 134–38.

12. Temperley, *The Whispering Gallery of Europe*, 311–12.

13. See Lefebure, *Scientific Disarmament*.

14. Quoted in Temperley, *The Whispering Gallery of Europe*, 192.

15. Timerbayev, *Verification*, 15–16.

16. Quoted in Bundy, *Danger and Survival*, 153.

17. The report was written by a board of scientific consultants led by David Lilienthal and heavily influenced by Robert Oppenheimer. It went to the secretary of state's Committee on Atomic Energy, headed by Dean Acheson.

18. Quoted in Herken, *The Winning Weapon*, 156 n.

19. U.S. Department of State, Committee on Atomic Energy, *A Report on the International Control of Atomic Energy*. Hereinafter cited as ALC.

20. Ibid., 4–5.

21. Dean Acheson, quoted in Schear, "Verifying Arms Agreements," 89.

22. The plan assumed that the ADA could secure all sources of fissile material and find some irreversible way to "denature" it so that states could be given a supply of "harmless" material for medical or commercial uses.

23. ALC, xii.

24. Acheson, *Present at the Creation*, 152.

25. The report underestimated the Soviet program by judging that only the U.K. and Canada were technologically advanced enough to utilize the information revealed. See ALC, viii–ix.

26. Bundy, *Danger and Survival*, 164.

27. Reprinted in Erskine, "The Polls," 155–90.

28. On Baruch, see Herken, *The Winning Weapon*, 158–91. For Truman's beliefs, see Hewlett and Anderson, *The New World*, 455–56.

29. Felix Belair Jr., "Plea to Give Soviets Atom Secret Stirs Debate in Cabinet," *New York Times*, September 22, 1945, p. 13.

30. First Report of the United Nations Atomic Energy Commission (UNAEC), December 31, 1946, in *Documents on Disarmament*, vol. 1 (1945–56), 50–59. Hereinafter cited as *DoD/vi*.

31. Statement by Baruch to the UNAEC, June 14, 1946, *DoD/vi*, 7–16.

32. Ibid., 13.

33. The British also quietly opposed any plan that would hamper their efforts to obtain nuclear weapons without guaranteeing their security. See Gowing, *Britain and Atomic Energy*, 89–90.

34. Nogee, *Soviet Policy toward International Control of Atomic Energy*.

35. Bundy, *Danger and Survival*, 181.

36. The best source for background information on early negotiations is Bechhoeffer, *Postwar Negotiations for Arms Control*.

37. Bundy, *Danger and Survival*, 192–96.

38. NSC 112 is summarized in "The Disarmament Problem and U.S. Policy before the NSC, April 22, 1955," National Security Archives (NSA).

39. Sims, *Icarus Restrained*, 49–80.

40. Kokeyev and Androsov, *Verification*, 5.

41. This precaution turned out to be unnecessary. By the 1952 MIKE test (the first American thermonuclear device), the Soviets still lacked a formal monitoring system. Andrei Sakharov collected several cartons of newly fallen snow after the explosion, but an absent-minded colleague poured it down the drain before Sakharov could analyze it. Sakharov, *Memoirs*, 158.

42. The United States detected JOE I on September 9. Oppenheimer calculated that the test had occurred on August 29. Truman assumed greater uncertainty in the U.S. monitoring system, dating the test between August 19 and 21. Khrushchev's memoirs place the explosion in July. Herken, *Winning Weapon*, 252, 302.

43. The proposal is reprinted in York, *The Advisors*, 158–59.

44. Quoted in Bundy, *Danger and Survival*, 217.

45. Panel of Consultants on Disarmament, "The Timing of the Thermonuclear Test," undated (probably September 1952), in *FRUS*, 1952–54, vol. II, 1001–2; Minutes of (Second) Panel Meeting of Consultants, May 6, 1952, quoted in Bernstein, "Crossing the Rubicon," 141.

46. John Ferguson, deputy director of the State Department's Policy Planning Staff, quoted in Bernstein, "Crossing the Rubicon," 142.

47. See Erskine, "The Polls," 171.

48. Harold Stassen, Hearings before the Senate Committee on Foreign Relations (SCFR), *Control and Reduction of Armaments*, pt. 1, 84th Congress, 2nd Session (January 1956), 12.

49. Panel of Consultants, "Armaments and American Foreign Policy," *FRUS*, 1952–54, vol. II, 1056–91.

50. Ibid., 1089–90.

51. For attitudes toward arms control in the Eisenhower Administration, see Greb and Johnson, *Who's in Charge?*

52. See "Discussion at the 203rd Meeting of the National Security Council, June 23, 1954," NSA, 2. Hereinafter cited as NSC 6-23-54.

53. "Atoms for Peace" Proposal, December 8, 1953, *DoD/vi*, 400.

54. "The Disarmament Problem," Annex A.

55. Robert Bowie, director of the Policy Planning Staff, was one of the earliest State Department voices for serious arms control efforts. Over time, the secretary of state also came around to this position.

56. See Bloomfield et al., *Khrushchev and the Arms Race*; Evangelista, *Innovation and the Arms Race*, ch. 5; and Holloway, *The Soviet Union and the Arms Race*.

57. Snyder, *Myths of Empire*, 230–31.

58. Snyder, "International Leverage on Soviet Domestic Change," 17.

59. Khrushchev, *Report of the Central Committee to the 20th Congress of the CPSU*, 28.

60. Evangelista, "Cooperation Theory and Disarmament Negotiations in the 1950s," 506–13.

61. For details of BRAVO, see Voss, *Nuclear Ambush*, 37–44.

62. Inglis, "H-Bomb Control," 67–70.

63. See Divine, *Blowing on the Wind*, and Dokos, *Negotiations for a CTBT 1958–1994*.

64. Rosi, "Public Opinion and National Security Policy," 369.

65. "Discussions at the 199th Meeting of the NSC, May 27, 1954," NSA. Hereinafter cited as NSC 5-27-54.

66. "Memorandum for the Secretary of Defense from the Joint Chiefs of Staff, April 30, 1954," NSA.

67. NSC 6-23-54, 3.

68. Ibid., 2.

69. NSC 5-27-54, 12, emphasis in original.

70. NSC 6-23-54, 2.

71. NSC 5-27-54, 13.

72. Statement to the Democratic Party, October 6, 1958, quoted in Voss, *Nuclear Ambush*, 87.

73. "Text of Churchill's Statement on the Hydrogen Bomb Tests," *New York Times*, March 31, 1954, p. 4.

74. Baylis, *Anglo-American Defense Relations, 1939–84*, 66–72.

75. Soviet Draft Resolution on Use of Atomic, Hydrogen and Other Weapons of Mass Destruction, June 1, 1954, *DoD/vi*, 422.

76. "U.N. Atomic Control Plan Dead, France Declared at Secret Talks," *New York Times*, July 17, 1954, p. 1.

77. Anglo-French Memorandum, June 11, 1954, *DoD/vi*, 423–24.

78. Soviet Disarmament Proposal, May 10, 1955, *DoD/vi*, 456–76.

79. See Bloomfield et al., *Khrushchev and the Arms Race*, 46.

80. Soviet Bloc Proposal at the Geneva Surprise Attack Conference, December 12, 1958, *DoD/vi*, 1298–1303.

81. Statement by Stassen, September 6, 1955, *DoD/vi*, 511.

82. Efinger, "The Verification Policy of the Soviet Union," 336–37. According to a senior Soviet diplomat, however, Khrushchev doubted that Congress would let Soviet planes fly over Washington, D.C. He wanted to call Eisenhower's bluff by accepting the Open Skies proposal and "watch the White House squirm in the propaganda spotlight." Dobrynin, *In Confidence*, 37–38.

83. "Discussion at the 253rd Meeting of the National Security Council, June 30, 1955," 5–6, NSA. Hereinafter cited as NSC 6-30-55.

84. NSC 6-30-55, 11.

85. "Report of the Special Assistant to the President to the January 26, 1956 Session of the National Security Council," 5, NSA.

86. U.S. Working Paper on Technical Exchange Mission, March 21, 1956, *DoD/v1*, 599–600.

87. U.S. Working Paper on Demonstration Test Area, March 21, 1956, *DoD/v1*, 600–601.

88. The JCS worried that the Soviets would stall conventional arms negotiations until they had approached nuclear parity with the United States. If they then agreed to limit conventional forces, the West would be "at a hell of a disadvantage." See "Memorandum of 275th Meeting of the National Security Council, February 7, 1956," 9, NSA. Hereinafter cited as NSC 2-7-56.

89. U.S. Memorandum, January 12, 1957, *DoD/v2*, 731–34.

90. Hewlett and Holl, *Atoms for Peace and War*; Freeman, *Britain's Nuclear Arms Control Policy*, 49–50; Scheinman, *Atomic Energy Policy in France under the Fourth Republic*.

91. On the 1956 campaign, see Divine, *Blowing on the Wind*, 84–112.

92. Since fission releases radioactive products whereas fusion does not, nuclear weapons can be made "cleaner" with designs that minimize reliance on fission processes.

93. *Newsweek*, October 29, 1956, p. 27; Bulganin to Eisenhower, October 17, 1956, *DoD/v1*, 694–97.

94. Hewlett and Holl, *Atoms for Peace and War*, 361.

95. Statement by Stassen, Nuclear Weapons and Testing, March 20, 1957, *DoD/v2*, 763–70.

96. Strauss's assistant for disarmament, quoted in Hewlett and Holl, *Atoms for Peace and War*, 385.

97. Ibid., 385–88.

98. "Summary of Important Provisions of 'Policy Recommendations to Washington,'" May 9, 1957," NSA.

99. Seaborg, *Kennedy*, 10.

100. "Defense Position on Test Limitations, April 20, 1957," NSA, and Hewlett and Holl, *Atoms for Peace and War*, 388–89.

101. Hewlett and Holl, *Atoms for Peace and War*, 399.

102. "Memorandum from the Director of the CIA regarding the Effectiveness of Nuclear Test Detection System, May 11, 1957," NSA.

103. "Letter from Lewis Strauss to John Foster Dulles, June 5, 1957," NSA.

104. U.S. Department of State, *Disarmament*, 40–41.

105. Western Statement on Nuclear Test Suspension, July 2, 1957, *DoD/v2*, 802–3.

106. Bechhoeffer, *Postwar Negotiations*, 354–55.

107. "Telegram for the Secretary of State from Stassen, July 2, 1957," NSA.

108. "Informal Memorandum from Harold Stassen to the Secretary of State, September 23, 1957," and "Letter from Charles Wilson, Secretary of Defense, to the Secretary of State, around July 10, 1957," NSA.

109. Strauss to Dulles, June 5, 1957, NSA.

110. "Report of the NSC Ad Hoc Working Group on the Technical Feasibility of a Cessation of Nuclear Testing, March 27, 1958, Appendix A: Concealment and Detection of Nuclear Tests Underground," NSA. Hereinafter cited as the Bethe Report.

111. Voss, *Nuclear Ambush*, 128.

112. Quoted in Divine, *Blowing on the Wind*, 188.

113. Statement by Stassen, Suspension of Nuclear Tests, August 21, 1957, *DoD/v2*, 845–48.

114. Soviet Statement, August 27, 1957, *DoD/v2*, 849–68.

115. See Bechhoeffer, *Postwar Negotiations*, 410–13.

116. On reserve, if not resistance, toward test cessation by the military and heavy industry, see Jönsson, *Soviet Bargaining Behavior*, 145–47.

117. "Western Working Paper Submitted to the Disarmament Subcommittee: Proposal for Measures of Disarmament, August 29, 1957," *DoD/v2*, 868–74.

118. Bechhoeffer, *Postwar Negotiations*, 401–2.

119. James Reston, "Leader Says Control Depends on Accord for Coexistence," *New York Times*, October 8, 1957, p. 10.

120. "Secretary Dulles' News Conference," June 11, 1957, U.S. Department of State *Bulletin*, 37 (July 1, 1957): 9.

121. "Proposed U.S. Position on Nuclear Tests, around February 1958," NSA.

122. Joint Chiefs of Staff, "Memorandum for the Secretary of Defense," March 13, 1958, NSA.

123. "Morning Conference on August 9, 1957," NSA.

124. Herken, *Cardinal Choices*, 101–23.

125. Herken, *Counsels of War*, 112–18.

126. This group was chaired by Hans Bethe, a physicist from Cornell University, and included representatives from the AEC, DOD, and the CIA.

127. Decree Discontinuing Soviet Tests, March 31, 1958, *DoD/v2*, 978–80.

128. Quoted in Greb and Johnson, *Who's in Charge?* 100.

129. See Erskine, "The Polls," 170, 185.

130. Khrushchev to Eisenhower, April 22, 1958, *DoD/v2*, 996–1004.

131. Eisenhower to Khrushchev, April 28, 1958, *DoD/v2*, 1006–7; Khrushchev to Eisenhower, May 9, 1958, *DoD/v2*, 1036–41.

132. Interview with Gerald Johnson, San Diego, October 13, 1989.

133. For details on the conference, see Jacobson and Stein, *Diplomats, Scientists, and Politicians*.

134. U.S. Department of State, *Bulletin*, 38:992 (June 30, 1958): 1085.

135. The head of the U.S. delegation's report to the NSC is summarized in "Discussion at the 378th Meeting of the National Security Council, August 27, 1958," NSA.

136. See "Letter from Herbert Loper, Assistant to the Secretary of Defense (Atomic Energy) to Dr. Killian, May 13, 1958," NSA.

137. The U.S. delegation consisted of James Fisk, Robert Bacher, and Ernest Lawrence. Teller was excluded, and Bethe attended only as an adviser.

138. Report of the Conference of Experts, August 21, 1958, *DoD/v2*, 1090–1111.

139. Rabinowitch, "Nuclear Bomb Tests," 287.

140. "Summary of Meeting Held in the State Department, August 13, 1958," NSA.

141. Statement by Eisenhower, August 22, 1958," *DoD/v2*, 1111–12.

142. *Pravda* interview with Khrushchev, August 29, 1958, *DoD/v2*, 1114–20.

143. The United States conducted 77 tests in 1958 compared with 117 previous shots, whereas the USSR detonated 35 blasts in 1958 and 49 before then. See "Factfile: Fifty Years of Nuclear Testing: Part II," 38.

144. On "ripeness," see Stein, *Getting to the Table*, 267–68.

Chapter Four   "Scientific" Approaches to Verification Decisions

1. Jacobson and Stein, *Diplomats, Scientists, and Politicians* is the best source for historical details on the first generation of CTB negotiations.

2. "Principal Arguments for Continuing Testing," around August 15, 1958, and "Principal Arguments against Continuing Testing," around August 21, 1958, in NSA.

3. This understanding, called the "Basic U.S. Position for Nuclear Test Suspension Negotiations with USSR," is discussed in "Letter from the Acting Secretary of Defense to the Secretary of State, late December 1958," NSA.

4. Groom, *British Thinking about Nuclear Weapons*, 357–62.

5. Wright, *Disarm and Verify*, 130.

6. Groom, *British Thinking about Nuclear Weapons*, 362–63.

7. Bloomfield et al., *Khrushchev and the Arms Race*, 154–55; Evangelista, "Sources of Moderation in Soviet Security Policy," 298–99.

8. Bloomfield et al., *Khrushchev and the Arms Race*, 157.

9. See Jonsson, *Soviet Bargaining*, 152, and Griffiths, "The Sources of American Conduct," 13–17.

10. G. Trofimenko, "The Struggle in the U.S.A. on Foreign Policy Questions," in Jonsson, *Soviet Bargaining*, 153.

11. Quoted in Gruliow, ed., *Current Soviet Policies III*, 203.

12. Jonsson, *Soviet Bargaining*, 143–61. The Presidium was the name used for the Politburo from 1952 to 1966.

13. See Griffiths, "The Sources of American Conduct," for different Soviet perspectives on international relations.

14. The Pugwash Conferences started in July 1957 to promote dialogue between Western and Soviet scientists about reducing nuclear dangers.

15. "Letter from Victor F. Weisskopf to James Killian, September 27, 1958," NSA.

16. Because the United States and the United Kingdom started their massive test series while the Soviet moratorium was in effect, the USSR argued that it could test until it matched the number of Western tests.

17. Quoted in Jónsson, *Soviet Bargaining*, 72.

18. Divine, *Blowing on the Wind*, 243.

19. See Finkelstein, "Arms Inspection."

20. Gehron, "Geneva Conference on the Discontinuance of Nuclear Weapons Tests," 486–87.

21. The West wanted forty foreign officials and twenty-one local support staff at more than 160 control posts. Additional people would be required for permanent OSI teams, daily air sampling flights, research and analysis teams, and other administrative duties. This would dwarf any other international organization—even the U.N. secretariat only had a staff of about four thousand.

22. "Memorandum from E. B. Skolnikoff to Killian re Summary of Discussion Regarding Nuclear Test Cessation Issues, November 18, 1958," NSA.

23. Details are in Greb and Johnson, *Who's in Charge?* 84.

24. Quoted in Jacobson and Stein, *Diplomats*, 195.

25. A. L. Latter, *A Method of Concealing Underground Nuclear Explosions* (RAND Corp. RM-2347-AFT, 1959). RAND is a think tank founded to do research for the air force. Fully decoupling a 10-kt shot by a factor of 300 would require a spherical hole with a diameter of 360 feet that was 3,000 feet underground, so a 400-kt test could not really be hidden in this manner.

26. Bethe, quoted in Voss, *Nuclear Ambush*, 155.

27. Katz, "Hiders and Finders," 423–24.

28. Quoted in Divine, *Blowing on the Wind*, 239.

29. Killian, *Sputnik, Scientists, and Eisenhower*, 168.

30. Teller, "Alternatives for Security," 204.

31. Few Americans knew about Project Argus and other high-altitude tests done in 1958 until the tests were publicized in a *New York Times* story in March 1959, a point that Soviet negotiators used to show that the United States could conduct clandestine tests. See Lang, *An Inquiry into Enoughness*, 48, and Gilpin, *American Scientists and Nuclear Weapons Policy*, 225.

32. Statement by PSAC Regarding Detection of Underground Nuclear Tests, January 5, 1959, *DoD/v2*, 1335–36.

33. "Letter from the Acting Secretary of Defense, late December 1958," NSA.

34. Killian, *Sputnik, Scientists, and Eisenhower*, 164–65.

35. Eisenhower, *Waging the Peace*, 479; and Divine, *Blowing on the Wind*, 246.

36. Jacobson and Stein, *Diplomats*, 155.

37. "Memorandum of Conversation with the President, January 12, 1959, 9:00 a.m.," NSA.

38. Latter's analysis was presented to PSAC in January 1959. It was not published for

internal government use until late March, not declassified until late October, and not released publicly until late December 1959.

39. Wadsworth, *The Price of Peace*, 24.

40. Statement by the USSR, January 22, 1959, *DoD/v2*, 1339–43.

41. "Letter from President Eisenhower to Prime Minister Macmillan, January 12, 1959," NSA.

42. "Memorandum of Conversation, January 12, 1959," NSA.

43. "Eisenhower to Macmillan, January 12, 1959," NSA.

44. For David Ormsby-Gore's account of this conversation, see Jacobson and Stein, *Diplomats*, 167.

45. Seaborg, *Kennedy*, 41.

46. Humphrey's letter is quoted in Voss, *Nuclear Ambush*, 292.

47. "Letter from Donald Quarles to the Secretary of State, December 30, 1958," NSA.

48. See Kistiakowsky, *A Scientist in the White House*, 6.

49. "Memorandum of conference between Eisenhower and Killian by Andrew Goodpaster, February 25, 1959," quoted in Divine, *Blowing on the Wind*, 252.

50. "Report of the United States Panel on Seismic Improvement," *DoD/v2*, 1378–92.

51. Subsequent experiments have shown that a decoupling factor of 50–70 is appropriate at low frequencies, that monitoring at high frequencies can reduce that to about a factor of 10, and that decoupling a 5-kt blast would require a spherical cavity whose diameter was larger than the Statue of Liberty is tall. See Fetter, *Toward a CTB*, 137–41, and Office of Technology Assessment (OTA), *Seismic Verification*, 100–101.

52. Compressional waves (P-waves) travel long distances at high speeds through the earth's interior. Teleseismic stations (located more than 2,000 kilometers from the event) can also detect two types of shear waves (S-waves)—transverse horizontal (SH) and transverse vertical (SV)—that go through the interior at slower speeds. Regional stations (often called in-country stations) can monitor two types of surface waves: Rayleigh (vertical) and Love (horizontal). In theory, an explosion in homogenous earth is a symmetrical source that would only generate P-waves, SV, and Rayleigh waves, whereas an earthquake would cause all types of waves. In practice, heterogeneity in the earth means that some vertical waves from explosions are converted into horizontal waves. The efficiency of the conversion decreases with increasing wave length, so the Berkner Panel predicted that earthquakes and explosions would have different proportions of long period Love and Rayleigh waves.

53. In comparison, the total annual amount spent on seismological research in the United States at that time was several hundred thousand dollars.

54. See Jacobson and Stein, *Diplomats*, 177–80, and Voss, *Nuclear Ambush*, 444–47.

55. "Letter from President Eisenhower to the Soviet Premier (Khrushchev), April 13, 1959," *DoD/v2*, 1392–93.

56. "Memorandum for the President: Voluntary Temporary Moratorium on Underground and High Altitude Tests, April 23, 1959," NSA.

57. "Macmillan Talks, Washington, March 19–23, 1959," NSA.

58. Bloomfield et al., *Khrushchev and the Arms Race*, 118.

59. Khrushchev to Eisenhower, April 23, 1959, *DoD/v2*, 1396–98.

60. Statement by the British Foreign Secretary to the House of Commons, April 27, 1959, *DoD/v2*, 1400–1401.

61. Quoted in Divine, *Blowing on the Wind*, 250.

62. *Congressional Record*, 55:4 (1959): 5347.

63. Letter from Eisenhower to Khrushchev, May 5, 1959, *DoD/v2*, 1403–5.

64. "Memorandum of Conference with the President, May 5, 1959," NSA.

65. Herken, *Cardinal Choices*, 116.

66. See Jacobson and Stein, *Diplomats*, 199–200.

67. Ambassador Wadsworth, quoted in Greb and Johnson, *Who's In Charge?* 104.

68. "Memorandum of Conference on May 5, 1959," NSA.

69. Wright complained that "for months on end, instructions were doled out to [the U.S. delegation] from Washington as a Victorian workhouse master might dole out the gruel" (*Disarm and Verify*, 120).

70. U.S. Congress, Joint Committee on Atomic Energy, *Hearings: Aspects of Detection and Inspection Controls of a Nuclear Weapons Test Ban*, 37. Hereinafter cited as JCAE 1960.

71. "Memorandum of Conference with the President, July 23, 1959," NSA.

72. "Letter from John McCone to James Killian, January 17, 1959," NSA. RAINER and the two underground tests in HARDTACK II were at NTS. McCone's claim that tests in other areas might reveal new problems with the Geneva System was disingenuous. Since the rock around NTS is an especially poor transmitter of seismic signals, tests elsewhere would most likely be easier to detect and identify.

73. A nuclear weapon is one-point safe if there would be no appreciable yield should an accident cause the high explosive to detonate. Kistiakowsky countered that the weapons of concern were one-point safe by the current definition, so "what is involved here is the establishment of a new, more severe test." Eisenhower accused the AEC of "setting up a straw man in order to knock it down." Nevertheless, he approved further study. See "Memorandum of Conference with the President, July 13, 1959," NSA.

74. Thorn and Westervelt, "Hydronuclear Experiments," 7.

75. Jönsson, *Soviet Bargaining*, 154–61.

76. Richter, *Khrushchev's Double Bind*, 119–23.

77. The superpowers wanted to prevent military activities in the region, yet the military was the only institution in many signatory states that could operate in the harsh conditions around the South Pole. The 1959 Antarctic Treaty lets the military provide logistical support for scientific endeavors but stipulates that all locations must be open to inspectors from any party to the treaty. See Shapley, "Antarctica: Why Success?"

78. Jacobson and Stein, *Diplomats*, 214.

79. Seaborg, *Kennedy*, 21.

80. Jacobson and Stein, *Diplomats*, 223–24.

81. Many of the Soviets' proposed criteria are routinely used now. For example, if the

epicenter of an event is in a densely populated area or below 2.5 km (the deepest test conducted to date), seismologists assume that it was an earthquake.

82. Statement by Eisenhower: Nuclear Weapons Tests, December 29, 1959, *DoD/v2*, 1590–91.

83. See Greb and Johnson, *Who's in Charge?* 105.

84. Erskine, "The Polls," 185.

85. Quoted in Divine, *Blowing on the Wind*, 296–97.

86. Statement by Wadsworth, February 11, 1960, *DoD/1960*, 33–39.

87. Since seismic events generate many different types of waves, the amount of energy released is measured in terms of the P-wave amplitude (m_b).

88. A "tamped" explosion fits tightly into the test hole, so that all of the blast's energy is transmitted to the surrounding walls.

89. Chemical and low-yield nuclear explosions have similar effects, which creates another identification problem for test-ban verification. Nuclear explosions would be preferable for studying decoupling because their much smaller mass-yield ratio would decrease the size of the cavity needed.

90. Seaborg, *Kennedy*, 22–23.

91. An account of the principals' meetings on March 22–23, 1960, is in Roberts, "The Hopes and Fears of an Atomic Test Ban."

92. "General Nuclear Test Negotiations: Meeting of Principals, March 23, 1960," NSA. In a last-ditch attempt to avoid both an uninspected moratorium and international opprobrium, Strauss (now commerce secretary) suggested that the United States counter the Soviet plan with a proposal to grant Swiss inspectors immediate and unquestioned access to any location during the moratorium. "Letter from Lewis Strauss to President Eisenhower, March 28, 1960," NSA.

93. "Joint Declaration by President Eisenhower and Prime Minister Macmillan on Nuclear Tests, March 29, 1960," *DoD/1960*, 77–78.

94. Wadsworth is quoted in Jacobson and Stein, *Diplomats*, 248.

95. The Soviets refused to conduct joint decoupled nuclear tests and are not believed to have conducted any fully decoupled nuclear tests of their own.

96. Kistiakowsky, *A Scientist at the White House*, 288.

97. JCAE 1960; for details, see Voss, *Nuclear Ambush*, 395–456.

98. Original estimates placed the decoupling factor at 100–150; this was later lowered to about 70. See OTA, *Seismic Verification*, 101.

99. Nathan, "A Fragile Détente," 97–104; and Pomerance, "The Anti-Test Ban Coalition," 51–54.

100. Snyder, "East-West Bargaining," 110–13.

101. Richter, *Khrushchev's Double Bind*, 125–26.

102. Goldman, *Verifying Arms Control Agreements*, 9.

103. Quoted in Beschloss, *Mayday*, 370.

104. See Jönsson, *Soviet Bargaining*, 162–64.

105. Dobrynin, *In Confidence*, 39–42.

106. Khrushchev, *Khrushchev Remembers*, 451.

107. U.S. Department of State, *Bulletin* 42:1092 (May 30, 1960): 851; Khrushchev, *Khrushchev Remembers*, 461.

108. Quoted in Richter, *Khrushchev's Double Bind*, 130.

109. Dobrynin, *In Confidence*, 41.

110. Kistiakowsky, *A Scientist in the White House*, 328.

111. Jacobson and Stein, *Diplomats*, 267.

112. Eisenhower, *Waging the Peace*, 263, 481.

113. Greb, "Survey of Past Nuclear Test Ban Negotiations," 100.

114. Quoted in Roberts, "Hopes and Fears," 23.

115. Killian, *Sputnik, Scientist, and Eisenhower*, 172.

116. This formula resembles the one used by the United States at the Disarmament Subcommittee in 1957. The West could still use verification to veto an extension, but concern for public opinion would make that hard to do lightly.

Chapter Five   The Corrosive Effects of Coercive Diplomacy

1. "Treaty Banning Nuclear Weapons Tests in the Atmosphere, in Outer Space, and Under Water, Signed August 5, 1963," *DoD/1963*, 291–93.

2. Dean, *Test Ban and Disarmament*, 89–90.

3. Details on Executive Branch divisions are in Terchek, *The Making of the Test Ban Treaty*, 29–48.

4. When ACDA was established in September 1961, Unilateralists constrained its resources and mandate, placed it under the direction of the secretary of state, and pressured it to include representatives from other agencies when doing research and developing policy recommendations.

5. For Wiesner's views, see Lang, *Inquiry*, 71–132.

6. Wiesner, *Where Science and Politics Meet*, 11.

7. Seaborg, *Kennedy*, 35. This section draws heavily on Seaborg's detailed account of the Kennedy administration's meetings on nuclear testing.

8. Jacobson and Stein, *Diplomats*, 338–41.

9. For more general evidence that Kennedy's attempts to pursue both arms control and strategic arms build-up caused the Soviets to misread his motives, see Larson, *Anatomy of Mistrust*, 107–54.

10. Statement by Tsarapkin, March 21, 1961, *DoD/1961*, 42–55. The French were testing unsophisticated devices, so the United States and the U.K. could learn little besides yield-to-magnitude ratios for the French test site. As the French program matured, though, their test data would be increasingly useful. Moreover, if the French continued to test (and encouraged China by example), a CTB would not achieve its main nonproliferation objectives.

11. The Soviets wanted to treat the United States and the United Kingdom as separate entities for the purposes of allocating verification burdens (such as number of OSIs,

budgetary contributions) but count them as a single unit when seeking parity between East and West in decision-making bodies. See Seaborg, *Kennedy*, 56.

12. Jönsson, *Soviet Bargaining*, 169.

13. Slusser, *The Berlin Crisis of 1961*.

14. Quoted in Jönsson, *Soviet Bargaining*, 185.

15. Anglo-American Draft Treaty, April 18, 1961, *DoD/1961*, 82–134.

16. Seaborg, *Kennedy*, 41.

17. Statement by Tsarapkin, April 28, 1961, *DoD/1961*, 134–42.

18. Recounted in Lang, *Inquiry*, 52–55.

19. See Jönsson, *Soviet Bargaining*, 33, and Divine, *Blowing on the Wind*, 287–88.

20. Jönsson, *Soviet Bargaining*, 168.

21. Schlesinger, *A Thousand Days*, 420; Voss, *Nuclear Ambush*, 467.

22. "Report of the Ad Hoc Panel on Nuclear Testing," July 21, 1961, NSA.

23. Schlesinger, *A Thousand Days*, 420.

24. Seaborg, *Kennedy*, 68–73.

25. Ibid., 76.

26. Kennedy, quoted ibid.

27. White House Statement, August 31, 1961, *DoD/1961*, 350.

28. Jacobson and Stein, *Diplomats*, 282.

29. See Erskine, "The Polls," 186.

30. Statement by Khrushchev, September 9, 1961, *DoD/1961*, 384–91.

31. Sakharov recollects arguing against test preparations in July 1961, only to have Khrushchev respond that "we have to conduct our policies from a position of strength. . . . I'd be a jellyfish and not Chairman of the Council of Ministers if I listened to people like Sakharov." Some scholars with a pluralistic view of Soviet policy making maintain, however, that Khrushchev took responsibility for the final decision to avoid looking as if he had lost control over foreign policy. See Sakharov, *Memoirs*, 216–17; Jönsson, *Soviet Bargaining Behavior*, 171–73; and Slusser, *The Berlin Crisis*, 148–69.

32. In Seaborg, *Kennedy*, 83.

33. See Schlesinger, *Thousand Days*, 425, and Seaborg, *Kennedy*, 77.

34. This test showed that Khrushchev was not bluffing about a 100-mt bomb, because the yield could have been that high if the bomb had been given a uranium casing. U.S. monitoring confirmed that the USSR had not cheated during the moratorium, because this test series followed logically from the last one. But the fallout had characteristics that U.S. analysts could not explain, suggesting that the USSR knew something they did not. Kennedy's advisers concluded that the United States was strong enough to "eat" one round of Soviet atmospheric testing but must not let a second series go unanswered. See Schlesinger, *A Thousand Days*, 448–52.

35. The West did not take this proposal seriously, but Jönsson suggests that it may have been a compromise between Khrushchev's desire to keep the idea of a test ban alive and his critics' wish to block an agreement. See *Soviet Bargaining*, 174–75.

36. The composition of the ENDC suited Soviet demands that East and West have equal representation and that nonaligned states also have a major role in international organizations. The new members were Brazil, Burma, Ethiopia, India, Mexico, Nigeria, Sweden, and the United Arab Emirates. Only seventeen states actually joined the ENDC test ban talks, though. France refused on the grounds that nuclear disarmament should be negotiated solely by the NWSs.

37. See Erskine, "The Polls," 188.

38. Seaborg notes that Kennedy was much more willing to accept risks and make compromises for a CTB than he seemed in public. See *Kennedy*, 128–29.

39. Jacobson and Stein, *Diplomats*, 347; Seaborg, *Kennedy*, 138–39.

40. In a speech in early March, Kennedy declared that the USSR would never agree to "a true test ban or mutual disarmament" if the West were weak. Support for atmospheric testing jumped from 46 percent to 66 percent. Twenty-five percent of respondents still opposed atmospheric tests, however, regardless of what the Soviet Union did. See Erskine, "The Polls," 186.

41. Quoted in Richter, *Khrushchev's Double Bind*, 148.

42. Jönsson, *Soviet Bargaining*, 188–89.

43. Jacobson and Stein, *Diplomats*, 353, 361.

44. Quoted in Seaborg, *Kennedy*, 148.

45. Sweden was the only nonaligned member with technical advisers as a permanent part of its delegation and considered capable of developing nuclear weapons. This underestimated India, which had a secret nuclear program since 1947 and had decided to pursue a nuclear weapons option after the first Chinese test in 1964. The Indian delegation, however, mainly offered legal arguments rather than technical analyses. For an account by the Indian representative, see Lall, *Negotiating Disarmament*.

46. Quoted in Lang, *Inquiry*, 62.

47. Eight Nation Joint Memorandum, April 16, 1962, *DoD/1962*, 334–36.

48. Jacobson and Stein, *Diplomats*, 395–96.

49. Ibid., 377.

50. Lall, *Negotiating Disarmament*, 22.

51. Quoted in Jönsson, *Soviet Bargaining*, 70. The head of the U.K. team maintained that most U.S. scientists were "open-minded and scrupulously objective" but acknowledged that some "found more pleasure in introducing sound technical arguments for putting a treaty out of court than for improving methods of detection." Wright, *Disarm and Verify*, 121–22.

52. Secretary of Defense, "Memorandum for the President: The US-USSR Military Balance With and Without a Test Ban," Summer 1962, NSA.

53. This reflected the French test's detection by many stations at teleseismic distances, the realization that fewer shallow earthquakes occurred in the USSR than had been calculated from records in the 1930s, and the discovery that signal-to-noise ratios could be improved by equipping seismometers with special filters and burying them in deep holes.

54. Schlesinger, *A Thousand Days*, 816.

55. "Anglo-American Proposal: Draft Treaty Banning Nuclear Weapons Tests in All Environments, August 27, 1962," *DoD/1962,* 792–807.

56. The new name stems from use by John McCloy (United States) and Valerian Zorin (USSR) of the word *verification* in their 1961 Statement of Agreed Principles, to avoid specifying whether disarmament inspections should cover only items being destroyed or also those permitted by an accord.

57. William Foster, "Memorandum to the President: U.S. Program Regarding a Treaty to Ban Nuclear Weapon Tests and Other Disarmament Proposals," July 30, 1962, NSA.

58. John Finney, "Legislators Back U.S. Test-Ban Plan," *New York Times,* August 3, 1962, pp. A1, 3.

59. Statement by Kuznetsov, August 29, 1962, *DoD/1962,* 820–29.

60. Khrushchev interview with *Pravda,* August 29, 1958, *DoD/1962,* 1116.

61. Schlesinger, *A Thousand Days,* 759–60.

62. See Bundy, *Danger and Survival,* 445–46.

63. Larson, *Anatomy of Mistrust,* 145–46.

64. Richter, *Khrushchev's Double Bind,* 159–60.

65. Quoted ibid., 159.

66. Griffiths, "The Soviet Experience of Arms Control," 81–82, 88.

67. Evangelista, "Sources of Moderation," 302.

68. Khrushchev to Kennedy, December 19, 1962, *DoD/1962,* 1239–42.

69. Quoted in Seaborg, *Kennedy,* 179.

70. Personal communication from Wiesner to Seaborg, *Kennedy,* 180–81.

71. Kennedy to Khrushchev, December 28, 1962, *DoD/1962,* 1277–79.

72. Cousins, "Notes on a 1963 Visit with Khrushchev," 21.

73. An AEC staff analysis concluded that the Soviet delegation had "no duty in the negotiations except to determine whether the United States would make concessions." Seaborg, *Kennedy,* 185.

74. Dean, *Test Ban and Disarmament,* 53.

75. Institute for Defense Analyses, "Verification and Response in Disarmament Agreements."

76. These books included Schelling and Halperin, *Strategy and Arms Control,* and Brennan, ed., *Arms Control, Disarmament, and National Security.* On the "Cambridge Approach" to arms control and verification, see Sims, *Icarus Restrained,* especially 226–27.

77. This passage was aimed at Unilateralists seeking espionage opportunities, as well as Arms Control Advocates hoping to set verification precedents that could be used for more significant disarmament measures.

78. See "Analysis of the On-Site Inspection Problem for a Test Ban Treaty," November 28, 1962, NSA, and Seaborg, *Kennedy,* 187–88.

79. Wiesner, *Where Science and Politics Meet,* 166–67; Wiesner quoted in Herken, *Cardinal Choices,* 140–41.

80. Anglo-American Memorandum, April 1, 1963, *DoD/1963,* 141–45.

81. Seaborg, *Kennedy,* 191. Reciprocal OSIs would have been expensive, so the United

States would probably not have done more than three a year. However, the United States wanted the right to conduct more OSIs than they planned so that the Soviets could not "spoof" them into using up their quota early in the year. Interview with Warren Heckrotte, August 20, 1994.

82. After the Cuban Missile Crisis, the Soviets quietly dropped their demands for an administrative troika for the U.N. and CTB verification.

83. Senator Joseph Clark, one of the few outspoken disarmament advocates in Congress, felt that Congress' refusal to sacrifice any sovereignty was the main reason for opposition to significant arms control proposals. See Clark, "Congress and Disarmament."

84. Senator Dodd, quoted in Jacobson and Stein, *Diplomats*, 444.

85. Senate Concurrent Resolution 21, *Congressional Record*, February 20, 1963, pp. 2604–5.

86. Alluvium is a porous material that would absorb much of the explosive energy from a test. The USSR had no areas with alluvium thick enough to muffle an explosion larger than 1 or 2 kt. See OTA, *Seismic Verification*, 97.

87. The goal was to bring the two sides close enough that failure to agree would be patently ridiculous but to let them work out the details so that they would feel responsible. See Lall, *Negotiating Disarmament*, 24–28.

88. Dean Rusk to McGeorge Bundy, March 16, 1963, quoted in Seaborg, *Kennedy*, 192.

89. Ibid., 202.

90. Rose, *U.S. Unilateral Arms Control Initiatives*, 62–73.

91. Statement by Khrushchev at Berlin, July 2, 1963, *DoD/1963*, 246.

92. On Wiesner's conviction that Kennedy intended to build on the LTBT for a CTBT in his second term, see Herken, *Cardinal Choices*, 145.

93. Richter, *Khrushchev's Double Bind*, 162–63.

94. Cousins, "Notes on a 1963 Visit with Khrushchev," 58.

95. Seaborg, *Kennedy*, 205.

96. Department of State, Bureau of Intelligence and Research, "The Soviet View of the Forthcoming Moscow Talks," June 14, 1963, p. 3, NSA.

97. ACDA, "Points to be Covered in Preparation of Forthcoming July 15 Mission of Governor Harriman to Moscow," June 20, 1963, NSA.

98. Harriman's account is quoted in Seaborg, *Kennedy*, 241.

99. Ibid., 192–93.

100. Quoted in Richter, *Khrushchev's Double Bind*, 148.

101. Kennedy's famous "Ich bin ein Berliner" speech said that those who thought Westerners could work with Communists should see the Berlin Wall and other symbols of the Cold War. Many in Kennedy's entourage were "surprised and dismayed" by his abrasive language. See Seaborg, *Kennedy*, 224–25.

102. Lall, *Negotiating Disarmament*, 27.

103. See testimony by Air Force Chief of Staff Curtis LeMay, Senate Committee on Foreign Relations, *Hearings: Nuclear Test Ban Treaty*, August 1963, p. 382. Hereafter cited as SCFR 1963.

104. The resolution urged the administration to make every effort to negotiate an immediate inspected ban on nuclear tests and, if that failed, to pledge not to test in the atmosphere or underwater as long as the Soviets refrained. See Schlesinger, *A Thousand Days*, 821.

105. Lall, *Negotiating Disarmament*, 27.

106. Sorenson, *Kennedy*, 745.

107. Harris Survey, *Washington Post*, September 16, 1963, p. 1.

108. After seeing the popularity of the LTBT even in conservative states, Kennedy told Wiesner that he should have tried harder for a CTBT. Communication from Wiesner to Benjamin Loeb, in Loeb, "The Limited Test Ban Treaty," 207.

109. On the final interagency meeting, see Seaborg, *Kennedy*, 228–29.

110. Manfred Efinger argues that the July 2 announcement reflected a decision at the highest level of Soviet leadership to accept satellite surveillance while continuing to denounce airplane overflights of the USSR, in "The Verification Policy of the Soviet Union," 338.

111. Terchek calls these groups "Peace Maximizers," "Security Maximizers," and "Power Maximizers." See *The Making of the Test Ban Treaty*, 167–72.

112. Daalder, "The Limited Test Ban Treaty," 11. For example, Strom Thurmond argued that the Soviets had decided to support an LTBT after realizing that data from their 1962 series would soon let them issue an ultimatum to the United States: "Either surrender or be destroyed" (*Congressional Record*, September 11, 1963, p. 15924).

113. State Department, "Administration Strategy toward Congress on Three Nuclear Arms Issues," 9.

114. SCFR 1963, 312–13.

115. Terchek, *The Making of the Test Ban Treaty*, 195–96.

116. SCFR 1963, 274–75.

117. *Congressional Record*, October 1, 1965, pp. 25842–43.

118. U.S. spending on underground tests increased steadily from $10.9 million in 1964 to $42.9 million in 1969. See Chayes, "Inquiry," 942.

119. "Factfile: Fifty Years of Nuclear Testing," 38.

120. Craig and Jungerman, *Nuclear Arms Race*, 6.

121. *Congressional Record*, February 21, 1963, p. 2799.

122. Robert Strausz-Hupé, Director, Foreign Policy Research Institute, University of Pennsylvania, SCFR 1963, p. 514.

123. Editorial, *New York Times*, August 23, 1963.

124. Only Albania voted against this resolution on November 27, 1963.

125. Seaborg, *Stemming the Tide*, 213.

126. "Letter from D. G. Brennan to 'Various Friends and Arms Controllers,'" November 25, 1964, NSA.

127. "Letter from Herbert Scoville, Jr. to Donald Brennan," around December 18, 1964, NSA.

Chapter Six   The Politics of Verification during Détente

1. Address by Secretary of State Haig, July 14, 1981, *DoD/1981*, 267.

2. Savel'yev and Detinov, *The Big Five*, 1–4.

3. Griffiths, "The Soviet Experience of Arms Control," 93–94.

4. Details on internal debates in the Johnson administration are in Seaborg, *Stemming the Tide*, 201–45.

5. Scientists had discovered that seismic arrays and seismometers on the ocean bottom could dramatically improve monitoring. See Bolt, *Nuclear Explosions*, 127.

6. Seaborg, *Stemming the Tide*, 221.

7. Statement by Foster, November 25, 1965, *DoD/1965*, 542–47.

8. Statement by Myrdal, March 10, 1966, *DoD/1966*, 130–39.

9. Statement by Adrian Fisher, April 4, 1968, *DoD/1966*, 190–99.

10. Statement by the Soviet representative (Roschin), August 9, 1966, *DoD/1966*, 530.

11. See Seaborg, *Stemming the Tide*, 273–75.

12. This was the first Soviet proposal for continuous international oversight of East bloc nuclear facilities. The idea may have come from East Germany, which wanted IAEA membership and de facto international recognition—the reverse of standard concerns that verification will reduce sovereignty! See ibid., 282–85.

13. Quoted ibid., 237.

14. Philip Farley, SCFR Subcommittee, *Hearings: Prospects for Comprehensive Nuclear Test Ban Treaty*, 14. Hereinafter cited as SCFR 1971.

15. The most famous evasion experiment was conducted in 1966, when a 5.3-kt explosion created a stable, free-standing cavity large enough to decouple a 0.38-kt test. This is the only full nuclear decoupling experiment reported in the open literature. Funds for Vela from 1962 to 1972 are in SCFR 1971, p. 116.

16. Interview with Jack Evernden, October 11, 1989.

17. The network of 120 stations was complete by 1967, at a cost to Vela of $10 million. Some key countries, including the USSR and China, did not participate. Congress stopped funding the WWSSN in 1968, so its capabilities dwindled throughout the 1970s. See Bolt, *Nuclear Explosions*, 113–19.

18. Ibid., 152.

19. Report of the Seismic Study Group of the Stockholm International Peace Research Institute (Summary), June 28, 1968, *DoD/1968*, 455–58.

20. See Clarke, *Politics of Arms Control*, 44–47, 169.

21. "Summary of ARPA Seismic Discrimination Meeting, July 20–23, 1970, at Woods Hole, Mass.," initial version, not approved for release. Appendix 8 in JCAE Subcommittee, *Hearings: Status of Current Technology to Identify Seismic Events as Natural or Man Made*, October 27 and 28, 1971. Hereinafter cited as JCAE 1971.

22. These maneuvers are described in SCFR 1971, pp. 58–61.

23. "Summary of ARPA Seismic Discrimination Meeting," version approved for release, JCAE 1971, Appendix 9.

24. SCFR 1971, p. 122.

25. Statement of June 29, 1971, reprinted in SCFR 1971, p. 59.

26. Farley testimony, SCFR 1971, p. 18.

27. ACDA opposed the amendment because Vela would have dwarfed the rest of its mission. The transfer would have also jeopardized ACDA's working relationship with DOD. See Clarke, *Politics of Arms Control*, 177–78.

28. See Jerome Spingarn, quoted in Boyer, "From Activism to Apathy," 829.

29. Griffiths, "The Soviet Experience," 93–98.

30. Garthoff, *Détente*, 36–68.

31. Holloway, *The Soviet Union*, 43–58.

32. Garthoff, *Détente*, 49. See also Evangelista, "Sources of Soviet Moderation," 302–13, and Rice, "SALT and the Search for a Security Regime," 293–306.

33. York, "The Great Test Ban Debate," 15–23.

34. Treaty between the United States of America and the Union of Soviet Socialist Republics on the Limitation of Underground Nuclear Weapon Tests, July 3, 1974, *DoD/1974*, 225–29.

35. Garthoff, *Détente*, 426–27.

36. News Conference by Iklé and Schlesinger, July 3, 1974, *DoD/1974*, 275–76.

37. ACDA, *Arms Control and Disarmament Agreements*, 165–66.

38. Seaborg wrote that a m_b 4.75 threshold would limit U.S. tests to 30–40 kt, but U.S. negotiators typically said that a m_b 4.75 threshold corresponded to 19–20 kt in hard rock. See *Stemming the Tide*, 218.

39. Testimony by Franklin Long, SCFR, *Hearings: Threshold Test Ban and Peaceful Nuclear Explosion Treaties*, July 28–September 15, 1977, pp. 127–29. Hereinafter cited as SCFR 1977.

40. Interview with Roland Timerbayev, May 17, 1995.

41. Heckrotte, "Verification of Test Ban Treaties," 65.

42. Interview with Milo Nordyke, October 9, 1989.

43. Interview with Warren Heckrotte, July 10, 1990.

44. "Treaty between the United States of America and the Union of Soviet Socialist Republics on Underground Nuclear Explosions for Peaceful Purposes, May 28, 1976," *DoD/1976*, 328–48.

45. If an electrical cable can be placed in a hole near the site of the explosion, the yield can be estimated by seeing how quickly the shock wave crushes the cable. See the discussion of CORRTEX in Chapter 7.

46. Heckrotte, "A Brief Historical Review of Verification for Arms Control," 58–59.

47. Heckrotte, "Verification of Test Ban Treaties," 67.

48. Interview with Herbert York, October 13, 1989.

49. Timerbayev, "Nuclear Explosions for Peaceful Purposes," 87.

50. Timerbayev, "A Hostage to Political Realities," 392.

51. Kissinger, *Years of Upheaval*, 1167; Remarks of President Ford, May 28, 1976," *DoD/1976*, 348–49.

52. Brennan, "A Comprehensive Test Ban," 155.

53. SCFR 1977, p. 93.

54. Testimony by Roger Batzel, SCFR 1977, p. 72.

55. Quoted in Don Oberdorfer, "Soviets Said 'Chiseling' on A-Test Pacts," *Washington Post*, October 15, 1976, p. A24.

56. Helm and Westervelt, "The New Test Ban Treaties," 176–77.

57. Ibid., 172.

58. SCFR 1977, pp. 36–37, 50, 39.

59. Ibid., 94.

60. Ibid., 122.

61. Ibid., 115.

62. Under Article 18 of the Vienna Convention on the Law of Treaties (signed in 1969), signatories must refrain from acts that would defeat a treaty's object and purpose unless they express the intention not to ratify.

63. Kissinger, *Years of Upheaval*, 1168.

64. Harris Poll, April 29, 1978. Unless otherwise noted, public opinion polls cited are available online from Public Opinion Location Library, Roper Center for Public Opinion Research, University of Connecticut.

65. York, *Making Weapons*, 282.

66. See Schear, "Verification, Compliance, and Arms Control," 273.

67. Schear, "Verifying Arms Agreements," 87.

68. Carter, "Three Steps toward Nuclear Responsibility."

69. Carter, *Keeping Faith*, 223.

70. Ibid., 213.

71. A CTB would have hindered modernization projects begun under Carter, such as the neutron bomb, the MX and Midgetman land-based missiles, and directed-energy third-generation warheads. Some of these projects could have adapted old warheads for new delivery vehicles, but others could not.

72. Thermonuclear weapons use a small fission explosion (the primary) to ignite the fusion part of the weapon (the secondary). Since primaries are the most crucial component, a clandestine test could raise confidence in the reliability of higher-yield weapons in the stockpile and increase the willingness to make minor modifications in warhead design without testing at full yield.

73. Brzezinski, *Power and Principle*, 172n.

74. Statement by Issraelyan, November 10, 1976, *DoD/1976*, 778–84.

75. Timerbayev, "A Hostage to Political Realities," 390.

76. York, *Making Weapons*, 313.

77. Address by Brezhnev, November 2, 1977, *DoD/1977*, 679–80.

78. Edmonds, "Proliferation and Test Bans," 78.

79. York, *Making Weapons*, 317.

80. Personal communication from Warren Heckrotte, September 12, 1994.

81. See Neidle, "Nuclear Test Bans," 191–92.

82. Interview with Warren Heckrotte, August 20, 1994.

83. Neidle estimates that negotiators had finished 90–95 percent of the main text and 50 percent of the SVAs by the spring of 1978. See Neidle, "Nuclear Test Bans," 182; Timerbayev, "A Hostage to Political Realities," 390; York, *Making Weapons*, 302, 320; and Edmonds, "A Complete Nuclear Test Ban," 379.

84. Neidle, "Nuclear Test Bans," 185.

85. The Committee on the Present Danger was a revived version of a group formed to mobilize support for the defense build-up prescribed by NSC 68. The 1976 group was led by Paul Nitze and Eugene Rostow, and included Ronald Reagan. By early 1979, the Coalition for Peace through Strength included 175 members of Congress and 89 special interest groups.

86. Bundy, *Danger and Survival*, 556–62; Garthoff, *Détente*, 730, 823.

87. Arms Control and Disarmament Act Amendments, August 17, 1977, *DoD/1977*, 523–26.

88. Hussein, "The Future of Arms Control: Part IV," 38.

89. Van der Vink and Paine, "The Politics of Verification," 273–74.

90. SCFR 1977, p. 86.

91. See Van Cleave and Cohen, *Nuclear Weapons, Policies, and the Test Ban Issue*, 84–85.

92. Richard Burt, "U.S. Complains to Soviet about Nuclear Violation," *New York Times*, September 19, 1980, p. A5.

93. Letter to Harold Brown, September 12, 1978, quoted in Greb, "Survey of Past Nuclear Test Ban Negotiations," 108.

94. York, *Making Weapons*, 287.

95. Interview with Harold Agnew, October 13, 1989.

96. "Statement by Kerr Before House Armed Services Committee, August 14, 1978," *DoD/1978*, 491–97.

97. Report on a Comprehensive Test Ban by a Panel of the House Armed Services Committee, October 13, 1978, *DoD/1978*, 609, emphasis added.

98. U.S. negotiators never defined a "permitted nuclear experiment" because policy makers could not reach internal agreement. The labs used four types of arguments to justify an exemption for very low yield explosions: (1) stockpile reliability; (2) new sources of energy; (3) verification difficulties; and (4) preservation of technical expertise and infrastructure to resume testing. Internal publications, however, emphasized the last point. This type of exemption would have favored the United States, which was a generation ahead of the USSR in simulation capabilities and other methods for operating in a no-test environment. See Pomerance, "The Comprehensive Test Ban at Last?" 10; and Neidle, "Nuclear Test Bans," 184.

99. York, *Making Weapons*, 318–19.

100. Ambassador Andronik Petrosyants, head of the Soviet delegation, objected to being treated like "a sixth-rate Arab country." As told by York, in Garthoff, *Détente*, 758.

101. According to Timerbayev, the Soviets wanted their expenditures to improve their own NSS manufacturing capabilities. The USSR would probably have accepted American-made NSSs if everything else in the negotiations had gone well. Interview with Roland Timerbayev, May 17, 1995.

102. Carter, *Keeping Faith*, 231.

103. Warnke, quoted in Dokos, *Negotiations for a CTBT*, 199n.

104. Timerbayev, "A Hostage to Political Realities," 390.

105. Quoted in Van Atta, "Inside a U.S.-Soviet Arms Negotiation," 666.

106. Freedman, *Britain and Nuclear Weapons*, 96.

107. Quoted in Van Atta, "Inside a U.S.-Soviet Arms Negotiation," 667.

108. Neidle, "Nuclear Test Bans," 182–83.

109. Quoted in Van Atta, "Inside a U.S.-Soviet Arms Negotiation," 688.

110. York, *Making Weapons*, 306.

111. Timerbayev, "A Hostage to Political Realities," 390.

112. York, *Making Weapons*, 308.

113. Interview with Peter Marshall, U.K. CTB Delegation, March 5, 1996.

114. York, *Making Weapons*, 307.

115. Timerbayev's suggestion is in Van Atta, "Inside a U.S.-Soviet Arms Negotiation," 668.

116. Interview with Roland Timerbayev, May 17, 1995.

117. Tripartite Report, July 30, 1980, *DoD/1980*, 317–21.

118. Neidle, "Nuclear Test Bans," 183.

Chapter Seven   Cooperative Verification at the Cold War's Conclusion

1. On arms control decision making in the first Reagan administration, see Talbott, *Deadly Gambits*.

2. "Second Anniversary of the Inauguration of the President," January 20, 1983, quoted in Garthoff, *The Great Transition*, 9.

3. Lehman and Weiss, *Beyond the SALT II Failure*, 81.

4. The United States put more strategic missiles at sea, whereas the USSR based more on land. Therefore, the Committee on the Present Danger claimed that the Soviets could use part of their MIRVed ICBMs to destroy most American missile silos. The president would face an unpalatable choice between surrendering or retaliating against Soviet cities, prompting attacks on U.S. cities in return. Unless the United States increased its land-based missiles, decreased their vulnerability, and improved the accuracy of its SLBMs, they argued, this scenario would embolden the Soviets and erode U.S. confidence. See Bundy, *Danger and Survival*, 556–59.

5. See Wirls, *Buildup*, 31–46.

6. ACDA was led by Eugene Rostow until early 1983 and then by Kenneth Adelman, two members of the Committee on the Present Danger. Reagan's science adviser was George Keyworth, a young protégé of Edward Teller.

7. Patrick Glynn, special assistant to the director of the ACDA, quoted in Genest, *Negotiating in the Public Eye*, 142.

8. Garthoff, *Détente*, 1012.

9. Yankelovich and Kaagan, "Assertive America," 696–713.

10. Wirls, *Buildup*, 35.

11. Statement by Rostow, October 21, 1981, *DoD/1981*, 487. The United States still called a CTB a "long term goal" but formally terminated negotiations in 1982.

12. Harris Poll, September 26, 1983.

13. In May 1983, the House passed a freeze resolution by a 278-149 vote, but the measure failed in the Senate.

14. Ladd, "The Freeze," 36.

15. Ibid., 39. See also Einhorn, "Treaty Compliance," 29.

16. An amendment to the FY84 ACDA Authorization Act required the president to report to Congress on Soviet arms-control compliance. The 1985 report accused the USSR of violating the LTBT by venting radioactive debris outside its territory. In fact, both superpowers were guilty of this. Venting usually indicates failure to follow adequate safety precautions but does not provide a military advantage. See Duffy, ed., *Compliance and the Future of Arms Control*, 52–58.

17. Heckrotte and Moulthrop, "Soviet High Yield Nuclear Weapons Tests and the Threshold Test Ban Treat," is an unclassified update of this work.

18. Statement by Rostow, July 29, 1982, *DoD/1982*, 475–78.

19. Interview with Warren Heckrotte, August 20, 1994.

20. Van der Vink and Paine, "The Politics of Verification," 285n.

21. Robert Barker, assistant secretary of defense for atomic energy, quoted in Van der Vink and Paine, "The Politics of Verification," 274.

22. See Sykes and Evernden, "The Verification of a Comprehensive Nuclear Test Ban." Perle belittled scientists who had helped to negotiate earlier test-ban treaties as "academics who couldn't negotiate a sabbatical" and dismissed current activists as a "bunch of seismologists feathering their own nests." See Judith Miller, "Sometimes I Say Things Differently," interview with Richard Perle, *New York Times*, March 13, 1987, p. A16; and KRON-4 TV, "Perle and the Scientists," 6.

23. Ackland, "Testing," 9.

24. Richard Perle to the air force assistant chief of staff for intelligence, April 15, 1985, quoted in KRON-4, "Perle and the Scientists," 5.

25. Michael Gordon, "CIA Changes Way That It Measures Soviet Atom Tests," *New York Times*, April 2, 1986.

26. Michael Gordon, "How Public Remarks Became Classified Data," *New York Times*, February 20, 1987.

27. Quoted in KRON-4, "Perle and the Scientists," 5.

28. Anson Franklin, "Letter to the Editor," *Science* 233 (September 26, 1986): 1367.

29. CORRTEX stands for "Continuous Reflectometry for Radius versus Time Experiments." Divisions in the interagency debate were complex. LANL pushed CORRTEX,

whereas LLNL scientists did not want Soviets present when they tested. The CIA wished to supplement CORRTEX with measures to improve seismic monitoring, but other U.S. officials accused them of seeking collateral information. See Michael Gordon, "Arms-Test Curbs Set Off a Dispute," *New York Times*, December 12, 1986, p. A9.

30. For details, see Lamb, "Monitoring Yields of Underground Nuclear Tests Using Hydrodynamic Methods."

31. Clark and Baruch, "Verification," 133.

32. U.S. Department of State, "Verifying Nuclear Testing Limitations," 5.

33. An asymmetrical blast might be used to develop directed energy weapons for strategic defenses. See Clark and Baruch, "Verification," 133.

34. Michael Gordon, "Atomic Test Data Weaken U.S. View," *New York Times*, September 11, 1988, p. A12.

35. Address by Reagan, September 24, 1984, *DoD/1984*, 689–93.

36. On the symbolic importance of verification, see Yankelovich and Smoke, "America's 'New Thinking.'"

37. The Soviets refused because exchanging observers would legitimate nuclear tests, not lead to their abolition. See Address by Gromyko, November 6, 1984, *DoD/1984*, 784–85.

38. Gaffney, "Test Ban Would Be Real Tremor to U.S. Security," 36–37.

39. Garthoff, *The Great Transition*, 505–7.

40. See Timerbayev, "Monitoring Arms Limitation Measures," 81–82, and Timerbayev, *Verification*, 81–97.

41. Statement by Issraelyan, February 21, 1984, *DoD/1984*, 94.

42. See Savel'yev and Detinov, *The Big Five*, 43–44, and Potter, "Soviet Attitudes," 205–6nn.

43. Savel'yev and Detinov, *The Big Five*, 77–79.

44. Except where noted, figures and quotes in this paragraph come from Yankelovich and Doble, "The Public Mood," 33–46.

45. Harris Poll, November 29, 1984.

46. Clark, "UK-USSR and US-USSR Joint Research Programs in Seismic Verification," 100.

47. Joint Declaration by the Leaders of Six Nations, May 22, 1984, *DoD/1984*, 420–21.

48. Statement by Issraelyan, August 21, 1984, *DoD/1984*, 592.

49. Meyer, "Gorbachev's New Political Thinking," and Stein, "Political Learning by Doing," 173–75.

50. Checkel, "Ideas, Institutions, and the Gorbachev Foreign Policy Revolution," and Evangelista, "The Paradox of State Strength."

51. Meyer, "Gorbachev's New Political Thinking," 133–55.

52. Snyder, "International Sources of Leverage."

53. Timerbayev, "A Soviet Official on Verification," 8.

54. Foreign Broadcast Information Service, *Soviet Union Daily Report*, January 27, 1986, p. C9.

55. Grinevsky, "The Verification of Arms Control."

56. Savel'yev and Detinov, *The Big Five*, 151–53.

57. See Potter, "The Evolution of Soviet Attitudes toward On-Site Inspection," 200, and Stovall, "The Stockholm Accord."

58. Dean, "Gorbachev's Arms Control Moves."

59. Gerald M. Boyd, "U.S. and Russians Make New Offers on Nuclear Tests," *New York Times*, July 30, 1985, p. 1.

60. Seth Mydans, "Soviet to Stop Atomic Tests; It Bids U.S. Same," *New York Times*, July 30, 1985, p. A6.

61. Raul Alfonsin et al., "To Reagan and Gorbachev," *New York Times*, October 30, 1985, p. A27.

62. Duncan, "How Many Soviet Tests Make a Flurry?" This series included a PNE for underground storage, which led to veiled accusations that the USSR had created a large cavity for decoupled explosions during the moratorium. See the comments by Paul Joachim von Stülpnagel, "Forum on Verification of a Comprehensive Test Ban," 27.

63. Adelman, "Nuclear Test Ban," 5, 7.

64. "Americans Rate Gorbachev's Nuclear Arms Reduction Proposals," *Gallup Report* 243 (December 1985): 8, and "Public Favors Halting A-Tests if Soviet Moratorium Continues," *Gallup Report* 248 (May 1986): 20–21.

65. *Congressional Quarterly Almanac 1985*, vol. 41, 177–78.

66. Von Hippel, "Arms Control Physics: The New Soviet Connection."

67. Velikhov, "Science and Scientists for a Nuclear-Weapon-Free World," 36.

68. When Evernden proposed putting a seismic network inside the USSR, DARPA offered to provide funds if the Soviets accepted; one of Evernden's superiors at the USGS stated that Evernden's initiative could be considered an "informal USGS proposal." See Smith, "Soviets Agree to Broad Seismic Test," 511–12. When NRDC representatives approached Deputy Secretary of State John Whitehead, he expressed concern about how the project related to official U.S. testing policy but did not oppose the effort. John C. Whitehead to Adrian DeWind, March 4, 1986 (author's files).

69. Schrag, *Listening for the Bomb*, 12–13.

70. Evangelista, "The Paradox of State Strength," 23–24.

71. Interview with Thomas Cochran, June 9, 1994.

72. Interview with Jacob Scherr, June 9, 1994.

73. Interview with Jacob Scherr, April 4, 1989.

74. The NRDC raised $4.5 million for the project, making this the largest private U.S.-Soviet scientific venture.

75. Schrag, *Listening for the Bomb*, 74, 78–79.

76. State Department press directive, quoted in Sweet, "NRDC and Soviet Academy Sign Unusual Test-Verification Pact," 64.

77. Some traditionalists had trouble tolerating the new openness in Soviet verification policy. See the comments by Oleg Grinevsky, head Soviet negotiator for the Stockholm Accord, in Oberdorfer, *The Turn*, 233.

78. Interview with Jacob Scherr, April 14, 1989.

79. The 1-kt threshold addressed concerns that a total moratorium could not be verified even with in-country monitoring. See *Congressional Quarterly Almanac 1986*, 461–62.

80. Interview with Chris Paine, April 12, 1989.

81. Ed Nawrocki, quoted in Schrag, *Listening for the Bomb*, 84.

82. After official support for Evernden was disclosed in conjunction with the NRDC-SAS project, government agencies disavowed him, describing Evernden's work as "a private trip to the Soviet Union at his own initiative . . . to pursue his own research." See the exchange in "Letters," *Science* 233 (September 26, 1986): 1367.

83. DARPA, "Natural Resources Defense Council Proposal to Place Seismic Monitoring Stations Near the Soviet Nuclear Test Site 3," June 26, 1986 (Memorandum to Richard Perle), in author's files.

84. Frank Gaffney, "Test Ban: The Quick Fix Won't Work," *Washington Post*, August 29, 1986, p. A15.

85. Knopf, "Beyond Two-Level Games," 610.

86. Quoted in Philip Taubman, "Moscow Says Its A-Test Halt Is Militarily Beneficial to U.S.," *New York Times*, August 26, 1986, p. A4.

87. Goldansky, "Verificational Deterrence and Nuclear Explosions," 31.

88. Interviews in Meyer, "Gorbachev's New Political Thinking," 163.

89. See Schrag, *Listening for the Bomb*, 89.

90. Archambeau, "Verification of a Very Low Yield Nuclear Test Ban," 279–80.

91. "Nuclear Glasnost," 17.

92. Goldman et al., *Verifying Arms Control*, 121–22.

93. Quoted in *Congressional Quarterly Almanac 1987*, 214.

94. Robert Park, "Bold Plan," *Washington Post*, January 22, 1989, p. D3.

95. Yankelovich and Smoke, "America's 'New Thinking,'" 3, 6.

96. Nolan, "Public and Congressional Attitudes toward On-Site Inspection," 173.

97. *Congressional Record* (August 8, 1986), 19914, 19915, and 19920.

98. Goldman et al., "Verifying Arms Control," 128.

99. Quoted in Isaacs, "House Challenges Reagan on Arms Control," 6.

100. Even these measures were not popular with the most ideologically anti-Soviet allies of the Reagan administration. For example, Senator Dan Quayle denounced a provision in the FY88 defense authorization bill ordering the DOE to study nontest methods of ensuring stockpile reliability as an example of "camels' noses under the tent" that would lead to further test restrictions. Quoted in *CQ Weekly Report*, July 30, 1988, p. 2092.

101. Interview with Gregory van der Vink, project director for the OTA study, April 12, 1989.

102. OTA, *Seismic Verification*.

103. Barker was rebutted by the head of the OTA, Van der Vink, and by scientists who participated in the study. See the House of Representatives, Committee on Foreign Affairs, "Nuclear Testing: Arms Control Opportunities," June 28, 1988. Hereinafter cited as HCFR 1988.

104. William Burns, director of the ACDA, HCFR 1988, p. 15.

105. Interview with Thomas Cochran, June 6, 1989.

106. Clark, "UK-USSR and US-USSR."

107. Interview with Holly Eisler, December 2, 1988.

108. Interview with Milo Nordyke, October 19, 1994.

109. When Congress increased funds for seismic verification, the money went through DARPA to the Incorporated Research Institute for Seismology (IRIS), a consortium of U.S. universities. The IRIS effort was run by seismologists from the NRDC-SAS project, and its first stations were located with the NRDC stations. The official objective was earthquake monitoring but improved monitoring of nuclear tests was implied by the phrase "mutual benefit of exchanging broad band digital seismological data for solving various seismological tasks." The text of this agreement is in HCFR 1988, pp. 113–15.

110. Kokeyev and Androsov, "Verification," 12.

111. Press background document for Moscow Summit (May 29–June 2, 1988), 78. To support his contention that the Soviets would not ultimately argue that CORRTEX was too disruptive or intrusive for the USSR, Barker refers to a similar statement by Ambassador Oleg Grinevsky at a U.N. verification conference in April 1988. See Barker's testimony in HCFR 1988, pp. 44–45.

112. Goldansky, "Verificational Deterrence," 28.

113. Rose, "Nuclear Test Ban," 20.

114. Goldansky, "Verificational Deterrence," 35.

115. Frank Carlucci, secretary of defense, *Annual Report to the Congress, Fiscal Year 1989,* February 18, 1988, p. 23.

116. Quoted in Robinson, "The Joint Verification Experiment," 91.

117. See the Reagan administration's response to questions submitted by Representative Dante Fascell in HCFR 1988, pp. 141, 144.

118. Michael Gordon, "U.S. Opposes Release of Soviet Nuclear Test Data," *New York Times,* March 23, 1989, p. A7.

119. R. Jeffrey Smith, "Soviets Catch U.S. Nuclear Inspectors," *Washington Post,* August 12, 1988, pp. A1, A6; R. Jeffrey Smith, "3 Inspectors Barred from Soviet A-Test," *Washington Post,* August 13, 1988, pp. A1, A6.

120. Panofsky, "Verification of the Threshold Test Ban," 6.

121. C. Paul Robinson, quoted in Michael Gordon, "U.S. Opposes Release of Soviet Nuclear Test Data," *New York Times,* March 23, 1989, p. A7.

122. An NRDC request for the JVE data was denied. The NRDC filed suit under the Freedom of Information Act to obtain the historical yield data exchanged for the JVE. The judge ruled unfavorably, saying that the JVE agreement required both parties to consent before data could be released to the public, and that the USSR could not approve the release because it no longer existed.

123. From Michael Gordon, "Soviet Test Data Rekindle Dispute," *New York Times,* October 30, 1988, p. 12. See also Michael Gordon, "Atomic Test Data Weaken U.S. View," *New York Times,* September 11, 1988, p. 12, and Scott, "Joint Nuclear Tests Raise Questions about Administration Policy," 26.

124. Quoted in Paine and Van der Vink, "The Politics of Verification," 281.

125. DOE would not reveal the radiochemical analysis done to ensure that the actual yield of the NTS shot was not much larger than expected, but the chief nuclear test negotiator confirmed that the detonation fell below 150 kt.

126. See Priestley et al., "Regional Seismic Recordings of the Soviet Nuclear Explosion of the Joint Verification Experiment."

127. Keeny, "Notes from the Underground," 2.

128. Robinson, "Verifying Testing Treaties—Old and New."

129. Robinson, "The Joint Verification Experiment."

130. See R. Jeffrey Smith, "U.S., Soviets Fail to Reach Nuclear Test Accord," *Washington Post*, December 16, 1988, p. A42.

131. Since Vice President Bush had shown no interest in a CTB, test ban activists sought to persuade the new administration to adopt a phased approach leading to a CTB before the 1995 NPT Extension Conference. See the NRDC's *Phasing Out Nuclear Weapons Tests*.

132. Quote in Krepon, "CIA, DIA at Odds over Soviet Threat," 6.

133. Testimony of Milo Nordyke, SCFR, *Hearings: Test Ban Issues*, October 6, 1988, 14–15. Hereinafter cited as SCFR 1988.

134. Reagan, "The Relationship between Progress in Other Areas of Arms Control and More Stringent Limitations on Nuclear Testing."

135. Warren Strobel, "U.S. Delays Talks on Underground Nuclear Tests," *Washington Times*, January 20, 1990, p. 9.

136. Lockwood, "Continued Testing 'Essential,' DOE Tells Congress," 29.

137. Resource constraints and conflicting priorities had forced DOE to cut the annual number of tests from seventeen in the early 1980s to eight in 1990. The laboratory directors wished to double the test rate but only received a 6 percent budget increase for FY91.

138. The 1990 TTBT protocol permits OSIs for test over 35 kt and OSIs, hydrodynamic yield estimation, and/or in-country seismic stations for tests over 50 kt. If no tests trigger these verification procedures, the other side can implement them for a set number of smaller tests each year.

139. See Norris and Arkin, "Soviet Testing Move," 56; and Peter Zheutlin, "Nevada, USSR."

140. George Butler, testimony quoted in SCFR, "Threshold Test Ban and Peaceful Nuclear Explosions Treaties," *Executive Report*, September 14, 1990, p. 19. Hereinafter cited as SCFR 1990.

141. SCFR 1990, pp. 19–21.

142. HCFR 1988, p. 51.

143. This effort is detailed in Schrag, *Global Action*.

144. Findlay, "A Comprehensive Nuclear Test Ban," 17.

145. *Congressional Quarterly Almanac 1992*, 517–18, 666.

146. Yankelovich and Smoke, "America's 'New Thinking,'" 15.

Chapter Eight   Working with the Politics of Verification

1. Quoted in Howard and Johnson, "A Comprehensive Test Ban," 9. The best source on the CD negotiations is the reports by Rebecca Johnson in the *Acronym* series, *Arms Control Today*, and *Bulletin of the Atomic Scientists*. Background information also comes from interviews by the author with policy makers and negotiators between February and October 1996. Because these interviews involved ongoing events, many had to be done on a not-for-attribution basis.

2. Lockwood, "Conference on Disarmament Sees Progress toward CTB Treaty," 17.

3. Address by John Holum, director of ACDA, to the Conference on Disarmament, January 25, 1994.

4. For details, see von Hippel and Collina, "Nuclear Junkies."

5. Arnett, ed., *Nuclear Weapons after the Comprehensive Test Ban*.

6. Robert Bell, quoted in "The Issues behind the CTB Treaty Ratification Debate," 6.

7. The decision to push for a CTB was accompanied by a directive that DOE should develop a program to preserve the core intellectual and technical competencies in nuclear weapons under a CTB. See Medalia, "Nuclear Weapons Stockpile Stewardship"; and Collina and Kidder, "Shopping Spree Softens Test Ban Sorrows."

8. The International Foundation, "Toward a Comprehensive Test Ban," 16.

9. Ironically, Russian weapons designers picked up the verification argument from their American counterparts at a conference sponsored by the NRDC—not the type of transnational collaboration that the NRDC had in mind! See Evangelista, "The Paradox of State Strength," 31–32.

10. France joined the voluntary moratorium in April 1992; the United Kingdom was constrained by the congressional ban on tests at NTS. See Yost, "France's Nuclear Dilemmas"; Lewis, "The United Kingdom"; and Zuckerman, "Prospects for a Comprehensive Test Ban."

11. Shen, "Toward a Nuclear-Weapon-Free World."

12. Hernandez, "Delivering Test-Ban Results by 1995."

13. Paine and Cochran, "So Little Time, So Many Weapons, So Much to Do," 15–16.

14. Sweet, "IRIS and Other Open Seismic Networks Could Be Crucial to Test-Ban Regime," 35.

15. Van der Vink and Park, "Nuclear Test Ban Monitoring," 634–35.

16. Basham and Dahlman, "International Seismological Verification," 187.

17. Van der Vink et al., *Nuclear Testing and Nonproliferation*, vi, 3–4.

18. Clements, "Prospects for a Comprehensive Test Ban Treaty," 24.

19. See Arnett, ed., *Implementing the Comprehensive Test Ban*.

20. R. Jeffery Smith, "Total Nuclear Test Ban Favored," *Washington Post*, January 31, 1995.

21. Johnson, "Nuclear Arms Control through Multilateral Negotiations."

22. GSETT-3 was designed to test a prototype global network feeding into an IDC in

Arlington, Virginia. By the end of 1995, GSETT-3 had forty-one primary and seventy-six auxiliary stations, about half of which were expected to be in the official IMS. The technical test identified some problems with software and information overload but showed that a single IDC was technically feasible and that current detection capabilities could go at least as low as 1 kt. See Johnson, "Comprehensive Test Ban Treaty," 21.

23. Costs and ambiguous events increase ten-fold for each magnitude unit that the monitoring threshold is lowered. See Van der Vink et al., *Nuclear Testing*, sec. VI, p. 5.

24. Hydroacoustic and infrasound sensors monitor signals from nuclear explosions in the water or atmosphere. Radionuclide detectors are useful for atmospheric tests or underground blasts that vent noble gases or radioactive debris. Satellites are used mainly to watch for suspicious activity around a test site or an ambiguous event, whereas electromagnetic pulse sensors can detect atmospheric explosions.

25. Preparatory commissions make implementation decisions after negotiations end until the Executive Council takes over after EIF.

26. Interview with member of U.S. delegation, March 4, 1996.

27. For example, an open seismic network near the Nevada Test Site detects about twenty small events each day that it cannot identify as earthquakes.

28. "The Issues behind the CTB Treaty Ratification Debate," 7.

29. The August 1997 event produced a seismic disturbance comparable to a nuclear test with a yield of 50 to 100 tons. Since scientists using only public data from a subset of IMS and auxiliary stations could provide overwhelming evidence that it was an earthquake, it is reasonable to believe that classified American monitoring capabilities go even lower. See Collina, "Test Ban One, Opposition Zero," 4.

30. Eckerman, "Inspection of Chinese Cargo Ship Yields No Evidence of Chemicals."

31. Perkovitch, "India's Nuclear Weapons Debate," 12.

32. The Pakistani representative maintained that his country must test if India did to avoid the impression that it lacked the technical expertise or political will for credible deterrence (interview with Munir Akram, March 7, 1996).

33. In hydronuclear experiments, some fissile material is replaced by passive material (e.g., natural or depleted uranium) so that the chain reaction goes more slowly and blows the device apart before much energy has been released. In hydrodynamic experiments, all the fissile material is replaced with inert material. Implosion and compression occur, but no chain reaction.

34. The U.S. decision was made after the JASONs, a group of independent consultants on defense issues, concluded that a stockpile stewardship program without HNEs could provide high confidence in the safety and reliability of U.S. weapons. An unclassified version of the study's summary and conclusions is reprinted as "JASON Nuclear Testing Study."

35. This was the initial Russian response to U.S. proposals for enhanced transparency regarding subcritical experiments. Such objections also parallel claims made during CWC hearings that rogue states could improve their own chemical warfare capabilities by taking advantage of provisions for the exchange of information about chemical weapons defenses. See "The Issues behind the CTB Treaty Ratification Debate," 11–12.

36. Grigori Berdennikov, Russian ambassador to the CD, quoted in Johnson, "Endgame Issues," 15.

37. Johnson, "Endgame Issues," 15.

38. Those who support the stockpile stewardship program argue that the United States would never take the risks involved in stockpiling a qualitatively new design that had never been tested. Critics contend that the program will preserve the ability to test on short notice and that pressures to do so will grow if "stewards" continue to hone their design skills and knowledge of weapons effects. For an example of this debate, see Gusterson, "NIF-TY Exercise Machine," and Cabasso and Burroughs, "End Run Around the NPT."

39. Johnson, "Nuclear Arms Control through Multilateral Negotiations," 109.

40. For a critique of the Indian decision by two Indian Arms Control Advocates, see Bidwai and Vanaik, *Testing Times.*

41. "Chairman's Draft Text of the Comprehensive Test Ban Treaty."

42. Alison Mitchell, "Clinton, At U.N., Signs Treaty Banning All Nuclear Testing," *New York Times,* September 25, 1996, p. 6.

43. Testimony by Harold Smith, Assistant to the Secretary of Defense for Atomic Energy, Senate Appropriations Subcommittee on Energy and Water Development, *Hearings on the CTBT and Maintenance of the U.S. Nuclear Stockpile,* October 29, 1997 (Federal News Service).

44. See testimony by Robert Barker, Senate Governmental Affairs Subcommittee on International Security, Proliferation, and Federal Services, October 27, 1997 (Federal News Service).

45. Steven Greenhouse, "Accord to Combat Sweatshop Labor Faces Obstacles," *New York Times,* April 13, 1997, p. A20.

Bibliography

Archival Material

National Security Archives. The National Security Archives, currently located at George Washington University, is a repository for declassified documents obtained through the Freedom of Information Act. Where NSA documents have formal titles, quotation marks are used; otherwise they are identified by a short descriptive title.

Government Documents

Defense Advanced Research Projects Agency. "Natural Resources Defense Council Proposal to Place Seismic Monitoring Stations Near the Soviet Nuclear Test Site 3." June 26, 1986 (memorandum to Richard Perle).

Foreign Broadcast Information Service. *Soviet Union Daily Report.*

Gehron, William J. "Geneva Conference on the Discontinuance of Nuclear Weapons Tests." Department of State *Bulletin* 43 (September 26, 1960): 486–87.

Goldman, Stuart D., Paul E. Gallis, and Jeanette M. Voas. *Verifying Arms Control Agreements: The Soviet View.* Washington, D.C.: Congressional Research Service, Report No. 87-316-F (April 15, 1987).

Institute for Defense Analyses. "Verification and Response in Disarmament Agreements." Woods Hole Summer Study 1962, Summary Report. Washington, D.C., November 1962.

Medalia, Jonathan. "Nuclear Weapons Stockpile Stewardship." *Congressional Research Service Report* 94–418 F, May 12, 1994.

Reagan, Ronald. "The Relationship Between Progress in Other Areas of Arms Control and More Stringent Limitations on Nuclear Testing." Report to Congress, White House Office of the Press Secretary, September 8, 1988.

U.S. Arms Control and Disarmament Agency. *Arms Control and Disarmament Agreements.* Washington, D.C.: ACDA, 1980.

———. *Documents on Disarmament.* Various volumes.

————. *Verification: The Critical Element of Arms Control.* Publication No. 85 (March 1976).

U.S. Congress, Joint Committee on Atomic Energy. *Hearings Before the Subcommittee on Research, Development, and Radiation.* 92nd Congress, 1st Session. Washington, D.C.: G.P.O., 1971.

————. Special Subcommittee on Radiation and the Subcommittee on Research and Development. *Hearings: Aspects of Detection and Inspection Controls of a Nuclear Weapons Test Ban.* 86th Congress, 2nd Session. Washington, D.C.: G.P.O., 1960.

————. Office of Technology Assessment. *Seismic Verification of Nuclear Testing Treaties* (OTA-ISC-361). Washington, D.C.: G.P.O., May 1988.

U.S. Congressional Budget Office. "U.S. Costs of Verification and Compliance under Pending Arms Treaties." September 1990.

U.S. House of Representatives, Committee on Foreign Affairs, Subcommittee of Arms Control, International Security and Science. *Hearings: Nuclear Testing: Arms Control Opportunities.* 100th Congress, 2nd Session, June 28, 1988.

U.S. Senate, Committee on Foreign Relations. *Hearings: Intermediate-Range Nuclear Forces Treaty.* 100th Congress, 2nd Session, 1988.

————. *Hearings: Nuclear Test Ban Treaty.* 88th Congress, 1st Session. Washington, D.C.: G.P.O., August 1963.

————. *Hearings: Prospects for Comprehensive Nuclear Test Ban Treaty.* 92nd Congress, First Session. Washington, D.C.: G.P.O., 1971.

————. *Hearings: Threshold Test Ban and Peaceful Nuclear Explosion Treaties.* 95th Congress, 1st Session, July 28–September 15, 1977.

————. *Hearings: Test Ban Issues.* 100th Congress, 2nd Session, October 6, 1988.

————. "Threshold Test Ban and Peaceful Nuclear Explosions Treaties." *Executive Report* 101–31, 101st Congress, 2nd Session, September 14, 1990. Washington, D.C.: G.P.O., 1992.

U.S. State Department. *Bulletin,* various issues.

————. *Disarmament: The Intensified Effort, 1955–58.* Pub. 6676, July 1958.

————. *Documents on Disarmament,* various volumes.

————. "Verifying Nuclear Testing Limitations: Possible U.S.-Soviet Cooperation." Special Report No. 152, August 14, 1986.

————. Committee on Atomic Energy. *A Report on the International Control of Atomic Energy.* Washington, D.C., March 16, 1946.

————. Office of the Historian. "Administration Strategy toward Congress on Three Nuclear Arms Issues (Limited Test Ban Treaty, Nonproliferation Treaty, Salt I Agreements)." Research Project No. 1189 (March 1978).

Van der Vink, Gregory, et al. *Nuclear Testing and Nonproliferation.* Report prepared by the IRIS Consortium for the Senate Committee on Governmental Affairs and the House Committee on Foreign Affairs, February 1994.

Articles and Books

Acheson, Dean. *Present at the Creation.* New York: Norton, 1969.

Ackland, Len. "Testing: Who Is Cheating Whom?" *Bulletin of the Atomic Scientists* 42:8 (October 1986): 9–11.

Adelman, Kenneth. "Nuclear Test Ban: A Long-Term Goal." *NATO Review* (April 1986): 5–6.

———. "Why Verification Is More Difficult (and Less Important)." *International Security* 14:4 (Spring 1990): 141–46.

Adler, Emanuel. "The Emergence of Cooperation: National Epistemic Communities and the International Evolution of the Idea of Nuclear Arms Control." *International Organization* 46:1 (Winter 1992): 101–45.

Algoni, Maria. "Verification and Congress: What Role for Politics." In Tower et al., eds. *Verification,* 26–34.

Archambeau, Charles. "Verification of a Very Low Yield Nuclear Test Ban." In Goldblat and Cox, eds., *Nuclear Weapons Tests,* 273–98.

Arnett, Eric, ed. *Implementing the Comprehensive Test Ban.* Oxford: Oxford University Press, 1994.

———, ed. *Nuclear Weapons after the Comprehensive Test Ban.* Oxford: Oxford University Press, 1996.

Barnet, Richard J., and Richard A. Falk, eds. *Security in Disarmament.* Princeton: Princeton University Press, 1965.

Basham, Peter, and Ola Dahlman. "International Seismological Verification." In Goldblat and Cox, eds. *Nuclear Weapons Tests,* 169–90.

Baylis, John. *Anglo-American Defense Relations, 1939–84.* 2nd ed. New York: St. Martin's Press, 1984.

Bechhoefer, Bernhard. *Postwar Negotiations for Arms Control.* Washington, D.C.: Brookings, 1961.

Bernstein, Barton. "Crossing the Rubicon." *International Security* 14:21 (Fall 1989): 132–60.

Beschloss, Michael. *Mayday.* New York: Harper and Row, 1986.

Bidwai, Praful, and Achin Vanaik. *Testing Times: The Global Stake in a Nuclear Test Ban.* Uppsala: Dag Hammarskjöld Foundation, 1996.

Blaker, James R. "On-Site Inspections: The Military Significance of an Arms-Control Proposal." *Survival* 26:3 (May–June 1984): 98–106.

Bloomfield, Lincoln P., Walter Clemens Jr., and Franklyn Griffiths. *Khrushchev and the Arms Race.* Cambridge: M.I.T. Press, 1966.

Bohn, Lewis C. "Non-Physical Inspection Techniques." In Brennan, ed., *Arms Control,* 347–64.

Bolt, Bruce. *Nuclear Explosions and Earthquakes.* San Francisco: W. H. Freeman, 1976.

Boyer, Paul. "From Activism to Apathy: The American People and Nuclear Weapons, 1963–1980." *Journal of American History* 70:4 (March 1984): 821–44.

Brams, Steven. *Superpower Games*. New Haven: Yale University Press, 1985.

Brennan, Donald. "A Comprehensive Test Ban: Everybody or Nobody." *International Security* 1:1 (Summer 1976): 92–117.

———, ed. *Arms Control, Disarmament, and National Security*. New York: George Braziller, 1961.

Brzezinski, Zbigniew. *Power and Principle*. New York: Farrar, Straus and Giroux, 1983.

Bühl, Hartmut. "Verification: Primarily a Political Problem." In O'Manique, ed., *A Proxy for Trust*, 55–64.

Bull, Hedley. "The Grotian Conception of International Society." In Martin Wight and Herbert Butterfield, eds. *Diplomatic Investigations*. Cambridge: Harvard University Press, 1968, 51–73.

———. *The Anarchical Society*. New York: Columbia University Press, 1977.

Bundy, McGeorge. *Danger and Survival*. New York: Random House, 1988.

Buzan, Barry. *People, States, and Fear*. 2nd ed. Boulder, Colo.: Lynne Reiner, 1991.

———. "From International System to International Society." *International Organization* 47:3 (Summer 1993): 327–51.

Caldwell, Dan. *The Dynamics of Domestic Politics and Arms Control*. Columbia, S.C.: University of South Carolina Press, 1991.

Carr, E. H. *The Twenty Years' Crisis, 1919–1939*. New York: Harper and Row, 1964.

Carroll, Berenice. "Germany Disarmed and Rearming, 1925–1935." *Journal of Peace Research* 3:2 (1966): 114–24.

Carter, Jimmy. "Three Steps toward Nuclear Responsibility." *Bulletin of the Atomic Scientists* 32:8 (October 1976): 8–14.

———. *Keeping Faith*. New York: Bantam Books, 1982.

Chayes, Abram. "An Inquiry into the Workings of Arms Control Agreements." *Harvard Law Review* 85:2 (March 1972): 906–69.

Chayes, Abram, and Antonia Handler Chayes. *The New Sovereignty*. Cambridge, Mass.: Harvard University Press, 1995.

Chayes, Antonia Handler, and Abram Chayes. "From Law Enforcement to Dispute Settlement." *International Security* 14:4 (Spring 1990): 147–64.

"Chairman's Draft Text of the Comprehensive Test Ban Treaty." *Arms Control Today* 26:6 (August 1996): 19–30.

Checkel, Jeff. "Ideas, Institutions, and the Gorbachev Foreign Policy Revolution." *World Politics* 45:2 (January 1993): 271–300.

Cheon, Seong W., and Niall M. Fraser. "Arms Control Verification: An Introduction and Literature Survey." *Arms Control* 9:1 (May 1988): 38–40.

Clark, Joseph. "Congress and Disarmament." *Bulletin of the Atomic Scientists* 19:7 (September 1963): 3–8.

Clark, Roger. "UK-USSR and US-USSR Joint Research Programs in Seismic Verification." In J. Altman and R. Rotblat, eds. *Verification of Arms Reductions*. Berlin: Springer-Verlag, 1989.

Clark, Roger, and John Baruch. "Verification of a Comprehensive Test Ban." In Frank Barnaby, ed. *A Handbook of Verification Procedures*. New York: St. Martin's, 1990, 37–178.

Clarke, Duncan. *Politics of Arms Control: The Role and Effectiveness of the U.S. Arms Control and Disarmament Agency*. New York: Free Press, 1979.

Clements, Kevin. "Prospects for a Comprehensive Test Ban Treaty." *Pacific Research*, November 1993.

Cohen, Stuart A. "The Evolution of Soviet Views on Verification." In Potter, ed., *Verification and SALT*, 49–75.

Collina, Tom Zamora. "Test Ban One, Opposition Zero." *Bulletin of the Atomic Scientists* 54:1 (January–February 1998): 4.

Collina, Tom Zamora, and Ray Kidder. "Shopping Spree Softens Test Ban Sorrows." *Bulletin of the Atomic Scientists* 50:4 (July–August 1994): 23–29.

Cousins, Norman. "Notes on a 1963 Visit with Khrushchev." *Saturday Review*, November 7, 1964, pp. 16–21+.

Craig, Paul, and John Jungerman. *Nuclear Arms Race*. New York: McGraw-Hill, 1986.

Croft, Stuart. *Strategies of Arms Control*. Manchester, U.K.: Manchester University Press, 1996.

Daalder, Ivo. "The Limited Test Ban Treaty." In Albert Carnesale and Richard Haass, eds., *Superpower Arms Control*. Cambridge, Mass.: Ballinger, 1987, 9–40.

Darilek, Richard. "Political Aspects of Verification: Arms Control in Europe." In O'Manique, ed., *A Proxy for Trust*, 65–74.

Dean, Arthur H. *Test Ban and Disarmament*. New York: Harper and Row, 1966.

Dean, Jonathan. "Gorbachev's Arms Control Moves." *Bulletin of the Atomic Scientists* 43:5 (June 1987): 34–40.

Divine, Robert. *Blowing on the Wind: The Nuclear Test Ban Debate, 1954–1960*. New York: Oxford University Press, 1978.

Dobrynin, Anatoly. *In Confidence*. New York: Random House, 1995.

Dokos, Thanos P. *Negotiations for a CTBT 1958–1994*. Lanham, Md.: University Press of America, 1995.

Downs, George W., David M. Rocke, and Peter Barsoom. "Is the Good News about Compliance Good News About Cooperation?" *International Organization* 50:3 (Summer 1996): 379–406.

Duffy, Gloria, ed. *Compliance and the Future of Arms Control*. Cambridge, Mass.: Ballinger, 1988.

Duncan, Jeffery. "How Many Soviet Tests Make a Flurry?" *Bulletin of the Atomic Scientists* 41:9 (October 1985): 8–9.

Dunn, Lewis. "Arms Control Verification: Living With Uncertainty." *International Security* 14:4 (Spring 1990): 165–84.

Dunn, Lewis, with Amy E. Gordon, eds. *Arms Control Verification and the New Role of On-Site Inspection*. Lexington, Mass.: D. C. Heath, 1990.

Eckerman, Celes. "Inspection of Chinese Cargo Ship Yields No Evidence of Chemicals." *Arms Control Today* 23:8 (October 1993): 19.

Eden, Lynn. "Contours of the Nuclear Controversy." In Eden and Miller, eds. *Nuclear Arguments*, 1–44.

Eden, Lynn, and Steven E. Miller, eds. *Nuclear Arguments*. Ithaca: Cornell University Press, 1989.

Edmonds, John. "Proliferation and Test Bans." In Josephine O'Conner Howe, ed., *The Search for World Security*. New York: St. Martin's Press, 1984.

———. "A Compete Nuclear Test Ban: Why Has It Taken So Long?" *Security Dialogue* 25:4 (December 1994): 375–88.

Eichenberg, Richard. "Dual Track and Double Trouble: The Two-Level Politics of INF." In Evans et al., eds. *Double-Edged Diplomacy*, 45–76.

———. "On Public Support." In Edward Kolodziej and Patrick Morgan, eds., *Security and Arms Control*. vol. 1. Westport, Conn.: Greenwood Press, 1989, 165–90.

Efinger, Manfred. "The Verification Policy of the Soviet Union." *Aussenpolitik* 40:4 (1989): 332–48.

Einhorn, Robert. "Treaty Compliance." *Foreign Policy* 45 (Winter 1981–2): 29–47.

Eisenhower, Dwight D. *Waging the Peace, 1956–1961*. Garden City, N.Y.: Doubleday, 1965.

Erskine, Hazel Gaudet. "The Polls: Atomic Weapons and Nuclear Energy." *Public Opinion Quarterly* 27:2 (Summer 1963): 155–90.

Evangelista, Matthew. *Innovation and the Arms Race*. Ithaca: Cornell University Press, 1988.

———. "Cooperation Theory and Disarmament Negotiations in the 1950s." *World Politics* 42:4 (July 1990): 502–28.

———. "Sources of Moderation in Soviet Security Policy." In Phillip Tetlock et al., eds. *Behavior, Society, and Nuclear War*. New York: Oxford University Press, 1991, 254–354.

———. "The Paradox of State Strength: Transnational Relations, Domestic Structures, and Security Policy in Russia and the Soviet Union." *International Organization* 49:1 (Winter 1995): 1–38.

Evans, Peter, Harold Jacobson, and Robert Putnam, eds. *Double-Edged Diplomacy*. Berkeley: University of California Press, 1993, 3–42.

"Factfile: Fifty Years of Nuclear Testing: Part II." *Arms Control Today* 25:7 (September 1995): 38.

Fetter, Steve. *Toward A Comprehensive Test Ban*. Cambridge, Mass.: Ballinger, 1988.

Findlay, Trevor. "A Comprehensive Nuclear Test Ban: Post-Cold War Prospects." *Working Paper*, No. 12. Canberra: Australian National University Peace Research Centre, 1992.

Finnemore, Martha. *National Interests in International Society*. Ithaca: Cornell University Press, 1996.

Finkelstein, Lawrence. "Arms Inspection." *International Conciliation*, No. 540 (November 1962): 5–89.

Florini, Ann. "The Evolution of International Norms." *International Studies Quarterly* 40:3 (September 1996): 363–90.

"Forum on Verification of a Comprehensive Test Ban." *Disarmament* 10 (Winter 1986–87): 15–39.

Freedman, Lawrence. *Britain and Nuclear Weapons*. London: Macmillan, 1980.

Freeman, J. P. G. *Britain's Nuclear Arms Control Policy in the Context of Anglo-American Relations*. New York: St. Martin's Press, 1986.

Gaffney, Frank. "Test Ban Would Be Real Tremor to U.S. Security." *Defense News*, September 5, 1988, pp. 35–36.

Gallagher, Nancy, ed. *Arms Control: New Approaches to Theory and Policy*. London: Frank Cass, 1998.

Garthoff, Raymond. *Détente and Confrontation*. Washington, D.C.: Brookings, 1985.

———. *The Great Transition*. Washington, D.C.: Brookings, 1994.

Genest, Marc A. *Negotiating in the Public Eye*. Stanford: Stanford University Press, 1995.

George, Alexander. "Case Studies and Theory Development: The Method of Structured, Focused Comparison." In Paul Gordon Lauren, ed., *Diplomacy*. New York: Free Press, 1979, 43–68.

———. *Bridging the Gap*. Washington, D.C.: U.S. Institute of Peace, 1993.

———, Philip Farley, and Alexander Dallin, eds. *U.S.-Soviet Security Cooperation*. New York: Oxford University Press, 1988.

Gilpin, Robert. *American Scientists and Nuclear Weapons Policy*. Princeton: Princeton University Press, 1962.

Glaser, Charles. "Why Do Strategists Disagree about the Requirements of Nuclear Deterrence?" In Eden and Miller, eds. *Nuclear Arguments*, 109–71.

Goldansky, Vitaliy. "Verificational Deterrence and Nuclear Explosions." *International Affairs* (June 1988): 27–35.

Goldblat, Jozef, and David Cox, eds. *Nuclear Weapon Tests: Prohibition or Limitation?* Oxford: Oxford University Press, 1988.

Goldstein, Judith, and Robert Keohane, eds. *Ideas and Foreign Policy*. Ithaca: Cornell University Press, 1993.

Gordon, Michael R. "All or Nothing." *National Journal*, April 14, 1984, p. 730.

Gourevitch, Peter. "The Second Image Reversed." *International Organization* 32:4 (Autumn 1978): 881–911.

Gowing, Margaret. *Britain and Atomic Energy, 1939–45*. London: Macmillan, 1964.

Gray, Colin. "Does Verification Really Matter? Facing Political Facts about Arms Control Compliance." *Strategic Review* 18:2 (Spring 1990): 32–42.

———. *House of Cards: Why Arms Control Must Fail*. Ithaca: Cornell University Press, 1992.

Graybeal, Sidney N., and Michael Krepon. "The Limitations of On-Site Inspection." *Bulletin of the Atomic Scientists* 43:10 (December 1987): 22–26.

Greb, G. Allen. "Survey of Past Nuclear Test Ban Negotiations." In Goldblat and Cox, eds., *Nuclear Weapon Tests*, 95–118.

Greb, G. Allen, and Gerald Johnson. "Who's in Charge? Arms Control Decision-Making in the United States, 1945–1970." Unpublished manuscript, 1996.

Grieco, Joseph. "Anarchy and the Limits of Cooperation." *International Organization* 42:3 (Summer 1988): 485–507.

Grier, Peter. "Poking and Prying for Peace." *Bulletin of the Atomic Scientists* 47:10 (December 1991): 25–29.

Griffiths, Franklyn. "The Sources of American Conduct: Soviet Perspectives and Their Policy Implications." *International Security* 9:2 (Fall 1984): 3–50.

———. "The Soviet Experience of Arms Control." In Stein, ed., *Getting to the Table*, 68–128.

Grinevsky, Oleg A. "The Verification of Arms Control, Disarmament Agreements, and Security." *Disarmament* 11:2 (Summer 1988): 12–19.

Groom, A. J. R. *British Thinking about Nuclear Weapons.* London: Frances Pinter, 1974.

Gruliow, Leo, ed. *Current Soviet Policy III.* New York: Columbia University Press, 1960.

Gumbel, E. J. "Disarmament and Clandestine Rearmament under the Weimar Republic." In Seymour Melman, ed. *Inspection for Disarmament.* New York: Columbia University Press, 1958, 203–19.

Gupta, Vipin. "Remote Sensing and Photogrammetry in Treaty Verification" *Photogrammetric Record* 14:83 (April 1994): 729–45.

Haas, Peter. *Saving the Mediterranean.* New York: Columbia University Press, 1990.

———. "Introduction: Epistemic Communities and International Policy Coordination." *International Organization* 46:1 (Winter 1992): 1–35.

Hampson, Fen Osler, with Michael Hart. *Multilateral Negotiations.* Baltimore: Johns Hopkins University Press, 1995.

Hasenclever, Andreas, Peter Mayer, and Volker Rittberger. "Interests, Power, and Knowledge." *Mershon International Studies Review* 40 (1996): 177–228.

Heckrotte, Warren. "Verification of Test Ban Treaties." In Potter, ed., *Verification and Arms Control*, 63–80.

———. "A Brief Historical Review of Verification for Arms Control." In Larry Costin, Mohsen Shahinpoor, and Mary Grizzard, eds., *Arms Control and Verification.* Albuquerque: TSI Press, 1992, 48–65.

Heckrotte, Warren, and Peter Moulthrop. "Soviet High Yield Nuclear Weapons Tests and the Threshold Test Ban Treaty." LLNL Preprint UCRL-101114.Rev1 (January 1990).

Helm, Robert, and Donald Westervelt. "The New Test Ban Treaties" *International Security* 1:3 (Winter 1977): 162–78.

Herken, Gregg. *The Winning Weapon.* New York: Alfred A. Knopf, 1980.

———. *Counsels of War.* New York: Oxford University Press, 1987.

———. *Cardinal Choices.* New York: Oxford University Press, 1992.

Hernandez, Sylvia. "Delivering Test-Ban Results by 1995." *Disarmament* 16:3 (1993): 19–34.

Hewlett, Richard, and Oscar Anderson. *The New World, 1939–1946.* University Park: Pennsylvania State University Press, 1962.

Hewlett, Richard, and Jack Holl. *Atoms for Peace and War, 1953–1961*. Berkeley and Los Angeles: University of California Press, 1989.

Higgins, A. Pearce. *The Hague Peace Conferences and Other International Conferences Concerning the Laws and Usages of War*. Cambridge: Cambridge University Press, 1909.

Holloway, David. *The Soviet Union and the Arms Race*, rev. ed. New Haven: Yale University Press, 1983.

Holls, Frederick. *The Peace Conferences at the Hague*. New York: Macmillan, 1900.

Holsti, Ole R. "Foreign Policy Viewed Cognitively." In Robert Axelrod, ed., *The Structure of Decision: The Cognitive Maps of Political Elites*. Princeton: Princeton University Press, 1976, 18–54.

Howard, Sean, and Rebecca Johnson. "A Comprehensive Test Ban: Disappointing Progress." *Acronym* 3 (September 1994).

Hussein, Farooq. "The Future of Arms Control: Part IV—The Impact of Weapons Test Restrictions." *Adelphi Papers* 165. London: International Institute for Strategic Studies, 1981.

Inglis, David. "H-Bomb Control." *Nation* 179 (July 24, 1954): 67–70.

International Foundation (Yevgeni Velikhov, Chair). "Toward a Comprehensive Test Ban." January 1991.

Isaacs, John. "House Challenges Reagan on Arms Control." *Bulletin of the Atomic Scientists* 42:8 (October 1986): 6–7.

"The Issues behind the CTB Treaty Ratification Debate." *Arms Control Today* 27:7 (October 1997): 6–13.

Jacobson, Harold K., and Eric Stein. *Diplomats, Scientists, and Politicians*. Ann Arbor: University of Michigan Press, 1966.

"JASON Nuclear Testing Study." *Arms Control Today* 25:7 (September 1995): 34–35.

Jervis, Robert. *Perception and Misperception in International Politics*. Princeton: Princeton University Press, 1976.

Johnson, Rebecca. "Nuclear Arms Control through Multilateral Negotiations." In Gallagher, ed., *Arms Control: New Approaches to Theory and Policy*, 83–115.

———. "Comprehensive Test Ban Treaty: The Endgame." *Acronym* 9 (April 1996).

———. "Endgame Issues in Geneva: Can the CD Deliver the CTBT in 1996?" *Arms Control Today* 26:3 (April 1996): 12–18.

Jonsson, Christer. *Soviet Bargaining Behavior*. New York: Columbia University Press, 1979.

Kapstein, Ethan B. "Is Realism Dead? The Domestic Sources of International Politics." *nternational Organization* 49:4 (Autumn 1995): 751–74.

Karkoszka, Andrzej. *Strategic Disarmament, Verification and National Security*. Stockholm: Swedish International Peace Research Institute, 1977.

Katz, Amrom. "Hiders and Finders." *Bulletin of the Atomic Scientists* 17:10 (December 1961): 423–24.

Katzenstein, Peter, ed. *The Culture of National Security*. New York: Columbia University Press, 1996.

Keeny, Spurgeon. "Notes from the Underground." *Arms Control Today* 18:5 (June 1988): 21–24.

Keohane, Robert. *After Hegemony*. Princeton: Princeton University Press, 1984.

———. "International Institutions: Two Approaches." *International Studies Quarterly* 32 (December 1988): 379–96.

Khrushchev, Nikita S. *Report of the Central Committee to the 20th Congress of the CPSU*. London: Soviet News Booklet, 1956.

———. *Khrushchev Remembers: The Last Testament*. Strobe Talbott, trans. Boston: Little, Brown, 1974.

Killian, James, Jr. *Sputnik, Scientists, and Eisenhower*. Cambridge: M.I.T. Press, 1977.

Kissinger, Henry. *Years of Upheaval*. Boston: Little, Brown, 1982.

Kistiakowsky, George. *A Scientist in the White House*. Cambridge, Mass.: Harvard University Press, 1976.

Knopf, Jeffrey. "Beyond Two-Level Games: Domestic-International Interaction in the Intermediate Range Nuclear Forces Negotiations." *International Organization* 47:4 (Autumn 1993): 599–628.

Kokeyev, Mikhail, and Andrei Androsov. *Verification: The Soviet Stance, Its Past, Present, and Future*. New York: UNIDIR, 1990.

Krass, Allan. "The Politics of Verification." *World Policy Journal* 4 (Fall 1985): 731–53.

———. *Verification: How Much Is Enough?* London: Taylor and Francis, 1985.

Krepon, Michael. "The Political Dynamics of Verification and Compliance Debates." In Potter, ed. *Verification and Arms Control*, 135–51.

———. "CIA, DIA at Odds over Soviet Threat." *Bulletin of the Atomic Scientists* 43:4 (May 1987): 6–7.

Krepon, Michael, and Dan Caldwell, eds. *The Politics of Arms Control Treaty Ratification*. New York: St. Martin's Press, 1991.

Krepon, Michael, and Mary Umberger, eds. *Verification and Compliance: A Problem Solving Approach*. Cambridge, Mass.: Ballinger, 1988.

KRON-4 TV. "Perle and the Scientists." Brian McTigue, producer. May 9, 1986.

Ladd, Everett Carll. "The Freeze Framework." *Public Opinion* 10 (August–September 1982).

Lall, Arthur. *Negotiating Disarmament: The Eighteen-Nation Disarmament Conference: The First Two Years, 1962–4*. Ithaca: Cornell University, Center for International Studies, 1964.

Lamb, F. K. "Monitoring Yields of Underground Nuclear Tests Using Hydrodynamic Methods." In Dietrich Schroeder and David Hafemeister, eds., *Nuclear Arms Technologies in the 1990s*. New York: American Institute of Physics, 1988, 109–48.

Lang, Daniel. *An Inquiry into Enoughness*. New York: McGraw Hill, 1965.

Larson, Deborah Welch. *The Origins of Containment*. Princeton: Princeton University Press, 1985.

———. *The Anatomy of Mistrust*. Ithaca: Cornell University Press, 1997.

Latter, A. L. *A Method of Concealing Underground Nuclear Explosions.* RAND Corp. RM-2347-AFT, 1959.

Lavoy, Peter. "Nuclear Myths and the Causes of Nuclear Proliferation." In Zachary S. Davis and Benjamin Frankel, eds., *The Proliferation Puzzle.* London: Frank Cass, 1993, 192–212.

Lebow, Richard Ned. *Between Peace and War.* Baltimore: Johns Hopkins University Press, 1981.

Lefebure, Victor. *Scientific Disarmament.* New York: Macmillan, 1931.

Lehman, John F., and Seymour Weiss. *Beyond the SALT II Failure.* New York: Praeger, 1981.

Lehman, Ronald F., II. "Lehman's Lessons: The Arms Control Agenda." *Arms Control Today* 21:10 (December 1991).

Leggett, Jeremy. "Recent Developments and Outlook for the Verification of a Nuclear Test Ban." In J. Altman and J Rotblat, eds., *Verification of Arms Reductions.* Berlin: Springer-Verlag, 1989.

"Letters to the Editor." *Science* 233 (September 26, 1986): 1367.

Levy, Jack. "Learning and Foreign Policy: Sweeping a Conceptual Minefield." *International Organization* 48:2 (Spring 1994): 279–312.

Lewis, Patricia. "The United Kingdom." In Arnett, ed., *Nuclear Weapons,* 99–115.

Litfin, Karen. *Ozone Discourses.* New York: Columbia University Press, 1994.

Lockwood, Dunbar. "Continued Testing 'Essential,' DOE Tells Congress." *Arms Control Today* 20:4 (May 1990): 29.

———. "Conference on Disarmament Sees Progress toward CTB Treaty." *Arms Control Today* 24:4 (May 1994): 17, 23.

Loeb, Benjamin. "The Limited Test Ban Treaty." In Krepon and Caldwell, eds., *The Politics of Treaty Ratification,* 167–227.

Lord, Carnes. "Verification: Reforming a Theology." *The National Interest* (Spring 1986): 50–60.

Lowenthal, Mark. "The Politics of Verification: What's New, What's Not." *Washington Quarterly* 14:1 (Winter 1991): 119–30.

Lowenthal, Mark, and Joel Witt. "The Politics of Verification." In Potter, ed., *Verification and Arms Control,* 153–68.

Marin-Bosch, Miguel (interview). "Achieving a Comprehensive Test Ban." *Arms Control Today* 24:5 (June 1994): 3–7.

McFate, Patricia Bliss, and Sidney N. Graybeal. "The Price for Effective Verification in an Era of Expanding Arms Control." *ANNALS* 500 (November 1988): 73–90.

Meyer, Stephen. "Verification and the ICBM Shell-Game." *International Security* 4:2 (Fall 1979): 40–68.

———. "Verification and Risk in Arms Control." *International Security* 8:4 (Spring 1984): 111–26.

———. "The Sources and Prospects of Gorbachev's New Political Thinking on Security." *International Security* 13:2 (Fall 1988): 124–63.

Miller, Steven E. "Politics over Promise: Domestic Impediments to Arms Control." *International Security* 8:4 (Spring 1984): 67–90.

Milner, Helen. "The Assumption of Anarchy in International Relations Theory." *Review of International Studies* 17 (January 1991): 67–85.

Molander, Johan. "The United Nations and the Elimination of Iraq's Weapons of Mass Destruction." In Tanner, ed., *From Versailles to Baghdad*, 137–59.

Moodie, Michael. "Ratifying the Chemical Weapons Convention." *Arms Control Today* 26:1 (February 1996): 3–9.

Moravcsik, Andrew. "Introduction: Integrating International and Domestic Theories of International Bargaining." In Evans, Jacobson, and Putnam, eds., *Double-Edged Diplomacy*, 3–42.

Morrocco, John D. "Verification Raises Cost, Technology Concerns." *Aviation Week and Space Technology* 133:6 (August 6, 1990): 44–60.

Myrdal, Alva. *The Game of Disarmament*. New York: Pantheon Books, 1976.

Nathan, James. "A Fragile Détente: The U-2 Incident Reconsidered." *Military Affairs* 39:3 (October 1974): 97–104.

Natural Resources Defense Council. *Phasing Out Nuclear Weapons Tests*. Washington, D.C.: NRDC, 1989.

Neidle, Alan. "Nuclear Test Bans: History and Future Prospects." In George et al., eds., *U.S.-Soviet Security Cooperation*, 175–214.

Nisbett, Richard, and Timothy Wilson. "Telling More than We Can Know." *Psychological Review* 84:3 (May 1977): 231–59.

Nogee, Joseph. *Soviet Policy toward International Control of Atomic Energy*. South Bend, Ind.: Notre Dame University Press, 1961.

Nolan, Janne. "Public and Congressional Attitudes toward On-Site Inspection." In Dunn, with Gordon, eds., *Arms Control Verification*, 161–84.

———, ed. *Global Engagement*. Washington, D.C.: Brookings, 1994.

Norris, Robert, and William Arkin. "Soviet Testing Move." *Bulletin of the Atomic Scientists* 46:4 (May 1990): 56.

"Nuclear Glasnost." *Amicus Journal* (Fall 1987): 14–19.

"Nuclear Weapon Safety" (symposium). *Bulletin of the Atomic Scientists* 47:3 (April 1991): 29–40.

Oberdorfer, Don. *The Turn*. New York: Simon and Schuster, 1991.

Oelrich, Ivan. "The Changing Rules of Arms Control Verification." *International Security* 14:4 (Spring 1990): 176–84.

O'Manique, John, ed. *A Proxy for Trust*. Ottawa: Norman Paterson School of International Affairs, Carleton University, 1985.

Osgood, Charles E. *An Alternative to War or Surrender*. Champaign: University of Illinois Press, 1962.

Ostrom, Elinor. *Governing the Commons*. New York: Cambridge University Press, 1990.

Oye, Kenneth, ed. *Cooperation Under Anarchy*. Princeton: Princeton University Press, 1996.

Paine, Christopher, and Thomas Cochran. "So Little Time, So Many Weapons, So Much to Do." *Bulletin of the Atomic Scientists* 48:1 (January–February 1992): 13–16.

Panofsky, Wolfgang. "Verification of the Threshold Test Ban." *Arms Control Today* 20:7 (September 1990): 3–6.

Panofsky, Wolfgang, and Spurgeon Keeny Jr. "MAD versus NUTS: Can Doctrine or Weaponry Remedy the Mutual Hostage Relationship of the Superpowers?" *Foreign Affairs*, 60:2 (Winter 1981–82): 287–304.

Perkovitch, George. "India's Nuclear Weapons Debate: Unlocking the Door to the CTBT." *Arms Control Today* 26:4 (May–June 1996): 11–16.

Pomerance, Jo. "The Anti-Test Ban Coalition." *Bulletin of the Atomic Scientists* 33:1 (January 1977): 51–54.

———. "The Comprehensive Test Ban at Last?" *Bulletin of the Atomic Scientists* 35:7 (September 1979): 9–10.

Pool, Ithiel de Sola. "Public Opinion and the Control of Armaments." In Brennan, ed., *Arms Control*, 333–46.

Potter, William, ed. *Verification and SALT: The Challenge of Strategic Deception*. Boulder, Colo.: Westview Press, 1980.

———. *Verification and Arms Control*. Lexington, Mass.: D. C. Heath, 1985.

Potter, William, with Leonid V. Belyaev and Mark Lay. "The Evolution of Soviet Attitudes toward On-Site Inspection." In Dunn with Gordon, eds., *Arms Control Verification*, 185–206.

Priestley, Keith, et al. "Regional Seismic Recordings of the Soviet Nuclear Explosion of the Joint Verification Experiment." *Geophysical Research Letters* 17:2 (February 1990): 179–82.

Rabinowitch, Eugene. "Nuclear Bomb Tests." *Bulletin of the Atomic Scientists* 14:8 (October 1958): 282–87.

Rice, Condoleeza. "SALT and the Search for a Security Regime." In George et al., eds., *U.S.-Soviet Security Cooperation*, 293–306.

Richards, Paul G. "Stages towards a New Test Ban." In Krepon and Umberger, eds., *Verification and Compliance*, 83–84.

Richter, James G. *Khrushchev's Double Bind*. Baltimore: Johns Hopkins University Press, 1994.

Risse-Kappen, Thomas, ed. *Bringing Transnational Relations Back In*. Cambridge: Cambridge University Press, 1995.

Roberts, Chalmers M. "The Hopes and Fears of an Atomic Test Ban." *The Reporter* 22:9 (April 28, 1960): 20–23.

Robinson, C. Paul. "The Joint Verification Experiment." *Disarmament* 12:2 (Summer 1989): 90–95.

———. "Verifying Testing Treaties—Old and New." *Arms Control Today* 20:6 (July–August 1990): 3–7.

Roddie, Stewart. *Peace Patrol*. London: Christophers, 1932.

Rose, Harald. "Nuclear Test Ban and Verification." *Disarmament* 12:3 (Fall 1989): 16–23.

Rose, William. *U.S. Unilateral Arms Control Initiatives*. Westport, Conn.: Greenwood Press, 1988.

Rosenau, James, and Ernst-Otto Czempiel, eds. *Governance without Government*. Cambridge: Cambridge University Press, 1992.

Rosi, Eugene J. "Public Opinion and National Security Policy: The Nuclear Testing Debate." In Rosi, ed., *American Defense and Detente*. New York: Dodd, Mead, 1973, 364–96.

Sakharov, Andrei. *Memoirs*. New York: Alfred A. Knopf, 1990.

Samuel, Peter. "Why the U.S. Insists on On-Site Checks of Nuclear Tests." *Defense Week* 6:32 (August 5, 1985): 1, 7.

Savel'yev, Aleksander G., and Nikolay N. Detinov. *The Big Five: Arms Control Decision-making in the Soviet Union*. Westport, Conn.: Praeger, 1995.

Schear, James. "Verifying Arms Control Agreements: Premises, Practices and Future Problems." *Arms Control* 3 (December 1982): 76–95.

———. "Verification, Compliance, and Arms Control: The Dynamics of the Domestic Debate." In Eden and Miller, eds. *Nuclear Arguments*, 264–321.

Scheffer, J. W. "Political Aspects of Verification." In O'Manique, ed., *A Proxy for Trust*, 75–84.

Scheinman, Lawrence. *Atomic Energy Policy in France under the Fourth Republic*. Princeton: Princeton University Press, 1965.

Schelling, Thomas, and Morton Halperin. *Strategy and Arms Control*. New York: Twentieth Century Fund, 1961.

Scherr, Alan B. *The Other Side of Arms Control*. Winchester, Mass.: Unwin Hyman, 1988.

Schlesinger, Arthur Jr. *A Thousand Days*. Greenwich, Conn.: Fawcett, 1965.

Schrag, Philip. *Listening for the Bomb*. Boulder, Colo.: Westview Press, 1989.

———. *Global Action*. Boulder, Colo.: Westview Press, 1992.

Scott, Robert T. "Joint Nuclear Tests Raise Questions about Administration Policy." *Arms Control Today* 18:8 (October 1988): 26.

Scribner, Richard, and Kenneth Luongo. *Strategic Nuclear Arms Control Verification: Terms and Concepts*. American Association for the Advancement of Science, Pub. No. 85-2 (January 1985).

Seaborg, Glenn, with Benjamin Loeb. *Stemming the Tide: Arms Control in the Johnson Years*. Lexington, Mass.: Lexington Books, 1987.

———. *Kennedy, Khrushchev, and the Test Ban*. Berkeley and Los Angeles: University of California Press, 1981.

Seay, Douglas. "What Are the Soviets' Objectives in Their Foreign, Military, and Arms Control Policies?" In Eden and Miller, eds., *Nuclear Arguments*, 47–108.

Shapley, Deborah. "Antarctica: Why Success?" In George et al., eds., *U.S.-Soviet Security Cooperation*, 307–35.

Shen, Dingli. "Toward a Nuclear-Weapon-Free World: A Chinese Perspective." *Bulletin of the Atomic Scientists* 50:2 (March–April 1994): 51–54.

Shimko, Keith. *Images and Arms Control*. Ann Arbor: University of Michigan Press, 1991.

Sims, Jennifer. *Icarus Restrained: An Intellectual History of Nuclear Arms Control, 1945–60.* Boulder, Colo.: Westview Press, 1990.

———. "Arms Control Process: The U.S. Domestic Context." In Jeffrey A. Larsen and Gregory J. Rattray, eds. *Arms Control toward the 21st Century.* Boulder, Colo.: Lynne Reiner Press, 1996, 55–76.

Slocombe, Walter. "Verification and Negotiation." In Steven E. Miller, ed., *The Nuclear Weapons Freeze and Arms Control.* Cambridge, Mass.: Ballinger, 1984.

Slusser, Robert. *The Berlin Crisis of 1961: Soviet-American Relations and the Struggle for Power in the Kremlin.* Baltimore: Johns Hopkins University Press, 1973.

Smith, R. Jeffery. "Soviets Agree to Broad Seismic Test." *Science* 233 (August 1, 1986): 511–12.

Snyder, Glenn, and Paul Diesing. *Conflict Among Nations.* Princeton: Princeton University Press, 1977.

Snyder, Jack. "International Leverage on Soviet Domestic Change." *World Politics* 42:1 (October 1989): 1–30.

———. *Myths of Empire.* Ithaca: Cornell University Press, 1991.

———. "East-West Bargaining over Germany: The Search for Synergy in a Two-Level Game." In Evans et al., eds., *Double-Edged Diplomacy,* 104–27.

Solingen, Etel. "The Domestic Sources of Regional Regimes." *International Studies Quarterly* 38:2 (June 1994): 305–37.

Sorenson, Theodore C. *Kennedy.* New York: Harper and Row, 1965.

Stein, Arthur. *Why Nations Cooperate.* Ithaca: Cornell University Press, 1990.

Stein, Janice Gross, ed. *Getting to the Table.* Baltimore: Johns Hopkins University Press, 1989.

———. "Political Learning by Doing: Gorbachev as Uncommitted Thinker and Motivated Learner." *International Organization* 48:2 (Spring 1994): 155–83.

Stovall, Don. "The Stockholm Accord." In Dunn, with Gordon, eds., *Arms Control Verification,* 15–38.

Sur, Serge, ed. *Verification of Current Disarmament and Arms Limitation Agreements.* New York: UNIDIR, 1991.

Sweet, William. "NRDC and Soviet Academy Sign Unusual Test-Verification Pact." *Physics Today* 39:7 (July 1986): 63–64.

———. "IRIS and Other Open Seismic Networks Could Be Crucial to Test-Ban Regime." *Physics Today* (December 1993): 35–37.

Sykes, Lynn, and Jack Evernden. "The Verification of a Comprehensive Nuclear Test Ban." *Scientific American* 247:4 (October 1982): 47–55.

Talbott, Strobe. *Deadly Gambits.* New York: Vintage Books, 1985.

Tanner, Fred. "Versailles: German Disarmament after World War I." In Tanner, ed., *From Versailles to Baghdad.* New York: UNIDIR, 1992, 5–26.

Teller, Edward. "Alternatives for Security." *Foreign Affairs* 36:2 (January 1958): 201–8.

Temperley, A. C. *The Whispering Gallery of Europe.* London: Collins, 1926.

Terchek, Ronald. *The Making of the Test Ban Treaty.* The Hague: Martinus Nijhoff, 1970.

Thorn, Robert, and Donald Westervelt. "Hydronuclear Experiments." Los Alamos: LANL, LA-10902-MS UC-2, February 1987.

Timerbayev, Roland. *Verification of Arms Limitation and Disarmament.* Foreign Broadcast Information Service, 1984. Originally published as *Kontrol'za Ogranicheniyem Vooruzheniy i Razoruzheniyem.* Moscow: International Relations Publishing House, 1983.

———— (under the pseudonym of R. Zheleznov). "Nuclear Explosions for Peaceful Purposes." *International Affairs* 8 (August 1976): 81–87.

———— (under the pseudonym of R. Zheleznov). "Monitoring Arms Limitation Measures." *International Affairs* 7 (1982): 75–84.

————. "A Soviet Official on Verification." *Bulletin of the Atomic Scientists* 43:1 (January–February 1987): 8–10.

————. "A Hostage to Political Realities: A Russian Commentary." *Security Dialogue* 25:4 (December 1994): 389–92.

Tower, John G., James Brown, and William K. Cheek, eds. *Verification: The Key to Arms Control in the 1990s.* Washington, D.C.: Brassey's, 1992.

Towle, Philip. *Arms Control in East-West Relations.* New York: St. Martin's Press, 1983.

————. *Enforced Disarmament from the Napoleonic Campaign to the Gulf War.* Oxford: Oxford University Press, 1997.

Van Atta, Dale. "Inside a U.S.-Soviet Arms Negotiation." *Nation,* December 19, 1981, 666–68.

Van Cleave, William, and S. T. Cohen. *Nuclear Weapons, Policies, and the Test Ban Issue.* Wesptort, Conn.: Praeger, 1987.

Van der Vink, Gregory, and Christopher Paine. "The Politics of Verification: Limiting the Testing of Nuclear Weapons." *Science and Global Security* 3 (1993): 261–88.

Van der Vink, Gregory, and Jeffery Park. "Nuclear Test Ban Monitoring: New Requirements, New Resources." *Science* 263 (February 4, 1994): 634–35.

Velikhov, Evgeny. "Science and Scientists for a Nuclear-Weapon-Free World." *Physics Today* 42:11 (November 1989): 32–38.

Von Hippel, Frank. "Arms Control Physics: The New Soviet Connection." *Physics Today* 42:11 (November 1989): 39–46.

Von Hippel, Frank, and Tom Zamora Collina. "Nuclear Junkies: Testing, Testing, 1, 2, 3,— Forever." *Bulletin of the Atomic Scientists* 49:6 (July–August 1993): 28–32.

Voss, Earl. *Nuclear Ambush.* Chicago: Henry Regnery, 1963.

Wadsworth, James. *The Price of Peace.* New York: Praeger, 1962.

Waltz, Kenneth. *Theory of International Politics.* New York: Random House, 1979.

Weber, Steven. *Cooperation and Discord in U.S.-Soviet Arms Control.* Princeton: Princeton University Press, 1991.

————. "Interactive Learning in U.S.-Soviet Arms Control." In George W. Breslauer and Philip E. Tetlock, eds. *Learning in U.S. and Soviet Foreign Policy.* Boulder, Colo.: Westview Press, 1991, 784–824.

Wendt, Alexander. "The Agent-Structure Problem in International Relations." *International Organization* 41:3 (Summer 1987): 335–70.

———. "Anarchy Is What States Make of It: The Social Construction of Power Politics." *International Organization* 46:2 (Spring 1992): 391–425.

Wiesner, Jerome. *Where Science and Politics Meet.* New York: McGraw-Hill, 1965.

Wirls, Daniel. *Buildup.* Ithaca: Cornell University Press, 1992.

Wittman, Donald. "Arms Control Verification and Other Games Involving Imperfect Detection." *American Political Science Review* 83:3 (September 1989): 923–45.

Wright, Michael. *Disarm and Verify.* London: Chatto and Windus, 1964.

Yankelovich, Daniel, and John Doble. "The Public Mood: Nuclear Weapons and the U.S.S.R." *Foreign Affairs* 63:1 (Fall 1984): 33–46.

Yankelovich, Daniel, and Larry Kaagan. "Assertive America." *Foreign Affairs* (Special Issue "America and the World") 59:3 (1980): 696–713.

Yankelovich, Daniel, and Richard Smoke. "America's New Thinking." *Foreign Affairs* 67:1 (Fall 1988): 1–17.

York, Herbert. "The Great Test Ban Debate." *Scientific American* 227:5 (November 1972): 15–23.

———. *The Advisors.* Palo Alto: Stanford University Press, 1976.

———. *Making Weapons, Talking Peace.* New York: Basic Books, 1987.

Yost, David. "France's Nuclear Dilemmas." *Foreign Affairs* 75:1 (January–February 1996): 108–18.

Young, Oran. *Compliance and Public Authority.* Washington, D.C.: Resources for the Future, 1979.

Zartman, I. William, and Maureen R. Berman. *The Practical Negotiator.* New Haven: Yale University Press, 1982.

Zheutlin, Peter. "Nevada, USSR." *Bulletin of the Atomic Scientists* 46:2 (March 1990): 10–12.

Zuckerman, Lord. "Prospects for a Comprehensive Test Ban." *Nature* 361 (February 4, 1993): 392–96.

Index

Acheson-Lilienthal Committee (ALC), 60–64, 83, 89, 130, 162
acoustic monitoring, 65, 86, 87
Adelman, Kenneth, 6–7, 37, 196
Advanced Research Projects Agency (ARPA), 155, 156. *See also* Defense Advanced Research Projects Agency
aerial monitoring, 8, 74, 79, 83, 86, 135, 138, 257n
agenda-setting, 52, 71
Agnew, Harold, 166–7, 177
Air Force Technical Applications Center (AFTAC), 65, 80, 155, 157, 177
alliance politics, 42, 46, 75, 76, 78, 81–2, 94
ambiguity, 10, 39
anarchy, in world politics, 1, 37, 38, 215; and cooperation, 4–13, 26
Antarctic Treaty, 109, 165, 262n
antiballistic missile defenses, 50, 83, 108, 145, 151, 154, 158, 159, 186–7
Archambeau, Charles, 189, 205
arms control: all-or-nothing approach to, 65–7, 68, 71, 75; costs, benefits, and risks of, 9, 16, 22, 23–4, 39, 46, 54; dilemma, 4, 44, 46, 54; step-by-step approach to, 72, 91, 110, 147, 201, 203, 209
Arms Control Advocates, defined, 5, 41, 43–4
Arms Control and Disarmament Agency (ACDA), 42, 122, 129, 135, 138, 144, 151, 156, 186, 264n
arms race: major developments in, 72–3; and test bans, 146–8, 227; test restrictions to curb, 22, 94, 98

asymmetries, effects on negotiations, 36, 226, 231–2
atmospheric sampling, 22, 35, 65, 80
atmospheric testing: ban on, 98, 102, 104, 105, 106, 117, 126, 127–8; and bargaining, 128, 140; moratorium on, 85, 88
Atomic Energy Act (1946), 62, 72
Atomic Energy Commission (AEC), 122; General Advisory Committee of, 66; on partial limits, 82–3, 88, 105; and test limits, block of, 70–1, 77, 86–7, 104, 151; and underground testing, 80, 85. *See also* Department of Energy
Australia, 46, 210, 230, 236–7, 239

Baruch Plan, 62–63, 65, 68
Berkner, Lloyd, chair of PSAC panel, 103, 136
Berlin, superpower conflict over, 69, 113, 123, 125, 142
Bethe, Hans, 80, 99, 109
Bethe Report, 83–4, 99, 160
Biological and Toxic Weapons Convention (BWC), 32, 53
BRAVO test, 67, 70, 72
break out from treaty, fears of, 126–7, 166, 196, 236
Brezhnev, Leonid, 141, 149, 151, 158–9, 191
Britain: arms control calculations, 60, 72, 93–4, 173; compromise proposals by, 73, 87, 102; domestic divisions, 173, 180–1; Labour Party, 72, 76, 94, 141; in multilateral CTB negotiations, 228, 230, 236–8; nuclear weapons program, 72, 73, 173, 255n

Brown, Harold, 80, 103, 113, 172, 177
bureaucratic politics, models of, 41–2, 253n
Bush, George H. W., 32, 34, 209–11
Bush, Vannevar, 63, 66

Cautious Cooperators, defined, 5, 41, 43–4
Carter, Jimmy: administration of, 42, 172–3; arms control preferences of, 170, 171–2, 177; CTB policy of, 177–8, 181, 183; TTBT/PNET policy, 165, 179
case study methodology, 22, 23
Central Intelligence Agency (CIA), 79, 88, 93, 98, 138, 189, 209
chemical explosions, 87, 109, 181, 202–3, 263n
Chemical Weapons Convention (CWC), 2–3, 37, 45, 48, 192, 231
China, 83, 145; CTB participation, 109, 139, 159, 174; in multilateral CTB negotiations, 228, 231–3, 235–6; nuclear testing by, 150, 151; nuclear weapons program of, 73, 95, 104; on test ban verification, 46, 87; on test restrictions, 113; and USSR, 120, 135, 141
civilian-based verification, 35–6, 229, 234–5, 239, 251–2n
classification of information, political uses of, 167, 189, 207, 219
Clinton, William J., 37, 227, 230, 239
coalition-building strategies, theories of, 33; alignment, 21, 52, 54, 56, 70, 74, 221–2; alliance, 21, 52, 56, 70, 149, 169, 222; avoidance, 21, 52, 54–5, 56, 93, 154–5, 159–60, 183, 220; identification, 21, 52, 53, 56, 220–1; linkages, 21, 52; side payments, 21, 52, 53
Coalition for Peace Through Strength, 176, 179
coalitions, 42, 52; blocking, 14, 23, 26, 51, 64–7, 89, 120, 188, 204; building, 21, 23, 26, 28, 45, 49, 52, 53, 219–20; winning, 14, 49, 51, 92, 110, 115–7, 168–9, 223–4
Cochran, Thomas, 198
collateral information collection, 6, 31, 51, 74, 98, 107, 162, 207

Committee of Principals, 93, 122
Committee on the Present Danger, 176, 274n
compliance: with domestic laws, 4–5, 18, 27, 29, 31, 32; incentives for, 7, 11, 43; reports to Congress on, 176, 275n
compliance judgments, national control over, 164, 175, 232
Comprehensive Test Ban (CTB), 23–5; arms control characteristics of, 22–3; early proposals for, 70–2, 73, 76–7; Eisenhower negotiations for full ban, 97–110; Kennedy 1962 U.S. draft proposal, 132–4, 139, 142–3, 146; negotiations of 1978–80, 173–81; negotiations of 1994–96, 226–40; phased approach, 24, 91, 92, 104, 111–8, 123, 124
Comprehensive Test Ban Treaty (CTBT), 239–40; chair's text, 230, 238–9; ratification of, 3, 239–40; signing of, 239
computer simulations, 237, 273n
Conference of Experts, 24, 85–90, 99, 106–7, 109, 117, 129, 132
Conference on Disarmament (CD), 23, 181, 187, 226, 228–9
confidence-building function of verification, 11, 59, 137
Congress: arms control role, 42–3, 76, 122, 124, 171, 176, 197, 216; legislated test restrictions, 196, 198, 199–204, 211
constructivist theories, 38–9
consultative mechanisms, 10, 11, 35, 144, 160, 163, 181, 233, 240
conventional arms control, 45, 64, 73, 75, 76, 78, 81–2
Conventional Forces in Europe accord (CFE), 184, 195
cooperative monitoring, 8, 13
cooperative security, 10–2, 59, 231
cooperative verification, 7, 31, 163–4, 248n
CORRTEX, 189–91, 195–6, 200–3, 205, 275–6n
Cousins, Norman, 136, 141
crisis, effects of, 57, 217
Cuban Missile Crisis, 24, 119–20, 134–5, 136, 143, 148

data exchanges, 35, 63, 74; for CTB, 137, 144, 152–3, 181; for TTBT, 161, 168–9, 206

Dean, Arthur, 121, 126, 132, 136, 137

decision-making body for CTB, 20, 36, 97; Executive Council, 109, 112, 116, 130, 231, 254–5n; International Scientific Commission, 132–3, 139; troika proposal, 123, 124

decoupling, 84, 103, 105, 117, 229; "Big Hole" theory, 99, 101, 129; detection despite, 179; limitations on, 260n, 261n, 263n, 270n; Project Cowboy, 104, 109, 113

Defense Advanced Research Projects Agency (DARPA), 189, 198, 200, 205. See also Advanced Research Projects Agency

democratization, verification to promote, 11, 34, 64–5, 137, 211

Department of Defense (DOD): arms control opposition, 66, 68, 70–1, 75, 79–80, 122, 186, 200, 203; partial limits support, 103, 105, 112, 115, 210; verification information control, 133, 151, 157–8, 189

Department of Energy (DOE), 178, 189, 209, 280n. See also Atomic Energy Commission

depoliticization: calls for, 2, 14, 17–8, 92; impossibility of, 3, 36, 49–51, 56, 104–10, 117, 217–8

deterrence: debates, 16–8, 41–2, 112, 122, 159, 172–3; strategies, and test ban preferences, 22, 23, 33, 44–5, 49, 54, 70, 186–7

distrust, 117, 135; politics of verification exacerbated by, 24, 31, 65, 78, 97, 145–8, 181; politics of verification hindered by, 20, 30, 73–4, 116, 143–4; unreliable verification heightened by, 103, 153

Dodd, Thomas, 102, 139, 143, 146

dual use, of verification information, 61–2, 72, 86, 89, 107, 114, 124, 219, 254n

Dulles, John Foster, 71, 75, 78–9, 81–4, 86, 101, 104

duration of CTB, 97, 102, 174, 178–9

economics of verification, 31–2, 36, 52, 107, 138, 164, 179, 209, 238

education, 25, 243–4; insufficient, 48, 225–6; about nuclear testing, 67, 68, 128, 198; about verification, 67, 70, 77, 89, 133, 143, 189. See also learning

Eighteen-Nation Disarmament Committee (ENDC), 128–33, 136–7, 141, 147

Eisenhower, Dwight D., 24, 54, 121; administration of, 41–2, 68, 75–7, 82–3, 93–4, 98, 101, 105–6, 111–2; arms control overtures by, 68, 74, 84–5, 88, 102–4, 115; arms control preferences of, 68, 71, 79, 83, 84, 92, 93, 101, 105; and decision-making structure, 71, 83; testing decisions, 88, 108, 110

enforcement view of verification, 11, 14

entry-into-force conditions, 23, 147, 158–9, 237–40

epistemic communities, 50, 53, 54, 218

equipment controversies, 164, 178

evasion scenarios, 33, 92, 94, 99, 115, 145, 202, 229. See also decoupling

Evernden, Jack, 155, 156, 198

fallout fears, 70, 73, 76, 80, 94, 98, 115, 121, 128, 144–5; atmospheric ban to end, 116, 119; and "dirty" tests ban, 82–3

Farley, Phillip, 156, 157

Federation of American Scientists, 147, 167, 197

Federov, Yevgeni, 96, 102, 136

Fermi, Enrico, 66, 83

first principles, 42, 43, 49, 52–4; lack of consensus on, 45, 89, 104, 215–6, 243

fissile material controls, 33, 60, 62; difficulty of, 68, 73; production ban on, 76, 78–81, 84

Ford, Gerald, 165

Foster, William, 122, 138, 152, 154

France: arms control proposals by, 59, 72; CTB participation, 109, 139, 159, 174; in multilateral CTB negotiations, 228, 230, 232, 236–7; nuclear tests by, 123, 127, 264n; nuclear weapons program, 73, 95; test ban, resistance to, 76, 81, 88, 113

Gaffney, Frank, 190–1, 203, 211, 218
Gaither Committee, 83, 122
game theory, and verification policy, 137
General and Complete Disarmament
    (GCD), 65; proposals for, 65, 72–6, 78,
    80–2, 128; Soviets link CTB to, 124, 128,
    134
Geneva System, 87, 91, 93, 96, 106, 116, 130;
    attacks on, 99–102, 107; modifications
    to, 107–8; revised estimates of, 112, 113,
    132
Germany: disarmament after World War I,
    35–6, 59, 61, 75; nuclear weapons access,
    81, 95, 154
Gorbachev, Mikhail, 2, 7, 11, 25, 40, 53;
    arms control accomplishments, need
    for, 194, 198, 201–2; bargaining strategy
    of, 192–3, 195, 197, 202–4, 205–6, 212–3;
    bluff-calling by, 194, 206, 212–3; deci-
    sion-making style, 193; new thinking,
    193–5, 212–3, 226; security policy, 21,
    40–1, 193–4; unilateral initiatives by,
    194, 195, 253n
Gore, Albert, 98, 104, 126
grassroots activism, 20, 76, 82, 209, 216. See
    also NRDC-SAS in-country project
Group of Scientific Experts (GSE), 173,
    193, 210, 218, 219, 231, 281–2n

HARDTACK test series, 83, 88, 100, 109
Harriman, Averell, 142–4
Heckrotte, Warren, 136, 164, 175, 188
Herter, Christian, 104, 110, 113
high-altitude tests, 100, 108, 260n; moni-
    toring of, 86, 104, 120, 124, 132. See also
    Technical Working Group I
Hosmer, Craig, 133, 139, 146
Hot Line Agreement, 141
Humphrey, Hubert, 76, 80, 102, 105, 145
hydroacoustic monitoring, 132, 231
hydrodynamic experiment, 178, 236–7
hydronuclear experiments, 108, 127, 236,
    237, 282n

ideal types, use of, 5–6, 41, 43–8, 242–3
ideas: importance of, 3–14, 25; in verifica-
    tion arguments, 37–48, 52, 55

Iklé, Fred, 160, 186
India, 33, 46; arms control proposals by,
    70, 82, 131, 193; in multilateral CTB
    negotiations, 228, 233, 236, 237–9;
    nuclear explosion by, 161; nuclear
    weapons development by, 2, 155, 266
intelligence gathering, 1, 6, 25, 31, 32, 35,
    52, 65, 155, 200
intentions, verification as test of, 8, 34, 64,
    69, 101–2, 104, 126, 147, 188, 190, 193,
    198–9; Reagan reversal regarding, 201,
    206
Intermediate-Range Nuclear Forces
    (INF) Treaty, 42, 184, 192, 194, 203
International Atomic Energy Agency
    (IAEA), 35, 37, 130, 131, 141, 153–4, 192
International Data Center (IDC), 232, 238
International Monitoring System (IMS),
    229, 231–2, 237, 282n
Iraq, 33, 36, 37, 228
Israel, 33, 228, 233

Jackson, Henry, 139
Johnson, Gerald, 85, 179
Johnson, Lyndon, 151, 154
Joint Chiefs of Staff (JCS), 70, 75–6, 117,
    122, 138, 142–3, 144, 145–6, 151
Joint Committee on Atomic Energy
    (JCAE), 113, 115, 133, 139
joint research proposals, 111, 112, 124
Joint Verification Experiment (JVE), 25,
    185, 203, 205–10, 279n

Kennedy, John F., 24, 115, 119–49; adminis-
    tration of, 121–3, 138; American Uni-
    versity Speech, 140–1; arms control
    preferences, 119, 128–9, 134; coercive
    diplomacy of, 120, 121–3, 128, 143, 148,
    266n, 268n; domestic coalition build-
    ing by, 122, 129, 145–6, 148; military
    programs of, 123, 125
Khrushchev, Nikita, 34, 41, 69, 84–5, 102,
    104; arms control gains, need for, 104,
    108–9, 113, 123; arms control prefer-
    ences, 69–70, 92, 93; coercive diplo-
    macy of, 69, 110; domestic power of,
    72, 81, 95, 113–4, 123–4, 135, 141; and

mutual cooperation, 95, 135, 141; testing resumed by, 125–7, 265n
Killian, James, 83, 96, 100, 105, 115–6, 122
Kissinger, Henry, 156, 159, 160, 165, 169
Kistiakowsky, George, 103, 108, 110, 112, 114, 122
Kozlov, Frol, 96, 114, 123, 141
Kuznetsov, Vasily, 135, 136, 138

Latter, Albert, 99, 100, 101, 103, 109
Latter, Richard, 113, 115
Lawrence Livermore National Laboratory (LLNL), 85, 103, 104, 122, 166, 188, 205
leaks of information, to media, 132, 207, 219, 235–6
learning, 20, 37, 54. *See also* education
limited test ban, 1962 proposal for, 131–2
Limited Test Ban Treaty (LTBT), xii, 23, 24, 119–20; negotiation of, 140–4; ratification of, 140, 143–8
Los Alamos National Laboratory (LANL), 108, 122, 166, 188
lulling effect, 75, 81, 145, 176, 186

Macmillan, Harold, 92–4, 102, 104, 111, 120, 126, 128–9, 140–1
magnitude-yield relationships, 110, 111, 116, 161
Malenkov, Vyacheslav, 69, 81, 95
managerial verification, 11–4, 31, 37, 46, 59, 61, 242–4, 249n
Manhattan Project, 60, 96
McCone, John, 112, 122, 138
McNamara, Robert, 122, 138, 142, 151
media, leaks to, 132, 207, 219, 235–6
misperceptions, 10, 11, 14, 20
misrepresentation of Soviet verification policy, 150, 165–6, 195
missile gap, 95, 112, 114, 121, 125
mixed-motive problems, 8, 9, 13, 22, 24, 26, 43–4, 52, 55
mobile missiles, 31, 38
Molotov, Vyacheslav, 69, 81
monitoring technology, as determinant of cooperation, 2, 38, 56, 119–20, 184, 218–9

moratorium on testing: before CTB negotiations began, 78–9, 80, 84–5; during CTB negotiations, 88, 97, 108, 110, 115, 127; Gorbachev initiates, 195, 202, 197, 198, 201–2; myth of "broken," 120, 125–8, 145–6, 196; nuclear experiments during, 108, 110, 127; post–Cold War, 210; U.S. refusal to repeat, 129, 134, 195–6
Myrdal, Alva, 15, 152, 232
myths, 39, 41, 46, 47, 125–8, 171, 215, 225, 244

national intelligence, permitted for CTBT, 25, 235, 238–40
National Security Council, 70, 75, 77, 78, 93
National Security Council Memorandum, 64–66, 112
national technical means of verification (NTM), 8, 9, 13, 23, 34; defined, 248n; prohibition on interference with, 144, 160; sufficient for CTB, 77, 85, 129, 137, 151; sufficient for partial ban, 98, 126, 127, 132, 140, 146
nationality, of verification staff, 97, 116, 132, 138
Natural Resources Defense Council (NRDC), 198
Nehru, Jawaharlal, 70–1
neutrality, in verification, 124, 131, 138, 139, 153, 263n
Nevada Test Site (NTS), 80, 84, 111, 125–6, 160, 202–3, 207, 209–10
Nitze, Paul, 122, 138
Nixon, Richard M., 113, 156, 159, 160, 168
nonaligned states, 128, 132, 140, 147, 152; Eight Nation Memorandum, 130–1, 139; Five Continent Initiative, 193, 196, 197, 210; G-21 in multilateral negotiations, 232, 235
noncompliance, 16, 23, 31, 43, 44, 48, 49
noncompliance, accusations of Soviet, 166–7, 176–7, 188; responses to, 7, 11–12, 17, 28, 62, 63, 247n. *See also* Threshold Test Ban Treaty: compliance disputes

nonproliferation: as reason to ban tests, 22, 73, 95, 98, 121, 134, 138, 144, 147, 151, 230; as reason to feign interest in test ban, 150–5
Non-Proliferation Treaty (NPT), 32, 33; extension conference, 211, 226, 230, 238; review conferences, 155, 159, 181, 210; verification of, 153–4, 165
norms, 39, 227
North Atlantic Treaty Organization (NATO), 122, 140, 228; Soviet attempts to split, 73, 151
Novaya Zemlya, 209, 234–5, 237
NRDC-SAS in-country project, 25, 53, 185, 197–205
nuclear balance, 15, 38, 56, 149, 217; and test ban, 83, 94, 95, 134–5, 145
nuclear disarmament, 33, 45, 58, 63, 68, 71, 73, 75, 76, 228, 238–9
nuclear freeze, 42, 187, 192
nuclear testing, 63, 65–6, 73, 80, 88–9, 126–7, 146; incentives for, 22, 93–4, 108, 125–6, 151; as pressure for restraint, 70–2, 96–7, 127, 135; underground, 80, 85–7
Nuclear Testing Talks (NTT), 203
nuclear weapons development, 44, 83, 146; "clean" bombs, 76, 79, 161, 257n; MIRVed warheads, 151, 160; strategic modernization, 22, 186, 228, 272n; tactical weapons, 83, 95, 98, 144, 229; thermonuclear weapons, 66, 227

Office of Technology Assessment (OTA), 204–5, 218
on-site inspection (OSI), 8, 11, 23, 25, 35, 46, 60, 87; challenge, 152–3, 174–5, 181; eligibility criteria for, 106, 109, 110, 111, 116, 263n; managed-access for, 25, 53, 75, 136–7, 138, 175, 233; in PNET, 162–5, 167–8; procedures to initiate, 97, 102, 105, 109, 174–5, 233–4, 238–40; quota of, 99, 102–3, 104–6, 111–6, 124, 132, 136–7, 138, 140–2, 267–8n; report on, 138, 175, 207; rights and restrictions during, 116, 163, 165; routine, 63, 74; shortcomings of, 103, 113, 115, 233; voluntary, 59, 130–1; unrestricted, 80, 127
openness, verification to promote, 34, 61, 64–5, 98, 112, 197, 199–200
Oppenheimer, Robert, 66, 254n
outer space, tests in, 100, 145; monitoring of, 99, 104, 107, 124

Paine, Christopher, 200, 205
Pakistan, 228, 232, 233, 236, 237
Panofsky, Wolfgang, 107
peaceful nuclear energy, 60, 68, 161–2
peaceful nuclear explosions, 79, 88, 94, 108; exemption for, 109, 161, 228, 236; Soviet program, 162–5, 173, 174, 277n; U.S. program, 161
Peaceful Nuclear Explosions Treaty (PNET), xii, 23; negotiation of, 161–5; ratification of, 165–70
Perle, Richard, 186, 189, 190, 200, 203, 218
plausibility of verification arguments, 45, 82, 85, 117, 182, 206, 208, 211–2, 220
politics of verification: defined, ix–x, 1, 3, 215; as a derivative problem, 17–8, 19, 26, 56, 214, 241–2; first-wave research on, 2, 14–9, 21, 43, 45, 47, 49, 54, 211, 214; Grotian conceptions of, 5, 7–10, 12–3, 18, 20, 22, 27, 38; Hobbesian conceptions of, 5, 6–7, 12–3, 18, 20, 22, 27, 38; Kantian conceptions of, 5, 10–3, 18, 20, 22, 27, 35, 38
precedents, attention to, 116, 161–3, 167–9, 174–5, 224; cooperation favored by, 89, 98, 103, 144, 165, 199, 229; cooperation hindered by, 146, 168, 190–1
prenegotiation, 23, 56, 57–90, 173
President's Science Advisory Committee (PSAC), 83, 88, 92, 98, 101, 103, 115–6, 117, 125
principles before details, 97, 162–4, 173, 232
public opinion polls, 12, 105, 111, 216; in U.S., 45, 50, 54, 57, 62, 67, 70, 72, 143, 169, 187–8, 192–3, 204, 266n; worldwide, 82, 120
public relations, 58, 64, 66, 76–7, 93, 98, 102, 119–20, 128–9, 254n; domestic sup-

port for defense programs, 68–9, 126, 186; international approval, 72, 73, 75, 78–9, 94
Pugwash, 96, 136, 218, 259n

Rabbi, I. I., 66, 83
Rabinowitch, Eugene, 88
radionuclide monitoring, 87, 231, 237
RAINER test, 80, 85, 87, 101
RAND Corporation, 99, 100, 104, 113
ratification of arms accords, 8, 25, 40, 51, 56; as constraint, 110, 129, 142–3, 177; and verification requirement, 111, 136, 138, 173, 179–80, 234, 237
Reagan, Ronald: administration of, 42, 186–8, 209; arms control policy, 2, 23, 24–5, 28; attack on détente accords, 165, 186, 274n; coercive diplomacy of, 184–5; test ban policy, 187, 201, 203, 209; "trust but verify" coalition-building, 4, 37, 185; verification approach, 14, 16, 30, 31, 34, 184
reciprocal verification, 21, 46, 137–40, 144
reliability as negotiating partner, 148, 168; Soviet doubts about U.S., 102, 136, 142–3, 173, 179; U.S. doubts about USSR, 75, 81, 186
Rubik's cube, 241, 245
Rusk, Dean, 122, 138, 145, 151
Russia, 227–8, 231, 233, 236–7

sabotage techniques, 2, 15, 17–20, 25, 44, 47, 100, 229
safeguards, 9, 24, 66, 140, 224; for LTBT, 145–6, 148; for TTBT, 166, 167, 210
Sakharov, Andrei, 96, 255n
satellites, xii, 1, 7, 9, 22, 35, 51, 144, 232
Scherr, Jacob, 199
Schlesinger, James, 156, 159, 160, 172
science transcending politics, 30, 88, 92, 122, 130–1, 218
scientific advice, sources of, 71, 79, 83, 130–1, 156, 186
scientific consensus, for political impact, 61–2, 87, 90, 156

scientific evidence, manipulation of, 80, 156–7
scientific experts, 20, 43, 45, 49, 50, 59–60, 266n; political judgments by, 90, 107, 117
scientific research: to avoid action, 149, 151–2, 155–8, 195–6, 204; funding, 151, 155, 157–8
scientific talks, to avoid political disagreements, 59–60, 88, 131
scope of CTB, 178, 179, 230, 236–7, 238, 273n
Scoville, Herbert Jr., 147, 167–8
Seaborg, Glenn, 122, 140, 141, 147, 151
secrecy, as security asset, 31, 64, 112
seismic monitoring, 1, 22, 65, 261n; attempts to discredit, 188–9, 196, 200, 206–8, 219, 275n; discrimination, 80, 84, 100, 103–4, 155–7, 179; and geology, 84, 87, 111, 160, 271n; in-country, 23, 25, 53, 103, 136–7, 144, 163, 174, 197–205; National Seismic Stations (NSSs), 178–81; open stations, 155, 205, 229, 270n, 279n
Seismic Research Program Advisory Group (SRPAG), 112, 114
seismology, field of, 50, 219; state of knowledge in, 80, 87, 118, 149, 170
self-verification, 98, 164
Semipalatinsk, 198, 199, 204, 209
Senate, U.S., 45, 51, 121; arms control opposition in, 79, 139; arms control support in, 105, 120, 143
Senate Committee on Foreign Relations (SCFR), 76, 157, 165–9
Shevardnadze, Edward, 194
sinkers, in negotiations, 82, 102, 179–81, 183, 241
Smith, Gerard, 156
South Africa, 226, 228
sovereignty, 11, 29, 31–2, 37, 39, 59, 90, 244–5, 268n, 270n
Soviet Academy of Sciences, 25, 197. *See also* NRDC-SAS in-country project
Soviet Union: analyses of U.S. policy

Soviet Union (*continued*)
making, 81–2, 95, 120, 129, 142, 148, 191–2; decision-making, 21, 54, 193, 216–7; defense debates, 21, 69, 94–6, 135, 149, 159, 173, 193–5; espionage concerns, 32, 73, 90, 114, 129, 136, 140, 142, 153, 175, 179; *glasnost*, 21, 24, 34, 170; and international organizations, 80, 82, 123–4, 192, 251n, 266n; international relations institutes of, 96, 193; military of, 69, 96, 125, 199; misunderstood by U.S., 16–7, 70, 96, 114, 123, 127, 136, 142, 148; and on-site inspection, 65, 79, 165, 173; political culture of, 125, 145, 167, 172, 196; scientists, 86, 96, 125; shifts on verification, 73–4, 105, 165, 170, 185, 192, 194–5, 206, 269n; verification as political problem, 86, 106; verification preferences, 14, 21, 29, 30, 34, 35, 46, 53, 250n
Sputnik, 82, 83
Stalin, Joseph, 63, 64, 69, 70, 89
standards for verification: "adequate," 15–6, 18, 24, 99–100, 137, 176; "effective," 15, 17, 18, 176, 186, 188; "foolproof," 9, 33, 65, 67, 68, 71, 75, 99, 105, 117; relative risk assessments, 83, 86, 92, 105, 139, 144, 157; "smartproof," 100
Stassen, Harold, 71, 74, 75–6, 78, 80, 81, 82, 112
State Department, 66, 68, 71, 88, 98, 122, 141, 172, 186–7, 199; Panel of Consultants on Disarmament, 66, 68
Stevenson, Adlai, 76–77
Stockholm Accord, 184, 195
stockpile safety and reliability, 22, 108, 172, 177–8, 187, 204, 211, 262n, 272n, 278n
stockpile stewardship program, 227–8, 239–40, 281n, 282n, 283n
strategic arms accords: SALT I, 9, 158–60; SALT II, 9, 165, 178; START I, 184, 192, 195
Strauss, Lewis, 70, 75, 79, 80, 122
subcritical experiments, 178, 236–7
surprise attack: Soviet fears of, 74; U.S.

fears of, 68, 112; verification for warning of, 69, 75
Suslov, Mikhail, 96, 114, 141
Sweden, 46, 131, 152–3, 155–6, 157, 193, 266n
symbolic politics, 150–5, 156–8, 187, 219

Technical Working Group I (TWG I), 104, 106–8, 124
Technical Working Group II (TWG II), 109–10, 111, 117
technology export controls, 178, 199
Teller, Edward, 66, 99, 100, 107, 122
test preparations, ban on, 127, 129, 133, 237
thermonuclear weapons: and development ban, 66–7, 83; and test ban, 70, 76–77
threshold problem, 93, 100–1, 102–3, 106, 112
threshold test ban proposals: 10-kt ban, 103; m_b 4.75 limit, 144, 147; moratorium on high-yield (100 kt) tests, 77
Threshold Test Ban Treaty (TTBT), xii, 23, 24; compliance disputes, 84, 166–7, 176–7, 188–9, 196, 205, 207–8, 235; origins of, 158–60; ratification of, 165–9, 210; terms of, 160–1, 236; verification protocol for, 185, 188–9, 208–10
Timerbayev, Roland, 28, 36, 164–5
trade-offs in verification, 25, 32, 48, 72, 117, 120, 176, 194–5, 203, 208, 211
transnational coalitions, 25, 42, 53, 55, 193, 197–205, 212; against cooperation, 176, 180, 281n
transparency, 8–11, 13, 31, 30, 36, 39, 46, 51, 194, 243, 244; increase of, 69, 74, 75, 126, 237, 243, 282n
Truman, Harry S., 62, 64, 65, 68
trust, 2, 9, 12, 29, 56, 58, 89
Tsarapkin, Semyon, 86, 97, 123, 126, 127, 131, 136
two-level games: in practice, 78, 81, 82, 183, 197, 208, 223; in theory, 20, 37, 40–8, 241

U-2 incident, 91, 92, 110, 113–4, 123, 125
uncertainty, 39, 40, 50, 54, 55, 120, 242; as

justification for more tests, 108, 209, 227–8, 262n; scientific, 24, 86, 92, 98, 107, 115, 188–9, 207
unilateral arms control initiatives, 32, 53, 84–5, 109, 113, 125, 140, 142, 251n
Unilateralists, defined, 5, 41, 43–4
United Nations (UN), 36, 37, 58; Atomic Energy Commission, 62; Disarmament Commission, 64, 66, 80; Disarmament Subcommittee, 72, 76, 77, 80, 82, 84, 89; General Assembly (UNGA), 74, 82, 125, 135, 137, 142, 147, 151; Institute for Disarmament Research (UNIDIR), 36–7; Security Council, 63, 74; Special Commission (UNSCOM), 33, 36, 37
United States Geological Survey (USGS), 198

Vela, Project, 104, 107, 109, 132, 135, 143, 152, 155, 218
Velikhov, Evgeny, 197–9
verification: abuse, 31, 34, 54, 102, 195; adversarial assumptions, 11, 13, 24, 47, 64, 97–8, 117, 172, 176; as contested concept, 14, 33, 49; as control, 30, 33, 59; defined, ix, 1, 28–9, 248n; as deterrence, 33–4, 78, 83, 84, 92, 104, 105, 106, 110, 115, 117; functions, 32–4, 51, 56, 137; multilateral, 36, 46, 128, 130, 138; objective factors, 12, 14, 30; paradox, 7, 14, 18–9, 20, 49, 56; political risks of, 31, 125; scientific approach to, 15, 30, 86, 92, 101, 105–6, 115–6, 171–2, 204, 250n; scope, 31–2, 51, 56; self-help approach to, 8, 10, 13, 25, 36, 42, 46, 145; strategic incentives, 28, 41; structure of arguments over, 14–5, 43–8; subjective factors, 12; substantive dilemmas, 27–9, 30, 32, 41, 43, 45, 61–2, 63, 230–1, 244–5; theoretical importance, 1–26
verification-first approach, 50, 53, 65, 66–7, 74, 75, 84, 197
veto over verification, 63, 97, 102, 104, 105, 106, 116, 124
violations: military significance of, 9, 11, 15–6, 137, 144, 145, 160, 172–3; political significance of, 9, 16,
visas, 200–1, 202, 203
von Hippel, Frank, 197

Wadsworth, James, 101, 111
Warnke, Paul, 168, 172, 175, 179
Warsaw Pact, 184, 192, 270n
Weinberger, Caspar, 186, 203
Weisskopf, Victor, 96
Wiesner, Jerome, 83, 122, 130, 136, 138, 142
win-win solutions, 2, 49, 51, 119, 182
withdrawal, right to, 102, 133, 161, 227, 230
workable-tolerable dilemma, 3, 35, 64, 67, 72, 73, 110, 120
World Meteorological Association, 130, 210
worldviews, 18, 25, 30, 41
Worldwide Standardized Seismographic Network (WWSSN), 155, 173
worst-case assumptions, 33–4, 55, 99, 145, 148, 176, 210

yield estimation, 77, 163; bias correction for, 177, 189, 206; exaggeration of problems, 166, 188–9; on-site electrical equipment for, 163, 164, 271n. See also CORRTEX
York, Herbert, 83, 177, 179

Zorin, Valerian, 79, 80, 81, 131

Library of Congress Cataloging-in-Publication Data

Gallagher, Nancy W., 1961–
The politics of verification / Nancy W. Gallagher.
    p.   cm.
Includes bibliographical references (p.   ) and index.
ISBN 0-8018-6017-2 (alk. paper)
1. Nuclear disarmament. 2. Nuclear arms control—Verification. 3. United States—
Foreign relations. I. Title.
JZ5675.G35 1999
327.1'747'0973—dc21   98-36543
                                                                    CIP

Lightning Source UK Ltd.
Milton Keynes UK
UKHW041123070721
386773UK00001B/2